WITHDRAWN

STATISTICS FOR ECONOMICS, ACCOUNTING AND BUSINESS STUDIES

THE LEARNING CENTRE
HAMMERSMITH AND WEST
LONDON COLLEGE
GLIDDON ROAD
LONDON W14 9BL
0181 741 1688

Hammersmith and West London College

300143

STATISTICS FOR ECONOMICS, ACCOUNTING AND BUSINESS STUDIES

SECOND EDITION

Michael Barrow

LONGMAN

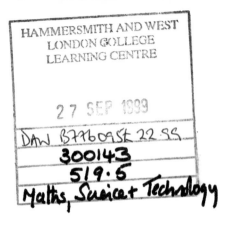

HAMMERSMITH AND WEST
LONDON COLLEGE
LEARNING CENTRE

27 SEP 1999

DAW B776095£ 22.99
300143
519·5
Maths, Science + Technology

Addison Wesley Longman Publishers Limited.,
Edinburgh Gate, Harlow,
Essex CM20 2JE, England
and Associated Companies throughout the world.

© Longman Group UK Limited 1988, 1996

All rights reserved; no part of this publication may be
reproduced, stored in a retrieval system, or transmitted
in any form or by any means, electronic, mechanical,
photocopying, recording, or otherwise without either the
prior written permission of the Publishers or a licence
permitting restricted copying in the United Kingdom issued
by the Copyright Licensing Agency Ltd.,
90 Tottenham Court Road, London W1P 9HE.

First published 1996
Reprinted 1998

ISBN 0 582 239532 PPR

British Library Cataloguing-in-Publication Data

A catalogue record for this book is
available from the British Library

Library of Congress Cataloging-in-Publication Data

Barrow, Michael.
  Statistics for economics, accountancy and business studies /
Michael Barrow. – 2nd. ed.
     p.   cm.
  Rev. ed of: Statistics for economics, accounting and business studies.
  Includes bibliographical references and index.
  ISBN 0-582-23953-2
  1. Economics – Statistical methods. 2. Commercial statistics.
I. Barrow, Michael. Statistics for economics, accounting and business
studies.   II. Title.
HB137.B37 1996
519.5'024'33–dc20   95-9388
                                                            CIP

Set by 8 in 10/12 pt Ehrhardt
Produced through Longman Malaysia, PP

300143

For Patricia, Caroline and Nicolas

CONTENTS

PREFACE TO THE SECOND EDITION

This text is aimed at students of economics and the closely related disciplines of accountancy and business, and provides examples and problems relevant to those subjects, using real data where possible. The book is at an elementary level and requires no prior knowledge of statistics, nor advanced mathematics. For those with a weak mathematical background and in need of some revision, some recommended texts are given at the end of this preface.

This is not a cookbook of statistical recipes; it covers all the relevant concepts so that an *understanding* of why a particular statistical test should be used is gained. These concepts are introduced naturally in the course of the text as they are required, rather than having sections to themselves. The book can form the basis of a one or two term course, depending upon the intensity of the teaching.

As well as explaining statistical concepts and methods, the different schools of thought about statistical methodology are discussed, giving the reader some insight into some of the debates that have taken place in the subject. The book uses the methods of classical statistical analysis, for which some justification is given in Chapter 6, as well as presenting criticisms which have been made of these methods.

An increasingly relevant question these days is the degree of integration of computing into teaching material for statistics. Most students nowadays will have access to a personal computer with spreadsheet software, or something more sophisticated. Therefore, this text does not come with associated specialist software nor a data diskette. It is better if students get used to industry-standard software; nor does it take long to type in reasonable amounts of data. Many of the examples in the text are illustrated using a spreadsheet for analysis (I use *Microsoft Excel*) and several screenshots are included. In addition, numerous tips are given about how to use computer software (usually a spreadsheet) for statistical analysis and each chapter contains one or two suggested computer-based exercises.

Changes since the first edition

Apart from a general updating of examples, the following major changes and additions have been made.

- Chapter 1 on descriptive statistics has been substantially revised to make it more attractive and introduce some new material. The distinction between cross-section and time-series data is emphasised.
- Simple and multiple regression each have their own chapters (9 and 10 respectively). An introductory course could omit multiple regression, if desired. There is new material about the diagnostic checking of regression results and about modelling in general.
- Chapter 8 contains an introduction to the analysis of variance (ANOVA) and the

F test, which is also useful when the *F* test is used in the regression context in Chapter 9.

- There are more exercises at the end of each chapter, including mini-projects and computer-based work. Questions come in matched pairs, except that odd-numbered exercises have the answers at the end of the book whilst even-numbered exercises do not and can therefore be used to evaluate student progress. Answers to the even-numbered exercises are available to instructors.

Mathematics requirements and texts

No more than elementary algebra is assumed in this text, any extensions being covered as they are needed in the book. It is helpful if students are comfortable at manipulating equations so if some revision is required I recommend one of the following books:

J. Black and J. Bradley, *Essential Mathematics for Economists*, 2nd edn, Wiley, 1980.
E. T. Dowling, *Mathematics for Economists*, Schaum's Outline Series in Economics, McGraw-Hill, 1986.
I. Jacques, *Mathematics for Economics and Business*, Addison-Wesley, 1992.

Acknowledge-ments

The publishers are grateful to the following for permission to reproduce copyright material: Blackwell Publishers for information from the *Economic Journal* and the *Economic History Review*; CSO for data extracts from CSO Databank, UK GDP, 1961–91, Investment Figures 1972–91, yield on Treasury Bills, Data from CSO Databank for 1973–93, Digest of UK Energy Statistics 1985, the General Household Survey, 1991, Family Expenditure Survey 1992, Economic Trends Annual Supplement 1993, Economic Trends 1993, Key data 1994–5 – data on road casualties, v/kms travelled; HMSO for data from Inland Revenue Statistics 1981, 1993, the Employment Gazette, September 1986, Local Management in Schools report, 1988, Annual Report of the National Food Survey Committee, 1990, General Household Survey, 1992, Digest of Energy Statistics 1993, Treasury Briefing February 1994, Employment Gazette, February 1995; Office of Health Economics for data from the Compendium of Health Statistics, 1992. Oxford University Press for extracts from *World Development Report* 1988 by the World Bank.

Though every effort has been made to trace the owners of copyright material, in a few cases this has proved impossible and we take this opportunity to apologise to any copyright holders whose rights have been unwittingly infringed.

INTRODUCTION

Statistics is a subject which can be (and is) applied to every aspect of our lives. A glance at the annual *Guide to Official Statistics*, published by the UK Central Statistical Office, for example, gives some idea of the range of material available. Under the letter 'S', for example, one finds entries for such disparate subjects as salaries, schools, semolina(!), shipbuilding, short-time working, spoons, and social surveys. It seems clear that whatever subject you wish to consider, there are data available to illuminate your study. However, it is a sad fact that many people do not understand the use of statistics, do not know how to draw proper inferences (conclusions) from them, or mis-represent them.

The subject of statistics may usefully be divided into two parts, descriptive statistics (Chapters 1, 2 and 11) and inferential statistics (Chapters 5–10), which are based upon the theory of probability (Chapters 3 and 4). Descriptive statistics are used to summarise information which would otherwise be too complex to take in, by use of such means as averages and graphs. The aim of this branch of statistics is to summarise the data in a way which does not distort the meaning which is contained within.

The subject of inferential statistics studies the relationship between a population (in the statistical sense) and a sample drawn from that population; in particular, the inferences which can be legitimately drawn about the population from the sample data. For example, the population might consist of all cars sold in the UK in the last decade, and it might be desired to know what proportion of them had been involved in an accident. It would be too expensive to collect information on all these cars, but some idea of the answer could be obtained from a sample drawn from the population. Data from the sample (e.g. the proportion of cars in the sample involved in an accident) can be used to make an estimate of a population parameter (e.g. the unknown proportion of all cars in the population involved in an accident) or to test particular hypotheses about the population (e.g. whether or not a majority of all cars have been involved in an accident). An important point to realise about this process is that there is still some uncertainty about the result obtained, because the sample may not properly represent the population under study. This can occur simply by chance or because of poor sampling technique. Chapters 5 and 6 (on estimation and hypothesis testing) discuss the issues involved in the chance element of sampling, while Chapter 7 (sampling methods) examines the sampling process to ensure good sample design.

The results of statistical analysis can be used in two ways: one is to aid decision making, the other is to inform one's belief in the truth of a hypothesis. In accountancy or business, statistics are more likely to be used in the first role (should the price of a product be reduced to increase sales and profitability?). Due to the inevitable uncertainty involved in random sampling, it is possible that the wrong decision will be made, on the basis of the evidence available. It is important to be aware of the costs of incorrect decisions, and to interpret statistical evidence in this light. It should be remembered that there are limitations to all statistical analyses, and that the statistics themselves do not make decisions, but are one input into the decision making process. One should not stop thinking about the problem at hand simply because some statistics are available.

In economics statistical evidence is usually used in a different way. Rarely is one piece of statistical work 'decisive'; rather, it is added to the body of evidence which researchers use to evaluate the worth of different economic theories. This is why there are so many statistical analyses of particular economic problems, such as the effects of unemployment benefits upon the level of unemployment.

These two purposes, decision making and persuasion, may be related to different schools of thought in statistics, which approach the subject in slightly different ways. Classical statistics (which is the approach adopted in this book) emphasises the making of decisions and the costs of making incorrect decisions. Bayesian statistics emphasises the degree of belief approach, rejecting the somewhat stark decision-based approach. However, the differences between the two approaches can be over-emphasised, and in this author's view what is more important is to understand the principles underlying the approach adopted so as to be able to interpret statistical results correctly. The differences between classical and Bayesian approaches are further discussed in Chapter 6.

This raises the important question about the relationship between the role of theory (be it economic, business, or otherwise) and evidence. It is often felt that debates may be settled 'by appeal to the facts', without any prior idea of what facts one is looking for. Unfortunately, it is not possible to look at statistical data in a vacuum in the hope that they will 'tell you something'. It is notoriously easy to read into data facts which are simply not there. For example, random data often seem to have patterns in them, containing some message to be extracted (see Table A1 in the Appendix if you wish to try this out). It is essential to have some theoretical understanding of the problem in hand in order to successfully evaluate available data. A knowledge of the theory of probability, and thus of how random data are generated, will help one to discriminate between meaningless (random) and meaningful data. This point is discussed in more detail throughout the text.

Finally it is worth adding a few words of general advice to the statistical beginner. Although it is important to gain a thorough understanding of the principles underlying statistical methods, one should not lose sight of common sense. Students are often over-impressed by sophisticated techniques, which they then apply inappropriately or unsuccessfully to a problem. A lot can be learned by a few simple techniques (carefully applied), such as drawing graphs, particularly in the preliminary stages of analysis. This can often give a useful overview of (or 'feel' for) the data which it is helpful to keep in mind when employing more sophisticated techniques later on.

A point that is often ignored, or given low priority, is the quality of the data being used. Very often, complex techniques are applied to data that are of poor quality, with the consequence that results of dubious value are obtained. This is not to say that sophisticated techniques should not be used, but that the researcher's time could sometimes be used more productively checking on, and trying to improve, the quality of the data. This is unglamorous, not to say tedious, work, but it is essential to good statistical research. In a programme of research into a particular problem, perhaps a third of the time available should be devoted to the collection and checking of the data. There is little which is more annoying than to have to recalculate all the results because of an error discovered in the data at a late stage.

With these warnings in mind, it is to be hoped that by the time you finish this book you will have not only a knowledge of how to apply statistical techniques and why they should be applied, but also an idea of the limitations and pitfalls involved, as well as a notion of the debates which have taken place regarding the proper use of statistical methods.

inevitable = unavoidable

1 DESCRIPTIVE STATISTICS

Introduction

The aim of descriptive statistical methods is simple: to present information in a clear, concise and accurate manner. The difficulty in analysing many phenomena, be they economic, social or otherwise, is that there is simply too much information for the mind to assimilate. The task of descriptive methods is therefore to summarise all this information and draw out the main features, without distorting the picture.

Consider, for example, the problem of presenting information about the wealth of British citizens (which follows later in this chapter). There are about 17 million households on which data are available and to present the data in raw form (i.e. the wealth holdings of each and every family) would be neither useful nor informative (it would take about 30,000 pages of a book, for example). It would be more useful to have much less information, but information which was still representative of the original data. In doing this, much of the original information would be deliberately lost; in fact, descriptive statistics might be described as the art of constructively throwing away much of the data!

There are many ways of summarising data and there are few hard and fast rules about how you should proceed. Newspapers and magazines often provide innovative (though not always successful) ways of presenting data. There are, however, a number of techniques which are tried and tested and these are the subject of this chapter. These are successful because (a) they tell us something useful about the underlying data, and (b) they are reasonably familiar to many people, so we can all talk in a common language. For example, the average tells us about the location of the data and is a familiar concept to most people. For example, my seven-year-old daughter already talks of her day at school being 'average'.

The appropriate method of analysing the data will depend on a number of factors: the type of data under consideration, the sophistication of the audience and the 'message' which it is intended to convey. One would use different methods to persuade academics of the validity of one's theory about inflation than one would use to persuade consumers that Brand X powder washes whiter than Brand Y. To illustrate the use of the various methods, three different topics are covered in this chapter. First we look at the relationship between educational attainment and employment prospects. Do higher qualifications improve your employment chances? The data come from people surveyed in 1991, so we have a sample of **cross-section** data giving a picture of the situation at one point in time. We look at the distribution of educational attainments amongst those surveyed, as well as the relationship to employment outcomes.

Secondly, we examine the distribution of wealth in the United Kingdom in 1988. The data are again cross-section, but this time we can use more sophisticated methods since wealth is measured on a **ratio scale**. Someone with £200,000 of wealth is twice as wealthy as someone with £100,000 for example, and there is a meaning to this ratio. In the case of education, one cannot say with any precision that one person is twice as educated as another. The educational categories may be ordered (so one person can be more educated than another) but we cannot measure the 'distance' between them. We refer to this as education being measured on **an ordinal** scale. In contrast, there is not an obvious natural ordering to the three employment categories (employed, unemployed, inactive), so this is measured on a **nominal** scale.

Thirdly, we look at investment over the period 1961 to 1991. This is **time series** data since we have a number of observations on the variable measured at different points in time. Here it is important to take account of the time dimension of the data: things would look different if the observations were in the order 1961, 1983, 1977... rather than in correct time order. We also look at the relationship between two variables, investment and output, over that period of time and find appropriate methods of presenting it.

In all three cases we make use of both graphical and numerical methods of summarising the data. Although there are some differences between the methods used in the three cases these are not watertight compartments: the methods used in one case might also be suitable in another, perhaps with slight modification. Part of the skill of the statistician is to know which methods of analysis and presentation are best suited to each particular problem.

Summarising data using graphical techniques
Education and employment, or, after all this, will you get a job?

We begin by looking at a question which should be of interest to you: how does education affect your chances of getting a job? With unemployment at high levels in many developed and developing countries around the world, one of the possible benefits of investing in education is that it reduces the chances of being out of work. But by how much does it reduce those chances? We shall use a variety of graphical techniques to explore the question.

The raw data for this investigation come from the 1991 UK *General Household Survey*, an annual survey of households. Some of these data are presented in Table 1.1 and show the numbers of males aged 20–29 by employment status (either in work, unemployed, or inactive, i.e. not seeking work) and by educational qualification (higher education, A-levels, other qualification, or no qualification). The table gives a **cross-tabulation** of employment status by educational qualification and is simply a count (the **frequency**) of the number of males falling into each of the 12 cells of the table. For example, the survey contained 270 young men in work who had experience of higher education. The overall sample size is 1,459 given at the bottom right-hand corner of the table.

Table 1.1   Economic status and educational qualifications: males aged 20–29

	Higher education	A levels	Other qualification	No qualification	Total
In work	270	255	552	161	1,238
Unemployed	18	22	72	77	189
Inactive	4	3	15	10	32
Sample size	292	280	639	248	1,459

The first graphical technique we shall use is the **bar chart** and this is shown in Fig. 1.1. This summarises the educational qualifications of those in work, i.e. the data in the first row of the table. The four educational categories are arranged along the horizontal (x) axis, while the frequencies are measured on the vertical (y) axis. The height of each bar represents the numbers in work for that category.

The biggest group is seen to be those with 'other qualifications' which is about as big as the 'higher education' and 'A-level' categories put together. The 'no qualifications' category is the smallest though it does make up a substantial fraction of those in work.

It would be interesting to compare this distribution with those for the unemployed and inactive. This is done in Fig. 1.2, which adds bars for these other two categories.

This **multiple bar chart** shows the size of the unemployed category getting larger, the lower the level of educational qualification obtained. The 'inactive' category is numerically unimportant relative to the others, but again gets larger at lower educational levels.

Figure 1.3 shows an alternative method of presentation: the **stacked bar chart**. In this case the bars are stacked one on top of another instead of being placed side by side.

A clearer picture emerges if the data are **transformed** to (column) percentages, i.e. the columns are expressed as percentages of the column totals. This makes it easier to directly compare the different educational categories. These figures are shown in Table 1.2.

Fig. 1.1 *Educational qualifications of males in work, aged 20–29*

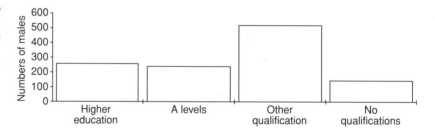

Note: The height of each bar is determined by the associated frequency. The first bar is 270 units high, the second is 255 units high, and so on. The ordering of the bars could be reversed (no qualifications becoming the first category) without altering the message.

Fig. 1.2 *Educational qualifications by employment category*

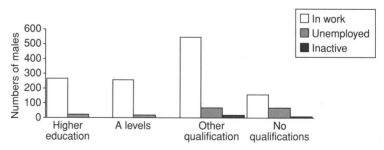

Note: The bars for the unemployed and inactive categories are constructed in the same way as for the employed: the height of the bar is determined by the frequency.

Fig 1.3 *Stacked bar chart of educational qualifications and employment status*

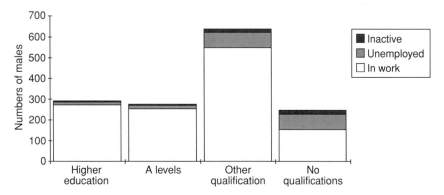

Note: The overall height of each bar is determined by the sum of the frequencies of the category, given in the final row of Table 1.1.

Table 1.2   Economic status and educational qualifications: column percentages

	Higher education	A levels	Other qualification	No qualification	Total
In work	92%	91%	86%	65%	85%
Unemployed	6%	8%	11%	31%	13%
Inactive	1%	1%	2%	4%	2%
Sample size	292	280	639	248	1,459

Note: The column percentages are obtained by dividing each frequency by the column total. For example, 92% is 272 divided by 292; 91% is 255 divided by 280, etc.

Having done this, it is easier to make a direct comparison of the different education categories (columns). This is shown in Fig. 1.4, where all the bars are of the same height (representing 100%) and the components of each bar now show the *proportions* of males in each educational category either in work, unemployed or inactive.

It is now clear how economic status differs according to education and the result is quite dramatic. In particular:

- The probability of unemployment increases rapidly with lower educational attainment (this interprets proportions as probabilities, i.e. if 10% are out of work then the probability that a person picked at random is unemployed is 10%).
- The biggest difference is between the no qualifications category and the other three, which have slight differences between them.

Fig 1.4 *Percentages in each employment category, by educational qualification*

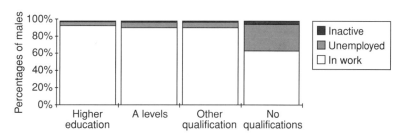

• The proportion inactive in any category is small, as one might expect for the 20–29 age group, though it is again largest in the category with no qualifications.

Can we safely conclude therefore that the probability of your being unemployed is significantly reduced by education? Could we go further and argue that the route to lower unemployment generally is via investment in education? The answer *may* be 'yes' to both questions, but we have not proved it. Two important considerations are as follows:

• Innate ability has been ignored. Those with higher ability are more likely to be employed *and* are more likely to receive more education. Ideally we would like to compare individuals of similar ability but with different amounts of education; however, it is difficult to get such data.
• Even if additional education does reduce a person's probability of becoming unemployed, this may be at the expense of someone else, who loses their job to the more educated individual. In other words, additional education does not reduce total unemployment but only shifts it around amongst the labour force. Of course it is still rational for individuals to invest in education if they do not take account of this externality.

The pie chart

Another useful way of presenting information graphically is the **pie chart**, which is particularly good at describing how a variable is distributed between different categories. For example, from Table 1.1 we have the distribution of working males according to educational qualification (the first row of the table). This can be shown in a pie chart as in Fig. 1.5.

The area of each slice is proportional to the respective frequency and the pie chart is an alternative means of presentation to the bar chart shown in Fig. 1.1. The percentages falling into each education category have been added around the chart, but this is not essential. For presentational purposes it is best not to have too many slices in the chart: beyond about six the chart tends to look crowded.

The chart reveals that nearly half of those employed fall into the 'other qualification' category, and that just 13% have no qualifications. This may be contrasted with Fig. 1.6 which shows a similar chart for the unemployed (the second row of Table 1.1).

Fig. 1.5 *Educational qualifications of males aged 20–29 in work*

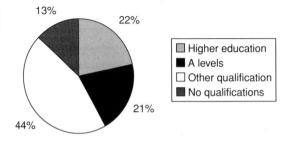

Note: If you have to draw a pie chart by hand, the angle of each slice can be calculated as follows: angle = $\dfrac{frequency}{total\ frequency} \times 360$. The angle of the first slice, for example, is $\dfrac{270}{1,238} \times 360 = 78.5°$.

Fig. 1.6 *Educational qualifications of the unemployed*

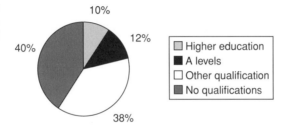

- ☐ Higher education
- ■ A levels
- ☐ Other qualification
- ▨ No qualifications

The 'other qualification' category is about the same size, but the 'no qualification' group now accounts for 40% of the unemployed and those with A-levels or a degree are less heavily represented.

Looking at cross-section data: wealth in the UK in 1988

Frequency tables and histograms

We now move on to examine data in a different form. The data on employment and education consisted simply of frequencies, where a characteristic (such as higher education) was either present or absent for a particular individual. We now look at the distribution of wealth, a variable which can be measured on a **ratio scale** so that a different value is associated with each individual. For example, one person might have £1,000 of wealth, another might have £1 million. Different presentational techniques will be used to analyse this type of data.

The data are given in Table 1.3 which shows the distribution of wealth in the UK for the year 1988 (the latest available at the time of writing), taken from *Inland Revenue Statistics* 1993. Wealth is difficult to define and to measure; the data shown here refer to *marketable* wealth (i.e. items such as the right to a pension, which cannot be sold, are excluded) and are estimates for the population as a whole based on taxation data.

Table 1.3   The distribution of marketable wealth: UK, 1988

Class interval	Numbers (thousands)	Amount (£m.)
0–9,999	3,330	15,472
10,000–24,999	3,186	55,251
25,000–39,999	2,876	91,963
40,000–49,999	1,204	53,649
50,000–59,999	1,003	54,974
60,000–79,999	1,663	115,709
80,000–99,999	1,267	113,721
100,000–199,999	1,793	243,621
200,000–299,999	390	94,465
300,000–499,999	211	80,387
500,000–999,999	77	51,792
1,000,000–1,999,999	17	22,443
2,000,000 or more	8	26,217
Totals	17,025	1,019,664

Note: It would be impossible to show the wealth of all 17 million individuals, so it has been summarised in this **frequency table**.

Wealth is divided into 13 **class intervals**: £0 up to (but not including) £10,000; £10,000 up to £24,999 etc. and the number of individuals within each class interval is shown. Note that the **class widths** vary up the wealth scale: the first is £10,000, the second £15,000; the third £15,000 also, and so on. This will prove an important factor when it comes to graphical presentation of the data.

This table has been constructed from the original 17,025,000 observations on individuals' wealth, so it is already a summary of the original data (note that all the frequencies have been expressed in thousands in the table) and much of the original information is lost. The first decision to make when drawing up such a frequency table from the raw data is how many class intervals to have, and how wide they should be. It simplifies matters if they are all of the same width but in this case it is not feasible: if 10,000 were chosen as the **standard width** there would be many intervals between 1,000,000 and 2,000,000 (100 of them in fact), most of which would have a zero or very low frequency. If 500,000 were the standard width there would be only a few intervals and the first (0–500,000) would contain 16,923 observations (99.4% of all observations) so almost all the interesting detail would be lost. A compromise between these extremes has to be found.

A useful rule of thumb is that the number of class intervals should equal the square root of the total frequency, subject to a maximum of about 12 intervals. Thus, for example, a total of 25 observations should be allocated to five intervals; 100 observations should be grouped into 10 intervals; and 17,025 should be grouped into about 12, as here. The class widths should be equal in so far as this is feasible, but should increase when the frequencies become very small. In Table 1.3 it might have been better if the author had chosen a constant width of 10,000 up to £60,000 of wealth. The increasing widths beyond £60,000 reflect the lower frequencies beyond this point.

To present these data graphically one could draw a bar chart as in the case of education above and this is presented in Fig. 1.7. Before reading on, spend some time looking at it and ask yourself what is wrong with it.

The answer is that the figure gives a completely misleading picture of the data! (Incidentally, this is the picture that you will get using a spreadsheet computer program, as I have done here. All the standard packages appear to do this, so beware. One wonders how many decisions have been influenced by data presented in this incorrect manner.)

Why is the figure wrong? It appears to show that there is a concentration of individuals above £60,000 (the frequency jumps from 1,003 to 1,663) and above

Fig. 1.7 *Bar chart of the distribution of wealth in the UK, 1988*

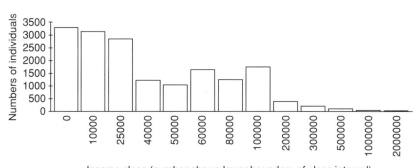

Income class (number shows lower boundary of class interval)

£100,000 (a jump from 1,267 to 1,793). But this is just the result of the change in the class width at these points (to 20,000 at £60,000 and to 100,000 at £100,000). Suppose that we divide up the £100,000–£200,000 class into two: £100,000 to £150,000 and £150,000 to £200,000. We divide the frequency of 1,793 equally between the two (this is an arbitrary decision but illustrates the point). The graph now looks like Fig. 1.8.

Fig. 1.8 *The wealth distribution with different class intervals*

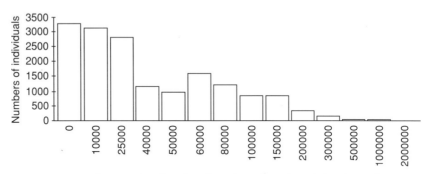

Income class (number shows lower boundary of class interval)

Comparing Figs 1.7 and 1.8 reveals a difference: the hump has now disappeared. But this is disturbing – it means that the shape of the distribution can be altered simply by altering the class widths. If so, how can we rely upon visual inspection of the distribution? A better method would make the shape of the distribution independent of how the class intervals are arranged. This can be done by drawing a **histogram**.

The histogram

A histogram is similar to a bar chart except that it corrects for differences in class widths. If all the class widths are identical then there is no difference between a bar chart and histogram. The calculations required to produce the histogram are shown in Table 1.4.

Table 1.4   Calculation of frequency densities

Range	Number	Class width	Frequency density
0–	3,330	10,000	0.33300
10,000–	3,186	15,000	0.21240
25,000–	2,876	15,000	0.19173
40,000–	1,204	10,000	0.12040
50,000–	1,003	10,000	0.10030
60,000–	1,663	20,000	0.08315
80,000–	1,267	20,000	0.06335
100,000–	1,793	100,000	0.01793
200,000–	703	3,800,000	0.00019
4,000,000–			

Note: As an alternative to the frequency density, one could calculate the frequency per 'standard' class width, with the standard width chosen to be 10,000 (the narrowest class). The values in column 4 would then be 3,330; 2,124; 1,917.3; etc. This would lead to the same shape of histogram as using the frequency density.

The new column in the table shows the **frequency density** which is defined as follows:

$$(1.1) \quad frequency \ density = \frac{frequency}{class \ width}$$

Using this formula corrects the figures for differing class widths. Thus $0.333 = 3,330/10,000$ is the first frequency density, $0.2124 = 3,186/15,000$ is the second, etc. Above £200,000 the class widths are very large and the frequencies small (too small to appear on the histogram), so these classes have been combined.

The width of the final interval is unknown, so has to be estimated in order to calculate the frequency density. It is likely be extremely wide since the wealthiest person may well have assets valued at several £m.; the value we assume will affect the calculation of the frequency density and therefore of the shape of the histogram. Fortunately it is in the tail of the distribution and only affects a small number of observations. Here we assume (arbitrarily) a width of £2m. to be a 'reasonable' figure, giving an upper class boundary of £4m.

The frequency density is then plotted on the vertical axis against wealth on the horizontal axis to give the histogram. One further point needs to be made: the scale on the wealth axis should be linear as far as possible, e.g. £50,000 should be twice as far from the origin as £25,000. However, it is difficult to fit all the values onto the horizontal axis without squeezing the graph excessively at lower levels of wealth, where most observations are located. Therefore the classes above £100,000 have been squeezed and the reader's attention is drawn to this. The result is shown in Fig. 1.9.

The effect of taking frequency densities is to make the *area* of each block in the histogram represent the frequency, rather than the height, which now shows the density. This has the effect of giving an accurate picture of the shape of the distribution. The actual frequencies have been written above the relevant blocks of the histogram since they can no longer be read off the vertical axis, though this is not an essential part of the chart and could be omitted if desired.

Having done all this, what does the histogram show?

- The histogram is heavily **skewed** to the right (i.e. the long tail is to the right).
- The **modal** class interval is £0–£10,000 (i.e. has the greatest density. No other £10,000 interval has more individuals in it).

Fig. 1.9 *Histogram of the distribution of wealth, UK, 1988*

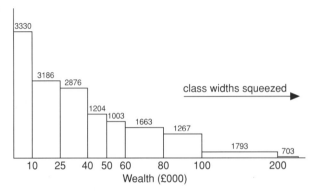

Note: A **frequency polygon** would be the result if, instead of drawing blocks for the histogram, one drew lines connecting the centres of the top of each block.

- The majority of people (55% in fact) have less than £40,000 of marketable wealth
- Few people have more than £200,000 of wealth.

The figure shows quite a high degree of inequality in the wealth distribution. Whether this is acceptable or even desirable is a value judgement. It should be noted that part of the inequality is due to differences in age: younger people have not yet had enough time to acquire much wealth and therefore appear worse off, although in life-time terms this may not be the case. To get a better picture of the distribution of wealth would require some analysis of the acquisition of wealth over the life-cycle. In fact, correcting for age differences does not make a big difference to the pattern of wealth distribution (on this point and on inequality in wealth in general, see Atkinson (1983), chs. 7 and 8).

Relative frequency and cumulative frequency distributions

The wealth distribution may also be illustrated using **relative** and **cumulative frequencies** of the data. These figures are calculated in Table 1.5.

Relative frequencies are shown in the third column, using the following formula:

$$(1.2) \quad \textit{Relative frequency} = \frac{\textit{frequency}}{\textit{sum of frequencies}} = \frac{f}{\sum f}$$

Note: If you are unfamiliar with the Σ notation then read Appendix 1A to this chapter before continuing.

The sum of the relative frequencies has to be 100% and this acts as a check on the calculations. The relative frequencies show the *proportion* of observations that fall into each class interval, so, for example, about 7% of individuals have wealth holdings between £40,000 and £50,000.

The cumulative frequencies, shown in the fourth column, are obtained by cumulating (successively adding) the frequencies. The cumulative frequencies show the

Table 1.5 Calculation of relative and cumulative frequencies

Range	Frequency	Relative frequency (%)	Cumulative frequency
0–	3,330	19.56	3,330
10,000–	3,186	18.71	6,516
25,000–	2,876	16.89	9,392
40,000–	1,204	7.07	10,596
50,000–	1,003	5.89	11,599
60,000–	1,663	9.77	13,262
80,000–	1,267	7.44	14,529
100,000–	1,793	10.53	16,322
200,000–	703	4.13	17,025
Totals	17,025	100.00	

Note: Relative frequencies are calculated in the same way as the column percentages in Table 1.2. Thus for example, 19.56% is 3,330 divided by 17,025. Cumulative frequencies are obtained by cumulating, or successively adding, the frequencies. For example, 6,516 is 3,330 + 3,186, 9,392 is 6,516 + 2,876, etc.

total number of individuals with wealth up to a given amount; for example, about ten and a half million people have less than £50,000 of wealth.

Both relative and cumulative frequency distributions can be drawn, in a similar way to the histogram. In fact, the relative frequency distribution has exactly the same shape as the frequency distribution but with different value labels for the blocks. This is shown in Fig. 1.10.

The cumulative frequency distribution is shown in Fig. 1.11, where the blocks increase in height as wealth increases. The simplest way to draw this is to cumulate the frequency densities (shown in the final column of Table 1.4) and to use these values as the *y*-axis co-ordinates. The labels for the blocks are the cumulative frequencies themselves.

Fig. 1.10 *The relative frequency distribution of wealth, UK, 1988*

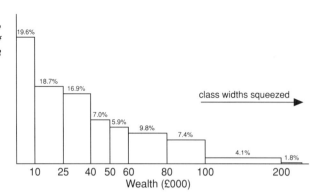

Fig. 1.11 *The cumulative frequency distribution of wealth, UK, 1988*

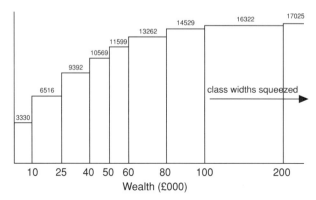

Note: The *y*-axis co-ordinates are obtained by cumulating the frequency densities in Table 1.4 above. The labels for the columns are from Table 1.5.

Summarising data using numerical techniques

Graphical methods are an excellent means of obtaining a quick overview of the data, but they are not particularly precise, nor do they lend themselves to further analysis. For this we must turn to numerical measures such as the average. There are a number of different ways in which we may describe a distribution such as that for wealth. If we think of trying to describe the histogram, it is useful to have:

- A **measure of location** giving an idea of whether people own a lot of wealth or a little. An example is the average, which gives some idea of where the distribution is located along the *x*-axis.

- A **measure of dispersion** showing how wealth is dispersed around (perhaps) the average; whether it is concentrated close to the average or is generally far away from it. An example here is the standard deviation.
- A **measure of skewness** showing how symmetric or not the distribution is, i.e. whether the left half of the distribution is a mirror image of the right half or not.

We consider each type of measure in turn.

Measures of location: the mean

The **arithmetic mean**, commonly called the average, is the most familiar measure of location, and is obtained simply by adding all the observations and dividing by the number of observations. If we denote the wealth of the *i*th household by x_i (so that the index *i* runs from 1 to *N*, where *N* is the number of observations) then the mean is given by the following formula:

$$(1.3) \quad \mu = \frac{\sum_{i=1}^{i=N} x_i}{N}$$

where μ (the Greek letter pronounced 'myu') denotes the mean and $\sum_{i=1}^{i=N} x_i$ (read 'sigma *x i*, from *i* = 1 to *N*', Σ being the Greek capital letter sigma) means the sum of the *x* values. We may simplify this to

$$(1.4) \quad \mu = \frac{\sum x}{N}$$

when it is obvious which *x* values are being summed (usually all the available observations).

Formula 1.3 can only be used when all the individual *x* values are known. The frequency table does not show all 17 million observations, however, but only the range of values for each class interval and the associated frequency. In this case of grouped data the following formula may be used:

$$(1.5) \quad \mu = \frac{\sum_{i=1}^{i=C} f_i x_i}{\sum_{i=1}^{i=C} f_i}$$

or, more simply,

$$(1.6) \quad \mu = \frac{\sum fx}{\sum f}$$

In this formula:

- *x* denotes the **mid-point** of each class interval, since the individual *x* values are unknown. The mid-point is used as the representative *x* value. This will cause a slight inaccuracy – because the distribution is so skewed, there are more households below the mid-point than above it in every class interval except, perhaps, the first. We ignore this problem here, and it is less of a problem for most distributions which are less skewed than this one.

- The summation runs from 1 to C, the number of class intervals, or distinct x values.
- $\Sigma f_i = N$ gives the total number of observations, the sum of the individual frequencies.

The calculation of μ for the wealth data is shown in Table 1.6.

Table 1.6 Calculation of average wealth

Range	Mid-point x (£000)	f	fx
0–	5	3,330	16,650
10,000–	17.5	3,186	55,755
25,000–	32.5	2,876	93,470
40,000–	45	1,204	54,180
50,000–	55	1,003	55,165
60,000–	70	1,663	116,410
80,000–	90	1,267	114,030
100,000–	150	1,793	268,950
200,000–	250	390	97,500
300,000–	400	211	84,400
500,000–	750	77	57,750
1,000,000–	1,500	17	25,500
2,000,000–	3,000	8	24,000
Totals		17,025	1,063,760

Note: The *fx* column gives the product of the values in the *f* and *x* columns (so, for example, $5 \times 3,330 = 16,650$ which is the total wealth held by those in the first class interval). The sum of the *fx* values gives total wealth.

Hence: $\mu = \dfrac{1,063,760}{17,025} = 62.48223$

Note that the x values are expressed in £000, so we must remember that the mean will also be in £000; the average wealth holding is therefore £62,482. Note that the frequencies have also been divided by 1,000 but this has no effect upon the calculation of the mean since f appears in both numerator and denominator of the formula for the mean.

   This value may seem surprising, since the histogram clearly shows most people have wealth below this point (approximately 70% of individuals are below the mean, in fact). The mean does not seem to be typical of the wealth that most people have. The reason the mean has such a high value is that there are some individuals whose wealth is way above the figure of £62,482 – up into the £millions, in fact. The mean is the 'balancing point' of the distribution – if the histogram were a physical model, it would balance on a fulcrum placed at 62,482. The few very high wealth levels exert a lot of leverage and counter-balance the more numerous individuals below the mean.

The mean as the expected value

We also refer to the mean as the **expected value** of x and write:

(1.7) $E(x) = \mu = 62,482$

$E(x)$ is read 'E of x' or 'the expected value of x'. The mean is the expected value in the sense that if we selected a household at random from the population we would 'expect' its wealth to be £62,482.

The expected value notation is particularly useful in keeping track of the effects upon the mean of certain data transformations (e.g. dividing wealth by 1,000 also divides the mean by 1,000); Appendix 1B provides a detailed explanation. Use is also made of the E operator in inferential statistics, to describe the properties of estimators (see Chapter 5).

The sample mean and the population mean

Very often we have only a sample of data, and it is important to distinguish this case from the one where we have all the possible observations. For this reason, the sample mean is given by:

$$(1.8) \quad \bar{x} = \frac{\sum x}{n} \text{ or } \bar{x} = \frac{\sum fx}{\sum f} \text{ for grouped data}$$

Note the distinctions between μ (the population mean) and $\bar{x}$ (the sample mean), and between N (the size of the population) and n (the sample size). Otherwise, the calculations are identical.

The weighted average

Sometimes observations have to be given different weightings in calculating the average, as the following example. Consider the problem of calculating the average spending per pupil by an education authority. The figures for spending on primary (ages 5 to 11), secondary (11 to 16) and post-16 pupils are given in Table 1.7.

Clearly, significantly more is spent on secondary and post-16 pupils (a general pattern throughout England and most other countries) and the overall average should lie somewhere between 890 and 1,910. However, taking a simple average of these values would give the wrong answer, because there are different numbers of children in the three age ranges. The numbers and proportions of children in each age group are given in Table 1.8.

Since there are relatively more primary school children than secondary, and relatively fewer post-16 pupils, the primary unit cost should be given greater weight in the averaging process and the post-16 unit cost the least. The **weighted average** is

Table 1.7 Cost per pupil in different types of school (£ p.a.)

	Primary	Secondary	Post-16
Unit cost	890	1,450	1,910

Table 1.8 Numbers and proportions of pupils in each age range

	Primary	Secondary	Post-16	Total
Numbers	8,000	7,000	3,000	18,000
Proportion	44%	39%	17%	

obtained by multiplying each unit cost figure by the proportion of children in each category and summing. The weighted average is therefore

(1.9) $0.44 \times 890 + 0.39 \times 1{,}450 + 0.17 \times 1{,}910 = 1{,}277.8$

The weighted average gives an answer closer to the primary unit cost than does the simple average of the three figures (1,416.7 in this case), which would be misleading. The formula for the weighted average is

(1.10) $\bar{x}_w = \sum_i w_i x_i$

where w represents the weights, *which must sum to one*, i.e.

(1.11) $\sum_i w_i = 1$

and x represents the unit cost figures.

The median

Returning to the study of wealth, the unrepresentative result for the mean suggests that we may prefer a measure of location which is not so strongly affected by outliers (extreme observations) and skewness.

The **median** is a measure of location which is more robust to such extreme values; it may be defined by the following procedure. Imagine everyone in a line from poorest to wealthiest. Go to the individual located half way along the line. Ask her what her wealth is. Her answer is the median. The median is clearly unaffected by extreme values, unlike the mean: if the wealth of the richest person were doubled (with no reduction in anyone else's wealth) there would be no effect upon the median. The calculation of the median is not so straightforward as for the mean, especially for grouped data.

For grouped data we must first identify the class interval which contains the median person. Then we must calculate where in the interval that person lies.

(1) To find the appropriate class interval: since there are 17,025,000 observations, we need the wealth of the person who is 8,512,500 in rank order. The table of cumulative frequencies (see Table 1.5 above) is the most suitable for this. There are 6,516,000 individuals with wealth of less than £25,000 and 9,392,000 with wealth of less than £40,000. The middle person therefore falls into the £25,000–40,000 class.

(2) To find the position in the class interval, we can now use formula (1.12):

(1.12) $median = x_L + \left(x_U - x_L\right)\left\{\dfrac{\dfrac{N+1}{2} - F}{f}\right\}$

where:

x_L = the lower limit of the class interval containing the median
x_U = the upper limit of this class interval
N = the number of observations (using $N+1$ rather than N in the formula is only important when N is relatively small)
F = the cumulative frequency of the class intervals up to (but not including) the one containing the median
f = the frequency for the class interval containing the median.

For the wealth distribution we have:

$$median = 25{,}000 + \left(40{,}000 - 25{,}000\right)\left\{\dfrac{\dfrac{17{,}025{,}000}{2} - 6{,}516{,}000}{2{,}876{,}000}\right\} = \pounds35{,}413$$

This alternative measure of location gives a very different impression: it is not much more than half the mean. Nevertheless, it is equally valid despite having a different meaning. It demonstrates that the person 'in the middle' has wealth of £35,413 and in this sense is typical of the UK population. Before going on to compare these measures further we examine a third, the mode.

Generalising the median – Quantiles

The idea of the median as the middle of the distribution can be extended: **quartiles** divide the distribution into four equal parts, **quintiles** into five, **deciles** into ten and finally **percentiles** divide the distribution into one hundred equal parts. Generically they are known as **quantiles**. We shall illustrate the idea by examining deciles (quartiles are covered below).

The first decile occurs one-tenth of the way along the line of people ranked from poorest to wealthiest. This means we require the wealth of the person ranked 1,702,500 ($= N/10$) in the distribution. From the table of cumulative frequencies, this person lies in the first class interval. Adapting formula (1.12), we obtain:

$$median = 0 + \left(10{,}000 - 0\right) \times \left\{\dfrac{1{,}702{,}500 - 0}{3{,}330{,}000}\right\} = 5{,}113$$

Thus we estimate that any household with less than £5,113 of wealth falls into the bottom 10% of the wealth distribution. In a similar fashion, the ninth decile can be found by calculating the wealth of the household ranked 15,322,500 ($= N \times 9/10$) in the distribution.

The mode

The **mode** is defined as that level of wealth which occurs with the greatest frequency. In this case 'level of wealth' means a class interval, corrected for width. From Table 1.4 it can be seen that this is the first interval, from £0 to £10,000, which has the highest frequency density. It is 'typical' of the distribution because it is the one which occurs most often (using the frequency densities, *not* frequencies). More people are like this in terms of wealth than anything else. Once again it is notable how different it is from both the median and the mean.

The three measures of location give different messages because of the skewness of the distribution: if it were symmetric they would all give approximately the same answer. Here we have a rather extreme case of skewness, but it does serve to illustrate how the different measures of location compare. When the distribution is skewed to the right, as here, they will be in the order mode, median, mean; if skewed to the left the ordering is reversed. If the distribution has more than one peak then this rule for orderings may not apply.

Which of the measures is 'correct' or most useful? In this particular case the mean is not very useful: it is heavily influenced by extreme values. The median is therefore often used when discussing wealth (and income) distributions. Where inequality is even more pronounced, as in some less developed countries, then the mean is even less informative. The mode is also quite useful in telling us about a large section of the population, although it can be sensitive to how the class intervals are arranged. If there were a class interval of £5,000 to £15,000 then this might well be the modal class, conveying a slightly different impression.

The three different measures of location are marked on the histogram in Figure 1.12. This brings out the substantial difference between the measures for a skewed distribution such as for wealth.

Fig. 1.12 *The histogram with the mean, median and mode marked*

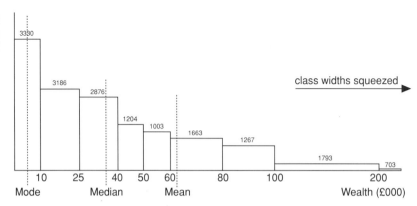

Measures of dispersion

Two different distributions might have the same mean yet look very different, as shown in Fig. 1.13 (the distributions have been drawn using smooth curves rather than bars to improve clarity). In one country everyone might have a similar level of wealth. In another, although the average is the same there might be extremes of great wealth and poverty. A measure of dispersion is a number which allows us to distinguish between these two situations.

The simplest measure of dispersion is the **range**, which is the difference between

Fig. 1.13 *Two distributions with different degrees of dispersion*

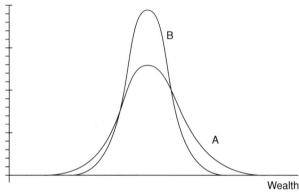

Note: Distribution A has a greater degree of dispersion than B, where everyone has similar levels of wealth.

the smallest and largest observations. It is impossible to calculate accurately from the table of wealth holdings since the largest observation is not available. In any case, it is not a very useful figure since it relies on two extreme values and ignores the rest of the distribution.

An improvement is the **inter-quartile range** which is the difference between the first and third quartiles. It therefore defines the limits of wealth of the middle half of the distribution. To calculate the first quartile (which we label Q_1) we have to go one-quarter of the way along the line of wealth holders (ranked from poorest to wealthiest) and ask the person in that position what their wealth is. The answer is the first quartile. The calculation is as follows:

- one-quarter of 17,025 is 4,256.25, which we may safely round down to 4,256
- the person ranked 4,256 is in the £10,000–25,000 class
- adapting formula (1.12):

$$(1.13) \quad Q_1 = 10,000 + \left(25,000 - 10,000\right)\left\{\frac{4,256 - 3,330}{3,186}\right\} = 14,359$$

The third quartile is calculated in similar fashion:

- three-quarters of 17,025 is 12,768.75, rounded up to 12,769
- the person ranked 12,769 is in the £60,000–80,000 class
- again using (1.12):

$$Q_3 = 60,000 + \left(80,000 - 60,000\right)\left\{\frac{12,769 - 11,599}{1,663}\right\} = 74,071$$

and therefore the inter-quartile range is $Q_3 - Q_1 = 74,071 - 14,359 = 59,712$.

This gives one summary measure of the dispersion of the distribution: the higher the value the more spread out is the distribution. Two different wealth distributions might be compared according to their inter-quartile ranges therefore, with the country having the larger figure exhibiting greater inequality. Note that the figures would have to be expressed in a common unit of currency for this comparison to be valid.

The variance

A more useful measure of dispersion is the **variance**, which makes use of all of the information in the sample. The variance is denoted by the symbol σ^2. σ is the Greek lower-case letter sigma, so σ^2 is read 'sigma squared'. It has a completely different meaning from Σ (capital sigma) used before. Its formula is:

$x_i - \mu$ measures the **deviation** of x_i from the mean. These deviations are first squared and then summed. Dividing by N gives the variance.

$$(1.14) \quad \sigma^2 = \frac{\sum\left(x_i - \mu\right)^2}{N}$$

The variance is the average of all the squared deviations from the mean. A more dispersed distribution (such as A in Figure 1.13) will tend to have larger deviations from the mean, and hence a larger variance. In comparing two distributions with similar means, therefore, we could examine their variances to see which of the two has the greater degree of dispersion. With grouped data the formula becomes:

$$(1.15) \quad \sigma^2 = \frac{\sum f(x_i - \mu)^2}{\sum f}$$

The calculation of the variance is shown in Table 1.9. Hence we obtain:

$$\sigma^2 = \frac{213,554,213.4}{17,025} = 12,543.56613$$

This calculated value is before translating back into the original units of measurement, as was done for the mean by multiplying by 1,000. In the case of the variance, however, we must multiply by 1,000,000 which is the *square* of 1,000. The variance is therefore 12,543,566,130. Multiplying by the square of 1,000 is a consequence of using squared deviations in the variance formula (see Appendix 1B on E and V operators for more details of this).

The standard deviation

In what units is the variance measured? Since we have used a squaring procedure in the calculation we end up with something like 'squared' £s, which is not very convenient. Because of this, we define the square root of the variance to be the **standard deviation**, which is therefore back in £s. The standard deviation is therefore given by:

$$(1.16) \quad \sigma = \sqrt{\frac{\sum(x_i - \mu)^2}{N}}$$

or, for grouped data:

$$(1.17) \quad \sigma = \sqrt{\frac{\sum f(x_i - \mu)^2}{\sum f}}$$

Table 1.9   Calculation of the variance of wealth

Range	Mid-point x (£000)	Frequency f	Deviation (x − μ)	(x − μ)²	f(x − μ)²
0–	5	3,330	−57.5	3,304.2	11,003,009.3
10,000–	17.5	3,186	−45.0	2,023.4	6,446,556.2
25,000–	32.5	2,876	−30.0	898.9	2,585,334.9
40,000–	45	1,204	−17.5	305.6	367,976.6
50,000–	55	1,003	−7.5	56.0	56,151.7
60,000–	70	1,663	7.5	56.5	93,987.5
80,000–	90	1,267	27.5	757.2	959,407.3
100,000–	150	1,793	87.5	7,659.4	13,733,232.0
200,000–	250	390	187.5	35,162.9	13,713,536.2
300,000–	400	211	337.5	113,918.2	24,036,749.4
500,000–	750	77	687.5	472,680.7	36,396,412.5
1,000,000–	1,500	17	1,437.5	2,066,457.3	35,129,774.7
2,000,000–	3,000	8	2,937.5	8,629,010.6	69,032,085.1
Totals		17,025			213,554,213.4

These are simply the square roots of (1.14) and (1.15). The standard deviation of wealth is therefore $\sqrt{12,543.56613} = 111.9980631$. This is in £000, so the standard deviation is actually £111,998 (note that this is the square root of 12,543,566,130, as it should be). On its own the standard deviation (and the variance) is not easy to interpret since it is not something we have an intuitive feel for, unlike the mean. It is more useful when used in a comparative setting. This will be illustrated later on.

The variance and standard deviation of a sample

As with the mean, a different symbol is used to distinguish a variance calculated from the population and one calculated from a sample. In addition, the sample variance is calculated using a slightly different formula from the one for the population variance. The sample variance is denoted by s^2 and its formula is given by equations (1.18) and (1.19) below:

$$(1.18) \quad s^2 = \frac{\sum\left(x - \bar{x}\right)^2}{n - 1}$$

$$(1.19) \quad s^2 = \frac{\sum f\left(x - \bar{x}\right)^2}{n - 1}$$

where n is the sample size. The reason $n-1$ is used in the denominator rather than n (as one might expect) is the following. Our real interest is in the population variance, and the sample variance is an estimate of it. The former is measured by the dispersion around μ, and the sample variance should ideally be measured around μ also. However, μ is unknown, so $\bar{x}$ is used instead. But the variation of the sample observations around $\bar{x}$ tends to be smaller than around μ. Using $n-1$ rather than n in the formula compensates for this and the result is an **unbiased**[1] (i.e. correct on average) estimate of the population variance.

Using the correct formula is more important the smaller is the sample size, as the proportionate difference between $n-1$ and n increases. For example, if $n = 10$, the adjustment amounts to 10% of the variance; when $n = 100$ the adjustment is only 1%.

The sample standard deviation is given by the square root of equation (1.18) or (1.19).

Alternative formulae for calculating the variance and standard deviation

The following formulae give the same answers as equations (1.14) to (1.17) but are simpler to calculate, either by hand or using a spreadsheet. For the population variance one can use

$$(1.20) \quad \sigma^2 = \frac{\sum x^2}{N} - \mu^2$$

or, for grouped data,

$$(1.21) \quad \sigma^2 = \frac{\sum fx^2}{\sum f} - \mu^2$$

---

[1] The concept of *bias* is treated in more detail in Chapter 5.

The calculation of the variance using equation (1.21) is shown in Fig. 1.14. The sample variance can be calculated using

$$(1.22) \quad s^2 = \frac{\sum x^2 - n\bar{x}^2}{n-1}$$

or, for grouped data,

$$(1.23) \quad s^2 = \frac{\sum fx^2 - n\bar{x}^2}{n-1}$$

The standard deviation may of course be obtained as the square root of these formulae.

Using a calculator or computer for calculation

Electronic calculators and (particularly) computers have simplified the calculation of the mean, etc. Figure 1.14 shows how to set out the above calculations in a spreadsheet (*Microsoft Excel* in this case) including some of the appropriate cell formulae.

The variance in this case is calculated using the formula $\sigma^2 = \dfrac{\sum fx^2}{\sum f} - \mu^2$

which is the formula given in equation (1.21) above. Note that it gives the same result.

The following formulae are contained in the cells:

D5:	=C5*B5	to calculate f times x
E5:	=D5*B5	to calculate f times x^2
H6:	=D18/C18	calculates $\Sigma fx / \Sigma f$
H7:	=E18/C18−H6^2	calculates $\Sigma fx^2 / \Sigma f - \mu^2$
H8:	=SQRT(H7)	calculates σ
H9:	=H8/H6	calculates σ/μ

Fig. 1.14 *Descriptive statistics calculated using Excel*

	A	B	C	D	E	F	G	H
1								
2		WEALTH DATA						
3	Wealth	Mid-point frequency						
4	Range	x	f	fx	fx sqd		Summary statistics	
5	0	5.0	3,330	16,650	83,250			
6	10,000	17.5	3,186	55,755	975,713		Mean	62.482
7	25,000	32.5	2,876	93,470	3,037,775		Variance	12543.57
8	40,000	45.0	1,204	54,180	2,438,100		Std. devn.	111.998
9	50,000	55.0	1,003	55,165	3,034,075		Coef. varn	1.792
10	60,000	70.0	1,663	116,410	8,148,700			
11	80,000	90.0	1,267	114,030	10,262,700			
12	100,000	150.0	1,793	268,950	40,342,500			
13	200,000	250.0	390	97,500	24,375,000			
14	300,000	400.0	211	84,400	33,760,000			
15	500,000	750.0	77	57,750	43,312,500			
16	1,000,000	1,500.0	17	25,500	38,250,000			
17	2,000,000	3,000.0	8	24,000	72,000,000			
18	Totals		17,025	1,063,760	280,020,313			

The coefficient of variation

The measures of dispersion examined so far are all measures of **absolute dispersion** and, in particular, their values depend upon the units in which the variable is measured. It is therefore difficult to compare the degrees of dispersion of two variables which are measured in different units. For example, one could not compare wealth in the UK with that in Germany if the former uses £s and the latter Deutschmarks for measurement. Nor could one compare the wealth distribution in one country between two points in time because inflation alters the value of the currency over time. The solution is to use a measure of **relative dispersion**, which is independent of the units of measurement. One such measure is the **coefficient of variation**, defined as:

$$(1.24) \quad \textit{Coefficient of variation} = \frac{\sigma}{\mu}$$

i.e. the standard deviation divided by the mean. Whenever the units of measurement are changed, the effect upon the mean and the standard deviation is the same, hence the coefficient of variation is unchanged. For the wealth distribution its value is $111.998/62.482 = 1.7925$, i.e. the standard deviation is 179% of the mean. This may be compared directly with the coefficient of variation of a different wealth distribution to see which exhibits a greater degree of dispersion.

The standard deviation of the logarithm

Another solution to the problem of different units of measurement is to use the logarithm[2] of wealth rather than the actual value. The reason why this works can best be illustrated by an example. Suppose that between 1979 and 1988 each individual's wealth doubled, so that $X_i^{88} = 2X_i^{79}$, where X_i^t indicates the wealth of individual i in year t. The standard deviation of X^{88} is therefore twice that of X^{79}. Taking logs, we have $\ln X_i^{88} = \ln 2 + \ln X_i^{79}$, so that the distribution of $\ln X^{88}$ is the same as that of $\ln X^{79}$ except that it is shifted to the right by $\ln 2$ units. The variances (and hence standard deviations) of the two logarithmic distributions are the same, indicating no change in the *relative* dispersion of the two wealth distributions.

The standard deviation of the logarithm of wealth is calculated from the data in Table 1.10. The variance is therefore:

$$\sigma^2 = \frac{228{,}081.885}{17{,}025} - \left(\frac{58{,}959.289}{17{,}025}\right)^2 = 1.4038$$

and the standard deviation $\sigma = 1.1848$. See below for a comparison with the 1979 figures.

Measuring deviations from the mean: z-scores

Imagine the following problem. A man and a woman are arguing over their career records. The man says he earns more than she does, so is more successful. The woman replies that women are discriminated against and that, relative to women, she is doing better than the man is, relative to other men. Can the argument be resolved?

Suppose the data are as follows: the average male salary is £19,500, the average female salary £16,800. The standard deviation of male salaries is £4,750, for women it is £3,800. The man's salary is £31,375 while the woman's is £26,800. The man is therefore £11,875 above the mean, the woman £10,000. However, women's salaries are less dispersed than men's, so the women has done well to get to £26,800.

One way to resolve the problem is to calculate the *z*-score, which gives the salary in terms of standard deviations from the mean. Thus for the man, the *z*-score is

$$(1.25) \quad z = \frac{X - \mu}{\sigma} = \frac{31{,}375 - 19{,}500}{4{,}750} = 2.50$$

---

[2] See Appendix 1C if you are unfamiliar with logarithms.

Table 1.10   Calculation of the standard deviation of the logarithm of wealth

Range	Mid-point x (£000)	$\ln(x)$	Frequency f	Deviation fx	fx^2
0–	5	1.609	3,330	5,359.428	8,625.667
10,000–	17.5	2.862	3,186	9,118.972	26,100.330
25,000–	32.5	3.481	2,876	10,012.046	34,854.338
40,000–	45	3.807	1,204	4,583.222	17,446.778
50,000–	55	4.007	1,003	4,019.355	16,106.895
60,000–	70	4.248	1,663	7,065.248	30,016.671
80,000–	90	4.500	1,267	5,701.259	25,654.580
100,000–	150	5.011	1,793	8,984.069	45,015.894
200,000–	250	5.521	390	2,153.370	11,889.747
300,000–	400	5.991	211	1,264.199	7,574.404
500,000–	750	6.620	77	509.746	3,374.553
1,000,000–	1,500	7.313	17	124.325	909.214
2,000,000–	3,000	8.006	8	64.051	512.815
Totals			17,025	58,959.289	228,081.885

Note: Use the 'ln' key on your calculator or the =LN() function in a spreadsheet to obtain natural logarithms of the data. You should obtain ln 5 = 1.609, ln 17.5 = 2.862, etc.

Thus the man is 2.5 standard deviations above the male mean salary. For the woman the calculation is

$$(1.26) \quad z = \frac{26{,}800 - 16{,}800}{3{,}800} = 2.632$$

The woman is 2.632 standard deviations above her mean and therefore wins the argument – she is nearer the top of her distribution than is the man and so is more of an outlier. Actually, this probably won't end the argument, but is the best the statistician can do. The z-score will be used again later in the book when we cover hypothesis testing (Chapter 6).

Chebyshev's inequality

Use of the z-score leads on naturally to **Chebyshev's inequality**, which tells us about the proportion of observations that fall into the tails of any distribution, regardless of its shape. The theorem is expressed as follows:

Chebyshev's inequality

(1.27)   At least $(1-1/k^2)$ of the observations in any distribution lie within k standard deviations of the mean

If we take the female distribution given above we can ask what proportion of women lie beyond 2.632 standard deviations from the mean (in both tails of the distribution). Setting $k = 2.632$, then $(1-1/k^2) = (1-1/2.632^2) = 0.8556$. So at least 85% of women have salaries within ±2.632 standard deviations of the mean, i.e. between £6,800 (= 16,800 − 2.632 × 3,800) and £26,800 (=16,800 + 2.632 × 3,800). 15% of women therefore lie outside this range.

Chebyshev's inequality is a very conservative rule since it applies to *any* distribution; if we know more about the shape of a particular distribution (for example, men's heights follow a Normal distribution – see Chapter 4) then we can make a more precise statement. In this example, over 99% of men are within 2.632 standard deviations of the average height, because there is a concentration of observations near the centre of the distribution.

Measuring skewness

The **skewness** of a distribution is the third characteristic that was mentioned earlier, in addition to location and dispersion. The wealth distribution is heavily skewed to the right, or **positively** skewed; it has its long tail in the right-hand end of the distribution. A measure of skewness gives a numerical indication of how asymmetric is the distribution.

One measure of skewness, known as the **coefficient of skewness**, is

(1.28) $$\frac{\sum f(x - \mu)^3}{N\sigma^3}$$

and it is based upon *cubed* deviations from the mean. The result of applying formula (1.28) is positive for a right skewed distribution (such as wealth), zero for a symmetric one, and negative for a left skewed one. Table 1.11 shows the calculation for the wealth data (some rows are omitted for brevity). Thus:

$$\frac{\sum f(x - \mu)^3}{N} = \frac{289{,}212{,}377{,}583.23}{17{,}025} = 16{,}987{,}511.16$$

and dividing by σ^3 gives $\dfrac{16{,}987{,}511.16}{111.9980631^3} = 12.092$, which is positive, as expected.

The measure of skewness is much less useful in practical work than measures of location and dispersion, and even knowing the value of the coefficient does not always give much idea of the shape of the distribution: two quite different distributions can share the same coefficient. In descriptive work it is probably better to draw the histogram itself.

Comparison of the 1988 and 1979 distributions of wealth

Some useful lessons may be learned by comparing the 1988 distribution with its counterpart from 1979 (at the start of the Conservative administration in the UK). This shows how useful the various summary statistics are when it comes to comparing two different distributions. The wealth data for 1979 are given in exercise 1.5 below, where you are asked to confirm the following calculations.

Table 1.11 Calculation of skewness of wealth data

Range	x	f	$x - \mu$	$(x - \mu)^3$	$f(x - \mu)^3$
0–	5.0	3,330	−57.482232	(189,933.193)	−632,477,533.42
10,000–	17.5	3,186	−44.982232	(91,017.102)	−289,980,487.24
⋮	⋮	⋮	⋮	⋮	⋮
1,000,000–	1,500.0	17	1,437.51777	2,970,569,133.382	50,499,675,267.50
2,000,000–	3,000.0	8	2,937.51777	25,347,872,067.072	202,782,976,536.57
Totals				28,688,838,597.660	289,212,377,583.23

Average wealth in 1979 was £16,399, just over a quarter of its 1988 value. The average increased substantially, therefore, but some of this was due to inflation rather than a real increase in the quantity of assets held. In fact between 1979 and 1988 the retail price index rose from 59.9 to 113.0, i.e. it roughly doubled, so there was a substantial increase in the real (i.e. after adjusting for price increases) value of assets held. The real value roughly doubled, and the nominal[3] increase (i.e. in cash terms, before any adjustment for rising prices) in wealth can be approximately equally divided between an inflationary component and a real one. Price indexes are covered in Chapter 2 where it is shown more formally how to divide a nominal increase into price and quantity components. It is likely that the extent of the real increase in assets is overstated here due to the use of the retail price index rather than an index of asset prices. A substantial part of the increase in asset values over the period is probably due to the very rapid rise in house prices (houses form a significant part of the wealth of many households).

The standard deviation is similarly affected by inflation. The 1979 value is 25,552 compared to 1988's 111,998, which is about 4.4 times larger. The spread of the distribution appears to have increased (even if we take account of the general price effect). Looking at the coefficient of variation, however, shows that it has increased from 1.56 to 1.79 which is not such a dramatic change. The spread of the distribution *relative to its mean* has not changed very much. Indeed, calculating the standard deviation of the logarithm for 1979 gives a figure of 1.31, *larger* than the 1988 figure (1.18) suggesting a reduction over time in the degree of relative dispersion. The fact that these results contradict each other suggests that (a) any change in relative dispersion over the period was not very large, and (b) it is difficult to find a definitive measure of dispersion. The standard deviation of the logarithm tends to give less weight to large observations (since the logarithmic transformation condenses the top of the distribution) than does the coefficient of variation; perhaps there has been a reduction of dispersion at the bottom of the distribution but an increase at the top.

The measure of skewness for the 1979 data comes out as 5.723, smaller that the 1988 figure. This suggests that the 1979 distribution is less skewed than is the 1988 one. Again, these two figures can be directly compared because they do not depend upon the units in which wealth is measured.

Time-series data: investment expenditures 1961–91

The data on the wealth distribution give a snapshot of the situation at particular points in time, and comparisons can be made between the 1979 and 1988 snapshots. Often, however, we wish to focus on the time-path of a variable and therefore we use **time-series data**. The techniques of presentation and summarising are slightly different than for cross-section data. As an example, we use data on investment in the UK for the period 1961–91. These data are taken from the UK *Economic Trends Annual Supplement*, 1993 edition, page 64. Investment expenditure is important to the economy because it is one of the prime determinants of growth. Since the UK economy's growth record since 1945 has been poor by international standards, lack of investment may be a cause. The variable studied is total gross (i.e. before depreciation is deducted) domestic fixed capital formation (GDFCF), measured in £m. The data are shown in Table 1.12.

---

[3] This is a different meaning of the term 'nominal' from that used earlier to denote data measured on a nominal scale, i.e. data grouped into categories without an obvious ordering. Unfortunately, both meanings of the word are in common (statistical) usage, though it should be obvious from the context which use is meant.

Table 1.12 UK investment, 1961–91

Year	GDFCF	Year	GDFCF	Year	GDFCF
1961	4,750	1972	11,940	1983	48,615
1962	4,904	1973	14,726	1984	54,967
1963	5,144	1974	17,497	1985	60,353
1964	6,123	1975	21,035	1986	64,514
1965	6,630	1976	24,504	1987	74,077
1966	7,063	1977	27,036	1988	89,857
1967	7,708	1978	31,060	1989	103,262
1968	8,506	1979	36,925	1990	106,028
1969	8,832	1980	41,561	1991	95,442
1970	9,736	1981	41,304		
1971	10,894	1982	44,824		

Note: Time–series data consist of observations on one or more variables over several time periods. The observations can be daily, weekly, monthly, quarterly or, as here, annually.

It should be remembered that the data are in current prices so that the figures reflect price increases as well as changes in the volume of physical investment. The series in Table 1.12 thus shows the actual amount of cash that was spent each year on investment. The techniques used below for summarising the investment data could equally well be applied to a series showing the volume of investment.

First of all we can use graphical techniques to gain an insight into the characteristics of investment. Figure 1.15 shows a **time-series graph** of investment. The graph plots the time periods on the horizontal axis and the investment variable on the vertical.

Plotting the data in this way brings out clearly some key features of the series:

- The **trend** in investment is upwards, with only two years in which there was either no increase or a decrease.
- The trend is **non-linear** – it follows an increasingly steep curve over time. This is essentially because investment grows by a *percentage* or *proportionate* amount each year. As we shall see shortly, it grows by about 10% each year. Therefore, as

Fig. 1.15 *Time-series graph of investment in the UK, 1961–91*

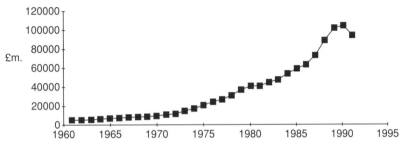

Note: The *X*, *Y* co-ordinates are the values {year, investment}; the first data point has the co-ordinates {1961, 4,750}, for example.

the level of investment increases each year, so does the increase in the level, giving a non-linear graph.

- Something fairly dramatic seems to occur in 1990–91, as investment expenditure diverges from its historical growth path. If we want to know what factors determine investment (or the effect of investment upon other economic magnitudes) we should get some useful insights from this period of the data.
- Successive values of the investment variable are similar in magnitude, i.e. the value in year t is similar to that in $t-1$. Investment does not change from £40bn in one year to £10bn the next, then back to £50bn, for instance. In fact, the value in one year appears to be based on the value in the previous year, plus (in general) 10% or so. We refer to this phenomenon as **serial correlation** and it is one of the aspects of the data that we might wish to investigate. The *ordering* of the data matters, unlike the case with cross-section data where the ordering is usually irrelevant. In deciding how to model investment behaviour, we might focus on *changes* in investment from year to year.
- The series seems 'smoother' in the earlier years (up to perhaps 1970) and exhibits greater volatility later on. In other words, there are greater fluctuations *around* the trend in the later years. We could express this more formally by saying that the variance of investment around its trend appears to change (increase) over time. This is known as **heteroscedasticity**; a constant variance is termed **homoscedasticity**.

We may gain further insight into how investment evolves over time by focusing on the *change* in investment from year to year. If we denote investment in year t by I_t then the change in investment, ΔI_t, is given by $I_t - I_{t-1}$. Table 1.13 shows the changes in investment each year and Fig. 1.16 provides a time-series graph.

The series is made up of mainly positive values, indicating that investment increases over time. It also shows that the increase grows each year, with perhaps some greater volatility (of the increase) towards the end of the period. The graph also shows dramatically the change that occurred in 1991.

Table 1.13   The change in investment

Year	ΔGDFCF	Year	ΔGDFCF	Year	ΔGDFCF
1961	518	1972	1,046	1983	3,791
1962	154	1973	2,786	1984	6,352
1963	240	1974	2,771	1985	5,386
1964	979	1975	3,538	1986	4,161
1965	507	1976	3,469	1987	9,563
1966	433	1977	2,532	1988	15,780
1967	645	1978	4,024	1989	13,405
1968	798	1979	5,865	1990	2,766
1969	326	1980	4,636	1991	−10,586
1970	904	1981	−257		
1971	1,158	1982	3,520		

Note: The change in investment is obtained by taking the difference between successive observations. For example, 154 is the difference between 4,904 and 4,750.

Fig. 1.16 *Time-series graph of the change in investment*

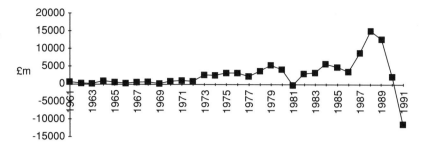

Outliers

Graphing data also allows you to see **outliers** (unusual observations). Outliers might be due to an error in inputting the data (e.g. typing 475 instead of 4750) or because something unusual happened (e.g. the investment figure for 1991). Either of these should be apparent from an appropriate graph. For example, the graph of the change in investment highlights the 1991 figure. In the case of a straight-forward error you should obviously correct it. If you are satisfied that the outlier is not simply a typo, you might want to think about the possible reasons for its existence and whether it distorts the descriptive picture you are trying to paint.

Another useful way of examining the data is to look at the **logarithm** of investment. This transformation has the effect of straightening out the non-linear investment series. Table 1.14 shows the transformed values and Fig. 1.17 graphs the series. In this case we use the natural (base *e*) logarithm.

This new series is much smoother than the original one and is helpful in showing the long-run trend, though it tends to mask some of the volatility of investment. The slope of the graph gives a close approximation to the average rate of growth of investment over the period (expressed as a decimal). This is calculated as follows:

Table 1.14 The logarithm of investment and the change in the logarithm

Year	ln GDFCF	Δln GDFCF	Year	ln GDFCF	Δln GDFCF	Year	ln GDFCF	Δln GDFCF
1961	8.466	0.115	1972	9.388	0.092	1983	10.792	0.081
1962	8.498	0.032	1973	9.597	0.210	1984	10.914	0.123
1963	8.546	0.048	1974	9.770	0.172	1985	11.008	0.093
1964	8.720	0.174	1975	9.954	0.184	1986	11.075	0.067
1965	8.799	0.080	1976	10.107	0.153	1987	11.213	0.138
1966	8.863	0.063	1977	10.205	0.098	1988	11.406	0.193
1967	8.950	0.087	1978	10.344	0.139	1989	11.545	0.139
1968	9.049	0.099	1979	10.517	0.173	1990	11.571	0.026
1969	9.086	0.038	1980	10.635	0.118	1991	11.466	−0.105
1970	9.184	0.097	1981	10.629	−0.006			
1971	9.296	0.112	1982	10.710	0.082			

Note: For 1961, 8.466 is the natural logarithm of 4,750, i.e. ln 4,750 = 8.466.

Fig. 1.17 *Time-series graph of the logarithm of investment expenditures*

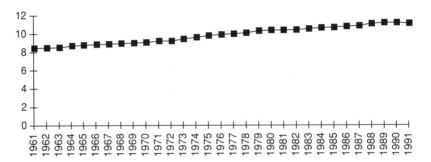

$$(1.29) \quad slope = \frac{change\ in\ (ln)\ investment}{number\ of\ years} = \frac{11.467 - 8.466}{30} = 0.100$$

i.e. 10% per annum. Note that although there are 31 observations, there are only 30 years of growth. A word of warning: you must use natural (base e) logarithms, not logarithms to the base 10, for this calculation to work. Remember also that the growth of the *volume* of investment will be less than 10% per annum, because part of it is due to price increases.

The logarithmic presentation is useful when comparing two different data series: when graphed in logs it is easy to see which is growing faster – just see which series has the steeper slope.

A corollory of equation (1.29) is that change in the natural logarithm of investment from one year to the next represents the *percentage* change in the data. For example, the natural logarithm of investment in 1961 is 8.466, while in 1962 it is 8.498. The difference is 0.032, so the rate of growth is 3.2%. You can verify this using the original data.

Finally we can graph the difference of the logarithm, as we graphed the difference of the level. This is shown in Fig. 1.18 (the calculations are in Table 1.14).

This is quite revealing. It shows the series fluctuating about the value of approximately 0.10 (the average calculated in equation (1.29) above), without a trend. Furthermore, the series does not seem to show increasing volatility over time, as the others did. The graph therefore demonstrates that in *proportionate* terms there is no increasing volatility; the variance of the series around 0.10 does not change much over time (though 1991 still seems to be an 'unusual' observation). We may loosely refer to this series as being **stationary** – it has a constant mean and variance. This is not a formal definition of the term, which imposes stricter conditions on the series, but it is a useful one to refer to.

Fig. 1.18 *Time-series graph of the difference of the logarithmic series*

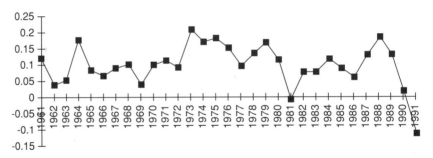

Graphing multiple series

Investment is made up of different categories: the table in exercise 1.14 presents investment data under four different headings: dwellings; other building and works; vehicles, ships and aircraft; and plant and machinery. Together they make up total investment. It is often useful to show all of the series together on one graph. Fig. 1.19 shows a **multiple time-series graph** of the investment data.

Construction of this type of graph is straightforward; it is just an extension of the technique for presenting a single series. It is easily, though laboriously, done by hand but most computer software can produce this type of chart very quickly. The only complication arises when the series are of different orders of magnitude and it is difficult to make all the series visible on the chart. In this case you can chart some of the series against a second vertical scale, on the right-hand axis. An example is shown in Fig. 1.20, plotting the investment data with the interest rate, which has much smaller numerical values.

Returning to the investment categories, Fig. 1.19 shows that 'plant and machinery' and 'other building and works' are the two largest categories and are of approximately equal size. This has not altered much over the period. All the series demonstrate generally similar patterns of behaviour over the time period. (One could also produce multiple plots of the logarithm of investment and of the change.)

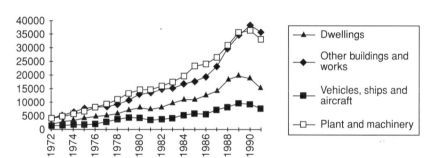

Fig. 1.19 *A multiple time-series graph of investment*

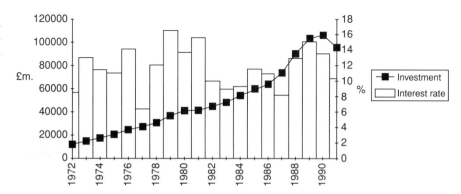

Fig. 1.20 *Time-series graph using two vertical scales: investment (LH scale) and the interest rate (RH scale), 1972–91*

Overlapping the ranges of the data series

The graph below, taken from the *Treasury Briefing*, February 1994, provides a nice example of how to plot multiple time-series and compare them. The aim is to compare the recessions and recoveries of 1974–78, 1979–83, and 1990–93. Instead of plotting time on the horizontal axis, the number of quarters since the start of each recession is used, so that the series overlap. This makes it easy to see the depth of the last recession and the long time before recovery commenced. By contrast, the 1974–78 recession ended quite quickly and recovery was quite rapid.

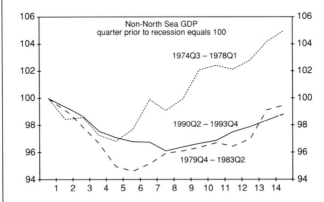

Number of quarters from onset of recession (0 is quarter prior to recession)

These series may also be illustrated by means of an **area graph**, which plots the four series stacked one on top of the other, as illustrated in Fig. 1.21.

This shows, for example, that construction (of all types) makes up about half of all investment and that this proportion has not changed significantly over the period shown.

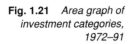

Fig. 1.21 *Area graph of investment categories, 1972–91*

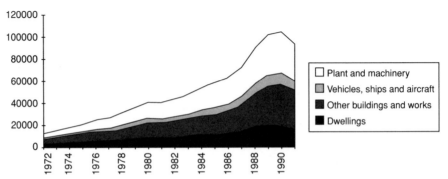

'Chart Junk'

With modern computer software it is easy to get carried away and produce a chart that actually hides more than it reveals. There is a great temptation to add some 3-D effects, liven it up with a bit of colour, rotate and tilt the viewpoint, etc. This sort of stuff is generally known as 'chart junk'. As an example, look at Fig. 1.22 which is an alternative to the area graph in Fig. 1.21 above. It was fun to create, but it doesn't get the message across at all! Taste is of course personal, but moderation is usually an essential part of it.

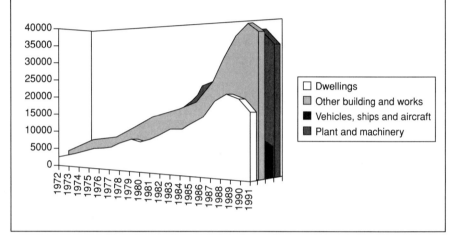

Fig. 1.22 *Over-the-top graph of investment*

Numerical summary statistics

The graphs have revealed quite a lot about the data already, but we can also calculate numerical descriptive statistics as we did for the cross-section data. First we consider the mean, then the variance and standard deviation.

The mean of a time series

We could calculate the mean of investment itself, but would this be helpful? Because the series is trended, it passes through the mean at some point between 1961 and 1991, but never returns to it. The mean of the series is actually £35.155bn, which is not very informative since it tells nothing about its value today, for instance. The problem is that the variable is trended, so that the mean is not typical of the series. The annual increase in investment is also trended, so is subject to the same criticism.

It is better to calculate the average growth rate, since this appears stationary (Fig. 1.18 above). This was calculated in equation (1.29) as approximately 10% per annum by calculating the slope of the graph of the ln investment series. We can get an accurate value in the following way:

(1) Calculate the overall **growth factor** of the series, i.e. x_T/x_1 where x_T is the final observation and x_1 is the initial observation.
(2) Take the $T-1$ root of the growth factor.
(3) Subtract 1 from the result in the previous step, giving the growth rate as a decimal.

For the investment data we have:

(1) $\dfrac{x_T}{x_1} = \dfrac{95{,}442}{4{,}750} = 20.09305$, i.e. investment expenditure is 20 times larger in 1991 than in 1961.

(2) $\sqrt[30]{20.09305} = 1.105185.$

(3) $1.105185 - 1 = 0.105185.$

Thus the average growth rate of investment is 10.5% per annum, rather than the 10% calculated earlier. (Step 2 can be performed on a scientific calculator by raising 20.09305 to the power 1/30, i.e. $20.09305^{(1/30)} = 1.105185$.)

(Note that we could have obtained the accurate answer from our earlier calculation as follows:

- the slope of the graph is 0.100012 (equation (1.29) above)
- calculate the anti-log (e^x) of this: $e^{0.100012} = 1.105185$
- subtract 1, giving a growth rate of $1.105185 - 1 = 0.105185 = 10.5\%$ p.a.)

Note that, since the calculated growth rate is based only upon the initial and final observations, it could be unreliable if either of these two values is an outlier.

The geometric mean   In calculating the average growth rate of investment we have implicitly calculated the **geometric mean** of a series. If we have a series of n values, then their geometric mean is calculated as the nth root of the *product* of the values, i.e.

The symbol Π (Greek 'pie') means 'the product of' in the same way as Σ means the sum.

$$(1.30) \quad geometric\ mean = \sqrt[n]{\prod_{i=1}^{n} x_i}$$

The x values in this case are the growth factors in each year, as in Table 1.15 (the values in intermediate years are omitted).

The product of the 30 growth factors is 20.09305 (the same as is obtained by dividing the final observation by the initial one – why?) and the 30th root of this is 1.105185. This latter figure, 1.105185, is the geometric mean of the growth factors and from it we can derive the growth rate of 10.5% p.a. by subtracting 1.

Table 1.15   Calculation of the geometric mean – annual growth factors

Year	GDFCF	Growth factors	
1961	4,750		
1962	4,904	1.032421	(= 4,904/4,750)
1963	5,144	1.048940	(= 5,144/4,904)
1964	6,123	1.190319	etc.
1965	6,630	1.082803	
⋮	⋮	⋮	
1986	64,514		
1987	74,077	1.148231	
1988	89,857	1.213022	
1989	103,262	1.149181	
1990	106,028	1.026786	
1991	95,442	0.900158	
Product		20.093050	

Note: Each growth factor simply shows the ratio of that year's investment to the previous year's.

Whenever one is dealing with growth data (or any series that is based on a multiplicative process) one should use the geometric mean rather than the arithmetic mean to get the answer. However, using the arithmetic mean in this case generally gives only a small error, as is indicated below.

Compound interest

The calculations we have performed relating to growth rates are analogous to computing **compound interest**. If we invest £100 at a rate of interest of 10% per annum, then the sum invested will grow at 10% p.a. (assuming all the interest is reinvested). Thus after one year the sum will have grown to £100 × 1.1 (£110), after two years to £100 × 1.1^2 (£121) and after t years to £100 × 1.1^t. The general formula for the terminal value S_t of a sum S_0 invested for t years at a rate of interest r is

(1.31) $S_t = S_0 (1+r)^t$

where r is expressed as a decimal. Rearranging (1.31) to make r the subject yields

(1.32) $r = \sqrt[t]{S_t \Big/ S_0} - 1$

which is precisely the formula for the average growth rate. To give a further example: suppose an investment fund turns an initial deposit of £8,000 into £13,500 over 12 years. What is the average rate of return on the investment? Setting $S_0 = 8$, $S_t = 13.5$, $t = 12$ and using (1.32) we obtain

$$r = \sqrt[12]{13.5 \Big/ 8} - 1 = 0.045$$

or 4.5% per annum.

Formula (1.32) can also be used to calculate the **depreciation rate** and the amount of annual depreciation on a firm's assets. In this case, S_0 represents the initial value of the asset, S_t represents the final or scrap value, and the annual rate of depreciation is given by r from equation (1.32).

An approximate way of obtaining the average growth rate

We have seen that when calculating rates of growth one should use the geometric mean, but if the growth rate is reasonably small then taking the arithmetic mean will give approximately the right answer. The arithmetic mean of the growth factors is

$$\frac{1.032421 + 1.048940 + \ldots + 1.0296786 + 0.900158}{30} = 1.107468$$

giving an estimate of the growth rate of 10.75% p.a. – not far off the correct value. Note also that one could equivalently take the average of the annual growth rates (0.032421, 0.048940, etc.), giving 0.107468, to get the same result. Use of the arithmetic mean is justified in this context if one needs only an approximation to the right answer and annual growth rates are reasonably small.

The variance of a time series

How should we describe the variance of a time series? The variance of the investment data can be calculated, but it would be uninformative in the same way as the mean. Since the series is trended, and this is likely to continue in the longer run (1991 notwithstanding), the variance is in principle equal to infinity. The calculated variance would be closely tied to the sample size: the larger it is, the larger the variance. Again it makes more sense to calculate the variance of the growth rate, which is a stationary series.

This variance can be calculated from the formula:

$$(1.33) \quad s^2 = \frac{\sum\left(x - \bar{x}\right)^2}{n-1} = \frac{\sum x^2 - n\bar{x}^2}{n-1}$$

where $\bar{x}$ is the (arithmetic) average rate of growth. The calculation is set out in Table 1.16 using the right-hand formula in (1.33).

The variance is therefore

$$s^2 = \frac{0.493517 - 30 \times 0.107468^2}{29} = 0.00507$$

and the standard deviation is 0.0712, the square root of the variance. The coefficient of variation is

$$cv = \frac{0.0712}{0.107468} = 0.663$$

i.e. the standard deviation of the growth rate is about 66% of the mean.

Note three things about this calculation: first, we have used the arithmetic mean (using the geometric mean makes very little difference); second, we have used the formula for the sample variance since the period 1961–91 constitutes a sample of all the possible data we could collect; and thirdly, we could have equally used the growth factors for the calculation of the variance (why?).

Table 1.16   Calculation of the variance of the growth rate

Year	GDFCF	Growth rate x	x^2
1961	4,750		
1962	4,904	0.032421	0.001051
1963	5,144	0.048940	0.002395
1964	6,123	0.190319	0.036221
1965	6,630	0.082803	0.006856
⋮	⋮	⋮	⋮
1986	64,514		
1987	74,077	0.148231	0.021973
1988	89,857	0.213022	0.045378
1989	103,262	0.149181	0.022255
1990	106,028	0.026786	0.000718
1991	95,442	−0.099840	0.009968
Totals		3.224034	0.493517

Graphing bivariate data: the scatter diagram

The analysis of investment is an example of the use of **univariate methods**: only a single variable is involved. However, we often wish to examine the relationship between two (or sometimes more) variables and we have to use **bivariate** (or **multivariate**) **methods**. To illustrate the methods involved we shall examine the relationship between investment expenditures and Gross Domestic Product (GDP). Table 1.17 provides data on GDP for the UK.

A **scatter diagram** (also called an **XY chart**) plots one variable (in this case investment) on the y axis, the other (GDP) on the x axis, and therefore shows the relationship between them. For example, one can see whether high values of one variable tend to be associated with high values of the other. Figure 1.23 shows the relationship for investment and GDP.

The chart shows a very strong linear relationship between the two variables, but we must be wary about drawing conclusions from this. Both variables are in nominal terms, i.e. they take no account of inflation over the time period. This may be seen algebraically: investment expenditure is made up of the *volume* of investment (I) times its *price* (P_I). Similarly, nominal GDP is real GDP (Y) times its price (P_Y). Thus the scatter diagram actually charts $P_I I$ against $P_Y Y$. It is likely that the two prices follow a similar trend over time and that this dominates the movements in real investment and GDP. The chart then shows the relationship between a mixture of

Table 1.17   GDP data

Year	GDP	Year	GDP	Year	GDP
1961	27,432	1971	57,748	1981	254,927
1962	28,812	1972	64,663	1982	279,041
1963	30,586	1973	74,257	1983	304,456
1964	33,435	1974	83,862	1984	325,852
1965	36,035	1975	105,852	1985	357,344
1966	38,370	1976	125,247	1986	384,843
1967	40,400	1977	145,983	1987	423,381
1968	43,808	1978	168,526	1988	471,430
1969	47,153	1979	198,221	1989	515,957
1970	51,770	1980	231,772	1990	551,118
				1991	573,645

Fig. 1.23 *Scatter diagram of investment (vertical axis) against GDP (horizontal axis) (nominal values)*

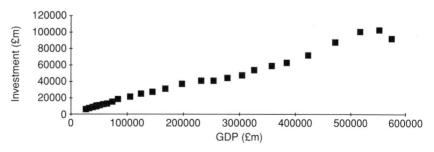

Note: The (x, y) co-ordinates of each point are given by the values of investment and GDP respectively. Thus the first (1961) data point is drawn 4,750 units above the horizontal axis and 27,432 units from the vertical one.

prices and quantities, when the more interesting relationship is between the quantities of investment and output.

Data transformations

In analysing employment and investment data in the examples above we have often changed the variables in some way in order to bring out the important characteristics. In statistics one usually works with data that have been transformed in some way rather than using the original numbers. It is therefore worthwhile to bring these together to summarise the reasons for the various transformations, and the implications in each case. We briefly deal with the following transformations:

- rounding
- grouping
- dividing or multiplying by a constant
- differencing
- taking logarithms
- taking the reciprocal
- deflating

Rounding

Rounding improves readability. Too much detail can hide the message, so rounding the answer makes it more memorable. To give an example, the average wealth holding calculated earlier in this chapter is actually £62,482.23201. How much should this be rounded for presentational purposes? Remember that the figures have already been effectively rounded by allocation to classes of width 10,000 or more (all observations have been rounded to the mid-point of the interval). However, much of this rounding is offsetting, i.e. numbers rounded up offset those rounded down, so the mean is reasonably accurate. Rounding to £62,500 makes the figure much easier to remember, and is only a change of 0.03% (62,482/62,500 = 0.9997), so is a reasonable compromise. In the text above the answer was not rounded to such an extent since the purpose was to highlight the methods of calculation.

Rounding is a 'trap door' function: you cannot obtain the original value from the transformed (rounded) value. Therefore, if you are going to need the original value in further calculations you should not round your answer. Furthermore, small rounding errors can cumulate, leading to a large error in the final answer. Therefore, you should never round an intermediate answer, only the final one. Even if you only round the intermediate answer by a small amount, the final answer could be grossly inaccurate. Try the following: calculate $60.29 \times 30.37 - 1831$ both before and after rounding the first two numbers to integers. In the first case you get 0.0073, in the second -31.

Grouping

When there is too much data to present easily, grouping solves the problem, although at the cost of hiding some of the information. The examples relating to education and unemployment and to wealth used grouped data. Using the raw data would have given us far too much information, so grouping is a first stage in data analysis. Grouping is another trap door transformation: once it's done you cannot recover the original information.

Dividing/multiplying by a constant

This transformation is carried out to make numbers more readable or to make calculation simpler by removing trailing zeroes. The data on wealth were divided by 1,000 to ease calculation; otherwise the fx^2 column would have contained extremely large values. Some summary statistics (e.g. the mean) will be affected by the transformation, but not all (e.g. the coefficient of variation). Try to remember which are affected! E and V operators (see Appendix 1B) can help. The transformation is easy to reverse.

Differencing

In time-series data there may be a trend, and it is better to describe the features of the data relative to the trend. The result may also be more economically meaningful, e.g. governments are often more concerned about the growth of output than about its level. Differencing is one way of eliminating the trend (see Chapter 11 for other methods of de-trending data). Differencing was used for the investment data for both of these reasons. One of the implications of differencing is that information about the *level* of the variable is lost and cannot be recovered.

Taking logarithms

Taking logarithms is used to linearise a non-linear series, in particular one that is growing at a constant rate. It is often easier to see the important features of such a series if the logarithm is graphed rather than the raw data. The logarithmic transformation is also useful in regression (see Chapter 9) because it yields estimates of *elasticities* (e.g. of demand). Taking the logarithm of the investment data linearised the series and tended to smooth it. The inverses of the logarithmic transformations are 10^x (for common logarithms) and e^x (for natural logarithms) so one can recover the original data.

Taking the reciprocal

The reciprocal of a variable might have a useful interpretation and provide a more intuitive explanation of a phenomenon. The reciprocal transformation will also turn a linear series into a non-linear one. The reciprocal of turnover in the labour market (i.e. the number leaving unemployment divided by the number unemployed) gives an idea of the duration of unemployment. If a half of those unemployed find work each year (turnover = 0.5) then the average duration of unemployment is 2 years (= 1/0.5). If a graph of turnover shows a linear decline over time, then the average duration of unemployment will be rising, at a faster and faster rate. Repeating the reciprocal transformation recovers the original data.

Deflating

Deflating turns a nominal series into a real one, i.e. one that reflects changes in quantities without the contamination of price changes. This is dealt with in more detail in the next chapter. It is often more meaningful in economic terms to talk about a real variable than a nominal one. Consumers are more concerned about their real income than about their money income, for example.

Confusing real and nominal variables is dangerous! For example, someone's nominal (money) income may be rising yet their real income falling (if prices are rising faster than money income). It is important to know which series you are dealing with (this is a common failing among students new to statistics and economics). An income series that is growing at 2–3% per annum is probably a real series; one that is growing at 10% per annum or more is likely to be nominal.

EXERCISES

Exercise 1

The following data show the education and employment status of women aged 20–29 (from the 1991 *General Household Survey*):

	Higher education	A levels	Other qualification	No qualification	Total
In work	209	182	577	92	1,060
Unemployed	12	9	68	32	121
Inactive	17	34	235	136	422
Sample	238	225	880	260	1,603

(a) Draw a bar chart of the numbers in work in each education category. Can this be easily compared with the similar diagram for males (Fig. 1.1)?

(b) Draw a stacked bar chart using all the employment states, similar to Fig. 1.3. Comment upon any similarities and differences from the diagram for men in the text.

(c) Convert the table into (column) percentages and produce a stacked bar chart similar to Fig. 1.4. Comment upon any similarities and differences.

(d) Draw a pie chart showing the distribution of educational qualifications of those in work and compare it to Fig. 1.5 in the text.

Exercise 2

The data below show the median weekly earnings (in £s) of those in full-time employment in Great Britain in 1992, by category of education.

	Degree	Other higher education	A level	GCSE A–C	GCSE D–G	None
Males	433	310	277	242	226	220
Females	346	278	201	183	173	146

(a) In what fundamental way do the data in this table differ from those in exercise 1?

(b) Construct a bar chart showing male and female earnings by education category. What does it show?

(c) Why would it be inappropriate to construct a stacked bar chart of the data? How should one graphically present the combined data for males and females? What extra information is necessary for you to do this?

Exercise 3

Using the data from exercise 1:

(a) Which education category has the highest proportion of people in work? What is the proportion?

(b) Which category of employment status has the highest proportion of people with a degree? What is the proportion?

Exercise 4

Using the data from exercise 2:

(a) What is the premium, in terms of median earnings, of a degree over A levels? Does this differ between men and women?

(b) Would you expect *mean* earnings to show a similar picture? What differences, if any, might you expect?

Exercise 5

The distribution of marketable wealth in 1979 in the UK is shown in the table below (taken from *Inland Revenue Statistics 1981*, p.105):

Range	Number 000s	Amount £m
0–	1,606	148
1,000–	2,927	5,985
3,000–	2,562	10,090
5,000–	3,483	25,464
10,000–	2,876	35,656
15,000–	1,916	33,134
20,000–	3,425	104,829
50,000–	621	46,483
100,000–	170	25,763
200,000–	59	30,581

Draw a bar chart and histogram of the data (assume the final class interval has a width of 200,000). Comment on the differences between the two. Comment on any differences between this histogram and the one for 1988 given in the text.

Exercise 6

The data below show the number of manufacturing plants in the UK in 1991/92 arranged according to employment:

Number of employees	Number of firms
1–	95,409
10–	15,961
20–	16,688
50–	7,229
100–	4,504
200–	2,949
500–	790
1,000–	332

Draw a bar chart and histogram of the data (assume the midpoint of the last class interval is 2,000). What are the major features apparent in each and what are the differences?

Exercise 7

Using the data from exercise 5:

(a) Calculate the mean, median and mode of the distribution. Why do they differ?

(b) Calculate the inter-quartile range, variance, standard deviation and coefficient of variation of the data.

(c) Calculate the skewness of the distribution.

(d) From what you have calculated, and the data in the chapter, can you draw any conclusions about the degree of inequality in wealth holdings, and how this has changed?

(e) What would be the effect upon the mean of assuming the final class width to be £10m? What would be the effects upon the median and mode?

Exercise 8

Using the data from exercise 6:

(a) Calculate the mean, median and mode of the distribution. Why do they differ?

(b) Calculate the inter-quartile range, variance, standard deviation and coefficient of variation of the data.

(c) Calculate the coefficient of skewness of the distribution.

Exercise 9

A motorist keeps a record of petrol purchases on a long journey, as follows:

Petrol station	1	2	3
Litres purchased	33	40	25
Price per litre	55.7	59.6	57.0

Calculate the average petrol price for the journey.

Exercise 10

Demonstrate that the weighted average calculation given in equation (1.9) is equivalent to finding the total expenditure on education divided by the total number of pupils.

Exercise 11

On a test taken by 100 students, the average mark is 65, with variance 144. Student A scores 83, student B scores 47.

(a) Calculate the z-scores for these two students.

(b) What is the maximum number of students with a score either better than A's or worse than B's?

(c) What is the maximum number of students with a score better than A's?

Exercise 12

The average income of a group of people is £8,000. 80% of the group have incomes within the range £6,000–10,000. What is the minimum value of the standard deviation of the distribution?

Exercise 13

The following data show car registrations in the UK during 1970–91 (source: *ETAS 1993*, p.57):

Year	Registrations	Year	Registrations	Year	Registrations
1970	91.4	1978	131.6	1986	156.9
1971	108.5	1979	142.1	1987	168.0
1972	177.6	1980	126.6	1988	184.2
1973	137.3	1981	124.5	1989	192.1
1974	102.8	1982	132.1	1990	167.1
1975	98.6	1983	150.5	1991	133.3
1976	106.5	1984	146.6		
1977	109.4	1985	153.5		

(a) Draw a time-series graph of car registrations. Comment upon the main features of the series.

(b) Draw time-series graphs of the change in registrations, the (natural) log of registrations, and the change in the ln. Comment upon the results.

Exercise 14

The table below shows the different categories of investment, 1972–91.

Year	Dwellings	Other building and works	Vehicles, ships and aircraft	Plant and machinery	Interest rate
1972	2,566	4,012	1,321	4,041	8.48
1973	3,150	5,063	1,621	4,892	12.82
1974	3,786	6,224	1,786	5,701	11.30
1975	4,682	7,645	1,989	6,719	10.93
1976	5,450	8,434	2,285	8,335	13.98
1977	5,699	8,479	3,151	9,707	6.39
1978	6,325	9,285	4,004	11,446	11.91
1979	7,649	11,053	4,684	13,539	16.49
1980	8,674	13,363	4,566	14,958	13.58
1981	8,138	14,253	3,846	15,067	15.39
1982	8,920	15,323	4,285	16,296	9.96
1983	10,447	15,703	4,530	17,935	9.04
1984	11,718	17,319	5,664	20,266	9.33
1985	11,854	18,190	6,439	23,870	11.49
1986	13,622	19,980	6,222	24,690	10.94
1987	15,274	23,925	7,805	27,073	8.38
1988	19,354	30,150	8,849	31,504	12.91
1989	20,986	35,570	10,324	36,382	15.02
1990	19,906	38,991	9,969	37,162	13.50
1991	16,645	36,529	8,452	33,816	10.45

Use appropriate graphical techniques to analyse the properties of any one of the investment series. Comment upon the results.

Exercise 15

Using the data from exercise 13:

(a) Calculate the average rate of growth of the series.

(b) Calculate the standard deviation around the average growth rate.

(c) Does the series appear to be more or less volatile than the investment figures used in the chapter? Suggest reasons.

Exercise 16

Using the data from exercise 14:

(a) Calculate the average rate of growth of the series for dwellings.

(b) Calculate the standard deviation around the average growth rate.

(c) Does the series appear to be more or less volatile than the investment figures used in the chapter? Suggest reasons.

Exercise 17

How would you *expect* the following time-series variables to look when graphed? (e.g. trended? Linear trend? Trended up or down? Stationary? Homoscedastic? Autocorrelated? Cyclical? Anything else?)

(a) Nominal national income.

(b) Real national income.

(c) The nominal interest rate.

Exercise 18

How would you expect the following time-series variables to look when graphed?

(a) The price level.

(b) The inflation rate.

(c) The £/$ exchange rate.

Exercise 19

(a) A government bond is issued, promising to pay the bearer £1,000 in five years' time. The prevailing market rate of interest is 7%. What price would you expect to pay now for the bond? What would its price be after two years? If, after two years, the market interest rate jumped to 10%, what would the price of the bond be?

(b) A bond is issued which promises to pay £200 per annum over the next five years. If the prevailing market interest rate is 7%, how much would you be prepared to pay for the bond? Why does the answer differ from the previous question? (Assume interest is paid at the end of each year.)

Exercise 20

A firm purchases a machine for £30,000 which is expected to last for 10 years, after which it will be sold for its scrap value of £3,000. Calculate the average rate of depreciation per annum, and calculate the written down value of the machine after one, two and five years.

Exercise 21

Depreciation of BMW and Mercedes cars is given in the following table:

Age	BMW 525i	Mercedes 200E
Current	22,275	21,900
1 year	18,600	19,700
2 years	15,200	16,625
3 years	12,600	13,950
4 years	9,750	11,600
5 years	8,300	10,300

(a) Calculate the average rate of depreciation of each type of car.

(b) Use the calculated depreciation rates to estimate the value of the car after 1, 2, etc. years of age. How does this match the actual values?

(c) Graph the values and estimated values for each car.

Exercise 22

A bond is issued which promises to pay £400 per annum in perpetuity. How much is the bond worth now, if the interest rate is 5%? (Hint: the sum of an infinite series of the form

$$\frac{1}{1+r} + \frac{1}{\left(1+r\right)^2} + \frac{1}{\left(1+r\right)^3} + \dots$$

is $1/r$, as long as $r > 0$.)

Exercise 23

Demonstrate, using Σ notation, that $E(x+k) = E(x)+k$.

Exercise 24

Demonstrate, using Σ notation, that $V(kx) = k^2 V(x)$.

Exercise 25

Criticise the following statistical reasoning: the average price of a dwelling is £54,150. The average mortgage advance is £32,760. So purchasers have to find £21,390, that is, about 40% of the purchase price. On any basis that is an enormous outlay which young couples, in particular, who are buying a house for the first time would find incredibly difficult, if not impossible, to raise.

Exercise 26

Criticise the following statistical reasoning: amongst arts graduates 10% fail to find employment. Amongst science graduates only 8% remain out of work. Therefore, science graduates are better than arts graduates. (Hint: imagine there are two types of job: popular and unpopular. Arts graduates tend to apply for the former, scientists for the latter.)

Exercise 27

Project 1: It has been claimed that, in spite of the UK government's desire to see lower taxation, the level of taxation in 1994 is higher than in 1979. Is this claim correct?

You should gather data which you think appropriate to the task, summarise it as necessary and write a brief report of your findings. You might like to consider the following points:

Should one consider tax revenue, or revenue as a proportion of GNP?

Should one distinguish between tax rates and the tax base (i.e. what is taxed)?

Has the balance between direct and indirect taxation changed?

Have different sections of the population fared differently?

You might like to consider other points, and do the exercise for a different country. Suitable data sources for the UK are: *Inland Revenue Statistics*, *UK National Accounts*, *Annual Abstract of Statistics* or *Financial Statistics*.

Exercise 28

Project 2: Is the employment and unemployment experience of the UK economy worse than that of its competitors? Write a report on this topic in a similar manner to the project above. You might consider rates of unemployment in the UK and other countries; trends in unemployment in each of the countries; the growth in employment in each country; the structure of employment (e.g. full-time/part-time) and unemployment (e.g. long-term/short-term).

You might use data for a number of countries, or concentrate on two in more depth. Suitable data sources are: *OECD Main Economic Indicators*; *European Economy* (published by the European Commission); *Employment Gazette*.

**Appendix 1A:
Σ notation**

The Greek symbol Σ (capital sigma) means 'add up' and is a shorthand way of writing what would otherwise be long algebraic expressions. For example, given the following observations on x:

x_1	x_2	x_3	x_4	x_5
3	5	6	4	8

then

$$\sum_{i=1}^{5} x_i = x_1 + x_2 + x_3 + x_4 + x_5 = 3 + 5 + 6 + 4 + 8 = 26$$

To expand the sigma expression, the subscript i is replaced by successive integers, beginning with the one below the Σ sign and ending with the one above it. Similarly

$$\sum_{i=2}^{4} x_i = x_2 + x_3 + x_4 = 5 + 6 + 4 = 15$$

When it is clear what range of values i takes, the formula can be simplified to

$$\sum_i x_i \text{ or } \sum x_i \text{ or even } \sum x.$$

When frequencies are associated with each of the observations, as in the data below:

i	1	2	3	4	5
x_i	3	5	6	4	8
f_i	2	2	4	3	1

then

$$\sum_{i=1}^{i=5} f_i x_i = f_1 x_1 + \ldots + f_5 x_5 = 2 \times 3 + \cdots + 1 \times 8 = 60$$

and

$$\sum f_i = 2 + 2 + 4 + 3 + 1 = 12$$

Thus the sum of the 12 observations is 60 and the mean is

$$\frac{\sum fx}{\sum f} = \frac{60}{12} = 5$$

Further examples are:

$$\sum x^2 = x_1^2 + x_2^2 + \cdots + x_5^2 = 150$$
$$\left(\sum x\right)^2 = \left(x_1 + x_2 + \cdots + x_5\right)^2 = 676$$
$$\sum fx^2 = f_1 x_1^2 + f_2 x_2^2 + \cdots + f_5 x_5^2 = 2 \times 3^2 + 2 \times 5^2 + \cdots + 1 \times 8^2 = 324$$

Using Σ notation we can see the effect of transforming x by dividing by 1,000, as was done in calculating the average level of wealth. Instead of working with x we used kx, where $k = 1/1,000$. In finding the mean we calculated

$$(1.34) \quad \frac{\sum kx}{N} = \frac{kx_1 + kx_2 + \cdots}{N} = \frac{k\left(x_1 + x_2 + \cdots\right)}{N} = k\frac{\sum x}{N}$$

so to find the mean of the original variable x we had to divide by k again, i.e. multiply by 1,000. In general, whenever each observation in a sum is multiplied by a constant, the constant can be taken outside the summation operator, as in (1.34) above.

EXERCISES ON Σ NOTATION

Exercise A1

Given the following data on x_i: {4, 6, 3, 2, 5}, evaluate:

$$\sum x_i, \ \sum x_i^2, \ \left(\sum x_i\right)^2, \ \sum\left(x_i - 3\right), \ \sum x_i - 3, \ \sum_{i=2}^{4} x_i$$

Exercise A2

Given the following data on x_i: $\{8, 12, 6, 4, 10\}$, evaluate:

$$\sum x_i, \ \sum x_i^2, \ \left(\sum x_i\right)^2, \ \sum(x_i - 3), \ \sum x_i - 3, \ \sum_{i=2}^{4} x_i$$

Exercise A3

Given the following frequencies, f_i, associated with the x values in exercise A1: $\{5, 3, 3, 8, 5\}$, evaluate:

$$\sum fx, \ \sum fx^2, \ \sum f(x-3), \ \sum fx - 3$$

Exercise A4

Given the following frequencies, f_i, associated with the x values in exercise 1A.2: $\{10, 6, 6, 16, 10\}$, evaluate:

$$\sum fx, \ \sum fx^2, \ \sum f(x-3), \ \sum fx - 3$$

Exercise A5

Given the pairs of observations on x and y,

x	4	3	6	8	12
y	3	9	1	4	3

evaluate $\sum xy, \ \sum x(y-3), \ \sum(x+2)(y-1)$.

Exercise A6

Given the pairs of observations on x and y,

x	3	7	4	1	9
y	1	2	5	1	2

evaluate $\sum xy, \ \sum x(y-2), \ \sum(x-2)(y+1)$.

Exercise A7

Demonstrate that $\dfrac{\sum f(x-k)}{\sum f} = \dfrac{\sum fx}{\sum f} - k$ where k is a constant.

Exercise A8

Demonstrate that $\dfrac{\sum f(x-\mu)^2}{\sum f} = \dfrac{\sum fx^2}{\sum f} - \mu^2$

Appendix 1B: E and V operators

These operators are an extremely useful form of notation that we shall make use of later in the book. It is quite easy to keep track of the effects of data transformations using them. There are a few simple rules for manipulating them that allow some problems to be solved quickly and elegantly.

$E(x)$ is the mean of a distribution and $V(x)$ is its variance. We showed above in (1.34) that multiplying each observation by a constant k multiplies the mean by k. Thus we have:

(1.35) $E(kx) = kE(x)$

If a constant is added to every observation the effect is to add that constant to the mean (see exercise 1.23):

(1.36) $E(x + a) = E(x) + a$

(Graphically, the whole distribution is shifted a units to the right and hence so is the mean.) Combining (1.35) and (1.36):

(1.37) $E(kx + a) = kE(x) + a$

Similarly for the variance operator it can be shown that:

(1.38) $V(x + k) = V(x)$

Proof:

$$V(x + k) = \frac{\sum\left((x + k) - (\mu + k)\right)^2}{N} = \frac{\sum\left((x - \mu) + (k - k)\right)^2}{N} = \frac{\sum(x - \mu)^2}{N} = V(x)$$

(A shift of the whole distribution leaves the variance unchanged.) Also (see exercise 1.24):

(1.39) $V(kx) = k^2\, V(x)$

This is why, when the wealth figures were divided by 1,000, the variance became divided by $1,000^2$. Applying (1.38) and (1.39):

(1.40) $V(kx + a) = k^2\, V(x)$

Finally we should note that V itself can be expressed in terms of E:

(1.41) $V(x) = E(x - E(x))^2$

Appendix 1C: Using logarithms

Logarithms are less often used now that cheap electronic calculators are available. Formerly logarithms were an indispensable aid to calculation. However, the logarithmic transformation is useful in other contexts in statistics and economics so its use is briefly set out here.

The logarithm (to the base 10) of a number x is defined as the power to which 10 must be raised to give x. For example, $10^2 = 100$, so the log of 100 is 2 and we write $\log_{10} 100 = 2$ or simply $\log 100 = 2$.

Similarly, the log of 1,000 is 3 ($1,000 = 10^3$), of 10,000 it is 4, etc. We are not restricted to integer (whole number) powers of 10, so for example $10^{2.5} = 316.227766$ (try this if you have a scientific calculator), so the log of 316.227766 is 2.5. Every number x can therefore be represented by its logarithm.

Multiplication of two numbers

We can use logarithms to multiply two numbers x and y, based on the property

$\log xy = \log x + \log y$

For example, to multiply 316.227766 by 10:

$$\log (316.227766 \times 10) = \log 316.227766 + \log 10$$
$$= 2.5 + 1$$
$$= 3.5$$

The *anti-log* of 3.5 is given by $10^{3.5} = 3{,}162.27766$ which is the answer.

Taking the anti-log (i.e. 10 raised to a power) is the inverse of the log transformation. Schematically we have:

$$x \to \text{take logarithms} \to a \ (= \log x) \to \text{raise 10 to the power } a \to x$$

Division

To divide one number by another we subtract the logs. For example, to divide 316.227766 by 100:

$$\log (316.227766/100) = \log 316.227766 - \log 100$$
$$= 2.5 - 2$$
$$= 0.5$$

and $10^{0.5} = 3.16227766$.

Powers and roots

Logarithms simplify the process of raising a number to a power. To find the square of a number, multiply the logarithm by 2, e.g. to find 316.227766^2:

$$\log(316.227766^2) = 2 \log (316.227766) = 5$$

and $10^5 = 100{,}000$.

To find the square root of a number (equivalent to raising it to the power $\frac{1}{2}$) divide the log by 2. To find the nth root, divide the log by n. For example, in the text we have to find the 30th root of 20.09305:

$$\frac{\log(20.09305)}{30} = 0.0434349$$

and $10^{0.0434349} = 1.105185$.

Common and natural logarithms

Logarithms to the base 10 are known as common logarithms but one can use any number as the base. *Natural* logarithms are based on the number e (= 2.71828. . .) and we write ln x instead of log x to distinguish them from common logarithms. So, for example,

$$\ln 316.227766 = 5.756462732$$

since $e^{5.756462732} = 316.227766$.

Natural logarithms can be used in exactly the same way as common logarithms and have the same properties. Use the 'ln' key on your calculator just as you would the 'log' key, but remember that the inverse transformation is e^x rather than 10^x.

EXERCISES ON LOGARITHMS

Exercise C1

Find the common logarithms of: 0.15, 1.5, 15, 150, 1500, 83.7225, 9.15, -12.

Exercise C2   Find the log of the following values: 0.8, 8, 80, 4, 16, -37.

Exercise C3   Find the natural logarithms of: 0.15, 1.5, 15, 225, -4.

Exercise C4   Find the ln of the following values: 0.3, e, 3, 33, -1.

Exercise C5   Find the anti-log of the following values: -0.823909, 1.1, 2.1, 3.1, 12.

Exercise C6   Find the anti-log of the following values: -0.09691, 2.3, 3.3, 6.3.

Exercise C7   Find the anti-ln of the following values: 2.70805, 3.70805, 1, 10.

Exercise C8   Find the anti-ln of the following values: 3.496508, 14, 15, -1.

Exercise C9   Evaluate: $\sqrt[2]{10}$, $\sqrt[4]{3.7}$, $4^{1/4}$, 12^{-3}, $25^{-3/2}$.

Exercise C10   Evaluate: $\sqrt[3]{30}$, $\sqrt[6]{17}$, $8^{1/4}$, 15^0, 12^0, $3^{-1/3}$.

References
A. B. Atkinson, *The Economics of Inequality*, 2nd edn, Oxford University Press, 1983.

B. Goffe, Resources for economists on the Internet, *Journal of Economic Perspectives*, Summer 1994.

R. Summers and A. Heston, The Penn World Table (Mark 5): an expanded set of international comparisons, 1950–1987, *Quarterly Journal of Economics*, pp. 1–41 (May 1991).

2 INDEX NUMBERS

Introduction

'The Retail Price Index in the second quarter of 1994 was 114.6, up 2.6% on its value a year earlier.'

The retail price index (RPI) referred to above is an example of an **index number**, which summarises a whole mass of information about the prices of different goods and services. Index numbers can also summarise information about quantities of goods and services. An index number is similar in purpose to other summary statistics such as the mean, and shares their advantages and disadvantages: it provides a useful overview of the data but misses out the finer detail.

Index numbers are most commonly used for following trends in data over time, such as the RPI measuring the price level or the index of industrial production (IIP) measuring the output of industry. The RPI also allows calculation of the rate of inflation, which is simply the rate of change of the price index; and from the IIP it is easy to measure the rate of growth of output. Index numbers are also used with cross-section data, for example an index of regional house prices would summarise information about the different levels of house prices in different regions of the country at a particular point in time. There are many other examples of index numbers in use, common ones being the Financial Times All Share index, the trade weighted exchange rate index, and the index of the value of retail sales.

This chapter will explain how index numbers are constructed from original data and the problems which arise in doing this. There is also a brief discussion of the RPI to illustrate some of these problems and to show how they are resolved in practice. Finally, a different set of index numbers is examined, which are used to measure inequality, such as inequality in the distribution of income, or in the market shares held by different firms competing in a market.

A simple index number

We begin with the simplest case, where we wish to construct an index number series for a single commodity. In this case, we shall construct an index number series representing the price of coal to industrial users, for the years 1988–92. The raw data are given in Table 2.1 (taken from the Digest of UK Energy Statistics, 1993). The index will show how the price of coal changes over the period. We assume that the product itself has not changed from year to year, so that the index provides a fair representation of costs. This means, for example, that the quality of coal has not changed during the period.

To construct a price index from these data we choose one year as the **reference year** (1988 in this case) and set the price index in that year equal to 100. The prices in the other years are then measured *relative* to the reference year figure of 100. The index, and its construction, are presented in Table 2.2.

The price index in Table 2.2 presents the same information as Table 2.1 but in a slightly different form. We have (perhaps) gained some degree of clarity, but we have lost the original information about the actual level of prices. Since it is usually *relative* prices that are of interest, this loss of information about the actual price level is not too serious, and information about relative prices is retained by the price index. For example, using either the index or actual prices, we can see that the price of coal was 2.9% lower in 1992 than in 1988.

The choice of reference year is arbitrary and we can easily change it for a different year. If we choose 1990 to be the reference year, then we set the price in that year equal to 100 and again measure all other prices relative to it. This is shown in Table 2.3 which can be derived from Table 2.2 or directly from the original data on prices. You should choose whichever reference year is most convenient for your purposes. Whichever year is chosen, the informational content is the same.

A price index with more than one commodity

In practice of course, industry uses other sources of energy as well as coal, such as gas, petroleum and electricity. Suppose that an index of the cost of all fuels used by industry is wanted, rather than just for coal (in the late 1980's, for example, industrialists were complaining about the high cost of *energy* in the U.K.). This is a more common requirement in reality, rather than the simple index number series calculated above. If the price of each fuel were rising at the same rate, say at 5% per year, then it is straightforward to say that the price of energy to industry is also rising at 5% per year. But supposing, as is likely, that the prices are all rising at different rates, as shown in Table 2.4. Is it now possible to say how fast the price of energy is

Table 2.1 The price of coal, 1988–92

	1988	1989	1990	1991	1992
Price (£/tonne)	44.76	43.74	44.67	43.87	43.48

Table 2.2 The price index for coal, 1988 = 100

Year	Index	
1988	100.0	(= 44.76/44.76 × 100)
1989	97.7	(= 43.74/44.76 × 100)
1990	99.8	etc.
1991	98.0	
1992	97.1	

Table 2.3 The price index for coal, 1990 = 100

Year	Index	
1988	100.2	(=44.74/44.67 × 100)
1989	97.9	(=43.74/44.67 × 100)
1990	100.0	etc
1991	98.2	
1992	97.3	

increasing? Several different prices now have to be combined in order to construct an index number, a more complex process than the simple index number calculated above.

From the data presented in Table 2.4 we can calculate that the price of coal has fallen by 2.9% over the four-year period, petrol has risen by 3.1%, electricity has risen by 16.9% and gas has fallen by 2.7%. It is difficult to see whether the overall price of energy is rising or falling, given these figures.

Using base year weights: the Laspeyres index

We tackle the problem by taking a **weighted average** of the price changes of the individual fuels, the weights being derived from the quantities of each fuel used by the industry. Thus if industry uses relatively more coal than petrol, more weight is given to the rise in the price of coal in the calculation.

We put this principle into effect by constructing a hypothetical 'shopping basket' of the fuels used by industry, and measure how the cost of this basket has risen (or fallen) over time. Table 2.5 gives the quantities of each fuel consumed by industry in 1988 (again from the Digest of UK Energy Statistics, 1993) and it is this which forms the shopping basket. 1988 is referred to as the **base year** since it is the quantities consumed in this year which are used to make up the shopping basket.

The cost of the basket at 1988 prices therefore works out as shown in Table 2.6 (using Tables 2.4 and 2.5). The final column of the table shows the expenditure on

Table 2.4   Fuel prices to industry, 1988–92

	Coal ($£$/tonne)	Petroleum ($£$/tonne)	Electricity ($£$/MWh)	Gas ($£$/therm)
1988	44.76	62.4	34.73	0.2277
1989	43.74	70.05	37.29	0.2203
1990	44.67	76.16	37.18	0.2248
1991	43.87	66.9	38.25	0.2208
1992	43.48	64.34	40.61	0.2216

Table 2.5   Quantities of fuel used by industry, 1988

Coal (m. tonnes)	13.96
Petroleum (m. tonnes)	8.88
Electricity (m. MWh)	97.14
Gas (m. therms)	5442

Table 2.6   Cost of the energy basket, 1988

	Price	Quantity	Price × quantity
Coal ($£$/tonne)	44.76	13.96	624.8496
Petroleum ($£$/tonne)	62.40	8.88	554.1120
Electricity ($£$/MWh)	34.73	97.14	3,373.6722
Gas ($£$/therm)	0.23	5,442.00	1,239.1434
Total			5,791.7772

each of the four energy inputs and the total cost of the basket is 5,791.7772 (this is in £m. so altogether about £5.79 bn. was spent on energy by industry).

This sum may be written as:

$$\sum_i p_{0i} q_{0i} = 5,791.772$$

where the summation is calculated over all the four fuels. p refers to prices, q to quantities. The first subscript (0) refers to the year, the second (i) to each energy source in turn. We refer to 1988 as year 0, 1989 as year 1, etc., for brevity of notation. Thus, for example, p_{01} means the price of coal in 1988, q_{12} the consumption of petroleum by industry in 1989.

We now need to find what the 1988 basket of energy would cost in each of the subsequent years, using the prices pertaining to those years. For example, for 1989 we value the 1988 basket using the 1989 prices. This is shown in Table 2.7.

Firms would therefore have to spend an extra £262m. (6053 – 5791) in 1989 to buy the same quantities of energy as in 1988. The sum of £6,053m. may be expressed as $\Sigma p_{1i} q_{0i}$, since it is obtained by multiplying the prices in year 1 (1989) by quantities in year 0 (1988).

Similar calculations for subsequent years produce the costs of the basket as shown in Table 2.8.

It can be seen that *if* firms had purchased the same quantities of each energy source in the following years, they would have had to pay more in every subsequent year, apart from 1991 when there was a slight decrease in the cost. There was a general tendency for energy prices to rise, therefore.

To obtain the energy price index from these data we measure the cost of the basket in each year relative to its 1988 cost, i.e. we divide the cost of the basket in each successive year by $\Sigma p_{0i} q_{0i}$ and multiply by 100.

This index is given in Table 2.9 and is called the **Laspeyres price index** after its inventor. We say that it uses **base year weights** (i.e. quantities in the base year 1988 form the weights in the basket).

Table 2.7 The cost of the 1988 energy basket at 1989 prices

	1989 price	1988 quantity	Price × quantity
Coal (£/tonne)	43.74	13.96	610.6104
Petroleum (£/tonne)	70.05	8.88	622.0440
Electricity (£/MWh)	37.29	97.14	3,622.3506
Gas (£/therm)	0.22	5,442.00	1,198.8726
Total			6,053.8776

Table 2.8 The cost of the energy basket, 1988–92

1988	5,791.78
1989	6,053.88
1990	6,134.92
1991	6,123.70
1992	6,329.12

Table 2.9   The Laspeyres price index

Year	Index	
1988	100.0000	
1989	104.5254	(= 6,053.88/5,791.78 × 100)
1990	105.9247	(= 6,134.92/5,791.78 × 100)
1991	105.7309	etc.
1992	109.2777	

We have set the value of the index to 100 in 1988, i.e. the reference year and the base year coincide, though this is not essential.

The Laspeyres index for year n with the base year as year 0 is given by the following formula:

$$(2.1) \quad P_L^n = \frac{\sum p_{ni} q_{0i}}{\sum p_{0i} q_{0i}} \times 100$$

(Henceforth we shall omit the i subscript on prices and quantities in the formulae for index numbers, for brevity.) The index shows that energy prices increased by 9.3% over the period – obviously the rise in the prices of petroleum and electricity out-weighed the falls in coal and gas prices. The rise amounts to an average increase of 2.25% p.a. in the cost of energy. During the same period, prices in general rose by 6.7% p.a. so in relative terms energy was becoming cheaper.

The choice of 1988 as the base year for the index was an arbitrary one; any year will do. If we choose 1989 as the base year then the cost of the 1989 basket is evaluated in each year, and this will result in a slightly different Laspeyres index. The calculations are in Table 2.10. The final two columns of the table compare the Laspeyres index constructed using the 1989 and 1988 baskets respectively (the former adjusted to 1988 = 100). A slight difference can be seen, due to the different consumption patterns (electricity and gas are more important in the 1989 basket). The difference is numerically quite small, however, amounting to about 0.1% of the value of the index.

The Laspeyres price index shows the increase in the price of energy for the 'average' firm, i.e. one which consumes energy in the same proportions as the 1988 basket overall. There are probably very few such firms: most would use perhaps only one or two energy sources. Individual firms may therefore experience price rises quite

Table 2.10   The Laspeyres price index using the 1989 basket

	Cost of basket	Laspeyres index 1989 = 100	Laspeyres index 1989 = 100	Laspeyres index using 1988 basket
1988	5,804.1174	95.67	100.00	100.00
1989	6,067.1015	100.00	104.53	104.53
1990	6,143.1611	101.25	105.84	105.92
1991	6,141.1971	101.22	105.81	105.73
1992	6,354.2512	104.73	109.48	109.28

different from those shown here. For example, a firm depending upon electricity alone would face a 17% rise over the four years, significantly higher than the figure of 9% suggested by the Laspeyres index.

Using current year weights: the Paasche index

Firms do not of course consume the same basket of energy every year. One would expect them to respond to changes in the relative prices of fuels and to other factors. Technological progress means that the efficiency with which the fuels can be used changes, causing fluctuations in demand. Table 2.11 shows the quantities consumed in the years after 1988 and indicates that firms did indeed alter their pattern of consumption:

The Laspeyres is not the only index which it is possible to construct. As we shall see, it is impossible to construct the perfect index number, but we can get an approximation to it. The Laspeyres index is one such approximation. We have seen that it uses base year weights throughout the time period studied, effectively assuming that the same basket of inputs is purchased year after year. This might be thought an unlikely occurrence, especially as relative prices change over time.

Any of the years could be chosen as the base year in the construction of a Laspeyres price index. Each would give a slightly different index number series because the consumption pattern is different in each year. We note, for example, that there has been a large reduction in the consumption of gas. There is therefore a different basket of commodities for each year, and there is no more reason to take one year's basket as the basis of calculation than another year's. Whichever base year is chosen, there remains the problem that the shopping basket stays unchanged over time and thus after a while becomes unrepresentative of what firms are using.

The **Paasche index** (denoted P_P^n to distinguish it from the Laspeyres index) overcomes this problem by using **current year weights** to construct the index.

Suppose 1988 is to be the reference year, so $P_P^0 = 100$. To construct the Paasche index for 1989 we use the 1989 weights, for the 1990 value of the index we use the 1990 weights, and so on. An example will clarify matters.

The Paasche index for 1989 will be the cost of the 1989 basket at 1989 prices relative to its cost at 1988 prices, i.e.

$$P_P^1 = \frac{\sum p_1 q_1}{\sum p_0 q_1} \times 100$$

This gives:

$$P_P^1 = \frac{6,067.10}{5,804.12} \times 100 = 104.5$$

Table 2.11   Quantities of energy used, 1988–92

	Coal (m. tonnes)	Petroleum (m. tonnes)	Electricity (m. MWh)	Gas (m. therms)
1989	12.93	8.19	99.42	5,540
1990	12.27	7.64	100.64	5,712
1991	11.57	8.29	99.57	5,382
1992	12.18	7.83	110.91	4,997

The general formula for the Paasche index in year n is given in equation (2.2).

$$(2.2) \quad P_P^n = \frac{\sum p_n q_n}{\sum p_0 q_n} \times 100$$

Table 2.12 shows the calculation of this index for the later years.

The Paasche formula gives a slightly different result than does the Laspeyres, as is usually the case. What *is* unusual here is that the Paasche generally shows a larger increase than the Laspeyres, for it is normally the other way round. One would expect profit maximising firms to respond to changing relative prices by switching their consumption in the direction of the inputs which are becoming relatively cheaper. The Paasche index, by using the current weights, captures this change, but the Laspeyres, assuming fixed weights, does not. One would therefore expect the Paasche to show a slower rate of price increase.

However, in this case, firms' behaviour appears positively perverse. Electricity has risen in price the most, yet firms' consumption has increased substantially. Coal has fallen in price, yet so has its consumption. Are firms' managements irrational, therefore? Some might agree with this conclusion, but a more likely explanation is technological change. If firms are able to use electricity more efficiently in production they would be willing to pay more for it. Alternatively, shifts in the pattern of demand for goods could produce this result. If consumers are demanding less output from firms which use predominantly coal as an input, then coal usage could fall despite the fall in its price.

Is one of the indices more 'correct' than the other? The answer is that neither is definitively correct. It can be shown that the 'true' value lies somewhere between the two, but it is impossible to say exactly where. If all the items which make up the index increase in price at the same rate then the Laspeyres and Paasche indices would give the same answer, so it is the change in *relative* prices and the resultant change in consumption patterns which causes problems.

Units of measurement

It is important that the units of measurement in the price and quantity tables be consistent. Note that in the example, the price of coal was measured in £/tonne and the consumption was measured in millions of tonnes. The other fuels were similarly treated (in the case of electricity, one MWh equals one million watt-hours). But suppose we had measured electricity consumption in kWh instead of MWh (1 MWh = 1000 kWh), but still measured its price in £ per MWh? We would then have 1988

Table 2.12 The Paasche price index

Year	Cost of year's basket at current prices	Cost at 1988 prices	Index
1988	5,791.78	5,791.78	100.0
1989	6,067.10	5,804.12	104.5
1990	6,155.82	5,821.79	105.7
1991	6,059.08	5,718.72	106.0
1992	6,644.76	6,023.49	110.3

data of 34.73 for price as before, but 97,140 for quantity. It is as if electricity consumption has been boosted a thousand-fold, and this would seriously distort the results. The (Laspeyres) energy price index would be (by a similar calculation to the one above):

1988	1989	1990	1991	1992
100	107.4	107.1	110.1	116.9

This is incorrect, and shows a higher value than the proper Laspeyres index (because electricity is now given too much weight in the calculation, and electricity prices were rising relatively quickly).

It is possible to make some manipulations of the units of measurement (usually to make calculation easier) as long as all items are treated alike. If, for example, all prices were measured in pence rather than pounds (so all prices in Table 2.4 were multiplied by 100) then this would have no effect on the resultant index, as you would expect. Similarly, if all quantity figures were measured in thousands of tonnes, thousands of therms and thousands of MWh there would be no effects on the Laspeyres index, even if prices remained in £/tonne, etc. But if electricity were measured in pence per MWh, while all other fuels were in £/tonne, a wrong answer would again be obtained. Quantities consumed should also be measured over the same time period, e.g. millions of therms *per annum*. It does not matter what the time period is (days, weeks, months or years) as long as all the items are treated similarly.

Using expenditures as weights

On occasion the quantities of each commodity consumed are not available, but expenditures are, and a price index can still be constructed using slightly modified formulae. It is often easier to find the expenditure on a good than to know the actual quantity consumed (think of housing as an example). We shall illustrate the method with a simplified example, using the data on energy prices and consumption for the years 1988 and 1989 only. The data are repeated in Table 2.13.

The data for consumption are assumed to be no longer available, only the expenditure on each energy source as a percentage of total expenditure. Expenditure is derived as the product of price and quantity consumed.

The formula for the Laspeyres index can be easily manipulated to accord with the data as presented in Table 2.13.

Table 2.13 Expenditure shares, 1988

	Price	Quantity	Expenditure	Share
Coal	44.76	13.96	624.85	10.8%
Petroleum	62.40	8.88	554.11	9.6%
Electricity	34.73	97.14	3,373.67	58.2%
Gas	0.23	5,442.00	1,239.14	21.4%
Total			5,791.78	100.0%

Note: The 10.8% share on coal is calculated as $(624.85/5,791.78) \times 100$. Other shares are calculated similarly.

The Laspeyres index formula based on expenditure shares is given in equation (2.3):[1]

$$(2.3) \quad P_L^n = \sum \frac{p_n}{p_0} \times s_0$$

Equation (2.3) is made up of two component parts. The first, p_n/p_0, is simply the price in year n relative to the base year price for each energy source. The second component, $s_0 = p_0 q_0 / \Sigma p_0 q_0$, is the share or proportion of total expenditure spent on each energy source in the base year, the data for which are in Table 2.13. It should be easy to see that the sum of the s_0 values is 1, so that equation (2.3) calculates a weighted average of the individual price increases, the weights being the expenditure shares.

The calculation of the Laspeyres index for 1989 using 1988 as the base year is therefore:

$$P_L^n = \frac{43.74}{44.76} \times 0.108 + \frac{70.05}{62.4} \times 0.096 + \frac{37.29}{34.73} \times 0.582 + \frac{0.2203}{0.2277} \times 0.214 = 1.0453$$

giving the value of the index as 104.5, the same value as derived earlier using the more usual methods. Values of the index for subsequent years are calculated by appropriate application of equation (2.3) above. This is left as an exercise for the reader, who may use Table 2.9 to verify the answers.

The Paasche index may similarly be calculated from data on prices and expenditure shares, as long as these are available for each year for which the index is required. The formula for the Paasche index is

$$(2.4) \quad P_P^n = \frac{1}{\sum \dfrac{p_0}{p_n} s_n} \times 100$$

The calculation of the Paasche index is also left as an exercise.

Comparison of the Laspeyres and Paasche indices

The advantages of the Laspeyres index are that it is easy to calculate and that it has a fairly clear intuitive meaning, i.e. the cost each year of a particular basket of goods. The Paasche index involves more computation, and it is less easy to envisage what it refers to. As an example of this point, consider the following simple case. The Laspeyres index values for 1990 and 1991 are 105.9 and 105.7. The ratio of these two numbers, 0.998, would suggest that prices fell by 0.2% between these years. What does this figure actually represent? The 1991 Laspeyres index has been divided by the same index for 1990, i.e.

$$\frac{P_L^3}{P_L^2} = \frac{\sum p_3 q_0}{\sum p_0 q_0} \bigg/ \frac{\sum p_2 q_0}{\sum p_0 q_0} = \frac{\sum p_3 q_0}{\sum p_2 q_0}$$

which is the ratio of the cost of the 1988 basket at 1991 prices to its cost at 1990 prices. This makes some intuitive sense. Note that it is not the same as the

---

[1]   See the appendix to this chapter for the derivation of this formula.

Laspeyres index for 1991 with 1990 as base year, which would require using q_2 in the calculation.

If the same is done with the Paasche index numbers an *increase* of 0.28% is obtained between 1990 and 1991. But the meaning of this is not so clear, for

$$\frac{P_P^3}{P_P^2} = \frac{\sum p_3 q_3}{\sum p_0 q_3} \bigg/ \frac{\sum p_2 q_2}{\sum p_0 q_2}$$

which does not simplify further. This is a curious mixture of 1990 and 1991 quantities, and 1988, 1990 and 1991 prices!

The major advantage of the Paasche index is that the weights are continuously updated, so that the basket of goods never becomes out of date. In the case of the Laspeyres index the basket remains unchanged over a period, becoming less and less representative of what is being bought by consumers. When revision is finally made there may therefore be a large change in the weighting scheme. The extra complexity of calculation involved in the Paasche index is less important now that computers do most of the work.

Quantity and expenditure indices

Just as one can calculate price indices, it is also possible to calculate **quantity** and **value indices**. We first concentrate on quantity indices, which provide a measure of the total quantity of energy consumed by industry each year. The problem again is that we cannot easily aggregate the different sources of energy. It makes no sense to add together tonnes of coal and petroleum, therms of gas and megawatts of electricity. Some means has to be found to put these different fuels on a comparable basis. We now reverse the roles of prices and quantities: the quantities of the different fuels are weighted by their different prices (prices represent the value to the firm, at the margin, of each different fuel). As with price indices, one can construct both Laspeyres and Paasche quantity indices.

The Laspeyres quantity index

The Laspeyres quantity index for year n is given by

$$(2.5) \quad Q_L^n = \frac{\sum q_n p_0}{\sum q_0 p_0} \times 100$$

i.e. it is the ratio of the cost of the year n basket to the cost of the year 0 basket, both valued at year 0 prices. Note that it is the same as equation (2.1) but with prices and quantities reversed.

Using 1988 as the base year, the cost of the 1989 basket at 1988 prices is:

$$\sum q_1 p_0 = 12.93 \times 44.76 + 8.19 \times 62.40 + 99.42 \times 34.73 + 5,540 \times 0.23 = 5,804.1174$$

and the cost of the 1988 basket at 1988 prices is 5,791.7772 (calculated earlier). The value of the quantity index for 1989 is therefore

$$Q_L^1 = \frac{5,804.1174}{5,791.7772} \times 100 = 100.21$$

In other words, if prices had remained constant between 1988 and 1989, industry would have consumed 0.21% more energy.

The value of the index for subsequent years is shown in Table 2.14, using the formula given in equation (2.5).

The Paasche quantity index

Just as there are Laspeyres and Paasche versions of the price index, the same is true for the quantity index. The Paasche quantity index is given by

$$(2.6) \quad Q_P^n = \frac{\sum q_n p_n}{\sum q_0 p_n} \times 100$$

and is the analogue of equation (2.2) with prices and quantities reversed. The calculation of this index is shown in Table 2.15.

This shows a similar trend to the Laspeyres index in Table 2.14. Normally one would expect the Paasche to show a slower increase than the Laspayres quantity index: firms should switch to inputs whose relative prices fall; the Paasche gives lesser weight (current prices) to these quantities than does the Laspeyres (base year prices) and thus shows a slower rate of increase. Just as with the price indices, we get the opposite result here, presumably due to the same factors.

Expenditure indices

The **expenditure** or **value index** is simply an index of the cost of the year n basket at year n prices and so it measures how expenditure changes over time. The formula for the index in year n is

$$(2.7) \quad E^n = \frac{\sum p_n q_n}{\sum p_0 q_0}$$

There is obviously only one value index and one does not distinguish between Laspeyres and Paasche formulations. The index can be easily derived from Table 2.16.

Table 2.14 Calculation of the Laspeyres quantity index

	$\Sigma p_0 q_i$	Index	
1988	5,791.7772	100.00	
1989	5,804.1174	100.21	$(= 5,804.1174/5,791.7772 \times 100)$
1990	5,821.7908	100.52	$(= 5,821.7908/5,791.7772 \times 100)$
1991	5,718.7167	98.74	etc.
1992	6,023.4900	104.00	

Table 2.15 Calculation of the Paasche quantity index

	$\Sigma q_n p_n$	$\Sigma q_0 p_n$	Index
1988	5,791.78	5,791.78	100.0
1989	6,067.10	6,053.88	100.2
1990	6,155.82	6,134.92	100.3
1991	6,059.08	6,123.70	98.9
1992	6,644.76	6,329.12	105.0

Note: The final column is calculated as the ratio of the previous two columns.

Table 2.16   The expenditure index

	$\Sigma p_n q_n$	Index
1988	5,791.7772	100.0
1989	6,067.1015	104.8
1990	6,155.8161	106.3
1991	6,059.0750	104.6
1992	6,644.7589	114.7

Note: The expenditure index is a simple index of the expenditures in the previous column.

The expenditure index shows how industry's expenditure on energy is changing over time. Thus expenditure in 1992 was 14.7% higher than in 1988. What the value index does not show is how that increased expenditure may be divided up into price and quantity changes. This decomposition is shown in the next section.

Relationships between price, quantity and expenditure indices

Just as multiplying a price by a quantity gives total value, or expenditure, the same is true of index numbers. The value index can be decomposed as the product of a price index and a quantity index. In particular, it is the product of a Paasche quantity index and a Laspeyres price index, *or* the product of a Paasche price index and a Laspeyres quantity index. This can be very simply demonstrated using Σ notation:

$$(2.8) \quad E^n = \frac{\sum p_n q_n}{\sum p_0 q_0} = \frac{\sum p_n q_n}{\sum p_n q_0} \times \frac{\sum p_n q_0}{\sum p_0 q_0} = Q_P^n \times P_L^n$$

or

$$(2.9) \quad E^n = \frac{\sum p_n q_n}{\sum p_0 q_0} = \frac{\sum p_n q_n}{\sum p_0 q_n} \times \frac{\sum p_0 q_n}{\sum p_0 q_0} = P_P^n \times Q_L^n$$

Thus increases in value or expenditure can be decomposed into price and quantity effects. Two decompositions are possible and give slightly different answers.

It is also evident that a quantity index can be constructed by dividing a value index by a price index, since by simple manipulation of (2.8) and (2.9) we obtain

$$(2.10) \quad Q_P^n = E^n / P_L^n$$

and

$$(2.11) \quad Q_L^n = E^n / P_P^n$$

Note that dividing the expenditure index by a Laspeyres price index gives a Paasche quantity index, and dividing by a Paasche price index gives a Laspeyres quantity index. This is known as **deflating** a series and is a widely used and very useful technique. We shall reconsider our earlier data in the light of this. Table 2.17 provides the detail. Column 2 of the table shows the expenditure on fuel at **current prices** or in **cash terms**. Column 3 contains the Laspeyres price index repeated from Table 2.9 above. Deflating (dividing) column 2 by column 3 and multiplying by 100 yields

Table 2.17 Deflating the expenditure series

	Expenditure at current prices	Laspeyres price index	Expenditure in volume terms	Index
1988	5,791.78	100.0	5,791.78	100.0
1989	6,067.10	104.5	5,804.43	100.2
1990	6,155.82	105.9	5,811.50	100.3
1991	6,059.08	105.7	5,730.66	98.9
1992	6,644.76	109.3	6,080.62	105.0

column 4 which shows expenditure on fuel in **quantity** *or* **volume terms**. The final column gives an index of energy expenditure in volume terms.

This index is equivalent to a Paasche quantity index, as illustrated by equation (2.7) and in Table 2.15 above.

Trap!

A common mistake is to believe that once a series has been turned into an index, it is inevitably in real terms. This is *not* the case. One can have an index of a nominal series (e.g. in Table 2.16 above) *or* of a real series (the final column of Table 2.17). An index number is just a means of combining a number of different series and presenting the result; it is not the same as deflating the series.

In the example above we used the price index for energy to deflate the expenditure series. However, it is also possible to use a *general* price index (such as the retail price index or the *GDP* deflator) to deflate. This gives a slightly different result, both in numerical terms and in its interpretation. Deflating by a general price index yields a series of expenditures in **constant prices** or in **real terms**. Deflating by a specific price index (e.g. of energy) results in a **quantity** or **volume** series.

An example should clarify this (see exercise 2.11 for data). The government spends billions of pounds each year on the health service. If this cash expenditure series is deflated by a general price index (e.g. the *GDP* deflator) then we obtain expenditure on health services at constant prices, or real expenditure on the health service. If the *NHS* pay and prices index is used as a deflator, then the result is an index of the quantity or volume of health services provided. Since the *NHS* index tends to rise more rapidly than the *GDP* deflator, the volume series rises more slowly than the series of expenditure at constant prices. This can lead to an interesting, if pointless, political debate. The government claims it is spending more on the health service, in real terms, while the opposition claims that the health service is getting fewer resources. As we have seen, both can be right.

The real rate of interest

Another example of 'deflating' is the real rate of interest. This adjusts the actual rate of interest for changes in the value of money, i.e. inflation. If you earn a 7% rate of interest on your money over a year, but the price level rises by 5% at the same time, you are clearly not 7% better off. The real rate of interest in this case would be given by:

(2.12)   real interest rate $= \dfrac{1 + 0.07}{1 + 0.05} - 1 = 0.019 = 1.9\%$

In general, if r is the interest rate and i is the inflation rate, the real rate of interest is given by

(2.13)   real interest rate $= \dfrac{1 + r}{1 + i} - 1$

A simpler method is often used in practice, which gives virtually identical results for small values of r and i. This is to subtract the inflation rate from the interest rate, giving $7\% - 5\% = 2\%$ in this case.

Chain indices

Whenever an index number series over a long period of time is wanted, it is usually necessary to link together a number of separate indices, resulting in a **chain index**. Without access to the original raw data it is impossible to construct a proper Laspeyres or Paasche index, so the result will be a mixture of different types of index number but it is the best that can be done in the circumstances.

Suppose that the following two index number series are available. Access to the original data is assumed to be impossible.

Laspeyres price index for energy, 1988–92 (from Table 2.9):

1988	1989	1990	1991	1992
100	104.5	105.9	105.7	109.3

Laspeyres price index for energy, 1984–88 (from exercise 2.3):

1984	1985	1986	1987	1988
100	104.2	85.9	83.0	79.4

The two series have different reference years and use different shopping baskets of consumption. The first index measures the cost of the 1988 basket in each of the subsequent years. The second measures the price of the 1984 basket in subsequent years. There is an 'overlap' year which is 1988. How do we combine these into one continuous index covering the whole period?

The obvious method is to use the ratio of the costs of the two baskets in 1988, $79.4/100 = 0.794$, to alter one of the series. To base the continuous series on $1984 = 100$ requires multiplying each of the post-1988 figures by 0.794 as is demonstrated in Table 2.18.

Table 2.18 A chain index of energy prices, 1984–92

	'Old' index	'New' index	Chain index
1984	100		100
1985	104.2		104.2
1986	85.9		85.9
1987	83.0		83.0
1988	79.4	100	79.4
1989		104.5	83.0
1990		105.9	84.1
1991		105.7	83.9
1992		109.3	86.8

Note: After 1988, the chain index values are calculated by multiplying the 'new' index by 0.794; e.g. $83.0 = 104.5 \times 0.794$ for 1989.

The continuous series could just as easily be based on 1980 = 100 by a simple rescaling, which would be equivalent to dividing the 'old' series by 0.794 and leaving the 'new' series unchanged.

The continuous series is not a proper Laspeyres index number as can be seen if we examine the formulae used. We shall examine the 1992 figure, 86.8, by way of example. This figure is calculated as $86.8 = 109.3 \times 79.4/100$ which in terms of our formulae is

$$(2.14) \quad \frac{\sum p_{92} q_{88}}{\sum p_{88} q_{88}} \times \frac{\sum p_{88} q_{84}}{\sum p_{84} q_{84}} \Big/ 100$$

The proper Laspeyres index for 1992 using 1984 weights is

$$(2.15) \quad \frac{\sum p_{92} q_{84}}{\sum p_{84} q_{84}} \times 100$$

There is no way that this latter equation can be derived from equation (2.14), proving that the former is not a properly constructed Laspeyres index number. Although it is not a proper index number series it does have the advantage of the weights being revised and therefore more up to date.

Similar problems arise when deriving a chain index from two Paasche index number series. Investigation of this is left to the reader; the method follows that outlined above for the Laspeyres case.

The Retail Price Index

The UK **Retail Price Index** is one of the most sophisticated of index numbers, involving the recording of the prices of 350 items each month, and weighting them on the basis of households' expenditure patterns as revealed by the annual Family Expenditure Survey (the *FES* is explained in more detail in Chapter 7 on sampling methods). The principles involved in the calculation are the same as set out above, but they are not strictly adhered to for a variety of reasons.

The RPI is something of a compromise between a Laspeyres and a Paasche index. It is calculated monthly, and within each calendar year the weights used remain constant, so that it takes the form of a Laspeyres index. Each January, however, the weights are updated on the basis of evidence from the *FES*, so that the index is in fact a set of chain-linked Laspeyres indices, the chaining taking place in January each year. Despite the formal appearance as a Laspeyres index, the RPI measured over a period of years has the characteristics of a Paasche index, due to the annual change in the weights.

Another departure from principle is the fact that about 14% of households are left out when expenditure weights are calculated. These consist of most pensioner households (10%) and the very rich (4%), because they tend to have significantly different spending patterns to the rest of the population and their inclusion would make the index too unrepresentative. A separate RPI is calculated for pensioners, while the very rich have to do without one.

A change in the quality of goods purchased can also be problematic, as alluded to earlier. If a manufacturer improves the quality of a product and charges more, is it fair to say that the price has gone up? Sometimes it is possible to measure improvement (if the power of a vacuum cleaner is increased, for example), but other cases are more difficult, such as if the punctuality of a train service is improved. By how much has quality improved? In many circumstances the statistician has to make a judgement about the best procedure to adopt.

Table 2.19 shows how prices have changed over the longer term. The 'inflation adjusted' column shows what the item would have cost if it had risen in line with the overall retail price index. It is clear that some relative prices have changed substantially and you can try to work out the reasons.

Table 2.19   Prices 80 years ago and today

Item	1914 price	Inflation adjusted price	1994 price
Car	£730	£36,971	£6,995
London–Manchester 1st class rail fare	£2.45	£124.08	£130
Pint of beer	1p	53p	£1.38
Milk (quart)	1.5p	74p	70p
Bread	2.5p	£1.21	51p
Butter	6p	£3.06	68p
Double room at Savoy Hotel, London	£1.25	£63.31	£195

Discounting and present values

Deflating makes expenditures in different years comparable by correcting for the effect of inflation. The future sum is deflated (reduced) because of the increase in the price level. **Discounting** is a similar procedure for comparing amounts across different years, correcting for **time preference**. For example, suppose that by investing £1,000 today a firm can receive £1,100 in a year's time. To decide if the investment is worthwhile, the two amounts need to be compared.

If the prevailing interest rate is 12%, then the firm could simply place its £1,000 in the bank and earn £120 interest, giving it £1,200 at the end of the year. Hence the firm should not invest in this particular project; it does better keeping money in the bank. The investment is not undertaken because

$$£1,000 \times (1+r) > £1,100$$

where r is the interest rate, 12%. Alternatively, this inequality may be expressed as

$$£1,000 > \frac{£1,100}{(1+r)}$$

The expression on the right-hand side of the inequality sign is the **present value** (*PV*) of £1,100 received in one year's time. r is the rate of discount and is equal to the rate of interest in this example because this is the rate at which the firm can transform present into future income, and vice-versa. In what follows, we use the terms interest rate and discount rate interchangeably. The term $1/(1+r)$ is known as the **discount factor**. Multiplying an amount by the discount factor results in the present value of the sum.

We can also express the inequality as follows (by subtracting £1,000 from each side):

$$0 > -£1,000 + \frac{£1,100}{(1+r)}$$

The right-hand side of this expression is known as the **net present value** (*NPV*) of the project. It represents the difference between the initial outlay and the present value of the return generated by the investment. Since this is negative the investment is not worthwhile (the money would be better placed on deposit in a bank). The general rule is to invest if the *NPV* is positive.

Similarly, the present value of £1,100 to be received in two years' time is

$$PV = \frac{£1,100}{(1+r)^2} = \frac{£1,100}{(1+0.12)^2} = £876.91$$

when $r = 12\%$. In general, the *PV* of a sum S to be received in t years is

$$PV = \frac{S}{(1+r)^t}$$

The *PV* may be interpreted as the amount a firm would be prepared to pay today to receive an amount S in t years' time. Thus a firm would not be prepared to make an outlay of more than £876.91 in order to receive £1,100 in two years' time. It would gain more by putting the money on deposit and earning 12% interest per annum.

Most investment projects involve an initial outlay followed by a *series* of receipts over the following years, as illustrated by the figures in Table 2.20.

In order to decide if the investment is worthwhile, the present value of the income stream needs to be compared to the initial outlay. The *PV* of the income stream is obtained by adding together the present value of each year's income. Thus we calculate

This present value example has only four terms but in principle there can be any number of terms stretching into the future.

$$(2.16) \quad PV = \frac{S_1}{(1+r)} + \frac{S_2}{(1+r)^2} + \frac{S_3}{(1+r)^3} + \frac{S_4}{(1+r)^4}$$

or more concisely, using Σ notation:

$$(2.17) \quad PV = \sum \frac{S_t}{(1+r)^t}$$

Table 2.20 The cash flows from an investment project

Year			Discount factor	Discounted income
1990	Outlay	−1,000		
1991	Income	300	0.893	267.86
1992		400	0.797	318.88
1993		450	0.712	320.30
1994		200	0.636	127.10
Total				1,034.14

Columns 3 and 4 of the table show the calculation of the present value. The discount factors, $1/(1+r)^t$, are given in column 3. Multiplying column 2 by column 3 gives the individual elements of the PV calculation (as in equation (2.16) above) and their sum is 1,034.14, which is the present value of the returns. Since the PV is greater than the initial outlay of 1,000 the investment generates a return of at least 12% and so is worthwhile.

An alternative investment criterion: the internal rate of return

The investment rule can be expressed in a different manner, using the **internal rate of return** (*IRR*). This is the rate of discount which makes the *NPV* equal to zero, i.e. the present value of the income stream is equal to the initial outlay. An *IRR* of 10% equates £1,100 received next year to an outlay of £1,000 today. Since the *IRR* is less than the market interest rate (12%) this indicates that the investment is not worthwhile: it only yields a rate of return of 10%. The rule 'invest if the *IRR* is greater than the market rate of interest' is equivalent to the rule 'invest if the net present value is positive, using the interest rate to discount future revenues'.

In general it is difficult to find the *IRR* of a project with a stream of future income, except by trial and error methods. The *IRR* is the value of *r* which sets the *NPV* equal to zero, i.e. it is the solution to

$$(2.18) \quad NPV = -S_0 + \sum \frac{S_t}{(1+r)^t} = 0$$

where S_0 is the initial outlay. Fortunately, most spreadsheet programs have an internal routine for its calculation. This is illustrated in Fig. 2.1 which shows the calculation of the IRR for the data in Table 2.20 above.

Cell C13 contains the formula '=*IRR*(C6:C10)' – this can be seen just above the column headings – which is the function used in *Excel* to calculate the internal rate of return. The *IRR* for this project is therefore 13.7% which is indeed above the market interest rate of 12%. The final two columns show that the *PV* of the income stream, when discounted using the internal rate of return, is equal to the initial outlay. The discount factors in the penultimate column are calculated using $r = 13.7\%$.

The *IRR* is easy to calculate if the income stream is a constant monetary sum. If the initial outlay is S_0 and a sum S is received each year in perpetuity, then the *IRR* is simply

$$IRR = \frac{S}{S_0}$$

Fig. 2.1   *Calculation of IRR*

| | | C13 | | =IRR(C6:C10) | | | | |
	A	B	C	D	E	F	G	H
						Discount		
				Discount	Discounted	factor	Discounted	
5	Year			factor	income	using IRR	income	
6	1990	Outlay	-1000					
7	1991	Income	300	0.893	267.86	0.880	263.96	
8	1992		400	0.797	318.88	0.774	309.66	
9	1993		450	0.712	320.30	0.681	306.52	
10	1994		200	0.636	127.10	0.599	119.86	
11	Total				1034.14		1000	
12								
13	Internal rate of return		13.7%					
14								

Note: Note that the first term in the series is the initial outlay (cell C6) and that it is entered as a *negative* number. If a positive value is entered, the *IRR* function will not work.

For example, if an outlay of £1,000 yields a permanent income stream of £120 p.a. then the *IRR* is 12%. This should be intuitively obvious, since investing £1,000 at an interest rate of 12% would give you an annual income of £120.

Nominal and real interest rates

If an income stream has already been deflated to real terms then the present value should be obtained by discounting by the **real interest rate**, not the nominal (market) rate. Table 2.21 illustrates the principle.

Column 1 repeats the income flows in cash terms from Table 2.20. Assuming an inflation rate of $i = 7\%$ per annum gives the price index shown in column 2, based on 1990 = 100. This is used to deflate the cash series to real terms, shown in column 3. This is in constant (1990) prices. To obtain the present value of *this* series, it has to be discounted by the real interest rate r_r, defined by

$$(2.19)\quad 1 + r_r = \frac{1+r}{1+i}$$

Table 2.21   Discounting a real income stream

Year			Price index	Real income	Real discount factor	Discounted sums
1990	Outlay	−1,000	100			
1991	Income	300	107.0	280.37	0.955	267.86
1992		400	114.5	349.38	0.913	318.88
1993		450	122.5	367.33	0.872	320.30
1994		200	131.1	152.58	0.833	127.10
Total						1,034.14

With a (nominal) interest rate of 12% and an inflation rate of 7% this gives

$$(2.20) \quad 1 + r_r = \frac{1+0.12}{1+0.07} = 1.0467$$

so that the real interest rate is 4.67%. The discount factors used to discount the real income flows are shown in column 4 of the table, based on the real interest rate, the discounted sums are in column 5 and the present value of the series is £1,034.14. This is the same as was found earlier, by discounting the cash figures by the nominal interest rate. Thus one can discount *either* the nominal (cash) values using the nominal discount rate, *or* the real flows by the real interest rate. *Make sure you do not confuse the nominal and real interest rates.*

The real interest rate can be approximated by subtracting the inflation rate from the nominal interest rate, i.e.12% − 7% = 5%. This gives a reasonably accurate approximation for low values of the interest and inflation rates (below about 10% p.a.). Because of the simplicity of the calculation, this method is often preferred.

Inequality indices

A separate set of index numbers is used specifically in the measurement of inequality, such as inequality in the distribution of income. We have already seen how we can measure the dispersion of a distribution via the variance and standard deviation. This is based upon the deviations of the observations about the mean. An alternative idea is to measure the difference between *every pair* of observations, and this forms the basis of a statistic known as the **Gini coefficient**. This would probably have remained an obscure measure, due to the complexity of calculation, were it not for Konrad Lorenz, who showed that there is an attractive visual interpretation of it, now known as the **Lorenz curve**, and a relatively simple calculation of the Gini coefficient, based on this curve.

We start off by constructing the Lorenz curve, based on data for the UK income distribution in 1992, and proceed then to calculate the Gini coefficient. We then use these measures to look at inequality both over time (in the UK) and across different countries.

We then examine another manifestation of inequality, in terms of market shares of firms. For this analysis we look at the calculation of **concentration ratios** and at their interpretation.

The Lorenz curve

Table 2.22 shows the data for the distribution of income in the UK based on data from the *Family Expenditure Survey* 1992, published by the CSO. The data report the gross normal weekly income of each household, which means the income is recorded after any cash benefits from the state (e.g. a pension) have been received but before any taxes have been paid.

The table indicates a substantial degree of inequality. For example, the poorest 10% of households earn £80 per week, or less, while the richest 6% (458 out of 7,418) earn ten times as much. Although these figures give some idea of the extent of inequality, they relate only to relatively few households at the extremes of the distribution. A **Lorenz curve** is a way of graphically presenting the whole distribution. A typical Lorenz curve is shown in Fig. 2.2.

Households are ranked along the horizontal axis, from poorest to richest, so that the median household, for example, is halfway along the axis. On the vertical axis is measured the cumulative share of income, which goes from 0% to 100%. A point

Table 2.22   The distribution of gross income in the UK, 1992

Range of weekly household income	Mid-point of interval	Numbers of households
£0–	40	909
£80–	105	949
£130–	165	955
£200–	240	905
£280–	325	1,020
£370–	455	1,356
£540–	670	866
£800–	1,000	458
Total		7,418

Fig. 2.2 *Typical Lorenz curve*

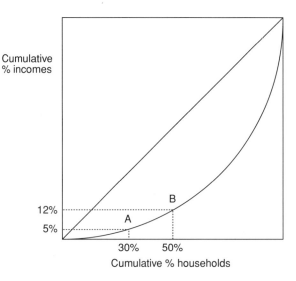

such as A on the diagram indicates that the poorest 30% of households earn 5% of total income. Point B shows that the poorest half of the population earn only 12% of income (and hence the other half earn 88%). Joining up all such points maps out the Lorenz curve.

A few things are immediately obvious about the Lorenz curve:

- Since 0% of households earn 0% of income, and 100% of households earn 100% of income, the curve must run from the origin up to the opposite corner.
- Since households are ranked from poorest to richest, the Lorenz curve must lie below the 45° line, which is the line representing complete equality. The further away from the 45° line is the Lorenz curve, the greater is the degree of inequality.
- The Lorenz curve must be concave from above: as we move to the right we encounter successively richer individuals, so the cumulative income grows faster.

Table 2.23 shows how to generate a Lorenz curve for the data given in Table 2.22. The task is to calculate the $\{x, y\}$ coordinates for the Lorenz curve. These are given in columns 6 and 8 respectively of the table. Column 5 of the table calculates the

Table 2.23   Calculation of the Lorenz curve co-ordinates

Range of income	Mid-point x	f (House-holds)	fx	% f	% Cumulative f	% Income	% Cumulative income
(1)	(2)	(3)	(4)	(5)	(6)	(7)	(8)
£0–	40	909	36,360	12.25%	12.25%	1.46%	1.46%
£80–	105	949	99,645	12.79%	25.05%	3.99%	5.45%
£130–	165	955	157,575	12.87%	37.92%	6.31%	11.76%
£200–	240	905	217,200	12.20%	50.12%	8.70%	20.45%
£280–	325	1,020	331,500	13.75%	63.87%	13.27%	33.73%
£370–	455	1,356	616,980	18.28%	82.15%	24.70%	58.43%
£540–	670	866	580,220	11.67%	93.83%	23.23%	81.66%
£800–	1,000	458	458,000	6.17%	100.00%	18.34%	100.00%
Totals		7,418	2,497,480	100.00%		100.00%	

Notes:
Column 4 = column 2 × column 3
Column 5 = column 3 ÷ 7,418
Column 6 = column 5 cumulated
Column 7 = column 4 ÷ 2,497,480
Column 8 = column 7 cumulated

proportion of households in each income category (i.e. the relative frequencies, as in Chapter 1), and these are then cumulated in column 6. These are the figures which are used along the horizontal axis. Column 4 calculates the total income going to each income class (by multiplying the class frequency by the mid-point). The proportion of total income going to each class is then calculated in column 7 (class income divided by total income). Column 8 cumulates the values in column 7.

Using columns 6 and 8 of the table we can see, for instance, that the poorest 12% of the population have about 1.5% of total income; the poorer half have about 20% of income; and the top 6% have about 18% of total income.

Figure 2.3 shows the Lorenz curve plotted, using the data in columns 6 and 8 of the table above. This shows a fairly smooth Lorenz curve, with perhaps a greater degree of inequality at the bottom of the distribution than at the top.

Fig 2.3 *Lorenz curve for data*

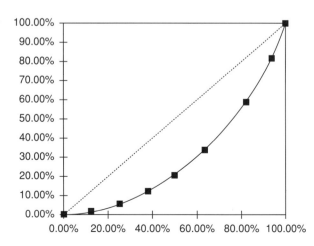

The Gini coefficient

The Gini coefficient is a numerical representation of the degree of inequality in a distribution and can be derived directly from the Lorenz curve. The Lorenz curve is illustrated once again in Fig. 2.4 and the Gini coefficient is simply the ratio of area A to the sum of areas A and B.

Denoting the Gini coefficient by G, we have

$$(2.21) \quad G = \frac{A}{A+B}$$

and it should be obvious that G must lie between 0 and 1. When there is total equality the Lorenz curve coincides with the 45° line, area A then disappears, and $G = 0$. With total inequality (one household having all the income), area B disappears, and $G = 1$. Neither of these extremes is likely to occur in real life; instead one will get intermediate values, but the lower the value of G, the less inequality there is (though see the *caveats* listed below). One could compare two countries, for example, simply by examining the values of their Gini coefficients.

The Gini coefficient may be calculated from the following formulae for areas A and B:

$$(2.22) \quad B = \frac{1}{2}\Big\{\big(x_1 - x_0\big)\times\big(y_1 + y_0\big)$$
$$+ \ \big(x_2 - x_1\big)\times\big(y_2 + y_1\big)$$
$$\vdots$$
$$+ \ \big(x_k - x_{k-1}\big)\times\big(y_k + y_{k-1}\big)\Big\}$$

where $x_0 = y_0 = 0$ and $x_k = y_k = 100$ (i.e. the coordinates of the two end-points of the Lorenz curve) and the other x and y values are the coordinates of the intermediate

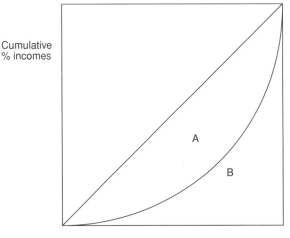

Fig. 2.4 *Calculation of the Gini coefficient from the Lorenz curve*

Cumulative % incomes

A

B

Cumulative % households

points. k is the number of classes for income in the frequency table. Area A is then given by:[2]

(2.23) $A = 5,000 - B$

and the Gini coefficient is then calculated as:

(2.24) $G = \dfrac{A}{A+B}$ or $\dfrac{A}{5,000}$

Thus for the data in Table 2.23 we have:

$$
\begin{aligned}
(2.25)\quad B = \tfrac{1}{2} \times \{ & (12.25 - 0) \times (1.46 + 0) \\
+ & (25.05 - 12.25) \times (5.45 + 1.46) \\
+ & (37.92 - 25.05) \times (11.76 + 5.45) \\
+ & (50.12 - 37.92) \times (20.45 + 11.76) \\
+ & (63.87 - 50.12) \times (33.73 + 20.45) \\
+ & (82.15 - 63.87) \times (58.43 + 33.73) \\
+ & (93.83 - 82.15) \times (81.66 + 58.43) \\
+ & (100 - 98.83) \times (100 + 81.66) \} \\
= & \ 2,953.55
\end{aligned}
$$

Therefore area $A = 5,000 - 2,953.55 = 2,046.45$ and we obtain

(2.26) $G = \dfrac{2,046.45}{5,000} = 0.40929$

or approximately 41%.

This method implicitly assumes that the Lorenz curve is made up of straight line segments connecting the observed points, which is in fact not true. Since the straight lines will lie inside the true Lorenz curve, area B is *over*-estimated and the so the calculated Gini coefficient is biased downwards. The true value of the Gini coefficient is slightly greater than 41% therefore. The bias will be greater (a) the fewer the number of observations and (b) the more concave is the Lorenz curve (i.e. the greater is inequality).

An alternative method of calculating G is simply to draw the Lorenz curve on gridded paper and count squares. This has the advantage that you can draw a smooth line joining the observations and avoid the bias problem mentioned above. This alternative method can prove reasonably quick and accurate, but has the disadvantage that you can't use a computer to do it!

Is inequality increasing?

The Gini coefficient is only useful as a comparative measure, for looking at trends in inequality over time, or for comparing different countries or regions. Table 2.24, taken from *Economic Trends* 1993, shows the value of the Gini coefficient for the UK over the past 14 years and shows how it has been affected by the tax system. The results are based on *equivalised* income, i.e. after making a correction for differences in family size.[3] For this reason there is a slight difference from the Gini coefficient

---

[2] The value 5,000 is correct if one uses percentages, as here (it is $100 \times 100 \times \tfrac{1}{2}$, the area of the triangle). If one uses percentages expressed as decimals, then $A = 0.5 - B$.

[3] This is because a larger family needs more income to have the same living standard as a smaller one.

Table 2.24   Gini coefficients for the UK, 1977–91

	Original income	Gross income	Disposable income	Post-tax income
1977	43	29	27	29
1979	44	30	27	29
1981	46	31	28	31
1983	48	32	28	31
1985	49	32	29	32
1987	51	36	33	36
1989	50	36	34	37
1991	51	37	35	39

Note: Gross income is original income plus certain state benefits, such as pensions. Taking off direct taxes gives disposable income and subtracting other taxes gives post-tax income.

calculated above, which uses unadjusted data. Using equivalised income appears to lower the Gini coefficient a little, since poorer households tend to have fewer members.

The table shows essentially two things:

(1) There appears to have been an increase in inequality over the period and this is true whatever definition of income one uses.
(2) The biggest reduction in inequality comes through cash benefits paid out by the state, rather than through taxes. In fact, the tax system appears to *increase* inequality rather than to reduce it, primarily because of the effects of indirect taxes. Johnson and Webb (1993) provide more detail on the changes in inequality (and their causes) in the UK over the period 1979–88.

The recent increase in inequality is a reversal of the historical trend. The figures presented in Table 2.25, from L. Soltow,[4] provide estimates of the Gini coefficient in earlier times. These figures suggest that a substantial decline in the Gini coefficient has occurred in the last century or so, perhaps related to the process of economic development. It is difficult to compare Soltow's figures directly with the modern ones because of such factors as the quality of data and different definitions of income. Adelman[5] also cites evidence to show that inequality has worsened in many parts of the world since 1960.

Table 2.25   Gini coefficients in past times

Year	Gini
1688	0.55
1801–03	0.56
1867	0.52
1913	0.43–0.63

[4]   Long run changes in British income inequality, *Economic History Review*, 1968.
[5]   A poverty-focused approach to development policy, in J. P. Lewis and V. Kalab (eds), *Development Strategies Reconsidered*, 1986.

A simpler formula for the Gini coefficient

Kravis, Heston and Summers[6] provide estimates of 'world' GDP by decile and these figures, presented in Table 2.26, will be used to illustrate another method of calculating the Gini coefficient.

These figures show that the poorer half of the world population earns only about 10% of world income and that a third of world income goes to the richest 10% of the population. This suggests a higher degree of inequality than for a single country such as Britain, as one might expect.

Table 2.26   The world distribution of income by decile

Decile	1	2	3	4	5	6	7	8	9	10
% GDP	1.5	2.1	2.4	2.4	3.3	5.2	8.4	17.1	24.1	33.5
Cumulative %	1.5	3.6	6.0	8.4	11.7	16.9	25.3	42.4	66.5	100.0

When the class intervals contain equal numbers of households (for example when the data are given for deciles of the income distribution, as here) formula (2.22) for area B simplifies to:

$$(2.27) \quad B = \frac{100}{2k}\left(y_0 + 2y_1 + 2y_2 + \ldots + 2y_{k-1} + y_k\right) = \frac{100}{k}\left(\sum_{i=0}^{i=k} y_i - 50\right)$$

where k is the number of intervals (e.g. 10 in the case of deciles, 5 for quintiles). Thus you simply sum the y values, subtract 50,[7] and divide by the number of classes k. The y values for the Kravis *et al.* data appear in the final row of Table 2.26, and their sum is 282.3. We therefore obtain

$$(2.28) \quad B = \frac{100}{10}(282.3 - 50) = 2{,}323$$

Hence

$$(2.29) \quad A = 5{,}000 - 2{,}323 = 2{,}677$$

and

$$(2.30) \quad G = \frac{2{,}677}{5{,}000} = 0.5354$$

or about 53%. This is surprisingly similar to the figure for original income in the UK, but, of course, differences in definition, measurement, etc. may make direct comparison invalid. While the Gini coefficient may provide some guidance when comparing inequality over time or across countries, one needs to take care in its interpretation.

[6] Real GDP per capita for more than one hundred countries, *Economic Journal*, 1978.
[7] If using decimal percentages, subtract 0.5.

Inequality and Development

Table 2.27 presents figures for the income distribution in selected countries around the world. They are in approximately ascending order of national income.

Table 2.27   Income distribution figures in selected countries

	Year	1	2	3	4	5	Top 10%	Gini
Bangladesh	1981–82	6.6	10.7	15.3	22.1	45.3	29.5	0.36
Kenya	1976	2.6	6.3	11.5	19.2	60.4	45.8	0.51
Côte d'Ivoire	1985–86	2.4	6.2	10.9	19.1	61.4	43.7	0.52
El Salvador	1976–77	5.5	10.0	14.8	22.4	47.3	29.5	0.38
Brazil	1972	2.0	5.0	9.4	17.0	66.6	50.6	0.56
Hungary	1982	6.9	13.6	19.2	24.5	35.8	20.5	0.27
Korea, rep.	1976	5.7	11.2	15.4	22.4	45.3	27.5	0.36
Hong Kong	1980	5.4	10.8	15.2	21.6	47	31.3	0.38
New Zealand	1981–82	5.1	10.8	16.2	23.2	44.7	28.7	0.37
UK	1979	7	11.5	17	24.8	39.7	23.4	0.31
Netherlands	1981	8.3	14.1	18.2	23.2	36.2	21.5	0.26
Japan	1979	8.7	13.2	17.5	23.1	37.5	22.4	0.27

Source: World Development Report 1988.

The table shows that countries have very different experiences of inequality, even for similar levels of income (compare Bangladesh and Kenya, for example). Hungary, the only (former) communist country, shows the greatest equality, although whether income accurately measures peoples' access to resources in such a regime is perhaps debatable. Note that countries with fast growth (such as Korea and Hong Kong) do not have to have a high degree of inequality. Developed countries seem to have uniformly low Gini coefficients.

Concentration ratios

The concentration ratio is commonly used to examine the distribution of market shares among firms competing in a market. Of course it would be possible to measure this using the Lorenz curve and Gini coefficient, but the concentration ratio has the advantage that it can be calculated on the basis of less information and tends to focus attention on the largest firms in the industry. The concentration ratio is often used as a measure of the competitiveness of a particular market but, as with all statistics, it requires careful interpretation.

A market is said to be concentrated if most of the demand is met by a small number of suppliers. The limiting case is monopoly where the whole of the market is supplied by a single firm. We shall measure the degree of concentration by the **five-firm concentration ratio**, which is the proportion of the market held by the largest five firms, and it is denoted C_5. The larger is this proportion, the greater the degree of concentration and potentially the less competitive is that market. Table 2.28 gives the sales figures of the ten firms in a particular industry.

For convenience the firms have already been ranked by size from A (the largest) to J (smallest). The output of the five largest firms is 482, out of a total of 569, so the

Table 2.28   Sales figures for an industry (millions of units)

Firm	A	B	C	D	E	F	G	H	I	J
Sales	180	115	90	62	35	25	19	18	15	10

five-firm concentration ratio is $C_5 = 84.7\%$, i.e 84.7% of the market is supplied by the five largest firms.

Without supporting evidence it is hard to interpret this figure. Does it mean that the market is not competitive and the consumer being exploited? Some industries, such as the computer industry, have a very high concentration ratio yet it is hard to deny that they are very competitive. On the other hand, some industries with no large firms have restrictive practices, entry barriers, etc. which mean that they are not very competitive (lawyers might be one example). A further point is that there may be a *threat* of competition from outside the industry which keeps the few firms acting competitively.

Concentration ratios can be calculated for different numbers of largest firms, e.g. the three-firm or four-firm concentration ratio. Straightforward calculation reveals them to be 67.7% and 78.6% respectively for the data given in Table 2.28. There is little reason in general to prefer one measure to the others, and they may give different pictures of the degree of concentration in an industry.

The concentration ratio calculated above relates to the quantity of output produced by each firm, but it is possible to do the same with sales revenue, employment, investment or any other variable for which data are available. The interpretation of the results will be different in each case. For example, the largest firms in an industry, while producing the majority of output, might not provide the greater part of employment if they use more capital-intensive methods of production. Concentration ratios obviously have to be treated with caution, therefore, and are probably best combined with case studies of the particular industry before conclusions are reached about the degree of competition.

EXERCISES

Exercise 1

The data below show exports and imports for the UK, 1987–92, in £bn at current prices.

	1987	1988	1989	1990	1991	1992
Exports	120.6	121.2	126.8	133.3	132.1	135.5
Imports	122.1	137.4	147.6	148.3	140.2	148.3

(a)   Construct index number series for exports and imports, setting the index equal to 100 in 1987 in each case.

(b)   Is it possible, using only the two indices, to construct an index number series for the balance of trade? If so, do so; if not, why not?

Exercise 2   The following data show the gross trading profits of companies, 1987–92, in the UK, in £m.

1987	1988	1989	1990	1991	1992
61,750	69,180	73,892	74,405	78,063	77,959

(a) Turn the data into an index number series with 1987 as the reference year.

(b) Transform the series so that 1990 is the reference year.

(c) What increase has there been in profits between 1987 and 1992? Between 1990 and 1992?

Exercise 3   The following data show energy prices and consumption in 1984–88 (analogous to the data in the chapter for the years 1988–92).

Prices	Coal (£/tonne)	Petroleum (£/tonne)	Electricity (£/MWh)	Gas (£/therm)
1984	49.60	149.70	28.89	0.2634
1985	51.00	151.75	30.02	0.2841
1986	49.64	72.98	30.07	0.2378
1987	47.50	78.10	28.92	0.2196
1988	43.10	55.04	30.02	0.2175

Quantities	Coal (m. tonnes)	Petroleum (m. tonnes)	Electricity (m. MWh)	Gas (m. therms)
1984	12.72	10.26	78.64	6,044
1985	14.62	9.12	79.53	6,185
1986	14.58	9.67	80.09	5,647
1987	15.12	8.61	83.89	6,182
1988	15.77	9.61	88.13	5,636

(a) Construct a Laspeyres price index using 1984 as the base year.

(b) Construct a Paasche price index. Compare this result with the Laspeyres index. Do they differ significantly?

(c) Construct Laspeyres and Paasche quantity indices. Check that they satisfy the conditions that $E^n = P_L \times Q_P$ etc.

Exercise 4   The prices of different house types in south-east England are given in the table below:

Year	Terraced houses	Semi-detached	Detached	Bungalows	Flats
1991	59,844	77,791	142,630	89,100	47,676
1992	55,769	73,839	137,053	82,109	43,695
1993	55,571	71,208	129,414	82,734	42,746
1994	57,296	71,850	130,159	83,471	44,092

(a) If the numbers of each type of house in 1991 were 1898, 1600, 1601, 499 and 1702 respectively, calculate the Laspeyres price index for 1991–94, based on 1991 = 100.

(b) Calculate the Paasche price index, based on the following numbers of dwellings:

Year	Terraced houses	Semi-detached	Detached	Bungalows	Flats
1992	1,903	1,615	1,615	505	1,710
1993	1,906	1,638	1,633	511	1,714
1994	1,911	1,655	1,640	525	1,717

(c) Compare Paasche and Laspeyres price series.

Exercise 5

(a) Using the data in exercise 3, calculate the expenditure shares on each fuel in 1984 and the individual price index number series for each fuel, with 1984 = 100.

(b) Use these data to construct the Laspeyres price index using the expenditures shares approach. Check that it gives the same answer as in exercise 3(a).

Exercise 6

The following table shows the weights in the Retail Price Index and the values of the index itself, for 1990 and 1994.

	Food	Alcohol and tobacco	Housing	Fuel and light	House-hold items	Clothing	Personal goods	Travel	Leisure
Weights									
1990	205	111	185	50	111	69	39	152	78
1994	187	111	158	45	123	58	37	162	119
Prices									
1990	121.0	120.7	163.7	115.9	116.9	115.0	122.7	121.2	117.1
1994	139.5	162.1	156.8	133.9	132.4	116.0	152.4	150.7	145.7

(a) Calculate the Laspeyres price index for 1994, based on 1990 = 100.

(b) Draw a bar chart of the expenditure weights in 1990 and 1994 to show how spending patterns have changed. What major changes have occurred? Do individuals seem to be responding to changes in relative prices?

(c) The pensioner price index is similar to the general index calculated above, except that it excludes housing. What effect does this have on the index? What do you think is the justification for this omission?

(d) If consumers spent, on average, £188 per week in 1990 and £240 per week in 1994, calculate the real change in expenditure on food.

(e) Do consumers appear rational, i.e. do they respond as one would expect to relative price changes? If not, why not?

Exercise 7

Construct a chain index from the following data series:

	1988	1989	1990	1991	1992	1993	1994
Series 1	100	110	115	122	125		
Series 2			100	107	111	119	121

What problems arise in devising such an index and how do you deal with them?

Exercise 8

Using the price index series calculated in exercise 3, and the series calculated in the chapter, construct a chain index of energy prices for the period 1984–92 based on the Paasche indices. Are there significant differences between the Laspeyres and Paasche versions?

Exercise 9

Industry is complaining about the rising price of energy. It demands to be compensated for any rise over 2% in energy prices between 1991 and 1992. How much would this compensation cost? Which price index should be used to calculate the compensation and what difference would it make?

Exercise 10

Using the data in exercise 6 above, calculate how much the average consumer would need to be compensated for the rise in prices between 1990 and 1994.

Exercise 11

The following data show expenditure on the National Health Service (in cash terms), the GDP deflator, the NHS pay and prices index, population, and population of working age:

Year	NHS expenditure (£m) (1)	GDP deflator 1973=100 (2)	NHS pay and price index 1973=100 (3)	Population (000) (4)	Population of working age (000) (5)
1987	21,495	442	573	56,930	34,987
1988	23,601	473	633	57,065	35,116
1989	25,906	504	678	57,236	35,222
1990	28,534	546	728	57,411	35,300
1991	32,321	585	792	57,801	35,467

(In all the following answers, set your index to 1987=100.)

(a) Turn the expenditure cash figures into an index number series.

(b) Calculate an index of 'real' NHS expenditure using the GDP deflator. How does this alter the expenditure series?

(c) Calculate an index of the volume of NHS expenditure using the NHS pay and prices index. How and why does this differ from the answer arrived at in (b)?

(d) Calculate indices of real and volume expenditure *per capita*. What difference does this make?

(e) Suppose that those not of working age cost twice as much to treat, on average, as those of working age. Construct an index of the need for health care and examine how health care expenditures have changed relative to need.

(f) How do you think the needs index calculated in (e) could be improved?

Exercise 12

(a) If w represents the wage rate and p the price level, what is w/p?

(b) If Δw represent the annual growth in wages and i is the inflation rate, what is $\Delta w - i$?

(c) What does $\ln(w) - \ln(p)$ represent? ($\ln$ = natural logarithm.)

Exercise 13

A firm is investing in a project and wishes to receive a rate of return of at least 15% on it. The stream of net income is:

Year	1	2	3	4
Income	600	650	700	400

(a) What is the Present Value of this income stream?

(b) If the investment costs £1,600 should the firm invest? What is the Net Present Value of the project?

Exercise 14

A firm uses a discount rate of 12% for all its investment projects. Faced with the following choice of projects, which yields the higher NPV?

Project	Outlay	Income stream					
		1	2	3	4	5	6
A	5,600	1,000	1,400	1,500	2,100	1,450	700
B	6,000	800	1,400	1,750	2,500	1,925	1,200

Exercise 15

Calculate the internal rate of return for the project in exercise 13. Use either trial and error methods or a computer to solve.

Exercise 16

Calculate the internal rates of return for the projects in exercise 14.

Exercise 17

(a) Draw a Lorenz curve and calculate the Gini coefficient for the wealth data in Chapter 1 (Table 1.4).

(b) Why is the Gini coefficient typically larger for wealth distributions than for income distributions?

Exercise 18

(a) Draw a Lorenz curve and calculate the Gini coefficient for the 1979 wealth data contained in exercise 5 of Chapter 1. Draw the Lorenz curve on the same diagram as you used in exercise 17.

(b) How does the answer compare to 1988?

Exercise 19

The following table shows the income distribution by quintile for the UK in 1991, for various definitions of income:

Quintile	Income measure			
	Original	Gross	Disposable	Post-tax
1 (bottom)	2.0%	6.7%	7.2%	6.6%
2	7.0%	10.0%	11.0%	11.0%
3	16.0%	16.0%	16.0%	16.0%
4	26.0%	23.0%	23.0%	23.0%
5	50.0%	44.0%	42.0%	44.0%

(a) Use equation (2.27) to calculate the Gini coefficient for each of the four categories of income.

(b) For the 'original income' category, draw a smooth Lorenz curve on a piece of gridded paper and calculate the Gini coefficient using the method of counting squares. How does your answer compare to that for part (a)?

Exercise 20

For the Kravis, Heston and Summers data (Table 2.26), combine the deciles into quintiles and calculate the Gini coefficient from the quintile data. How does your answer compare with the answer given in the text, based on deciles? What do you conclude about the degree of bias?

Exercise 21

Calculate the three-firm concentration ratio for employment in the following industry:

Firm	A	B	C	D	E	F	G	H
Employees	3,350	290	440	1,345	821	112	244	352

Exercise 22

Compare the degrees of concentration in the following two industries. Can you say which is likely to be more competitive?

Firm	A	B	C	D	E	F	G	H	I	J
Sales	337	384	696	321	769	265	358	521	880	334
Sales	556	899	104	565	782	463	477	846	911	227

Exercise 23

Project: The World Development Report contains data on the income distributions of many countries around the world (by quintile). Use these data to compare income distributions across countries, focusing particularly on the differences between poor countries, middle income, and rich countries. Can you see any pattern emerging? Are there countries which do not fit into this pattern? Write a brief report summarising your findings.

Appendix: Deriving the expenditure share form of the Laspeyres price index

We can obtain the expenditure share version of the formula from the standard formula given in equation (2.1):

$$P_L^n = \frac{\sum p_n q_0}{\sum p_0 q_0} = \frac{\sum \dfrac{P_n}{p_0} p_0 q_0}{\sum \dfrac{p_0}{p_0} p_0 q_0}$$

$$= \frac{\sum \dfrac{p_n}{p_0} \dfrac{p_0 q_0}{\sum p_0 q_0}}{\sum \dfrac{p_0}{p_0} \dfrac{p_0 q_0}{\sum p_0 q_0}} = \sum \frac{p_n}{p_0} \frac{p_0 q_0}{\sum p_0 q_0}$$

$$= \sum \frac{p_n}{p_0} \times s_0$$

which is equation (2.3) in the text.

References

P. Johnson and S. Webb (1993), Explaining the growth in UK income inequality: 1979–88. *Economic Journal*, 103, pp. 429–35.

3 PROBABILITY

Probability theory and statistical inference

In October 1985 Mrs Evelyn Adams of New Jersey, USA, won $3.9 million in the State lottery at odds of 1 in 3,200,000. In February 1986 she again won, though this time only (!) $1.4 million at odds of 1 in 5,200,000. The odds against both these wins were calculated at about 1 in 17,300 billion. Mrs Adams is quoted as saying 'They say good things come in threes, so. . .'.

The above story illustrates the principles of probability at work. The same principles underlie the theory of statistical inference. Statistical inference is the task of drawing conclusions (inferences) about a population from a sample of data drawn from that population. For example, we might have a survey which shows that 30% of a sample of 100 families intend to take a holiday abroad next year. What can we conclude from this about *all* families? The techniques set out in this and subsequent chapters show how to accomplish this.

Why is knowledge of probability necessary for the study of statistical inference? In order to be able to say something about a population on the basis of some sample evidence we must first examine how the sample data are collected. In many cases, the sample is a random one, i.e. the observations making up the sample are chosen at random from the population. If a second sample were selected it would almost certainly be different from the first. Each member of the population has a particular probability of being in the sample (in simple random sampling the probability is the same for all members of the population). To understand sampling procedures, and the implications for statistical inference, we must therefore first examine the theory of probability.

As an illustration of this, suppose we wish to know if a coin is fair, i.e. equally likely to fall heads or tails. The coin is tossed ten times and ten heads are recorded. This constitutes a random sample of tosses of the coin. What can we infer about the coin? *If* it is fair, the probability of getting ten heads is 1 in 1,024, so a fairly unlikely event seems to have happened. We might reasonably infer therefore that the coin is biased.

The definition of probability

The first task is to define precisely what is meant by probability. This is not as easy as one might imagine and there are a number of different schools of thought on the subject. Consider the following questions:

- What is the probability of 'heads' occurring on the toss of a coin?
- What is the probability of a driver having an accident in a year of driving?
- What is the probability of a country such as Peru defaulting on its international loan repayments (as Mexico did in the 1980s)?

We shall use these questions as examples when examining the different schools of thought on probability.

The frequentist view   Considering the first question above, the **frequentist view** would be that the probability is equal to the **proportion** of heads obtained from a coin in the long run, i.e. if the coin were tossed many times. The first few results of such an experiment might be:

H, T, T, H, H, H, T, H, T ...

After a while, the proportion of heads settles down at some particular fraction and subsequent tosses will individually have an insignificant effect upon the value. Figure 3.1 shows the result of tossing a coin 250 times and recording the proportion of heads (actually, this was simulated on a computer: life is too short to do it for real).

This shows the proportion settling down at a value of about 0.50, which indicates an unbiased coin (or rather, an unbiased computer!). This value is the probability, according to the frequentist view. To be more precise, the probability is the proportion of heads obtained as the number of tosses *approaches infinity*. In general we can define Pr(*H*), the probability of event *H* (in this case heads) occurring, as

$$\mathrm{Pr}(H) = \frac{\text{number of occurrences of } H}{\text{number of trials}} \quad \textit{as the number of trials approaches infinity}$$

In this case, each toss of the coin constitutes a trial.

This definition gets round the obvious question of how many trials are needed before the probability emerges, but means that the probability of an event cannot strictly be obtained in finite time.

Although this approach appears attractive in theory, it does have its problems. One couldn't actually toss the coin an infinite number of times. Or, what if one took a different coin, would the results from the first coin necessarily apply to the second?

Perhaps more seriously, the definition is of less use for the second and third questions posed above. Calculating the probability of an accident is not too problematic: it may be defined as the proportion of all drivers having an accident during the year. However, this may not be relevant for a *particular* driver, since drivers vary so much in their accident records. And how would you answer the third question? There is no long run that we can appeal to. We cannot re-run history over and over again to see

Fig. 3.1 *Proportion of heads in 250 tosses of a coin*

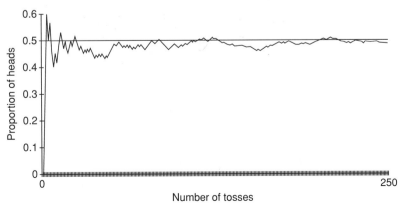

in what proportion of cases the country defaults. Yet this is what lenders want to know and credit-rating agencies have to assess. Maybe another approach is needed.

The subjective view

According to this view, probability is a **degree of belief** that someone holds about the likelihood of an event occurring. It is inevitably subjective and therefore some argue that it should be the degree of belief that it is *rational* to hold, but this just shifts the argument to what is meant by 'rational'. Some progress can be made by distinguishing between **prior** and **posterior** beliefs. The former are those held before any evidence is considered; the latter are the modified probabilities in the light of the evidence. For example, one might initially believe a coin to be fair (the prior probability of heads is one half), but not after seeing only five heads in fifty tosses (the posterior probability would be less than a half).

Although it has its attractions, this approach (which is the basis of **Bayesian** statistics) also has its drawbacks. It is not always clear how one should arrive at the prior beliefs, particularly when one really has no prior information. Also, these methods often require the use of sophisticated mathematics, which may account for the limited use made of them.

There is not universal agreement therefore as to the precise definition of probability. We do not have space here to explore the issue further, so we will ignore the problem! The probability of an event occurring will be defined as a certain value and we won't worry about the precise meaning. This is an **axiomatic** approach: we simply state what the probability is, without justifying it, and then examine the consequences.

Probability theory: the building blocks

We start with a few definitions, to establish a vocabulary:

- An **experiment** is an action such as flipping a coin, which has a number of possible **outcomes** or **events**, such as heads or tails.
- A **trial** is a single performance of the experiment, with a single outcome.
- The **sample space** consists of all the possible outcomes of the experiment. The outcomes for a single toss of a coin are {heads, tails}, for example. The outcomes in the sample space are **mutually exclusive**, which means that the occurrence of one rules out all the others. One cannot have both heads and tails in a single toss of a coin. If a single card is drawn at random from a pack, then the sample space may be drawn as in Fig. 3.2. Each point represents one card in the pack and there are 52 points altogether.
- With each outcome in the sample space we can associate a **probability**, which is the chance of that outcome occurring. The probability of heads is one half; the probability of drawing the Ace of Spades from a pack of cards is one in 52, etc.

There are restrictions upon the probabilities we can associate with the outcomes in

Fig. 3.2 *The sample space for drawing from a pack of cards*

	A	K	Q	J	10	9	8	7	6	5	4	3	2
♠	•	•	•	•	•	•	•	•	•	•	•	•	•
♥	•	•	•	•	•	•	•	•	•	•	•	•	•
♦	•	•	•	•	•	•	•	•	•	•	•	•	•
♣	•	•	•	•	•	•	•	•	•	•	•	•	•

the sample space. These are needed to ensure that we do not come up with self-contradictory results; for example, it would be odd to arrive at the conclusion that we could expect heads more than half the time *and* tails more than half the time. The restrictions are as follows:

- The probability of an event must lie between 0 and 1, i.e.

    (3.1) $0 \leq \Pr(A) \leq 1$, for any event A

    The explanation is straightforward. If A is certain to occur it occurs in 100% of all trials and so its probability is 1. If A is certain not to occur then its probability is 0, since it never happens however many trials there are. Since one cannot be more certain than certain, probabilities of less than 0 or more than 1 can never occur, and (3.1) follows.
- The sum of the probabilities associated with all the outcomes in the sample space is 1. Formally

    (3.2) $\Sigma P_i = 1$

    where P_i is the probability of event i occurring. This follows from the fact that one, and only one, of the outcomes *must* occur, since they are mutually exclusive and also **exhaustive**, i.e. they define all the possibilities.
- Following on from (3.2) we may define the **complement** of an event as everything in the sample space apart from that event. The complement of heads is tails, for example. If we write the complement of A as not-A then it follows that $\Pr(A) + \Pr(\text{not-}A) = 1$ and hence

    (3.3) $\Pr(\text{not-}A) = 1 - \Pr(A)$

Compound events

Most practical problems require the calculation of the probability of a set of outcomes rather than just a single one, or the probability of a series of outcomes in separate trials. For example, the probability of drawing a spade at random from a pack of cards encompasses 13 points in the sample space (one for each spade). This probability is 13 out of 52, or one-quarter, which is fairly obvious; but for more complex problems the answer is not immediately evident. We refer to such sets of outcomes as **compound events**. Some examples are getting a five *or* a six on a throw of a die or drawing an Ace *and* a Queen to complete a 'straight' in a game of poker.

It is sometimes possible to calculate the probability of a compound event by examining the sample space, as in the case of drawing a spade above. However, in many cases this is not so, for the sample space is too complex or even impossible to write down. For example, the sample space for three draws of a card from a pack consists of over 140,000 points! An alternative method is needed. Fortunately there are a few simple rules for manipulating probabilities which help us to calculate the probabilities of compound events.

If the previous examples are examined closely it can be seen that outcomes are being compounded using 'or' and 'and': '. . .five *or* six on a single throw. . .'; '. . .an Ace *and* a Queen. . .'. 'And' and 'or' act as *operators*, and compound events are made up of simple events compounded by these two operators. The following rules for manipulating probabilities show how to handle these operators.

The addition rule

This rule is associated with 'or'. The probability of A or B occurring is given by

Fig 3.3 *The sample space for rolling a die*

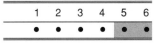

Fig 3.4 *The sample space for drawing a Queen or a Spade*

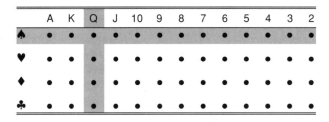

$$(3.4) \quad \Pr(A \text{ or } B) = \Pr(A) + \Pr(B)$$

So, for example, the probability of a five or a six on a roll of a die is

$$(3.5) \quad \Pr(5 \text{ or } 6) = 1/6 + 1/6 = 1/3$$

This answer can be verified from the sample space, as in Fig. 3.3. Each dot represents a simple event (one to six). The compound event is made up of two of the six points, shaded in Fig. 3.3, so the probability is 2/6 or 1/3.

However, (3.4) is not a general solution to this type of problem, as can be seen from the following example. What is the probability of a Queen or a Spade in a single draw from a pack of cards? $\Pr(Q) = 4/52$ (four queens in the pack) and $\Pr(S) = 13/52$ (13 spades), so applying (3.4) gives

$$(3.6) \quad \Pr(Q \text{ or } S) = \Pr(Q) + \Pr(S) = 4/52 + 13/52 = 17/52$$

However, if the sample space is examined the correct answer is found to be 16/52, as in Fig. 3.4. The problem is that one point in the sample space (the one representing the Queen of Spades) is double-counted, once as a Queen and again as a Spade. The event 'drawing a Queen *and* a Spade' is possible, and gets double counted. Equation (3.4) has to be modified by subtracting the probability of getting a Queen *and* a Spade. The correct answer is obtained from

$$(3.7) \quad \Pr(Q \text{ or } S) = \Pr(Q) + \Pr(S) - \Pr(Q \text{ and } S)$$
$$= 4/52 + 13/52 - 1/52$$
$$= 16/52$$

The general rule is therefore

$$(3.8) \quad \Pr(A \text{ or } B) = \Pr(A) + \Pr(B) - \Pr(A \text{ and } B)$$

Rule (3.4) worked for the die example because $\Pr(5 \text{ and } 6) = 0$ since a five and a six cannot both simultaneously occur.

In general, therefore, one should use (3.8), but when two events are mutually exclusive the rule simplifies to (3.4).

The multiplication rule

The multiplication rule is associated with 'and'. Consider a mother with two children. What is the probability that they are both boys? This is really a compound event: a boy on the first birth *and* a boy on the second. Assume that in a single birth a boy or girl is equally likely, so $\Pr(\text{boy}) = \Pr(\text{girl}) = 0.5$. Denote by $\Pr(B1)$ the probability of a boy on the first birth and by $\Pr(B2)$ the probability of a boy on the second. Thus the question asks for $\Pr(B1 \text{ and } B2)$ and this is given by:

$$(3.9) \quad \Pr(B1 \text{ and } B2) = \Pr(B1) \times \Pr(B2)$$
$$= 0.5 \times 0.5$$
$$= 0.25$$

Intuitively, the multiplication rule can be understood as follows. One-half of mothers have a boy on their first birth and of these, one-half will again have a boy on the second. Therefore a quarter of mothers have two boys.

Like the addition rule, the multiplication rule requires slight modification before it can be applied generally. The example assumes first and second births to be **independent events**, i.e. that having a boy on the first birth does not affect the probability of a boy on the second. This assumption is not always valid.

Write $\Pr(B2 \mid B1)$ to indicate the probability of the event $B2$ *given* that the event $B1$ has occurred. Let us drop the independence assumption and suppose the following:

$$(3.10) \quad \Pr(B1) = \Pr(G1) = 0.5$$

i.e. boys and girls are equally likely on the first birth, and

$$(3.11) \quad \Pr(B2 \mid B1) = \Pr(G2 \mid G1) = 0.6$$

i.e. a boy is more likely to be followed by another boy, and a girl by another girl. (It is easy to work out $\Pr(B2 \mid G1)$ and $\Pr(G2 \mid B1)$. What are they?)

Now what is the probability of two boys? Half of all mothers have a boy first, and of these, 60% have another boy. Thus 30% (60% of 50%) of mothers have two boys. This is obtained from the rule:

$$(3.12) \quad \Pr(B1 \text{ and } B2) = \Pr(B1) \times \Pr(B2 \mid B1)$$
$$= 0.5 \times 0.6$$
$$= 0.3$$

Thus in general we have:

$$(3.13) \quad \Pr(A \text{ and } B) = \Pr(A) \times \Pr(B \mid A)$$

which simplifies to

$$(3.14) \quad \Pr(A \text{ and } B) = \Pr(A) \times \Pr(B)$$

if A and B are independent.

Independence may therefore be defined as follows: two events, A and B, are independent if the probability of one occurring is not influenced by the fact of the other having occurred. Formally, if A and B are independent then

$$(3.15) \quad \Pr(B \mid A) = \Pr(B \mid \text{not } A) = \Pr(B)$$

and

$$(3.16) \quad \Pr(A \mid B) = \Pr(A \mid \text{not } B) = \Pr(A)$$

Combining the addition and multiplication rules

More complex problems can be solved by suitable combinations of the addition and multiplication formulae. For example, what is the probability of a mother having one child of each sex? This could occur in one of two ways: a girl followed by a boy or a boy followed by a girl. Therefore we have (assuming non-independence according to (3.11))

$$\Pr(1 \text{ girl, } 1 \text{ boy}) = \Pr((G1 \text{ and } B2) \text{ or } (B1 \text{ and } G2))$$
$$= \Pr(G1) \times \Pr(B2 \mid G1) + \Pr(B1) \times \Pr(G2 \mid B1)$$
$$= (0.5 \times 0.4) + (0.5 \times 0.4)$$
$$= 0.4$$

The answer can be checked if we remember (3.2) stating that probabilities must sum to 1. We have calculated the probability of two boys (0.3) and of a child of each sex (0.4). The only other possibility is of two girls. This probability must be 0.3, the same as two boys, since boys and girls are treated symmetrically in this problem (even with the non-independence assumption). The sum is therefore $0.3 + 0.4 + 0.3 = 1$, as it should be.

Tree diagrams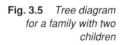

The preceding problem can be illustrated using a **tree diagram**, which often helps to clarify a problem. A tree diagram is an alternative way of enumerating all possible outcomes in the sample space, with the associated probabilities. The diagram for two children is shown in Fig. 3.5.

The diagram begins at the left and the first node shows the possible alternatives (boy, girl) at that point and the associated probabilities (0.5, 0.5). The next two nodes show the alternatives and probabilities for the second birth, given the sex of the first child. The final four nodes show the possible results: boy, boy; boy, girl; girl, boy; and girl, girl.

To find the probability of two girls, using the tree diagram, follow the lowest path, multiplying the probabilities along it to give $0.5 \times 0.6 = 0.3$. To find the probability of one child of each sex it is necessary to add the probabilities obtained from the paths boy, girl and girl, boy, giving $0.2 + 0.2 = 0.4$. This provides a graphical alternative to the formulae used above and may help comprehension.

The tree diagram can obviously be extended to cover third and subsequent children although the number of branches rapidly increases (in geometric progression). The difficulty then becomes not the calculation of the probability attached to each outcome, but sorting out which branches should be taken into account in the calculation. Suppose we consider a family of five children of whom three are girls. To simplify matters we again assume independence of probabilities. The appropriate tree diagram has $2^5 = 32$ end points, each with probability $1/32$. How many of these

Fig. 3.5 *Tree diagram for a family with two children*

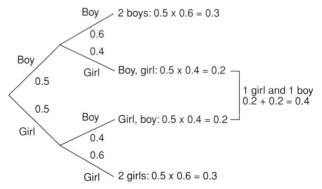

relate to families with three girls and two boys, for example? To find this out, we use the ideas of **combinations** and **permutations**.

Combinations and permutations

How can we establish the number of ways of having three girls and two boys? One way would be to write down all the possible orderings:

GGGBB	GGBGB	GGBBG	GBGGB	GBGBG
GBBGG	BGGGB	BGGBG	BGBGG	BBGGG

This shows that there are ten such orderings, so the probability of three girls and two boys in a family of five children is 10/32. In more complex problems this soon becomes difficult or impossible. The record number of children born to a British mother is 39(!) of whom 32 were girls. The appropriate tree diagram has over 5 thousand billion 'routes' through it, and drawing one line (i.e. for one child) per second would imply 17,433 years to complete the task! Rather than do this, we use the **combinatorial** formula. Suppose there are n children, r of them girls, then the number of orderings, denoted nCr, is obtained from

$n!$ is read 'n factorial' and is defined as the product of all the integers up to and including n.

$$(3.17) \quad nCr = \frac{n!}{r!(n-r)!} = \frac{n \times (n-1) \times \ldots \times 1}{\{r \times (r-1) \times \ldots \times 1\} \times \{(n-r) \times (n-r-1) \times \ldots \times 1\}}$$

In the above example $n = 5$, $r = 3$ so the number of orderings is

$$(3.18) \quad 5C3 = \frac{5 \times 4 \times 3 \times 2 \times 1}{\{3 \times 2 \times 1\} \times \{2 \times 1\}} = 10$$

If there were four girls out of five children then the number of orderings or combinations would be

$$(3.19) \quad 5C4 = \frac{5 \times 4 \times 3 \times 2 \times 1}{\{4 \times 3 \times 2 \times 1\} \times 1} = 5$$

This gives five possible orderings, i.e. the single boy could be the first, second, third, fourth or fifth born.

   Why does this formula work? Consider five empty places to fill, corresponding to the five births in chronological order. Take the case of three girls (call them Amanda, Bridget and Caroline for convenience) who have to fill three of the five places. For Amanda there is a choice of five empty places. Having 'chosen' one, there remain four for Bridget, so there are $5 \times 4 = 20$ possibilities (i.e. ways in which these two could choose their places). Three remain for Caroline, so there are 60 ($= 5 \times 4 \times 3$) possible orderings in all (the two boys take the two remaining places). Sixty is the number of **permutations** of three *named* girls in five births. This is written $5P3$ or in general nPr. Hence

$$5P3 = 5 \times 4 \times 3$$

or in general

$$(3.20) \quad nPr = n \times (n-1) \times \ldots \times (n-r+1)$$

A simpler formula is obtained by multiplying and dividing by $(n-r)!$

$$(3.21) \quad nPr = \frac{n \times (n-r) \times \ldots \times (n-r+1) \times (n-r)!}{(n-r)!}$$

$$= \frac{n!}{(n-r)!}$$

What is the difference between nPr and nCr? The latter does not distinguish between the girls; the two cases Amanda, Bridget, Caroline, boy, boy and Bridget, Amanda, Caroline, boy, boy are effectively the same (three girls followed by two boys). So nPr is larger by a factor representing the number of ways of ordering the three girls. This factor is given by $r! = 3 \times 2 \times 1 = 6$ (any of the three girls could be first, either of the other two second, and then the final one). Thus to obtain nCr one must divide nPr by $r!$, giving (3.17).

Bayes' theorem

Bayes' theorem is a factual statement about probabilities which in itself is uncontroversial. However, the use and interpretation of the result is at the heart of the difference between **classical** and **Bayesian** statistics. The theorem itself is easily derived from first principles.

$$(3.22) \quad \Pr(A \text{ and } B) = \Pr(A \mid B) \times \Pr(B)$$

hence

$$(3.23) \quad \Pr(A \mid B) = \frac{\Pr(A \text{ and } B)}{\Pr(B)}$$

Expanding both top and bottom of the right-hand side,

$$(3.24) \quad \Pr(A \mid B) = \frac{\Pr(B \mid A) \times \Pr(A)}{\Pr(B \mid A) \times \Pr(A) + \Pr(B \mid \text{not } A) \times \Pr(\text{not } A)}$$

Equation (3.24) is known as **Bayes' theorem** and is a statement about the probability of the event A, conditional upon B having occurred. The following example demonstrates its use.

Two bags contain red and yellow balls. Bag A contains six red and four yellow balls, bag B has three red and seven yellow balls. A ball is drawn at random from one bag and turns out to be red. What is the probability that it came from bag A?

Denoting:

$\Pr(A) = 0.5$ (the probability of choosing bag A at random) $= \Pr(B)$
$\Pr(R \mid A) = 0.6$ (the probability of selecting a red ball from bag A), etc.

we have

$$(3.25) \quad \Pr(A \mid R) = \frac{\Pr(R \mid A) \times \Pr(A)}{\Pr(R \mid A) \times \Pr(A) + \Pr(R \mid B) \times \Pr(B)}$$

using Bayes' theorem. Evaluating this gives

$$(3.26) \quad \Pr(A \mid R) = \frac{0.6 \times 0.5}{0.6 \times 0.5 + 0.3 \times 0.5}$$
$$= \frac{2}{3}$$

(You can check that $\Pr(B \mid R) = 1/3$ so that the sum of the probabilities is 1.)

Bayes' theorem can be extended to cover more than two bags: if there are five bags, for example, labelled A to E then

$$(3.27) \quad \Pr(A \mid R) = \frac{\Pr(R \mid A) \times \Pr(A)}{\Pr(R \mid A) \times \Pr(A) + \Pr(R \mid B) \times \Pr(B) + \ldots + \Pr(R \mid E) \times \Pr(E)}$$

In Bayesian language, $\Pr(A)$, $\Pr(B)$, etc. are known as the **prior** (to the drawing of the ball) probabilities, $\Pr(R \mid A)$, $\Pr(R \mid B)$, etc. are the **likelihoods** and $\Pr(A \mid R)$, $\Pr(B \mid R)$, etc. are the **posterior** probabilities. Bayes' theorem can alternatively be expressed as

$$(3.28) \quad \text{posterior probability} = \frac{\text{likelihood} \times \text{prior probability}}{\sum \left(\text{likelihoods} \times \text{prior probabilities} \right)}$$

This is illustrated below, by reworking the above example.

	Prior probabilities	Likelihoods	Prior × likelihood	Posterior probabilities
A	0.5	0.6	0.30	$0.30/0.45 = 2/3$
B	0.5	0.3	0.15	$0.15/0.45 = 1/3$
Total			0.45	

The general version of Bayes' theorem may be stated as follows. If there are n events labelled $E_1, \ldots E_n$ then the probability of the event i occurring, given the sample evidence S, is

$$(3.29) \quad \Pr(E_i \mid S) = \frac{\Pr(S \mid E_i) \times \Pr(E_i)}{\sum \left(\Pr(S \mid E_i) \times \Pr(E_i) \right)}$$

As stated earlier, dispute arises over the interpretation of Bayes' theorem. In the above example there is no difficulty because the probability statements can be interpreted as relative frequencies. If the experiment of selecting a bag at random and choosing a ball from it were repeated many times, then of those occasions when a red ball is selected, in two-thirds of them bag A will have been chosen. However, consider an alternative interpretation of the symbols:

A: a coin is fair
B: a coin is unfair
R: the result of a toss is a head

Then, given a toss (or series of tosses) of a coin, this evidence can be used to calculate the probability of the coin being fair. But this makes no sense according to the frequentist school: either the coin is fair or not; it is not a question of probability. The calculated value must be interpreted as a degree of belief and be given a subjective interpretation.

Decision analysis

The study of probability naturally leads on to the analysis of decision making where risk is involved. This is the realistic situation facing most firms and the use of probability can help to illuminate the problem. To illustrate the topic, we use the example of a firm facing a choice of three different investment projects. The uncertainty which the firm faces concerns the interest rate at which to discount the future flows of income. The question is: which project should the firm select? As we shall see, there is no unique, right answer to the question but, using probability theory we can see why the answer might vary.

Table 3.1 provides the data required for the problem. The three projects are imaginatively labelled A, B and C. There are four possible **states of the world**, i.e. future scenarios, each with a different interest rate, as shown across the top of the table. This is the only source of uncertainty, otherwise the states of the world are identical. The figures in the body of the table show the present value of each income stream at the given discount rate. Thus for example, if the interest rate turns out to be 4% then project A has a present value of £1,475,000 while B's is £1,500,000. If the discount rate turns out to be 5% the PV for A is £1,363,000 while for B it has changed to £1,380,000. Obviously, as the discount rate rises, the present value of the return falls. (Alternatively, we could assume that a higher interest rate increases the cost of borrowing to finance the project, which reduces its profitability.) We assume that each project requires a (certain) initial outlay of £1,100,000 with which the PV should be compared.

The final row shows the probabilities which the firm attaches to each interest rate. These are obviously someone's subjective probabilities and are symmetric around a central value of 4.5%. We assume no inflation in this example, so these are effectively real rates.

Decision criteria: maximising the expected value

We need to decide how a decision is to be made on the basis of these data. The first criterion involves the expected value of each project. This uses the E operator which was introduced in Chapter 1. In other words, we find the expected present value of each project, by taking a weighted average of the PV figures, the weights being the probabilities. The project with the highest expected return is chosen.

The expected values are calculated in Table 3.2. The highest expected present

Table 3.1 Data for decision analysis: present values of three investment projects at different interest rates (£000)

Project	4%	Future interest rate 5%	6%	7%
A	1,475	1,363	1,200	1,115
B	1,500	1,380	1,148	1,048
C	1,650	1,440	1,200	810
Probability	0.2	0.4	0.4	0.2

Table 3.2　Expected values of the three projects

Project	Expected value
A	1,543.2
B	1,520.8
C	1,548.0

value is £1,548,000, associated with project C. On this criterion therefore, C is chosen.

Is this a wise choice? You may notice that if the interest rate turns out to be 7% then C would be the *worst* project to choose and the firm would make a substantial loss in such circumstances. Project C is the most sensitive to the discount rate (it has the greatest *variance* of the four projects) and therefore the firm faces more risk by opting for C. Perhaps some alternative criteria should be looked at. These we look at next, in particular the **maximin**, **maximax** and **minimax regret** strategies.

Maximin, maximax and minimax regret

The **maximin** criterion looks at the worst case scenario for each project and then selects the project which does best in these circumstances. It is inevitably a pessimistic or cautious view therefore. Table 3.3 illustrates the calculation. This time we observe that project A is preferred. In the worst case (which occurs when $r = 7\%$ for all projects) then A does best, with a PV of £1,115,000 and therefore a slight profit.

The opposite criterion is the optimistic one where the **maximax** criterion is used. In this case one looks at the *best* circumstances for each project and chooses the best performing project. Each project does best when the interest rate is at its lowest level, 3%. Examining the first column of Table 3.1 shows that project C ($PV = 1,650$) performs best and is therefore chosen.

A final criterion is that of **minimax regret**. If project B were chosen but the interest rate turns out to be 7% then we would regret not having chosen A, the best project under these circumstances. Our *regret* would be the extent of the difference between the two, a matter of $1,115 - 1,048 = 67$. Similarly, the regret if we had chosen C would be $1,115 - 810 = 305$. We can calculate these regrets at the other interest rates too, always comparing the PV of a project with the best PV given that interest rate. This gives us Table 3.4.

The final column of the table shows the maximum regret for each project. The minimax regret criterion is to choose the minimum of these figures. This is given at the bottom of the final column; it is 150 which is associated with project B. A justification for using this criterion might be that you don't want to fall too far behind your

Table 3.3　The maximin criterion

Project	Minimum
A	1,115
B	1,048
C	810
Maximum	1,115

Table 3.4   The costs of taking the wrong decision

Project	4%	5%	6%	7%	Maximum
A	175	77	0	0	175
B	150	60	52	67	150
C	0	0	0	305	305
Minimum					150

competitors. If other firms are facing similar investment decisions, then the regret table shows the difference in *PV* (and hence profits) if they choose the best project while you do not. Choosing the minimax regret solution ensures that you won't fall too far behind.

You will probably have noticed that we have managed to find a justification for choosing all three projects! No one project comes out best on all criteria. Nevertheless, the analysis might be of some help: if the investment project is one of many small, independent investments the firm is making then this would justify use of the expected value criterion. On the other hand, if this is a big, one-off project which could possibly bankrupt the firm if it goes wrong, then the maximin criterion would be appropriate.

The expected value of perfect information

Often a firm can improve its knowledge about future possibilities via research, which costs money. This effectively means buying information about the future state of the world. The question arises: how much should a firm pay for such information? **Perfect information** would reveal the future state of the world with certainty – in this case, the future interest rate. In that case you could be sure of choosing the right project given each state of the world. If interest rates turn out to be 4%, the firm would invest in *C*, if 7% in *A*, and so on.

In such circumstances, the firm would expect to earn:

$$(0.2 \times 1,650) + (0.4 \times 1,440) + (0.4 \times 1,200) + (0.2 \times 1,115) = 1,609$$

i.e. the probability of each state of the world is multiplied by the *PV* of the *best* project for that state. This gives a figure which is substantially greater than the expected value calculated earlier, without perfect information, 1,548. The **expected value of perfect information** is therefore the difference between these two, 61. This sets a *maximum* to the value of information, for it is unlikely in the real world that any information about the future is going to be perfect.

EXERCISES

Exercise 1

Given a standard pack of cards, calculate the following probabilities:

(a) drawing an Ace
(b) drawing a court card (i.e. Jack, Queen or King)
(c) drawing a red card
(d) drawing three Aces without replacement
(e) drawing three Aces with replacement

Exercise 2

The following data give duration of unemployment by age, in July 1986.

Age	≤ 8	Duration of unemployment (weeks) 8–26	26–52	>52	Total	Economically active
		(Percentage figures)			(000s)	(000s)
16–19	27.2	29.8	24.0	19.0	273.4	1,270
20–24	24.2	20.7	18.3	36.8	442.5	2,000
25–34	14.8	18.8	17.2	49.2	531.4	3,600
35–49	12.2	16.6	15.1	56.2	521.2	4,900
50–59	8.9	14.4	15.6	61.2	388.1	2,560
≥60	18.5	29.7	30.7	21.4	74.8	1,110

The 'economically active' column gives the total of employed plus unemployed in each age category.

(a) In what sense may these figures be regarded as probabilities? What does the figure 27.2 (top left cell) mean following this interpretation?

(b) Assuming the validity of the probability interpretation, which of the following statements are true?
  (i) The probability of an economically active adult aged 25–34, drawn at random, being unemployed is 531.4/3,600.
  (ii) If someone who has been unemployed for over one year is drawn at random, the probability that they are aged 16–19 is 19%.
  (iii) For those aged 35–49 who became unemployed before July 1985, the probability of their still being unemployed is 56.2%.
  (iv) If someone aged 50–59 is drawn at random from the economically active population, the probability of their being unemployed for eight weeks or less is 8.9%.
  (v) The probability of someone aged 35–49 drawn at random from the economically active population being unemployed for between 8 and 26 weeks is $0.166 \times 521.2/4{,}900$.

(c) A person is drawn at random from the population and found to have been unemployed for over one year. What is the probability that they are aged between 16 and 19?

Exercise 3

'Odds' in horse race betting are defined as follows: 3/1 (three to one against) means a horse is expected to win once for every three times it loses; 3/2 means two wins out of five races; 4/5 (five to four *on*) means five wins for every four defeats, etc.

(a) Translate the above odds into 'probabilities' of victory.

(b) In a three-horse race, the odds quoted are 2/1, 6/4, and 1/1. What makes the odds different from probabilities? Why are they different?

(c) Discuss how much the bookmaker would expect to win in the long run at such odds, assuming each horse is backed equally.

Exercise 4

(a) Translate the following odds to 'probabilities': 13/8, 2/1 *on*, 100/30.

(b) In the 2.45 race at Plumpton on 18/10/94 the odds for the five runners were:

Philips Woody	1/1
Gallant Effort	5/2
Satin Noir	11/2
Victory Anthem	9/1
Common Rambler	16/1

Calculate the 'probabilities' and their sum.

(c) Should the bookmaker base his odds on the true probabilities of each horse winning, or on the amount bet on each horse?

Exercise 5

How might you estimate the probability of Peru defaulting on its debt repayments next year?

Exercise 6

How might you estimate the probability of a corporation reneging on its bond payments?

Exercise 7

Judy is 33, unmarried and assertive. She is a graduate in Political Science, involved in union activities and anti-discrimination movements. Which of the following statements do you think is more probable?

(a) Judy is a bank clerk.

(b) Judy is a bank clerk, active in the feminist movement.

Exercise 8

In March 1994 a news item revealed that a London 'gender' clinic (which reportedly enables you to choose the sex of your child) had just set up in business. Of its first six births, two were of the 'wrong' sex. Assess this from a probability point of view.

Exercise 9

A newspaper advertisement reads 'The sex of your child predicted, or your money back!'. Discuss this advertisement from the point of view of (a) the advertiser and (b) the client.

Exercise 10

'Roll six sixes to win a Mercedes!' is the announcement at a fair. You have to roll six dice. If you get six sixes you win the car, valued at £20,000. The entry ticket costs £1. What is your expected gain or loss on this game? The organisers of the fair have to take out insurance against the car being won. This costs £250 for the day. Does this seem a fair premium? If not, why not?

Exercise 11

At another stall, you have to toss a coin numerous times. If a head does not appear in 20 tosses you win £1 billion. The entry fee for the game is £100.

(a) What are your expected winnings?

(b) Would you play?

Exercise 12

A four-engine plane can fly as long as at least two of its engines work. A two-engine plane flies as long as at least one engine works. The probability of an individual engine failure is 1 in 1,000.

(a) Would you feel safer in a four- or two-engine plane, and why? Calculate the probabilities of an accident for each type.

(b) How much safer is one type than the other?

(c) What crucial assumption are you making in your calculation? Do you think it is valid?

Exercise 13

Which of the following events are independent?

(a) Two flips of a fair coin

(b) Two flips of a biased coin

(c) Rainfall on two successive days

(d) Rainfall on St Swithin's day and rain one month later.

Exercise 14

Which of the following events are independent?

(a) A student getting the first two questions correct in a multiple choice exam

(b) A driver having an accident in successive years

(c) IBM and DEC earning positive profits next year

(d) Arsenal Football Club winning on successive weekends.

How is the answer to (b) reflected in car insurance premiums?

Exercise 15

Manchester United beat Liverpool 4–2 at soccer, but you do not know the order in which the goals were scored. Draw a tree diagram to display all the possibilities and use it to find (a) the probability that the goals were scored in the order L, MU, MU, MU, L, MU, and (b) the probability that the score was 2–2 at some stage.

Exercise 16

An important numerical calculation on a spacecraft is carried out independently by three computers. If all arrive at the same answer it is deemed correct. If one disagrees it is overruled. If there is no agreement then a fourth computer does the calculation and, if its answer agrees with any of the others, it is deemed correct. The probability of an individual computer getting the answer right is 99%. Use a tree diagram to find:

(a) the probability that the first three computers get the right answer

(b) the probability of getting the right answer

(c) the probability of getting no answer

(d) the probability of getting the wrong answer.

Exercise 17

The French national lottery works as follows. Six numbers from the range 0 to 49 are chosen at random. If you have correctly guessed all six you win the first prize. What are your chances of winning if you are only allowed to choose six numbers? A single entry like this costs one franc. For 210 francs you can choose ten numbers and you win if the six selected numbers are among them. Is this better value than the single entry?

Exercise 18

The UK national lottery works as follows. You choose six (different) numbers in the range 1 to 49. If all six come up in the draw (in any order) you win the first prize, expected to be around £2m. (which could be shared if someone else chooses the six winning numbers).

(a) What is your chance of winning with a single ticket?

(b) You win a second prize if you get five out of six right, *and* your final chosen number matches the 'bonus' number in the draw (also in the range 1 to 49). What is the probability of winning a second prize?

(c) Calculate the probabilities of winning a third, fourth or fifth prize, where a third prize is won by matching five out of the six numbers, a fourth prize by matching four out of six and a fifth prize by matching three out of six.

(d) What is the probability of winning a prize?

(e) The prizes are as follows:

Prize	Value	
First	£2 million	(expected, possibly shared)
Second	£100,000	(expected, for each winner)
Third	£1,500	(expected, for each winner)
Fourth	£65	(expected, for each winner)
Fifth	£10	(guaranteed, for each winner)

Comment upon the distribution of the fund between first, second, etc. prizes.

(f) Why is the fifth prize guaranteed whereas the others are not?

(g) In the first week of the lottery, 49 million tickets were sold. There were 1,150,000 winners, of which seven won (a share of) the jackpot, 39 won a second prize, 2,139 won a third prize and 76,731 a fourth prize. Are you surprised by these results or are they as you would expect?

Exercise 19

A coin is either fair or has two heads. You initially assign probabilities of 0.5 to each possibility. The coin is then tossed twice, with two heads appearing. Use Bayes' theorem to work out the posterior probabilities of each possible outcome.

Exercise 20

A test for AIDS is 99% successful, i.e. if you are HIV+ it will detect it in 99% of all tests, and if you are not, it will again be right 99% of the time. Assume that about 1% of the population are HIV+. You take part in a random testing procedure, which gives a positive result. What is the probability that you are HIV+? What implications does your result have for AIDS testing?

Exercise 21

(a) Your initial belief is that a defendant in a court case is guilty with probability 0.5. A witness comes forward claiming he saw the defendant commit the crime. You know the witness is not totally reliable and tells the truth with probability p.

Use Bayes' theorem to calculate the posterior probability that the defendant is guilty, based on the witness's evidence.

(b) A second witness, equally unreliable, comes forward and claims she saw the defendant commit the crime. Assuming the witnesses are not colluding, what is your posterior probability of guilt?

(c) If $p < 0.5$, compare the answers to (a) and (b). How do you account for this curious result?

Exercise 22

A man is mugged and claims that the mugger had red hair. In police investigations of such cases, the victim was able to correctly identify the assailant's hair colour 80% of the time. Assuming that 10% of the population have red hair, what is the probability that the assailant in this case did in fact have red hair? Guess the answer first, then find the right answer using Bayes' theorem. What are the implications of your results for juries' interpretation of evidence in court, particularly in relation to racial minorities?

Exercise 23

A firm has a choice of three projects, with profits as indicated below, dependent upon the state of demand.

		Demand	
Project	Low	Middle	High
A	100	140	180
B	130	145	170
C	110	130	200
Probability	0.25	0.45	0.3

(a) Which project should be chosen on the expected value criterion?

(b) Which project should be chosen on the maximin and maximax criteria?

(c) Which project should be chosen on the minimax regret criterion?

(d) What is the expected value of perfect information to the firm?

Exercise 24

A firm can build a small, medium or large factory, with anticipated profits from each dependent upon the state of demand, as in the table below.

		Demand	
Factory	Low	Middle	High
Small	300	320	330
Medium	270	400	420
Large	50	250	600
Probability	0.3	0.5	0.2

(a) Which project should be chosen on the expected value criterion?

(b) Which project should be chosen on the maximin and maximax criteria?

(c) Which project should be chosen on the minimax regret criterion?

(d) What is the expected value of perfect information to the firm?

Exercise 25   There are 25 people at a party. What is the probability that there are at least two with a birthday in common? (Hint: the *complement* is (much) easier to calculate.)

Exercise 26   This problem is tricky, but amusing. Three gunmen, A, B and C, are shooting at each other. The probabilities that each will hit what they aim at are respectively 1, 0.75, 0.5. They take it in turns to shoot (in alphabetical order) and continue until only one is left alive. Calculate the probabilities of each winning the contest. (Assume they draw lots for the right to shoot first.)

Hint 1: Start with one-on-one gunfights, e.g. the probability of A beating B, or of B beating C.

Hint 2: You'll need the formula for the sum of an infinite series, given in Chapter 1.

4 PROBABILITY DISTRIBUTIONS

Introduction

In this chapter the probability concepts introduced in the last chapter are generalised by using the idea of a **probability distribution**. A probability distribution lists, in some form, all the possible outcomes and the probability associated with each one. For example, the simplest experiment is tossing a coin, for which the possible outcomes are heads or tails, each with probability one half. The probability distribution can be expressed in a variety of ways: in words, or in a graphical or mathematical form. For tossing a coin, the graphical form is shown in Fig. 4.1, and the mathematical form is

$\Pr(H) = \frac{1}{2}$
$\Pr(T) = \frac{1}{2}$

The different forms of presentation are equivalent but one might be more suited to a particular purpose.

Some probability distributions occur often and so are well known. Because of this they have names so we can refer to them easily; for example, the **Binomial distribution** or the **Normal distribution**. In fact, these are *families* of distributions. A single toss of a coin gives rise to one member of the Binomial distribution; two tosses would give rise to another member of that family. These two distributions differ only in the number of tosses. If a biased coin were tossed, this would lead to another Binomial distribution, but it would differ from the previous two because of the different probability of heads.

In order to understand fully the idea of a probability distribution a new concept is first introduced, that of a **random variable**. As will be seen later in the chapter, an important random variable is the sample mean, and to understand how to draw inferences from the sample mean it is important to recognise it as a random variable.

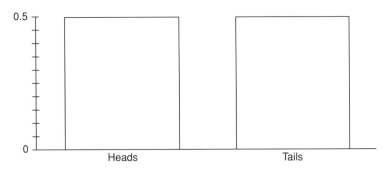

Fig. 4.1 *The probability distribution for the toss of a coin*

Random variables

Examples of random variables have already been encountered in the previous chapter, for example the result of the toss of a coin, or the number of boys in a family of five children. A random variable is one whose outcome or value is the result of chance and is therefore unpredictable, although the range of possible outcomes and the probability of each outcome may be known. It is impossible to know in advance the outcome of a toss of a coin for example, but it must be either heads or tails, each with probability one half. The number of heads in 250 tosses is another random variable which can take any value between zero and 250, although values near 125 are the most likely. You are very unlikely to get 250 heads from a fair coin!

The time of departure of a train is a random variable. It may be timetabled to depart at 11.15, but it probably (almost certainly!) won't leave at exactly that time. If a sample of ten basketball players were taken, and their average height calculated, this would be a random variable. In this latter case, it is the process of taking a sample that introduces the variability which makes the resulting average a random variable. If the experiment were repeated, a different sample and a different value of the random variable would be obtained.

The above examples can be contrasted with some things which are *not* random variables. If one were to take *all* basketball players and calculate their average height, the result would not be a random variable. This time there is no sampling procedure to introduce variability into the result. If the experiment were repeated the same result would be obtained, since the same people would be measured the second time (this assumes that the population does not change, of course). Just because the value of something is unknown does not mean it qualifies as a random variable. This is an important distinction to bear in mind, since it is legitimate to make probability statements about random variables ('the probability that the average height of a sample of basketball players is over six feet four is 60%) but not about parameters ('the probability that the Pope is over six feet is 60%'). Here again there is a difference of opinion between frequentist and subjective schools of thought. The latter group would argue that it is possible to make probability statements about the Pope's height. It is a way of expressing lack of knowledge about the true value.

The Binomial distribution

One of the simplest distributions which a random variable can have is the Binomial. This applies to the type of problem encountered in the previous chapter, concerning the the sex of children. It provides a general formula for calculating the probability of r boys in n births or, in more general terms, the probability of r 'successes' in n trials.[1] We shall use it to calculate the probabilities of 0, 1, . . . 5 boys in five births.

For the Binomial distribution to apply we first need to assume independence of successive events and we shall assume that, for any birth:

$$Pr(boy) = P = \tfrac{1}{2}$$

It follows that

$$Pr(girl) = 1 - Pr(boy) = 1 - P = \tfrac{1}{2}$$

Although we have $P = \tfrac{1}{2}$ in this example, the Binomial distribution applies for any value of P between 0 and 1.

First we consider the case of $r = 5$, $n = 5$, i.e. five boys in five births. This probability is found using the multiplication rule:

[1] The identification of a boy with 'success' is a purely formal one and is not meant to be pejorative!

$\text{Pr}(r{=}5) = P \times P \times P \times P \times P = P^5 = (\frac{1}{2})^5 = 1/32$

The probability of four boys (and then implicitly one girl) is

$\text{Pr}(r{=}4) = P \times P \times P \times P \times (1-P) = 1/32$

But this gives only one possible ordering of the four boys and one girl. There are five possible orderings (using the combinatorial formula, $5C4 = 5$) so the desired probability is $5/32$. The formula for four boys and one girl is therefore

$\text{Pr}(r{=}4) = 5C4 \times P^4 \times (1-P)$

For three boys we obtain

$\text{Pr}(r{=}3) = 5C3 \times P^3 \times (1-P)^2 = 10 \times 1/32 = 10/32$

In a similar manner

$\text{Pr}(r{=}2) = 5C2 \times P^2 \times (1-P)^3 = 10/32$
$\text{Pr}(r{=}1) = 5C1 \times P^1 \times (1-P)^4 = 5/32$
$\text{Pr}(r{=}0) = 5C0 \times P^0 \times (1-P)^5 = 1/32$

As a check on our calculations we may note that the sum of the probabilities equals 1, as they should since we have enumerated all possibilities.

A fairly clear pattern emerges. The probability of r boys in n births is given by

$\text{Pr}(r) = nCr \times P^r \times (1 - P)^{(n-r)}$

and this is known as the Binomial formula or distribution. The Binomial distribution is appropriate for analysing problems with the following characteristics:

- There is a number (n) of trials.
- Each trial has only two possible outcomes, 'success' (with probability P) and 'failure' (probability $1-P$) and the outcomes are independent between trials.
- The probability P does not change between trials.

The probabilities calculated by the Binomial formula may be illustrated in a diagram, as shown in Fig. 4.2. This is very similar to the relative frequency distribution which was introduced in Chapter 1. That distribution was based on empirical data (to do with wealth) while the Binomial probability distribution is a theoretical construction, built up from the basic principles of probability theory.

Fig. 4.2 *Probability distribution of the number of boys in five children*

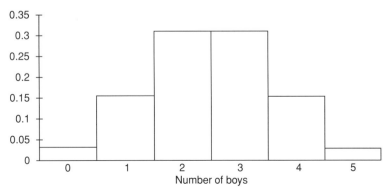

Number of boys

As stated earlier, the Binomial is in fact a family of distributions and each member of the family is distinguished by two **parameters**, n and P. The Binomial is thus a distribution with two parameters, and once their values are known the distribution is completely determined (i.e. $\Pr(r)$ can be calculated for all values of r). To illustrate the difference between members of the family of the Binomial distribution, Fig. 4.3 below presents three other Binomial distributions, for different values of P and n. It can be seen that for the value of $P = \frac{1}{2}$ the distribution is symmetric, while for all other values it is skewed to either the left or right.

Since the Binomial distribution depends only upon the two values n and P, a shorthand notation can be used. A random variable r, which has a Binomial distribution with the parameters n and P, can be written

Fig. 4.3 *Binomial distributions with different parameter values*

(a)

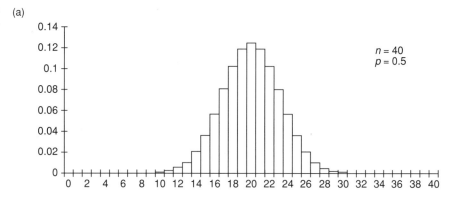

(b)

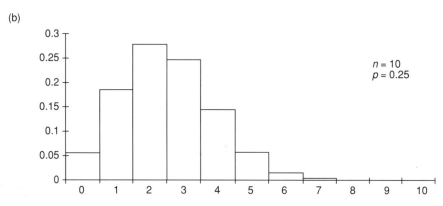

(c)

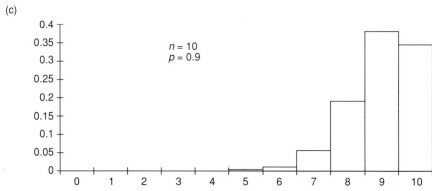

(4.1) $r \sim B(n, P)$

Thus for the previous example of children, where r represents the number of boys,

$r \sim B(5, \frac{1}{2})$

This is simply a brief and convenient way of writing down the information available; it involves no new problems of a conceptual nature.

By drawing up a relative frequency table based on the Binomial frequencies, we can find the mean and the variance of the Binomial distribution. This is shown in Table 4.1 for the values $n = 5$ and $P = \frac{1}{2}$.

Note that r is equivalent to x and $\Pr(r)$, the relative frequency, to $f(x)/\Sigma f(x)$. The mean of this distribution is given by

$$(4.2) \quad E(r) = \frac{\Sigma r \times \Pr(r)}{\Sigma \Pr(r)} = \frac{80/32}{32/32} = 2.5$$

and the variance is given by

$$(4.3) \quad V(r) = \frac{\Sigma r^2 \times \Pr(r)}{\Sigma \Pr(r)} - \mu^2 = \frac{240/32}{32/32} - 2.5^2 = 1.25$$

The mean value tells us that in a family of five children we would expect, on average, two and a half boys. Obviously no single family can be like this; it is the average over all such families. The variance is more difficult to interpret intuitively, but it tells us something about how the number of boys will be spread around the average of 2.5.

Alternatively, the mean of any Binomial distribution may simply be calculated as nP and the variance by $nP(1-P)$. It is readily verified that these give the values calculated above.

The Binomial distribution can be used to solve a variety of problems. For example, if a die is thrown four times, what is the probability of getting two or more sixes? This is a problem involving repeated experiments (rolling the die) with but two types of outcome for each roll: success (a six) or failure (anything but a six). The probability of success (one-sixth) does not vary from one experiment to another, and so use of the Binomial distribution is appropriate. The values of the parameters are $n = 4$ and $P = 1/6$. Denoting by r the random variable 'the number of sixes in four rolls of the die' then

(4.4) $r \sim B(4, \frac{1}{6})$

Table 4.1   Calculating the mean and variance of the Binomial distribution

r	$\Pr(r)$	$r \times \Pr(r)$	$r^2 \times \Pr(r)$
0	1/32	0	0
1	5/32	5/32	5/32
2	10/32	20/32	40/32
3	10/32	30/32	90/32
4	5/32	20/32	80/32
5	1/32	5/32	25/32
Totals	32/32	80/32	240/32

Hence

$$\Pr(r) = nCr \times P^r (1-P)^{(n-r)}$$

where $P = \frac{1}{6}$ and $n = 4$. The probabilities of two, three and four sixes are then given by

$$\Pr(r = 2) = 4C2 \left(\tfrac{1}{6}\right)^2 \left(\tfrac{5}{6}\right)^2 = 0.116$$
$$\Pr(r = 3) = 4C3 \left(\tfrac{1}{6}\right)^3 \left(\tfrac{5}{6}\right)^1 = 0.015$$
$$\Pr(r = 4) = 4C4 \left(\tfrac{1}{6}\right)^4 \left(\tfrac{5}{6}\right)^0 = 0.00077$$

Since these events are mutually exclusive, the probabilities can simply be added together to get the desired result, which is 0.132, or 13.2%. This is the probability of two or more sixes in four rolls of a die. What has been calculated is the area in the right-hand tail of the appropriate Binomial distribution, as illustrated in Fig. 4.4.

Many similar problems can be solved by calculating the area under the appropriate part of the Binomial distribution.

Having examined one particular probability distribution we now move on to the most important of all probability distributions, the Normal.

The Normal distribution

The Normal distribution is the most common and important distribution in statistics. It was discovered by the German mathematician Gauss in the nineteenth century (hence it is also known as the Gaussian distribution), in the course of his work on regression (see Chapter 9).

Many random variables turn out to be Normally distributed. Men's (or women's) heights are Normally distributed. IQ (the measure of intelligence) is also Normally distributed. Another example is of a machine producing (say) bolts with a nominal length of 5 cm which will actually produce bolts of slightly varying length (these differences would probably be extremely small) due to factors such as wear in the machinery, slight variations in the pressure of the lubricant, etc. These would result in bolts whose length is Normally distributed. This sort of process is extremely common, with the result that the Normal distribution often occurs in everyday problems. Many variables familiar in economics are not Normal, however. Incomes are not Normally distributed (though the logarithm of income is approximately Normal).

Fig. 4.4 *Probability of two or more sixes in four rolls of a die*

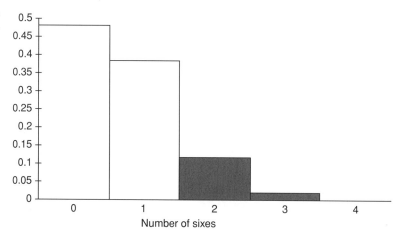

Note: The shaded area represents the probabilities of two or more sixes and together their area represents 13.2% of the whole distribution.

Having introduced the Normal distribution, what does it look like? It is presented below in mathematical and graphical forms. If x is a random variable which is Normally distributed its probability distribution is given in mathematical form by the formula

$$(4.5) \quad \Pr(x) = \frac{1}{\sigma\sqrt{2\pi}} e^{-\frac{1}{2}\left(\frac{x-\mu}{\sigma}\right)^2}$$

The mathematical formulation is not so formidable as it appears. μ and σ are the parameters of the distribution, like n and P for the Binomial (though they have different meanings); π is 3.1416 and e is 2.7183. If the formula is evaluated using different values of x the values of $\Pr(x)$ obtained will map out a Normal distribution.

The Normal distribution mapped out by this process will look like the one drawn in Fig. 4.5. The Normal distribution is a continuous one, unlike the Binomial which is discrete, so it can be evaluated for all values of x, not just for integers.

It should be noted that the Normal distribution is

- unimodal
- symmetric
- bell shaped and
- extends continuously over all the values of x from minus infinity to plus infinity, though the value of $\Pr(x)$ becomes extremely small as these values are approached (the pages of this book being of only finite width, this last characteristic is not faithfully reproduced!).

Like the Binomial, the Normal is a family of distributions differing from one another only in the values of the parameters μ and σ. Several Normal distributions are drawn in Fig. 4.6 for different values of the parameters.

Whatever value of μ is chosen turns out to be the centre of the distribution. Since the distribution is symmetric, μ is its mean. The effect of varying σ is to narrow (small σ) or widen (large σ) the distribution. σ turns out to be the standard deviation of the distribution. The Normal is another two-parameter family of distributions like the Binomial, and once the mean μ and the standard deviation σ (or equivalently the variance, σ^2) are known the whole of the distribution can be drawn. The shorthand notation for a Normal distribution is

$$(4.6) \quad x \sim N(\mu, \sigma^2)$$

Fig. 4.5 *The Normal distribution*

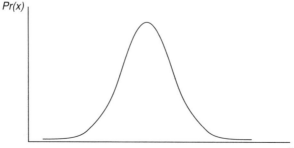

Fig. 4.6(a) *The Normal distribution, $\mu = 20$, $\sigma = 5$*

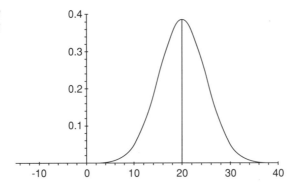

Fig. 4.6(b) *The Normal distribution, $\mu = 15$, $\sigma = 2$*

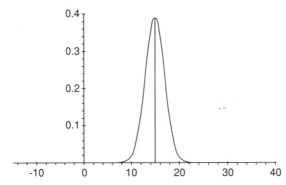

Fig. 4.6(c) *The Normal distribution, $\mu = 0$, $\sigma = 4$*

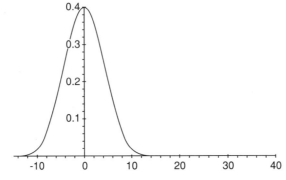

meaning 'the variable x is Normally distributed with mean μ and variance σ^2'. This is similar in form to the expression for the Binomial distribution, though the meaning of the parameters is different.

The Normal distribution can be used in practice to solve a wide variety of problems; a simple one is as follows. The height of adult males is Normally distributed with mean height $\mu = 174$ cm and standard deviation $\sigma = 9.6$ cm. Let x represent the height of adult males; then

(4.7) $x \sim N(174, 92.16)$

and this is illustrated in Fig. 4.7.

Fig. 4.7   *Illustration of mens height distribution*

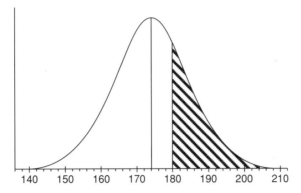

What proportion of men are over 180 cm in height? This requires calculating the area under the Normal distribution to the right of $x = 180$, i.e. the shaded area in Fig. 4.7. One way to find this would be to make use of equation (4.1), but this requires the use of sophisticated mathematics.

Since this is a frequently encountered problem, the answers have been set out in the tables of the **standard Normal distribution**. Since there is an infinite number of Normal distributions (for every combination of μ and σ^2) it would be an impossible task to tabulate them all. The standard Normal distribution, which has a mean of zero and variance of one, is therefore used to represent all Normal distributions. Before the table can be consulted, therefore, the data have to be transformed so that they accord with the standard Normal distribution.

The required transformation is the z-score, which was introduced in Chapter 1. Therefore we calculate

$$(4.8) \quad z = \frac{x - \mu}{\sigma}$$

and z is a Normally distributed random variable with mean 0 and variance 1, i.e. $z \sim N(0,1)$. This is the standard Normal distribution which is tabulated in Table A2 in the Appendix. It is easy to verify the mean and variance of z:

$$E\left(z\right) = E\left(\frac{x - \mu}{\sigma}\right) = \frac{1}{\sigma}\left(E\left(x\right) - \mu\right) = 0 \qquad \text{(since } E(x) = \mu\text{)}$$

$$V\left(z\right) = V\left(\frac{x - \mu}{\sigma}\right) = \frac{1}{\sigma^2}V\left(x\right) = \frac{\sigma^2}{\sigma^2} = 1$$

Thus the transformation shifts the distribution μ units to the left and then adjusts the dispersion by dividing through by σ. Evaluating the z-score we obtain

$$(4.9) \quad z = \frac{180 - 174}{9.6} = 0.63$$

This means that 180 is 0.63 standard deviations above the mean, 174, of the distribution. The problem now is to find the area under the standard Normal distribution to the right of 0.63 standard deviations above the mean. This answer can be read off directly from the table of the standard Normal distribution, Table A2. An excerpt from Table A2 is presented in Table 4.2.

Table 4.2   Areas of the standard Normal distribution (excerpt from Table A2)

z	0.00	0.01	0.02	0.03	...	0.09
0.0	.5000	.4960	.4920	.4880	...	.4641
0.1	.4602	.4562	.4522	.4483	...	.4247
⋮	⋮	⋮	⋮	⋮	...	⋮
0.5	.3085	.3050	.3015	.2981	...	.2776
0.6	.2743	.2709	.2676	.2643	...	.2451
0.7	.2420	.2389	.2358	.2327	...	.2148

The left-hand column gives the z-score to one place of decimals. The appropriate row of the table to consult is the one for $z = 0.6$, which is shaded. For the second place of decimals (0.03) we consult the appropriate column, also shaded. At their intersection we find the value 0.2643, which is the desired area and therefore probability. In other words, 26.43% of the distribution lies to the right of 0.63 standard deviations above the mean. Therefore 26.43% of men are over 180 cm in height.

Use of the standard Normal table is possible because although there is an infinite number of Normal distributions, they are all fundamentally the same, so that the area to the right of 0.63 standard deviations above the mean is the same for all of them. The process of standardisation turns all Normal distributions into a standard Normal distribution with a mean of zero and a variance of one. This process is illustrated in Fig. 4.8.

The area in the right-hand tail is the same for both distributions. It is the standard Normal distribution in Fig. 4.8(b) which is tabulated in Table A2. To demonstrate how standardisation turns all Normal distributions into the standard Normal, the earlier problem is repeated but taking all measurements in inches. The answer should obviously be the same. Taking 1 in = 2.54 cm the figures are

$$x = 70.87 \quad \sigma = 3.78 \quad \mu = 68.50$$

What proportion of men are over 70.87 inches in height? The appropriate Normal distribution is now

$$(4.10) \quad x \sim N(68.50, 3.78^2)$$

The z-score is

$$(4.11) \quad z = \frac{70.87 - 68.50}{3.78} = 0.63$$

which is the same z-score as before and therefore gives the same probability.

Since a great deal of use is made of the standard Normal tables, it is worth working through a couple more examples to reinforce the method. We have so far calculated that $\Pr(z > 0.63) = 0.2643$. Since the total area under the graph equals one (i.e. the sum of probabilities must be one), the area to the left of $z = 0.63$ must equal 0.7357, i.e. 73.57% of men are under 180 cm. It is fairly easy to manipulate areas under the graph to arrive at any required area. For example, what proportion of men are between 174 and 180 cm in height? It is helpful to refer to Fig. 4.9 at this point.

The size of area A is required. Area B has already been calculated as 0.2643. Since the distribution is symmetric the area A + B must equal 0.5, since 174 is at the centre (mean) of the distribution. Area A is therefore $0.5 - 0.2643 = 0.2357$. 23.57% is the desired result.

Fig. 4.8(a) *The Normal distribution*

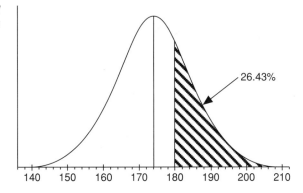

26.43%

Fig. 4.8(b) *The standard Normal distribution corresponding to Fig. 4.8(a)*

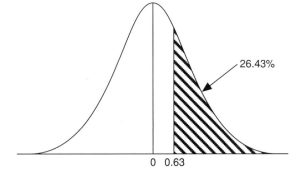

26.43%

Fig. 4.9

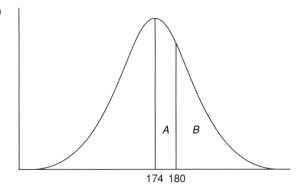

Using a computer to find areas under the standard Normal distribution

If you use a spreadsheet program you can probably look up the *z*-distribution directly and hence dispense with tables. In *Excel*, for example, the function = *NORMSDIST*(0.63) gives the answer 0.7357, i.e. the area to the *left* of the *z*-score. The area in the right-hand tail is then obtained by subtracting this value from 1, i.e. 1 − 0.7357 = 0.2643. Entering the formula =1-*NORMSDIST*(0.63) in a cell will give the area in the right-hand tail directly.

As a final exercise consider the question of what proportion of men are between 166 and 178 cm tall. As shown in Fig. 4.10 area C + D is wanted. The only way to find this is to calculate the two areas separately and then add them together. For area D the z-score associated with 178 is:

$$(4.12) \quad z_D = \frac{178 - 174}{9.6} = 0.42$$

Table A2 indicates that the area in the right-hand tail, beyond $z = 0.42$, is 0.3372, so area D = 0.5 − 0.3372 = 0.1628. For C, the z-score is

$$(4.13) \quad z_C = \frac{166 - 174}{9.6} = -0.83$$

The minus sign indicates that it is the left-hand tail of the distribution, below the mean, which is being considered. Since the distribution is symmetric, it is the same as if it were the right-hand tail, so the minus sign may be ignored when consulting the table. Looking up $z = 0.83$ in Table A2 gives an area of 0.2033 in the tail, so area C is therefore 0.5 − 0.2033 = 0.2967. Adding areas C and D gives 0.1628 + 0.2967 = 0.4595. So nearly one half of all men are between 166 and 178 cm in height. It is worth practising a few of these calculations to become proficient in them.

An alternative interpretation of the results obtained above is that if a man is drawn at random from the adult population, the probability that he is over 180 cm tall is 26.43%. This is in line with the frequentist school of thought. Since 26.43% of the population is over 180 cm in height, that is the probability of a man over 180 cm being drawn at random.

The sample mean as a Normally distributed variable

One of the most important concepts in statistical inference is the probability distribution of the mean of a random sample, since we often use the sample mean to tell us something about an associated population. Suppose that, from the population of adult males, a random sample of size $n = 36$ is taken, their heights measured, and the mean height of the sample calculated. This sample mean is a random variable because of the chance element of random sampling (different samples would yield different values of the sample mean). Since the sample mean is a random variable it must have associated with it a probability distribution.

Fig. 4.10 *The proportion of men between 166 cm and 178 cm tall*

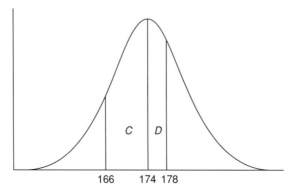

166   174 178

We therefore need to know, first, what is the appropriate distribution and, second, what are its parameters. From the definition of the sample mean we have

$$(4.14) \quad \bar{x} = \frac{1}{n}\left(x_1 + x_2 + \ldots + x_n\right)$$

where each observation, x_i, is itself a Normally distributed random variable, with $x_i \sim N(\mu, \sigma^2)$, because each comes from the parent distribution with such characteristics. We now make use of the following theorem to demonstrate that $\bar{x}$ is Normally distributed:

Theorem: Any linear combination of independent, Normally distributed random variables is itself Normally distributed.

A linear combination of two variables x_1 and x_2 is of the form $w_1 x_1 + w_2 x_2$ where w_1 and w_2 are constants. This can be generalised to any number of x values. As long as the observations are independently drawn, therefore, the sample mean is Normally distributed. In this case, the weight w on each observation is $1/n$.

We now need the parameters (mean and variance) of the distribution. For this we use the E and V operators once again:

$$(4.15) \quad E(\bar{x}) = \frac{1}{n}\left(E(x_1) + E(x_2) + \ldots + E(x_n)\right) = \frac{1}{n}\left(\mu + \mu + \ldots + \mu\right) = \frac{1}{n}n\mu = \mu$$

$$(4.16) \quad V(\bar{x}) = \frac{1}{n^2}\left(V(x_1) + V(x_2) + \ldots + V(x_n)\right) = \frac{1}{n^2}\left(\sigma^2 + \sigma^2 + \ldots + \sigma^2\right)$$

$$= \frac{1}{n}n\sigma^2 = \frac{\sigma^2}{n}$$

Putting all this together, we have

Don't worry if you didn't follow the derivation of this formula, just accept that it is correct.

$$(4.17) \quad \bar{x} \sim N\left(\mu, \frac{\sigma^2}{n^2}\right)$$

This we may summarise in the following theorem:

Theorem: The sample mean, $\bar{x}$, drawn from a population which has a Normal distribution with mean μ and variance σ^2, has a sampling distribution which is Normal, with mean μ and variance σ^2/n, where n is the sample size.

The meaning of this theorem is as follows. First of all it is assumed that the population from which the samples are to be drawn is itself Normally distributed (this assumption will be relaxed in a moment), with mean μ and variance σ^2. From this population many samples are drawn, each of sample size n, and the mean of each sample calculated. The samples are independent, meaning that the observations selected for one sample do not influence the selection of observations in the other samples. This gives many sample means, $\bar{x}_1$, $\bar{x}_2$ etc. If these sample means are treated as a new set of observations, then the probability distribution of these observations can be drawn. The theorem states that this distribution is Normal, with the sample means centred around μ, the population mean, and with variance σ^2/n. The argument is set out diagrammatically in Fig. 4.11.

Intuitively this theorem can be understood as follows. If the height of adult males is a Normally distributed random variable with mean $\mu = 174$ cm and variance $\sigma^2 = 92.16$, then it would be expected that a random sample of (say) nine males would yield a sample mean height of around 174 cm, perhaps a little more, perhaps a little less. In other words, the sample mean is centred around 174 cm, or the mean of the distribution of sample means is 174 cm.

The larger is the size of the individual samples (i.e. the larger n), the closer the sample mean would tend to be to 174 cm. For example, if the sample size is only two, a sample of two very tall people is quite possible, with a high sample mean as a result, well over 174 cm, e.g. 182 cm. But if the sample size were 20, it is very unlikely the 20 very tall males would be selected and the sample mean is likely to be much closer to 174. This is why the sample size n appears in the formula for the variance of the distribution of the sample mean, σ^2/n.

Note that, once again, we have transformed one (or more) random variables, the x_i's, with a particular probability distribution into another random variable, $\bar{x}$, with a (slightly) different distribution. This is common practice in statistics: transforming a variable will often put it into a more useful form, e.g. one whose probability distribution is well known.

The above theorem can be used to solve a range of statistical problems. For example, what is the probability that a random sample of nine adult males will have a mean height greater than 180 cm? The height of all adult males is known to be Normally distributed with mean $\mu = 174$ cm and variance $\sigma^2 = 92.16$. The theorem can be used to derive the probability distribution of the sample mean. For the population we have:

$$x \sim N(\mu, \sigma^2) \text{ i.e. } x \sim N(174, 92.16)$$

Hence for the sample mean:

$$\bar{x} \sim N(\mu, \sigma^2/n) \text{ i.e. } \bar{x} \sim N(174, 92.16/9)$$

This is shown diagrammatically in Fig. 4.12.

Fig. 4.11 *The parent distribution and the distribution of sample means*

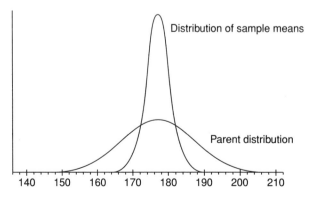

Note: The distribution of $\bar{x}$ is drawn for a sample size of $n = 9$. A larger sample size would widen the $\bar{x}$ distribution, a smaller sample size would narrow it.

Fig. 4.12 *The proportion of sample means greater than* $\bar{x} = 180$

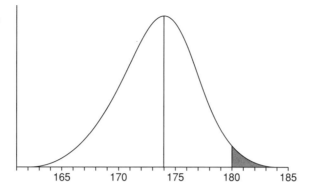

To answer the question posed, the area to the right of 180, shaded in Fig. 4.12, has to be found. This should by now be a familiar procedure. First the z-score is calculated:

$$(4.18) \quad z = \frac{\bar{x} - \mu}{\sqrt{\sigma^2 / n}} = \frac{180 - 174}{\sqrt{92.16 / 9}} = 1.88$$

Note that the divisor in the formula for the z-score now is σ^2/n, not σ^2. This is because it is the distribution of sample means which is being used, which has a variance of σ^2/n, not σ^2 which is the population variance. $\sqrt{\sigma^2/n}$ is known as the **standard error**, to distinguish it from σ, the standard deviation of the population.

Looking up the value of $z = 1.88$ in Table A2 gives an area of 0.0311 in the right-hand tail of the Normal distribution beyond $z = 1.88$. Thus 3.11% of sample means will be greater than or equal to 180 cm when the sample size is nine. The desired probability is therefore 3.11%.

Since this probability is quite small, we might consider the reasons for this. There are two possibilities:

(1) through bad luck, the sample collected is not very representative of the population as a whole, or
(2) the sample is representative of the population, but the population mean is not 174 cm. after all.

Only one of these two possibilities can be correct. How to decide between them will be taken up later on, in Chapter 6 on hypothesis testing.

It is interesting to examine the difference between the answer for a sample size of nine (3.11%) and the one obtained earlier for a single individual (26.43%). The latter may be considered as a sample of size one from the population. The examples illustrate the fact that the larger the sample size, the closer the sample mean is likely to be to the population mean. Thus larger samples tend to give better estimates of the population mean.

Sampling from a non-Normal population

The previous theorem and examples relied upon the fact that the population followed a Normal distribution. But what happens if it is not Normal? After all, it is not known for certain that the heights of all adult males are Normally distributed, and there are many populations which are not Normal (e.g. wealth, as shown in Chapter 1). What can be done in these circumstances? The answer is to use another theorem about the distribution of sample means (presented without proof). This is known as the **Central Limit Theorem**:

The Central Limit Theorem: The sample mean $\bar{x}$, drawn from a population with mean μ and variance σ^2, has a sampling distribution which approaches a Normal distribution with mean μ and variance σ^2/n, as the sample size approaches infinity.

This is very useful, since it allows the assumption that the population is Normally distributed to be dropped. Note that the distribution of sample means is only Normal as long as the sample size is infinite; for any finite sample size the distribution is only approximately Normal. However, the approximation is close enough for practical purposes if the sample size is larger than 25 or so observations. If the population distribution is itself nearly Normal then a smaller sample size would suffice. If the population distribution is particularly skewed then more than 25 observations would be desirable. Twenty-five observations constitutes a rule of thumb that is adequate in most circumstances. This is another illustration of statistics as an inexact science. It does not provide absolutely clear-cut answers to questions but, used carefully, helps us to arrive at sensible conclusions.

As an example of the use of the Central Limit Theorem, we return to the wealth data of Chapter 1. Recall that the mean level of wealth was 62.482 (measured in £000) and the variance 12,545. Suppose that a sample of $n = 50$ people were drawn from this population. What is the probability that the sample mean is greater than 75 (i.e. £75,000)?

On this occasion we know that the parent distribution is highly skewed so it is fortunate that we have 50 observations. This should be ample for us to justify applying the Central Limit Theorem. The distribution of $\bar{x}$ is therefore

(4.19) $\bar{x} \sim N(\mu, \sigma^2/n)$

and, inserting the parameter values, this gives[2]

(4.20) $\bar{x} \sim N(62.482, 12545/50)$

To find the area beyond a mean of 75 (£75,000), the z-score is first calculated:

(4.21) $z = \dfrac{75 - 62.482}{\sqrt{12545/50}} = 0.79$

Referring to the standard Normal tables, the area in the tail is then found to be 21.48%. This is the desired probability. So there is a probability of 21.48% of finding a sample of size 50 with mean of £75,000 or greater. This demonstrates that there is quite a high probability of getting a sample mean which is a long way from 62.482. This is a consequence of the high degree of dispersion in the distribution of wealth.

Extending this example, we can ask what is the probability of the sample mean lying within, say, £31,000 either side of the mean value of £62,482 (i.e. between 31,482 and 93,482)? Figure 4.13 illustrates the situation, with the desired area shaded. By symmetry, areas A and B must be equal, so we only need find one of them. For B, we calculate the z-score:

---

[2] Note that if we used 62,482 for the mean we would have 12,545,000,000 as the variance. Using £000 keeps the numbers more manageable.

Fig. 4.13 *The probability of $\bar{x}$ lying within £31,000 either side of £62,482*

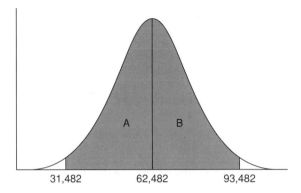

$$(4.22)\quad z = \frac{93.482 - 62.482}{\sqrt{12545/50}} = 1.96$$

From the standard Normal table, this cuts off 2.5% in the upper tail, so A = 0.475. Areas A and B together make up 95% of the distribution, therefore. There is thus a 95% probability of the sample mean falling within the range [31482, 93482] and we call this the **95% probability interval** for the sample mean. We write this:

$$(4.23)\quad \Pr(31,482 \le \bar{x} \le 93,482) = 0.95$$

or, in terms of the formulae we have used:

$$(4.24)\quad \Pr\left(\mu - 1.96\sqrt{\sigma^2/n} \le \bar{x} \le \mu + 1.96\sqrt{\sigma^2/n}\right) = 0.95$$

The relationship between the Binomial and Normal distributions

Many statistical distributions are related to one another in some way. This means that many problems can be solved by a variety of different methods (using different distributions), though usually one is more convenient than the others. This point may be illustrated by looking at the relationship between the Binomial and Normal distributions.

Recall that if a random variable r follows a Binomial distribution then

$$(4.1)\quad r \sim B(n, P)$$

and the mean of the distribution is nP and the variance $nP(1-P)$. It turns out that as n gets larger, the Binomial distribution becomes approximately the same as a Normal distribution with mean nP and variance $nP(1-P)$. This approximation is sufficiently accurate as long as $nP > 5$ and $n(1-P) > 5$, so the approximation may not be very good (even for large values of n) if P is very close to zero or one.

To demonstrate, the following problem is solved using both the Binomial and Normal distributions. Forty students take an exam in statistics which is simply graded pass/fail. If the probability, P, of any individual student passing is 60%, what is the probability of at least 30 students passing the exam?

The sample data are:

$P = 0.6$
$1 - P = 0.4$
$n = 40$

Binomial distribution method

To solve the problem using the Binomial distribution it is necessary to find the probability of exactly 30 students passing, plus the probability of 31 passing, plus the probability of 32 passing, etc. up to the probability of 40 passing (the fact that the events are mutually exclusive allows this). The probability of 30 passing is

$$Pr(r = 30) = nCr \times P^r (1-P)^{n-r}$$
$$= 40C30 \times 0.6^{30} \times 0.4^{10}$$
$$= 0.020$$

(N.B. This calculation assumes that the probabilities are independent, i.e. no copying!) This by itself is quite a tedious calculation, but Pr(31), Pr(32), etc. still have to be calculated. Calculating these and summing them gives the result of 3.52% as the probability of at least 30 passing. (It would be a useful exercise for you to do, if only to appreciate how long it takes.)

Normal distribution method

As stated above, the Binomial distribution can be approximated by a Normal distribution with mean nP and variance $nP(1-P)$. nP in this case is 24 and $n(1-P)$ is 16, both greater than 5, so the approximation can be safely used. Thus

$$r \sim N(nP, nP(1-P))$$

and inserting the parameter values gives

$$r \sim N(24, 9.6)$$

The usual methods are then used to find the appropriate area under the distribution. However, before doing so, there is one adjustment to be made (this only applies when approximating the Binomial distribution by the Normal). The Normal distribution is a continuous one while the Binomial is discrete. Thus 30 in the Binomial distribution is represented by the area under the Normal distribution between 29.5 and 30.5. 31 is represented by 30.5 to 31.5, etc. Thus it is the area under the Normal distribution to the right of 29.5, not 30, which must be calculated. This is known as the **continuity correction**. Calculating the z-score gives

$$(4.25) \quad z = \frac{29.5 - 24}{\sqrt{9.6}} = 1.78$$

This gives an area of 3.75%, not far off the correct answer as calculated by the Binomial distribution. The time saved and ease of calculation would seem to be worth the slight loss in accuracy.

Other examples can be constructed to test this method, using different values of P and n. Small values of n, or values of nP or $n(1-P)$ less than 5, will give poor results, i.e. the Normal approximation to the Binomial will not be very good.

The Poisson distribution

The section above showed how the Binomial distribution could be approximated by a Normal distribution under certain circumstances. The approximation does not work particularly well for very small values of P, when nP is less than 5. In these circumstances the Binomial may be approximated instead by the Poisson distribution, which is given by the formula

$$(4.26) \quad Pr(x) = \frac{\mu^x e^{-\mu}}{x!}$$

where μ is the mean of the distribution (like μ for the Normal distribution and nP for the Binomial). Like the Binomial, but unlike the Normal, the Poisson is a discrete probability distribution, so that equation (4.26) is only defined for integer values of x. Furthermore, it is applicable to a series of trials which are independent, as in the Binomial case.

The use of the Poisson distribution is appropriate when the probability of 'success' is very small and the number of trials large. Its use is illustrated by the following example. A manufacturer gives a two–year guarantee on the TV tubes he makes. From past experience he knows that 0.5% of his tubes will be faulty and fail within the guarantee period. What is the probability that of a consignment of 500 tubes (a) none will be faulty, (b) more than three are faulty?

The mean of the Poisson distribution in this case is $\mu = 2.5$ (0.5% of 500). Therefore

$$(4.27) \quad \Pr\left(x = 0\right) = \frac{2.5^0 e^{-2.5}}{0!} = 0.082$$

giving a probability of 8.2% of no failures. The answer to this problem via the Binomial method is

$$\Pr(r = 0) = 0.995^{500} = 0.0816$$

Thus the Poisson method gives a reasonably accurate answer. The Poisson approximation to the Binomial is satisfactory if nP is less than about 7.

The probability of more than three tubes expiring is calculated as

$$\Pr(x > 3) = 1 - \Pr(x = 0) - \Pr(x = 1) - \Pr(x = 2) - \Pr(x = 3)$$

$$\Pr\left(x = 1\right) = \frac{2.5^1 e^{-2.5}}{1!} = 0.205$$

$$\Pr\left(x = 2\right) = \frac{2.5^2 e^{-2.5}}{2!} = 0.256$$

$$\Pr\left(x = 3\right) = \frac{2.5^3 e^{-2.5}}{3!} = 0.214$$

So $\Pr\left(x > 3\right) = 1 - 0.082 - 0.205 - 0.256 - 0.214$

$$= 0.242$$

Thus there is a probability of about 24% of more than three failures. The Binomial calculation is much more tedious, but gives an answer of 24.2% also.

The Poisson distribution is also useful for queuing-type problems. If a shop receives, on average, 20 customers per hour, what is the probability of no customers within a five-minute period while the owner takes a coffee break?

The average number of customers per five-minute period is $20 \times 5/60 = 1.67$. The probability of a free five-minute spell is therefore

$$\Pr\left(x = 0\right) = \frac{1.67^0 e^{-1.67}}{0!} = 0.189$$

a probability of about 19%. Note that this problem cannot be solved by the Binomial method since n and P are not known separately, only their product.

EXERCISES

Exercise 1

Two dice are thrown and the sum of the two scores is recorded. Draw a graph of the resulting probability distribution of the sum and calculate its mean and variance. What is the probability that the sum is 9 or greater?

Exercise 2

Two dice are thrown and the absolute difference of the two scores recorded. Graph the resulting probability distribution and calculate its mean and variance. What is the probability that the absolute difference is 4 or more?

Exercise 3

Sketch the probability distribution for the time of departure of a train. Locate the timetabled departure time on your chart.

Exercise 4

A train departs every half hour. You arrive at the station at a completely random moment. Sketch the probability distribution of your waiting time. What is your expected waiting time?

Exercise 5

Sketch the probability distribution for the number of accidents on a stretch of road in one day.

Exercise 6

Sketch the probability distribution for the number of accidents on the same stretch of road in one year. How and why does this differ from your previous answer?

Exercise 7

Six dice are rolled and the number of sixes is noted. Calculate the probabilities of $0, 1, \ldots, 6$ sixes and graph the probability distribution.

Exercise 8

If the probability of a boy in a single birth is $\frac{1}{2}$ and is independent of the sex of previous babies then the number of boys in a family of 10 children follows a Binomial distribution with mean 5 and variance 2.5. In each of the following instances, describe how the distribution of the number of boys differs from the Binomial described above.

(a) The probability of a boy is 6/10.

(b) The probability of a boy is $\frac{1}{2}$ but births are not independent. The birth of a boy makes it more than an even chance that the next child is a boy.

(c) As (b) above, except that the birth of a boy makes it less than an even chance that the next child will be a boy.

(d) The probability of a boy is 6/10 on the first birth. The birth of a boy makes it a more than even chance that the next baby will be a boy.

Exercise 9

A firm receives components from a supplier in large batches, for use in its production process. Production is uneconomic if a batch containing 10% or more defective components is used. The firm checks the quality of each incoming batch by taking a sample of 15 and rejecting the whole batch if more than one defective component is found.

(a) If a batch containing 10% defectives is delivered, what is the probability of it being accepted?

(b) How could the firm reduce this probability of erroneously accepting bad batches?

(c) If the supplier produces a batch with 3% defective, what is the probability of the firm sending back the batch?

(d) What role does the assumption of a 'large' batch play in the calculation?

Exercise 10

The UK record for the number of children born to a mother is 39, 32 of them girls. Assuming the probability of a girl in a single birth is 0.5 and that this probability is independent of previous births,

(a) Find the probability of 32 girls in 39 births (you'll need a scientific calculator or a computer to help with this!).

(b) Does this result cast doubt on the assumptions?

Exercise 11

Using equation (4.5) describing the Normal distribution and setting $\mu = 0$ and $\sigma^2 = 1$, graph the distribution for the values $x = -2, -1.5, -1, -0.5, 0, 0.5, 1, 1.5, 2$.

Exercise 12

Repeat the previous exercise for the values $\mu = 2$ and $\sigma^2 = 4$. Use values of x from -2 to $+6$ in increments of 1.

Exercise 13

For the standard Normal variable z, find

(a) $\Pr(z > 1.64)$

(b) $\Pr(z > 0.5)$

(c) $\Pr(z > -1.5)$

(d) $\Pr(-2 < z < 1.5)$

(e) $\Pr(z = -0.75)$.

For (a) and (d), shade in the relevant areas on the graph you drew for exercise 11.

Exercise 14

Find the values of z which cut off

(a) the top 10%

(b) the bottom 15%

(c) the middle 50%

of the standard Normal distribution.

Exercise 15

If $x \sim N(10, 9)$ find

(a) $\Pr(x > 12)$

(b) $\Pr(x < 7)$

(c) $\Pr(8 < x < 15)$

(d) $\Pr(x = 10)$.

Exercise 16

IQ (the intelligence quotient) is Normally distributed with mean 100 and standard deviation 16.

(a) What proportion of the population has an IQ above 120?

(b) What proportion of the population has IQ between 90 and 110?

(c) In the past, about 10% of the population went to university. Now the proportion is about 30%. What was the IQ of the 'marginal' student in the past? What is it now?

Exercise 17

Ten adults are selected at random from the population and their IQ measured.

(a) What is the probability distribution of the sample average IQ?

(b) What is the probability that the average IQ of the sample is over 110?

(c) If many such samples were taken, in what proportion would you expect the average IQ to be over 110?

(d) What is the probability that the average IQ lies within the range 90 to 110? How does this answer compare to the answer to part (b) of exercise 16? Account for the difference.

(e) What is the probability that a random sample of ten university students has an average IQ greater than 110?

(f) The first adult sampled has an IQ of 150. What do you expect the average IQ of the sample to be?

Exercise 18

The average income of a country is known to be £10,000 with standard deviation £2,500. A sample of 40 individuals is taken and their average income calculated.

(a) What is the probability distribution of this sample mean?

(b) What is the probability of the sample mean being over £10,500?

(c) What is the probability of the sample mean being below £8,000?

(d) If the sample size were 10, why could you not use the same methods to find the answers to (a)–(c)?

Exercise 19

A coin is tossed ten times. Write down the distribution of the number of heads

(a) exactly, using the Binomial distribution,

(b) approximately, using the Normal distribution.

(c) Find the probability of four or more heads, using both methods. How accurate is the Normal method, with and without the continuity correction?

Exercise 20

A machine producing electronic circuits has an average failure rate of 15% (they're difficult to make). The cost of making a batch of 500 circuits is £8,400 and the good ones sell for £20 each. What is the probability of the firm making a loss on any one batch?

Exercise 21

An experienced invoice clerk makes an error once in every 100 invoices, on average.

(a) What is the probability of finding a batch of 100 invoices without error?

(b) What is the probability of finding such a batch with more than two errors?

Calculate the answers using both the Binomial and Poisson distributions. If you try to solve the problem using the Normal method, how accurate is your answer?

Exercise 22

A firm employing 100 workers has an average absenteeism rate of 4%. On a given day, what is the probability of (a) no workers, (b) one worker, (c) more than six workers being absent?

Exercise 23

Computer project: This exercise demonstrates the Central Limit Theorem at work. In your spreadsheet, use the $=RAND()$ function to generate a random sample of 25 observations (I suggest entering this function in cells A4:A28, for example). Copy these cells across 100 columns, to generate 100 samples. In row 29, calculate the mean of each sample. Now examine the distribution of these sample means.

(a) What distribution would you expect them to have?

(b) What is the parent distribution from which the samples are drawn?

(c) What are the parameters of the parent distribution and of the sample means?

(d) Do your results in (c) accord with what you would expect?

(e) Draw up a frequency table of the sample means and graph it. Does it look as you expected?

(f) Experiment with different sample sizes and with different parent distributions to see the effect that these have.

Exercise 24

Project: An extremely numerate newsagent (with a spreadsheet program, as you will need) is trying to work out how many copies of a newspaper he should order. The cost to him per copy is 15 pence, which he then sells at 45 pence. Sales are distributed Normally with an average daily sale of 250 and variance 625. Unsold copies cannot be returned for credit or refund; he has to throw them away, losing 15p per copy.

(a) What do you think the seller's objective should be?

(b) How many copies should he order?

(c) What happens to the *variance* of profit as he orders more copies?

(d)   Calculate the probability of selling *more than X* copies. (Create an extra column in the spreadsheet for this.) What is the value of this probability at the optimum number of copies ordered?

(e) What would the price–cost ratio have to be to justify the seller ordering X copies?

(f)   The wholesaler offers a sale or return deal, but the cost per copy is 16p. Should the seller take up this new offer?

(g) Are there other considerations which might influence the seller's decision?

Hints:
Set up your spreadsheet as follows:

col. A: (cells A10:A160)175, 176, . . . up to 325 in unit increments (to represent sales levels).

col. B: (cells B10:B160) the probability of sales falling between 175 and 176, between 176 and 177, etc. up to 325–326. (*Excel* has the =NORMDIST() function to do this – see the help facility.)

col. C: (cells C10:C160) total cost (= 0.15 × number ordered. Put the latter in cell F3 so you can reference it and change its value).

col. D: (cells D10:D160) total revenue (=MIN(sales, number ordered) × 0.45).

col. E: profit (revenue − cost).

col. F: profit × probability (i.e. col. E × col. B).

cell F161: the sum of F10:F160 (this is the expected profit).

Now vary the number ordered (cell F3) to find the maximum value in F161.

You can also calculate the variance of profit fairly simply, using an extra column.

5 ESTIMATION AND CONFIDENCE INTERVALS

Introduction

We now come to the heart of the subject of statistical inference. Up until now the following type of question has been examined: given the population parameters μ and σ^2, what is the probability of the sample mean $\bar{x}$, from a sample of size n, being greater than some specified value or within some range of values? The parameters μ and σ^2 are assumed to be known and the objective is to try to form some conclusions about possible values of $\bar{x}$. However, in practice it is usually the sample values $\bar{x}$ and s^2 that are known, while the population parameters μ and σ^2 are not. Thus a more interesting question to ask is: given the values of $\bar{x}$ and s^2, what can be said about μ and σ^2? Sometimes the population variance is known, and inferences have to be made about μ alone. For example, a sample of 50 British families finds an average weekly expenditure on food ($\bar{x}$) of £37.50 with a standard deviation (s) of £6.00; what can be said about the average expenditure (μ) of *all* British families?

Schematically this type of problem is shown as follows:

Sample information		Population parameters
$\bar{x}, s^2$	inferences about $\longrightarrow$	μ, σ^2

This chapter covers the **estimation** of population parameters such as μ and σ^2 while Chapter 6 describes **testing hypotheses** about these parameters. The two procedures are very closely related.

Point and interval estimation

There are basically two ways in which an estimate of a parameter can be presented. The first of these is a **point estimate**, i.e. a single value which is the best estimate of the parameter of interest. The point estimate is the one which is most prevalent in everyday usage; for example, the average Briton drinks 4.5 cups of tea per day. Although this is presented as a fact, it is actually an estimate, obtained from a survey of people's drinking habits. Since it is obtained from a sample there must be some doubt about its accuracy – the sample will probably not exactly represent the whole population. For this reason **interval estimates** are also used, which give some idea of the likely accuracy of the estimate. If the sample size is small, for example, then it is quite possible that the estimate will not be very close to the true value and this would be reflected in a wide interval estimate, for example that the average Briton drinks between 3 and 6 cups of tea per day. A larger sample, or a better method of estimation, would allow a narrower interval to be derived and thus a more precise estimate of the parameter to be obtained, such as an average consumption of between 4 and 5 cups. Interval estimates are better for the consumer of the statistics, since they not only show the estimate of the parameter but also give an idea of the confidence which the researcher has in that estimate. The following sections describe how to construct both types of estimate.

Rules and criteria for finding estimates

In order to estimate a parameter such as the population mean, a rule (or set of rules) is required which describes how to derive the estimate of the parameter from the sample data. Such a rule is known as an **estimator**. An example of an estimator for the population mean is 'use the sample mean'. It is important to distinguish between an estimator, a rule, and an estimate, which is the value derived as a result of applying the rule to the data.

There are many possible estimators for any parameter, so it is important to be able to distinguish between good and bad estimators. The following are all possible estimators of the population mean:

(1) the sample mean
(2) the smallest sample observation
(3) the first sample observation

A set of criteria is needed for discriminating between good and bad estimators. Which of the above three estimators is 'best'? Two important criteria by which to judge extimators are **bias** and **precision**.

Bias

It is impossible to know if a single estimate of a parameter, derived by applying a particular estimator to the sample data, gives a correct estimate of the parameter or not. The estimate might be too low or too high and, since the parameter is unknown, it is impossible to check this. What *is* possible, however, is to say whether an estimator gives the correct answer *on average*. An estimator which gives the correct answer on average is said to be unbiased. Another way of expressing this is to say that an unbiased estimator does not *systematically* mislead the researcher away from the correct value of the parameter. It is important to remember, though, that even using an unbiased estimator does not guarantee that a single use of the estimator will yield a correct estimate of the parameter.

Formally, an estimator is unbiased if its expected value is equal to the parameter being estimated. Consider trying to estimate the population mean using the three estimators suggested above. Taking the sample mean first, we have already learned that its expected value is μ, i.e.

$$E(\bar{x}) = \mu$$

which immediately shows that the sample mean is an unbiased estimator.

The second estimator (the smallest observation in the sample) can easily be shown to be biased, using the result derived above. Since the smallest sample observation must be less than the sample mean, its expected value must be less than μ. Denote the smallest observation by x_s, then

$$E(x_s) < \mu$$

so this estimator is biased downwards. It underestimates the population mean. The size of the bias is simply the difference between the expected value of the estimator and the value of the parameter, so the bias in this case is

(5.1) $\text{Bias} = E(x_s) - \mu$

For the sample mean $\bar{x}$ the bias is obviously zero.

Turning to the third rule (the first sample observation) this can be shown to be another unbiased estimator. Choosing the first observation from the sample is equivalent to taking a random sample of size one from the population in the first place. Thus the single observation may be considered as the sample mean from a random sample of size one. Since it is a sample mean it is unbiased, as demonstrated earlier.

Precision

Two of the estimators above were found to be unbiased, and in fact there are many unbiased estimators (the sample median is another). Some way of choosing between the set of all unbiased estimators is therefore required, which is where the second criterion of precision comes in. Unlike bias, precision is a relative concept, comparing one estimator to another. Given two estimators A and B, A is more precise than B if the estimates it yields (from all possible samples) are less spread out than those of estimator B. A precise estimator will tend to give similar estimates for all possible samples.

Consider the two unbiased estimators found above: how do they compare on the criteria of precision? It turns out that the sample mean is the more precise of the two, and it is not difficult to understand why. Taking just a single sample observation means that it is quite likely to be unrepresentative of the population as a whole, and thus leads to a poor estimate of the population mean. The sample mean on the other hand is based on all the sample observations and it is unlikely that all of them are unrepresentative of the population. The sample mean is therefore a good estimator of the population mean, being more precise than the single observation estimator.

Just as bias was related to the expected value of the estimator, so precision can be defined in terms of the variance. One estimator is more precise than another if it has a smaller variance. Recall that the probability distribution of the sample mean is

(5.2) $\bar{x} \sim N(\mu, \sigma^2/n)$

in large samples, so the variance of the sample mean is

$$V(\bar{x}) = \sigma^2/n$$

As the sample size n gets larger the variance of the sample mean becomes smaller, so the estimator becomes more precise. For this reason large samples give better estimates than small samples, and so the sample mean is a better estimator than taking just one observation from the sample. The two estimators can be compared in a diagram (see Fig. 5.1) which draws the probability distributions of the two estimators.

It is easily seen that the sample mean yields estimates which are *on average* closer to the population mean.

A related concept is that of **efficiency**. The efficiency of one estimator, relative to another, is given by the ratio of their sampling variances. Thus the efficiency of the first observation estimator, relative to the sample mean, is given by

(5.3) $\text{Efficiency} = \dfrac{\text{var}(\bar{x})}{\text{var}(\bar{x}_1)} = \dfrac{\sigma^2/n}{\sigma^2} = \dfrac{1}{n}$

Thus the efficiency is determined by the relative sample sizes in this case.

Fig. 5.1 *The sampling distribution of two estimators*

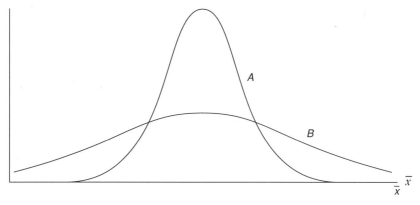

Note: Curve *A* shows the distribution of sample means, which is the more precise estimator. *B* shows the distribution of estimates using a single observation.

The trade-off between bias and precision: the Bill Gates effect

It should be noted that just because an estimator is biased does not necessarily mean that it is imprecise. Sometimes there is a trade-off between an unbiased, but imprecise, estimator and a biased, but precise, one. Figure 5.2 illustrates this.

Although estimator *A* is biased it will nearly always yield an estimate which is fairly close to the true value; even though the estimate is expected to be wrong, it is not likely to be far wrong. Estimator *B*, though unbiased, can give estimates which are far away from the true value, so that *A* might be the preferred estimator.

As an example of this, suppose we are trying to estimate the average wealth of the US population. Consider the following two estimators:

(1) Use the mean wealth of a random sample of Americans.
(2) Use the mean wealth of a random sample of Americans but, if Bill Gates is in the sample, omit him from the calculation.

Bill Gates is the founder and Chairman of Microsoft Corporation, the leading computer software company. Because of this, he is a dollar billionaire ($6bn according to a recent report). His presence in a sample of, say, 30 observations would swamp the sample and give a highly misleading result. Assuming Bill Gates has $6bn and the others each have $200,000 of wealth, the average wealth would be estimated at about $200 million, which is unlikely to be true.

The first rule could therefore give us a wildly incorrect answer, although the rule is unbiased. The second rule is clearly biased but does rule out the possibility of such an unlucky sample. We can work out the approximate bias. It is the difference between the average wealth of all Americans and the average wealth of all Americans except Bill Gates. If the average of all 250 million Americans is about $200,000, then total wealth is $50,000bn. Subtracting Bill's $6bn leaves $49,994bn to be shared amongst the rest, giving $199,976 each, an error of 0.01%.

It might seem worthwhile therefore to accept this degree of bias in order to improve the precision of the estimate. Furthermore, if we did use the biased rule, we could always adjust the sample mean upwards by 0.01% to get an approximately unbiased estimate.

Of course, this point applies to any exceptionally rich person, not just Bill Gates. It points to the need to ensure that the rich are not over- (nor under-) represented in the sample. Chapter 7 on sampling methods investigates this point in more detail. In

Fig. 5.2 *The trade-off between bias and precision*

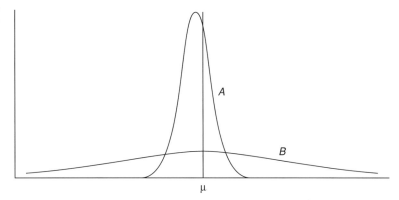

the rest of this book only unbiased estimators are considered, the most important being the sample mean.

Maximum likelihood estimation

Another justification for using the sample mean to estimate the population mean is that it is the **maximum likelihood estimator** of the parameter. Suppose we have a sample of data with a mean of 100. We can ask the question: what value of the population mean gives the greatest probability of obtaining a sample with a mean of 100? Intuitively it seems clear that a population mean of 10 is unlikely to give a high probability of such a sample mean. A population mean of 50 should give a higher probability, but still not a very good one.

It turns out that (subject to certain assumptions) a population mean of 100 gives the greatest probability of obtaining a sample mean of 100. No other value of the parameter gives such a high probability of obtaining the sample evidence. This would seem to be a further useful justification for using the sample mean as an estimator. The assumption required to justify this is that the population itself is Normally distributed. Note that this is a (much) stronger assumption than is required to demonstrate unbiasedness. The Central Limit Theorem showed that no assumption about the shape of the population distribution was required for unbiasedness.

Estimation with large samples

For the type of problem encountered in this chapter the method of estimation differs according to the size of the sample. 'Large' samples, by which is meant sample sizes of 25 or more, are dealt with first, while small samples are considered in the following section. The reason why different methods are required will be dealt with in a later section.

Estimating a mean

To demonstrate the principles and practice of estimating the population mean, we shall take the example of estimating the average wealth of the British population, the full data for which were given in Chapter 1. Suppose that we didn't have this information but were required to estimate the average wealth from a sample of data. In particular, let us suppose that the sample size is $n = 100$, the sample mean is $\bar{x} = 60$ (in £,000) and the sample variance is $s^2 = 12,500$. Obviously, this sample has got pretty close to the true values (see Chapter 1). What can we infer about the population mean μ from the sample data alone?

For the point estimate of μ the sample mean is a good candidate since it is unbiased, and it is more precise than other sample statistics such as the median. The point estimate of μ is simply £60,000, therefore.

The point estimate does not give an idea of the uncertainty associated with the estimate. We are not *absolutely* sure that the mean is £60,000 (in fact it isn't – see Chapter 1). The interval estimate will be centred around the sample mean, but give some idea of the confidence we attach to the estimate.

To obtain the interval estimate we first require the probability distribution of $\bar{x}$, first established in Chapter 4:

(5.4) $\bar{x} \sim N(\mu, \sigma^2/n)$

From this, it was calculated that there is a 95% probability of the sample mean lying within 1.96 standard errors of μ, i.e.

See equation (4.24) in Chapter 4 to remind yourself of this. Remember that ±1.96 is the *z*-score which cuts off 2.5% in each tail of the Normal distribution.

$$\Pr\left(\mu - 1.96\sqrt{\sigma^2/n} \le \bar{x} \le \mu + 1.96\sqrt{\sigma^2/n}\right) = 0.95$$

This statement can be turned around to say that μ lies within 1.96 standard errors of $\bar{x}$ with **95% confidence**, i.e. one can be 95% confident that

(5.5) $\left[\bar{x} - 1.96\sqrt{\sigma^2/n}, \bar{x} + 1.96\sqrt{\sigma^2/n}\right]$

Diagrammatically these two arguments may be presented as shown in Figs 5.3(a) and 5.3(b).

The interval shown in equation (5.5) is called the **95% confidence interval** and this is the interval estimate for μ. In this example the value of σ^2 is unknown, but in large ($n \ge 25$) samples it can be replaced by s^2 from the sample. s^2 is here used as an estimate of σ^2 which is unbiased and sufficiently precise in large samples. The 95% confidence interval is therefore

The two values are the lower and upper limits of the interval.

(5.6) $\left[\bar{x} - 1.96\sqrt{s^2/n} \le \mu \le \bar{x} + 1.96\sqrt{s^2/n}\right]$

$= \left[60 - 1.96\sqrt{12,500/100}, 60 + 1.96\sqrt{12,500/100}\right]$

$= \left[38.1, 81.9\right]$

Thus we are 95% confident that the true average level of wealth lies between £38,100 and £81,900. It should be noted that £60,000 lies exactly at the centre of the interval (because of the symmetry of the Normal distribution).

By examining equation (5.6) one can see that the confidence interval is wider

(1) the smaller the sample size,
(2) the greater the standard deviation of the sample.

The greater uncertainty which is associated with smaller sample sizes is manifested in a wider confidence interval estimate of the population mean. This occurs because a smaller sample has more chance of being unrepresentative (just because of an unlucky sample).

Greater variation in the sample data also leads to greater uncertainty about the population mean and a wider confidence interval. Greater sample variation suggests greater variation in the population so, again, a given sample could include observations which are a long way off the mean.

Fig. 5.3(a) *The 95% probability interval for $\bar{x}$ around the population mean μ*

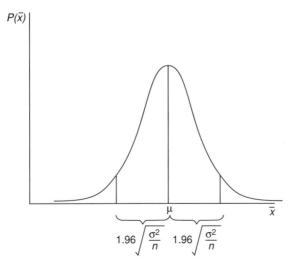

Fig. 5.3(b) *The 95% confidence interval for μ around the sample mean $\bar{x}$*

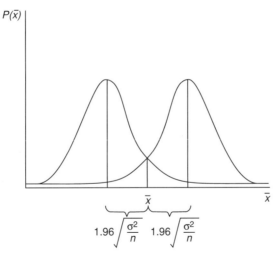

Note that the width of the confidence interval does *not* depend upon the population size – a sample of 100 observations reveals as much about a population of 10,000 as it does about a population of 10,000,000. This point will be discussed in more detail in Chapter 7 on sampling methods.

A question which arises at this point is why the term 'confidence' is used when referring to the estimate, rather than the term 'probability'. Why not say that μ lies within the interval with 95% probability? The answer to this goes back to the definition of probability. According to the frequentist view, probability statements can be made about random variables but not about population parameters. Since μ is a parameter one cannot make probability statements about it. The true value of μ either lies in the interval or it does not; it cannot be 95% in it. To emphasise this point the term 'confidence' rather than 'probability' is used. This may seem like a semantic difference, but it is important to understand the reason for it. Those who adhere to the subjective belief definition of probability and use Bayesian methods of analysis would regard it as legitimate to talk of a probability interval, reflecting one's belief about the location of μ. Classical statistics continues to emphasise the difference between a random variable, with its probability distribution, and a population parameter.

A second question is why use a probability (and hence a confidence level) of 95%? In fact, one can choose any confidence level, and thus confidence interval. The 90% confidence interval can be obtained by finding the z-score which cuts off 10% of the Normal distribution (5% in each tail). From Table A2 this is $z = 1.64$, so the 90% confidence interval is

(5.7) $$\left[\bar{x} - 1.64\sqrt{s^2/n}, \ \bar{x} + 1.64\sqrt{s^2/n} \right]$$
$$= \left[60 - 1.64\sqrt{12,500/100}, \ 60 + 1.64\sqrt{12,500/100} \right]$$
$$= \left[41.7, \ 78.3 \right]$$

Notice that this is narrower than the 95% confidence level. The greater the degree of confidence required, the wider the interval has to be. Any confidence level may be chosen, and by careful choice of this level the confidence interval can be made as wide or as narrow as wished. This would seem to undermine the purpose of calculating the confidence interval, which is to obtain some idea of the uncertainty attached to the estimate. This is not the case, however, because the reader of the results can interpret them appropriately, as long as the confidence level is made clear. To simplify matters, the 95% and 99% confidence levels are the most commonly used and serve as conventions. Beware of the researcher who calculates the 76% confidence interval – this may have been chosen in order to obtain the desired answer rather than in the spirit of scientific enquiry! The general formula for the $(100-\alpha)$% confidence interval is

(5.8) $$\left[\bar{x} - z_\alpha \sqrt{s^2/n}, \ \bar{x} + z_\alpha \sqrt{s^2/n} \right]$$

where z_α is the z-score which cuts off the extreme α% of the Normal distribution.

Estimating a proportion

It is often the case that we wish to estimate the **proportion** of the population that has a particular characteristic (e.g. is unemployed), rather than wanting an average. Given what we have already learned this is fairly straightforward and is based on similar principles. Suppose that, following Chapter 1, we wish to estimate the proportion of educated men who are unemployed. We have a random sample of 200 men, of whom 15 are unemployed. What can we infer?

The sample data are $n = 200$ and $p = 0.075 \ (= 15/200)$. We denote the population proportion by the Greek letter π and it is this that we are trying to estimate using data from the sample. The sample data are:

$p = 0.075$
$n = 200$

The key to solving this problem is recognising p as a random variable just like the sample mean. This is because its value depends upon the sample drawn and will vary from sample to sample. Once the probability distribution of this random variable is established the problem is quite easy to solve, using the same methods as were used for the mean. The sampling distribution of p is[1]

$$(5.9) \quad p \sim N\left(\pi, \frac{\pi(1-\pi)}{n}\right)$$

Having derived the probability distribution of p the same methods of estimation can be used as for the sample mean. Since the expected value of p is π, the sample proportion is an unbiased estimate of the population parameter. The point estimate of π is simply p, therefore. Thus it is estimated that 7.5% of educated men are unemployed.

Given the sampling distribution for p in equation (5.9) above, the formula for the 95% confidence interval for π can immediately be written down as:

As usual, the 95% confidence interval limits are given by the point estimate plus and minus 1.96 standard errors.

$$(5.10) \quad \left[p - 1.96\sqrt{\frac{\pi(1-\pi)}{n}}, \ p + 1.96\sqrt{\frac{\pi(1-\pi)}{n}} \right]$$

Since the value of π is unknown the confidence interval cannot yet be calculated, so the sample value of 0.075 has to be used instead. Like the case of the sample mean above, this is acceptable in large samples. Thus the 95% confidence interval becomes

$$(5.11) \quad \left[p - 1.96\sqrt{\frac{0.075(1-0.075)}{200}}, \ p + 1.96\sqrt{\frac{0.075(1-0.075)}{200}} \right]$$

$$= \left[0.075 - 0.037, \ 0.075 + 0.037 \right]$$

$$= \left[0.038, \ 0.112 \right]$$

We say that we are 95% confident that the true proportion of unemployed, educated men lies between 3.8% and 11.2%.

It can be seen that these two cases apply a common method. The 95% confidence interval is given by the point estimate plus or minus 1.96 standard errors. For a different confidence level, 1.96 would be replaced by the appropriate value from the standard Normal distribution.

With this knowledge two further cases can be swiftly dealt with.

Estimating the difference between two means

Sixty pupils from school 1 scored an average mark of 62% in an exam, with a standard deviation of 18%; 35 pupils from school 2 scored an average of 70% with standard deviation 12%. Estimate the true difference between the two schools in the average mark obtained.

This is a more complicated problem than those previously treated since it involves two samples rather than one. An estimate has to be found for $\mu_1 - \mu_2$ (the true difference in the mean marks of the schools), in the form of both point and interval

---

[1] See the appendix to this chapter for the derivation of this formula.

estimates. The pupils taking the exams may be thought of as samples of all pupils in the schools who could potentially take the exams.

Notice that this is a problem about sample means, not proportions, even though the question deals in percentages. The point is that each observation in the sample (i.e. each student's mark) can take a value between 0 and 100, and one can calculate the standard deviation of the marks. For this to be a problem of sample proportions the mark for each pupil would each have to be of the pass/fail type, so that one could only calculate the proportion who passed.

It might be thought that the way to approach this problem is to derive one confidence interval for each sample (along the lines set out above), and then to somehow combine them; for example, the degree of overlap of the two confidence intervals could be assessed. This would be the wrong approach. It is sometimes a good strategy, when faced with an unfamiliar problem to solve, to translate it into a more familiar problem and then solve it using known methods. This is the procedure which will be followed here. The essential point is to keep in mind the concept of a random variable and its probability distribution.

Problems involving a single random variable have already been dealt with above. The current problem deals with two samples and therefore there are two random variables to consider, i.e. the two sample means $\bar{x}_1$ and $\bar{x}_2$. Since the aim is to estimate $\mu_1 - \mu_2$, an obvious candidate for an estimator is the difference between the two sample means, $\bar{x}_1 - \bar{x}_2$. We therefore need to establish the sampling distribution of $\bar{x}_1 - \bar{x}_2$. This is derived in the Appendix to this chapter and results in equation (5.12):

$$(5.12) \quad \bar{x}_1 - \bar{x}_2 \sim N\left(\mu_1 - \mu_2, \frac{\sigma_1^2}{n_1} + \frac{\sigma_2^2}{n_2}\right)$$

This is illustrated in Fig. 5.4. Equation (5.12) shows that $\bar{x}_1 - \bar{x}_2$ is an unbiased estimator of $\mu_1 - \mu_2$. The difference between the sample means will therefore be used as the point estimate of $\mu_1 - \mu_2$. Thus the point estimate of the true difference between the schools is

$$\bar{x}_1 - \bar{x}_2 = 62 - 70 = -8\%$$

The 95% confidence interval estimate is derived in the same manner as before, making use of the standard error of the random variable. The formula is

The term under the square root sign is the standard error for $\bar{x}_1 - \bar{x}_2$.

$$(5.13) \quad \left[\bar{x}_1 - \bar{x}_2 - 1.96\sqrt{\frac{s_1^2}{n_1} + \frac{s_2^2}{n_2}}, \ \bar{x}_1 - \bar{x}_2 + 1.96\sqrt{\frac{s_1^2}{n_1} + \frac{s_2^2}{n_2}}\right]$$

Since the values of σ^2 are unknown they have been replaced in equation (5.13) by their sample values. As in the single sample case, this is acceptable in large samples. The 95% confidence interval for $\mu_1 - \mu_2$ is therefore

$$\left[(62-70)-1.96\sqrt{\frac{18^2}{60}+\frac{12^2}{35}}, \ (62-70)+1.96\sqrt{\frac{18^2}{60}+\frac{12^2}{35}}\right]$$

$$= [-14.05, -1.95]$$

Fig. 5.4 *The distribution of $\bar{x}_1 - \bar{x}_2$*

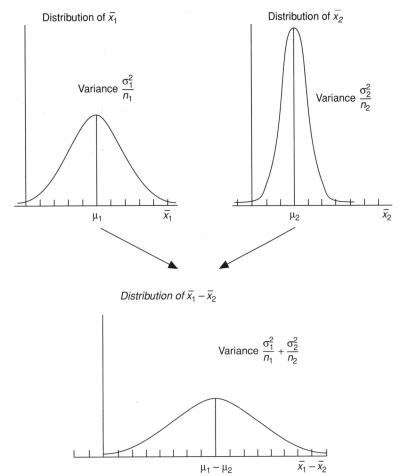

Distribution of $\bar{x}_1$

Variance $\dfrac{\sigma_1^2}{n_1}$

μ_1 $\bar{x}_1$

Distribution of $\bar{x}_2$

Variance $\dfrac{\sigma_2^2}{n_2}$

μ_2 $\bar{x}_2$

Distribution of $\bar{x}_1 - \bar{x}_2$

Variance $\dfrac{\sigma_1^2}{n_1} + \dfrac{\sigma_2^2}{n_2}$

$\mu_1 - \mu_2$ $\bar{x}_1 - \bar{x}_2$

The estimate is that school 2's average mark is between 1.95 and 14.05 percentage points above school 1's. Notice that the confidence interval does not include the value zero, which would imply equality of the two schools' marks. Equality of the two schools can thus be ruled out with 95% confidence.

Estimating the difference between two proportions

A survey of 80 Britons showed that 23 owned personal computers. A similar survey of 50 Swedes showed 10 with computers. Are personal computers more widespread in Britain than Sweden?

Here the aim is to estimate $\pi_1 - \pi_2$, the difference between the two population proportions, so the probability distribution of $p_1 - p_2$ is needed, the difference of the sample proportions. The derivation of this follows similar lines to those set out above for the difference of two sample means, so is not repeated. The probability distribution is

$$(5.14) \quad p_1 - p_2 \sim N\left(\pi_1 - \pi_2, \; \frac{\pi_1(1-\pi_1)}{n_1} + \frac{\pi_2(1-\pi_2)}{n_2}\right)$$

Again, the two samples must be independently drawn for this to be correct (it is difficult to see how they could not be in this case).

Since the difference between the sample proportions is an unbiased estimate of the true difference, this will be used for the point estimate. The point estimate is therefore

$$p_1 - p_2 = 23/80 - 10/50$$
$$= 0.0875$$

or 8.75%. The 95% confidence interval is given by

$$(5.15) \quad \left[p_1 - p_2 - 1.96\sqrt{\frac{\pi_1(1-\pi_1)}{n_1} + \frac{\pi_2(1-\pi_2)}{n_2}}, \right.$$

$$\left. p_1 - p_2 + 1.96\sqrt{\frac{\pi_1(1-\pi_1)}{n_1} + \frac{\pi_2(1-\pi_2)}{n_2}} \right]$$

π_1 and π_2 are unknown so have to be replaced by p_1 and p_2 for purposes of calculation, so the interval becomes

$$(5.16) \quad \left[0.29 - 0.2 - 1.96\sqrt{\frac{0.29 \times 0.71}{80} + \frac{0.2 \times 0.8}{50}}, \right.$$

$$\left. 0.29 - 0.2 + 1.96\sqrt{\frac{0.29 \times 0.71}{80} + \frac{0.2 \times 0.8}{50}} \right]$$

$$= \left[-0.06, \ 0.24 \right]$$

The 95% confidence interval is fairly wide in this case, ranging from a negative to a positive value. We cannot even be 95% confident that there is any true difference at all between the two countries.

Estimation with small samples: the _t_ distribution

So far only large samples (defined as sample sizes in excess of 25) have been dealt with, which means that (by the Central Limit Theorem) the sampling distribution of $\bar{x}$ follows a Normal distribution, whatever the distribution of the parent population. Remember, from the two theorems of Chapter 4, that

- if the population follows a Normal distribution, $\bar{x}$ is also Normally distributed, and
- if the population is not Normally distributed, $\bar{x}$ is approximately Normally distributed in large samples ($n \geq 25$).

In both cases, confidence intervals were constructed based on the fact that

$$(5.17) \quad \frac{\bar{x} - \mu}{\sqrt{\sigma^2 / n}} \sim N(0, 1)$$

and so the standard Normal distribution is used to find the values which cut off the extreme 5% of the distribution. In practical examples, we had to replace σ by its estimate, s. Thus the confidence interval was based on the fact that

$$(5.18) \quad \frac{\bar{x} - \mu}{\sqrt{s^2 / n}} \sim N(0, 1)$$

For small sample sizes, equation (5.18) is no longer true. Instead, the relevant distribution is the t distribution and we have[2]

$$(5.19) \quad \frac{\bar{x} - \mu}{\sqrt{s^2 / n}} \sim t_{n-1}$$

The random variable defined in equation (5.19) has a t distribution with $n-1$ degrees of freedom. As the sample size gets larger, the t distribution approaches the standard Normal, so the latter can be used for large samples.

The t distribution was derived by W S Gossett in 1908 while conducting tests on the average strength of Guinness beer (who says statistics has no impact on the real world?). He published his work under the pseudonym 'Student', since the company did not allow its employees to publish under their own names, so the distribution is sometimes also known as the Student distribution.

The t distribution is in many ways similar to the standard Normal, insofar as it is

- unimodal
- symmetric
- centred on zero
- bell shaped
- extends from minus infinity to plus infinity.

The differences are that it is more spread out (has a larger variance) than the standard Normal distribution, and has only one parameter rather than two: the **degrees of freedom**, denoted by the Greek letter v (pronounced 'nu'[3]). In problems involving the estimation of a sample mean the degrees of freedom are given by the sample size minus one, i.e. $v = n - 1$.

The t distribution is drawn in Fig. 5.5 for various values of the parameter v. Note that the fewer the degrees of freedom (smaller sample size) the more dispersed is the distribution.

Fig. 5.5 *The t distribution drawn for differing degrees of freedom*

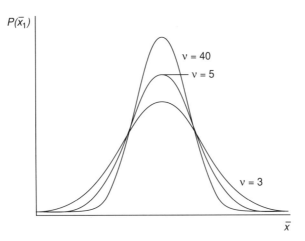

---

[2] We also require the assumption that the parent population is Normally distributed.

[3] Actually, the Greeks pronounce this 'ni'. They also pronounce π 'pee' rather than 'pie' as the English do. This makes statistics lectures in English hard for Greeks to understand!

To summarise the argument so far, when

- the sample size is small, *and*
- the sample variance is used to estimate the population variance

then the t distribution should be used for constructing confidence intervals, not the standard Normal. This results in a slightly wider interval than would be obtained using the standard Normal distribution. This reflects the slightly greater uncertainty involved when s^2 is used as an estimate of σ^2 if the sample size is small.

Apart from this, the methods are exactly as before and are illustrated by the examples below.

Estimating a mean

The following would seem to be an appropriate example. A sample of 15 bottles of beer showed an average specific gravity of 1035.6, with standard deviation 2.7. Estimate the true specific gravity of the brew.

The sample information may be summarised as

$\bar{x} = 1{,}035.6$
$s = 2.7$
$n = 15$

The sample mean is still an unbiased estimator of μ (this is true regardless of the distribution of the population) and serves as point estimate of μ. The point estimate of μ is therefore 1,035.6.

Since σ is unknown, the sample size is small and it can be assumed that the specific gravity of all bottles of beer is Normally distributed (numerous small random factors affect the specific gravity). Thus:

$$(5.20) \quad \frac{\bar{x} - \mu}{\sqrt{s^2 / n}} \sim t_{n-1}$$

and the t distribution should be used to construct the interval.

The 95% confidence interval estimate is given by

$$(5.21) \quad \left[\bar{x} - t_{n-1}\sqrt{s^2 / n}, \ \bar{x} + t_{n-1}\sqrt{s^2 / n} \right]$$

where t_{n-1} is the value of t which cuts off the extreme 5% (2.5% in each tail) of the t distribution with v degrees of freedom . Table A3 gives percentage points of the t distribution and part of it is reproduced in Table 5.1.

The structure of the t distribution table is different from that of the standard Normal table. The first column of the table gives the degrees of freedom. In this example we want the row corresponding to $v = n - 1 = 14$. The appropriate column of the table is the one headed '0.025' which indicates the area cut off in *each* tail. At the intersection of this row and column we find the appropriate value, $t_{14} = 2.145$. Therefore the confidence interval is given by

$$\left[1035.6 - 2.145\sqrt{2.7^2 / 15}, \ 1035.6 + 2.145\sqrt{2.7^2 / 15} \right]$$

which when evaluated gives

$[1034.10, 1037.10]$

Table 5.1   Percentage points of the *t* distribution (excerpt from Table A3)

v	0.4	0.25	0.10	0.05	0.025	0.01	0.005
			Area (α) in each tail				
1	0.325	1.000	3.078	6.314	12.706	31.821	63.656
2	0.289	0.816	1.886	2.920	4.303	6.965	9.925
$\vdots$	$\vdots$	$\vdots$	$\vdots$	$\vdots$	$\vdots$	$\vdots$	$\vdots$
13	0.259	0.694	1.350	1.771	2.160	2.650	3.012
14	0.258	0.692	1.345	1.761	2.145	2.624	2.977
15	0.258	0.691	1.341	1.753		2.602	2.947

Note: The appropriate *t* value for constructing the confidence interval is found at the intersection of the shaded row and column.

We can be 95% confident that the true specific gravity lies within this range. If the Normal distribution had (incorrectly) been used for this problem then the *t* value of 2.145 would have been replaced by a *z*-score of 1.96, giving a confidence interval of

[1034.23, 1036.97]

This underestimates the true confidence interval and gives the impression of a more precise estimate than is actually the case. Use of the Normal distribution leads to a confidence interval which is 8.7% too narrow.

Estimating the difference between two means

As in the case of a single mean the *t*-distribution needs to be used in small samples when the population variances are unknown. Again, both parent populations must be Normally distributed and in addition it must be assumed that the population variances are equal, i.e. $\sigma_1^2 = \sigma_2^2$ (this is required in the mathematical derivation of the *t* distribution). This latter assumption was not required in the large sample case using the Normal distribution. Consider the following example.

A sample of 20 Labour controlled local authorities shows that they spend an average of £175 per taxpayer on administration with a standard deviation of £25. A similar survey of 15 Conservative controlled authorities finds an average figure of £158 with standard deviation of £30. Estimate the true difference in expenditure between Labour and Conservative authorities.

The sample information available is

$$\bar{x}_1 = 175 \qquad \bar{x}_2 = 158$$
$$s_1 = 25 \qquad s_2 = 30$$
$$n_1 = 20 \qquad n_2 = 15$$

We wish to estimate $\mu_1 - \mu_2$ The point estimate of this is $\bar{x}_1 - \bar{x}_2$ which is an unbiased estimate. This gives $175 - 158 = 17$ as the expected difference between the two sets of authorities.

For the confidence interval, the *t* distribution has to be used since the sample sizes are small and the population variances unknown. It is assumed that the populations are Normally distributed and that the samples have been independently drawn. We also assume that the population variances are equal, which seems justified since s_1 and s_2 do not differ by much (this kind of assumption is tested in Chapter 6). The confidence interval is given by the formula:

$$(5.22) \quad \left[\bar{x}_1 - \bar{x}_2 - t_v \sqrt{\frac{S^2}{n_1} + \frac{S^2}{n_2}} , \ \bar{x}_1 - \bar{x}_2 + t_v \sqrt{\frac{S^2}{n_1} + \frac{S^2}{n_2}} \right]$$

where

$$(5.23) \quad S^2 = \frac{\left(n_1 - 1\right)s_1^2 + \left(n_2 - 1\right)s_2^2}{n_1 + n_2 - 2}$$

is the **pooled variance** and

$$v = n_1 + n_2 - 2$$

gives the degrees of freedom associated with the t distribution.

S^2 is an estimate of the (common value of) the population variances. It would be inappropriate to have the differing values s_1^2 and s_2^2 in the formula for the t distribution, for this would be contrary to the assumption that $\sigma_1^2 = \sigma_2^2$, which is essential for the use of the t distribution. The estimate of the common population variance is just the weighted average of the sample variances, using degrees of freedom as weights. Each sample has $n - 1$ degrees of freedom, and the total number of degrees of freedom for the problem is the sum of the degrees of freedom in each sample.

To evaluate the 95% confidence interval we first calculate S^2:

$$S^2 = \frac{\left(20 - 1\right) \times 25^2 + \left(15 - 1\right) \times 30^2}{20 + 15 - 2} = 741.6$$

Inserting this into equation [5.22] gives

$$\left[17 - 2.042 \sqrt{\frac{741.6}{20} + \frac{741.6}{15}}, \ 17 + 2.042 \sqrt{\frac{741.6}{20} + \frac{741.6}{15}} \right]$$

$$= \left[-1.99, \ 35.99 \right]$$

Thus the true difference is quite uncertain and the evidence is even consistent with Conservative authorities spending more than Labour authorities. The large degree of uncertainty arises because of the small sample sizes and the quite wide variation within each sample.

One should be careful about the conclusions drawn from this test. The greater expenditure on administration could be either because of inefficiency of because of a higher level of services provided. To find out which is the case would require further investigation. The statistical test carried out here examines the levels of expenditure, but not whether they are productive or not.

Estimating proportions

Estimating proportions when the sample size is small cannot be done with the t distribution. Recall that the distribution of p was derived from the distribution of r (the number of successes in n trials), which followed a Binomial distribution. In large samples the distribution of r is approximately Normal, thus giving a Normally distributed sample proportion. In small samples it is inappropriate to approximate the Binomial distribution with the t distribution, and indeed is unnecessary, since the Binomial itself can be used. Small sample methods for the sample proportion should be based on the Binomial distribution, therefore, as set out in Chapter 4. These methods are not discussed further here, therefore.

EXERCISES

Exercise 1   (a)   Why is an interval estimate better than a point estimate?

(b)   What factors determine the width of a confidence interval?

Exercise 2   Is the 95% confidence interval (a) twice as wide, (b) more than twice as wide, (c) less than twice as wide, as the 47.5% interval? Explain your reasoning.

Exercise 3   Explain the difference between an estimate and an estimator. Is it true that a good estimator always leads to a good estimate?

Exercise 4   Explain why an unbiased estimator is not always to be preferred to a biased one.

Exercise 5   A random sample of two observations x_1 and x_2 is drawn from a population. Prove that $w_1 x_1 + w_2 x_2$ gives an unbiased estimate of the population mean as long as $w_1 + w_2 = 1$. (Hint: Prove that $E(w_1 x_1 + w_2 x_2) = \mu$.)

Exercise 6   Following the previous question, prove that the most precise unbiased estimate is obtained by setting $w_1 = w_2 = \frac{1}{2}$. (Hint: Minimise $V(w_1 x_1 + w_2 x_2)$ with respect to w_1 after substituting $w_2 = 1 - w_1$. You will need a knowledge of calculus to solve this.)

Exercise 7   Given the sample data

$$\bar{x} = 40 \quad s = 10 \quad n = 36$$

calculate the 99% confidence interval estimate of the true mean. If the sample size were 20, how would the method of calculation and width of the interval be altered?

Exercise 8   A random sample of 100 record shops found that the average weekly sale of a particular record was 260 copies, with standard deviation of 96. Find the 95% confidence interval to estimate the true average sale for all shops. To compile the record chart it is necessary to know the correct average weekly sale to within 5% of its true value. How large a sample size is required?

Exercise 9   Given the sample data $p = 0.4$, $n = 50$, estimate the 99% confidence interval estimate of the true proportion.

Exercise 10   A political opinion poll questions 1,000 people. 464 declare they will vote Conservative. Find the 95% confidence interval estimate for the Conservative share of the vote.

Exercise 11

Given the sample data

$$\bar{x}_1 = 25 \qquad \bar{x}_2 = 22$$
$$s_1 = 12 \qquad s_2 = 18$$
$$n_1 = 80 \qquad n_2 = 100$$

estimate the true difference between the means with 95% confidence.

Exercise 12

(a) A sample of 200 women from the labour force found an average wage of £6,000 p.a. with standard deviation £2,500. A sample of 100 men found an average wage of £8,000 with standard deviation £1,500. Estimate the true difference in wages between men and women.

(b) A different survey, of men and women doing similar jobs, obtained the following results:

$$\bar{x}_W = £7,200 \qquad \bar{x}_M = £7,600$$
$$s_W = £1,225 \qquad s_M = £750$$
$$n_W = 75 \qquad n_M = 50$$

Estimate the difference between male and female wages using these new data. What can be concluded from the results of the two surveys?

Exercise 13

67% out of 150 pupils from school A passed an exam, 62% of 120 pupils at school B passed. Estimate the 99% confidence interval for the true difference between the proportions passing the exam.

Exercise 14

(a) A sample of 954 adults in early 1987 found that 23% of them hold shares. Given a UK adult population of 41 million and assuming a proper random sample was taken, find the 95% confidence interval estimate for the number of shareholders in the UK.

(b) A 'similar' survey the previous year had found a total of 7 million shareholders. Assuming 'similar' means the same sample size, find the 95% confidence interval estimate of the increase in shareholders between the two years.

Exercise 15

A sample of 16 observations from a Normally distributed population yields a sample mean of 30 with standard deviation 5. Find the 95% confidence interval estimate of the population mean.

Exercise 16

A sample of 12 families in a town reveals an average income of £15,000 with standard deviation £6,000. Why might you be hesitant about constructing a 95% confidence interval for the average income in the town?

Exercise 17

Two samples were drawn, each from a Normally distributed population, with the following results:

$$\bar{x}_1 = 45 \qquad s_1 = 8 \qquad n_1 = 12$$
$$\bar{x}_2 = 52 \qquad s_2 = 5 \qquad n_2 = 18$$

Estimate the difference between the population means, using the 95% confidence level.

Exercise 18

The heights of 10 men and 15 women were recorded, with the following results:

	Mean	Variance
Men	173.5	80
Women	162	65

Estimate the true difference between men's and women's heights. Use the 95% confidence level.

Exercise 19

Project: Estimate the average weekly expenditure upon alcohol by students. Ask a (reasonably) random sample of your fellow students for their weekly expenditure on alcohol. From this, calculate the 95% confidence interval estimate of such spending by all students.

Appendix: Derivations of sampling distributions

Derivation of the sampling distribution of p

The sampling distribution of p is fairly straightforward to derive, given what we have already learned. The sampling distribution of p can be easily derived from the distribution of r, the number of successes in n trials of an experiment, since $p = r/n$. The distribution of r for large n is approximately Normal (from Chapter 4):

$$(5.24) \quad r \sim N(nP, nP(1 - P))$$

Knowing the distribution of r, is it possible to find that of p? Since p is simply r multiplied by a constant, $1/n$, it is also Normally distributed. The mean and variance of the distribution can be derived using the E and V operators. The expected value of p is

$$(5.25) \quad E\left(p\right) = E\left(r/n\right) = \frac{1}{n}E\left(r\right) = \frac{1}{n}nP = P = \pi$$

The expected value of the sample proportion is equal to the population proportion (note that the probability P and the population proportion π are the same thing and may be used interchangeably). The sample proportion therefore gives an unbiased estimate of the population proportion.

For the variance:

$$(5.26) \quad V\left(p\right) = V\left(\frac{r}{n}\right) = \frac{1}{n^2}V\left(r\right) = \frac{1}{n^2}nP\left(1 - P\right) = \frac{\pi\left(1 - \pi\right)}{n}$$

Hence the distribution of p is given by

$$(5.27) \quad p \sim N\left(\pi, \frac{\pi\left(1 - \pi\right)}{n}\right)$$

Derivation of the sampling distribution of $\bar{x}_1 - \bar{x}_2$

This is the difference between two random variables so is itself a random variable. Since any linear combination of Normally distributed, independent random variables is itself Normally distributed, the difference of sample means follows a Normal distribution. The mean and variance of the distribution can be found using the E and V operators. Letting

$$E\left(\bar{x}_1\right) = \mu_1, \; V\left(\bar{x}_1\right) = \sigma_1^2 / n \quad \text{and}$$
$$E\left(\bar{x}_2\right) = \mu_2, \; V\left(\bar{x}_2\right) = \sigma_2^2 / n_2$$

then

$$(5.28) \quad E\left(\bar{x}_1 - \bar{x}_2\right) = E\left(\bar{x}_1\right) - E\left(\bar{x}_2\right) = \mu_1 - \mu_2$$

and

$$(5.29) \quad V\left(\bar{x}_1 - \bar{x}_2\right) = V\left(\bar{x}_1\right) + V\left(\bar{x}_2\right) = \frac{\sigma_1^2}{n_1} + \frac{\sigma_2^2}{n_2}$$

Equation (5.29) assumes $\bar{x}_1$ and $\bar{x}_2$ are independent random variables. The probability distribution of $\bar{x}_1 - \bar{x}_2$ can therefore be summarised as:

$$(5.30) \quad \bar{x}_1 - \bar{x}_2 \sim N\left(\mu_1 - \mu_2, \frac{\sigma_1^2}{n_1} + \frac{\sigma_2^2}{n_2}\right)$$

This is equation (5.12) in the text.

6 HYPOTHESIS TESTING

Introduction

This chapter deals with problems very similar to those of the previous chapter on estimation, but examines them in a different way. The estimation of population parameters and the testing of hypotheses about those parameters are similar techniques (indeed they are formally equivalent in a number of respects), but there are important differences in the interpretation of the results arising from each method. The process of estimation is appropriate when measurement is involved, such as measuring the true average expenditure on food; hypothesis testing is better when decision making is involved, such as whether to accept that a supplier's products are up to a specified standard. Hypothesis testing is also used to make decisions about the truth or otherwise of different theories, such as whether rising prices are caused by rising wages; and it is here that the issues become contentious. It is sometimes difficult to interpret correctly the results of hypothesis tests in these circumstances. This is discussed further below.

The concepts of hypothesis testing

In many ways hypothesis testing is analogous to a criminal trial. In a trial there is a defendant who is *initially presumed innocent*. The *evidence* against the defendant is then presented and, if the jury finds this convincing *beyond all reasonable doubt*, he is found guilty; the presumption of innocence is overturned. Of course, mistakes are sometimes made: an innocent person is convicted or a guilty person set free. Both of these errors involve costs (not only in the monetary sense), either to the defendant or to society in general, and the errors should be avoided if at all possible. The laws under which the trial is held may help avoid such errors. The rule that the jury must be convinced 'beyond all reasonable doubt' helps to avoid convicting the innocent, for instance.

The situation in hypothesis testing is similar. First there is a **maintained** or **null hypothesis** which is initially *presumed* to be true. The empirical evidence, usually data from a random sample, is then gathered and assessed. If the evidence seems inconsistent with the null hypothesis, i.e. it has a low probability of occurring *if* the hypothesis were true, then the null hypothesis is *rejected* in favour of an alternative. Once again there are two types of error one can make, either rejecting the null hypothesis when it is really true, or not rejecting it when in fact it is false. Ideally one would like to avoid both types of error.

An example helps to clarify the issues and the analogy. Suppose that you are thinking of taking over a small business franchise. The current owner claims the weekly turnover of each existing franchise is £5,000 and at this level you are willing to take on a franchise. You would be more cautious if the turnover is less than this figure. You examine the books of 26 franchises chosen at random and find that the average turnover was £4,900 with standard deviation £280. What do you do?

The null hypothesis in this case is that average weekly turnover is £5,000 (or more; that would be even more to your advantage). The **alternative hypothesis** is that turnover is strictly less than £5,000 per week. We may write these more succinctly as follows:

$H_0: \mu = 5,000$
$H_1: \mu < 5,000$

H_0 is conventionally used to denote the null hypothesis, H_1 for the alternative. Initially, H_0 is presumed to be true and this presumption will be tested using the sample evidence. Note that the sample evidence is *not* used as part of the hypothesis.

You have to decide whether the owner is telling the truth (H_0) or not (H_1). The two types of error you could make are as follows

- **Type I error** – reject H_0 when it is in fact true. This would mean missing a good business opportunity.
- **Type II error** – not rejecting H_0 when it is in fact false. You would go ahead and buy the business and then find out that it is not as attractive as claimed. You would have overpaid for the business.

The situation is set out in Fig. 6.1.

Obviously a good decision rule would give a good chance of making a correct decision and rule out errors as far as possible. Unfortunately it is impossible to completely eliminate the possibility of errors. As the decision rule is changed to reduce the probability of a Type I error, the probability of making a Type II error inevitably increases. The skill comes in balancing these two types of error.

Again a diagram is useful in illustrating this. Assuming that the null hypothesis is true, then the sample observations are drawn from a population with mean 5,000 and some variance, which we shall assume is accurately measured by the sample variance. The distribution of $\bar{x}$ is then given by

$$(6.1) \quad \bar{x} \sim N(\mu, \sigma^2/n) \text{ or}$$
$$\bar{x} \sim N(5000, 280^2/26)$$

Under the alternative hypothesis the distribution of $\bar{x}$ would be the same except that it would be centred on a value less than 5,000. These two situations are illustrated in Fig. 6.2. The distribution of $\bar{x}$ under H_1 is shown by a dashed curve to signify that its exact position is unknown, only that it lies to the left of the distribution under H_0.

A **decision rule** amounts to choosing a point on the horizontal axis in Fig. 6.2. If the sample mean lies to the left of this point then H_0 is rejected (the sample mean is too far away from H_0 for it to be credible) in favour of H_1 and you do not buy the firm. If $\bar{x}$ lies above this decision point then H_0 is not rejected and you go ahead with

Fig. 6.1 *The two different types of error*

	True situation	
Decision	H_0 true	H_0 false
Accept H_0	Correct decision	Type II error
Reject H_0	Type I error	Correct decision

Fig. 6.2 *The sampling distributions of $\bar{x}$ under H_0 and H_1*

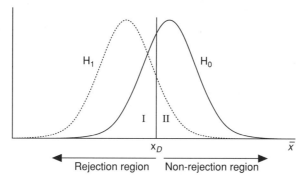

Rejection region   Non-rejection region

the purchase. Such a decision point is shown in Fig. 6.2, denoted by x_D. To the left of x_D lies the **rejection (of H_0) region**; to the right lies the **non-rejection region**.

Based on this point, we can see the probabilities of Type I and Type II errors. The area under the H_0 distribution to the left of x_D, labelled I, shows the probability of rejecting H_0 given that it is in fact true: a Type I error. The area under the H_1 distribution to the right of x_D, labelled II, shows the probability of a Type II error: not rejecting H_0 when it is in fact false (and H_1 is true).

Shifting the decision line to the right or left alters the balance of these probabilities. Moving the line to the right increases the probability of a Type I error but reduces the probability of a Type II error. Moving the line to the left has the opposite effect.

The Type I error probability can be calculated for any value of x_D. Suppose we set x_D to a value of 4,950. Using the distribution of $\bar{x}$ given in equation (6.1) above, the area under the distribution to the left of 4,950 is obtained using the z-score:

$$(6.2) \quad z = \frac{x_D - \mu}{\sqrt{s^2/n}} = \frac{4,950 - 5,000}{\sqrt{280^2/26}} = -0.91$$

From the tables of the standard Normal distribution we find that the probability of a Type I error is 18.1%. Unfortunately, the Type II error probability cannot be established because the exact position of the distribution under H_1 is unknown. Therefore we cannot decide on the appropriate position of x_D by some balance of the two error probabilities.

The convention therefore is to set the position of x_D by using a Type I error probability of 5%, known as the **significance level**[1] of the test. In other words, we are prepared to accept a 5% probability of rejecting H_0 when it is in fact true. This allows us to establish the position of x_D. From Table A2 we find that $z = -1.64$ cuts off the bottom 5% of the distribution, so the decision line should be 1.64 standard errors below 5,000. The value -1.64 is known as the **critical value** of the test. We therefore obtain

$$(6.3) \quad x_D = 5,000 - 1.64\sqrt{280^2/26} = 4,910$$

Since the sample mean of 4,900 lies below 4,910 we reject H_0 *at the 5% significance*

[1] The term **size** of the test is also used, not to be confused with the sample size. We use the term significance level in this text.

level or equivalently we reject *with 95% confidence*. The significance level is generally denoted by the symbol α and the complement of this, given by $1 - \alpha$, is known as the confidence level (as used in the confidence interval).

An equivalent procedure would be to calculate the z-score associated with the sample mean, known as the **test statistic**, and then compare this to the critical value of the test. This allows the hypothesis testing procedure to be broken down into five neat steps:

(1) Write down the null and alternative hypotheses:

$H_0: \mu = 5{,}000$
$H_1: \mu < 5{,}000$

(2) Choose the significance level of the test, conventionally $\alpha = 0.05$ or 5%.
(3) Look up the critical value of the test from statistical tables, based on the chosen significance level. $z^* = 1.64$ is the critical value in this case.
(4) Calculate the test statistic:

$$(6.4) \quad z = \frac{\bar{x} - \mu}{\sqrt{s^2 / n}} = \frac{-100}{\sqrt{280^2 / 26}} = -1.82$$

(5) Decision rule. Compare the test statistic with the critical value: if $z < -z^*$ reject H_0 in favour of H_1. Since $-1.82 < -1.64$ H_0 is rejected with 95% confidence. Note that we use $-z^*$ here because we are dealing with the left-hand tail of the distribution.

One tail and two tail tests

In the above example the rejection region for the test consisted of one tail of the distribution of $\bar{x}$, since the buyer was only concerned about turnover being less than claimed. For this reason it is known as a **one tail test**. Suppose now that an accountant is engaged to sell the franchise and wants to check the claim about turnover before advertising the business for sale. In this case she would be concerned about turnover being either below *or* above 5,000.

This would now become a **two tail test** with the null and alternative hypotheses being

$H_0: \mu = 5{,}000$
$H_1: \mu \neq 5{,}000$

The null hypothesis is a **simple** hypothesis since it concerns only a unique value of μ. The alternative is a **composite** hypothesis which refers to a range of possible values of μ, all values except 5,000 in fact. Now there are two rejection regions for the test. Either a very low sample mean *or* a very high one will serve to reject the null hypothesis. The situation is presented graphically in Fig. 6.3.

The distribution of $\bar{x}$ under H_0 is the same as before, but under the alternative hypothesis the distribution could be shifted either to the left or to the right, as depicted. If the significance level is still chosen to be 5%, then the *two* rejection regions consist of the two extremes of the distribution under H_0, containing 2.5% in each tail (hence 5% in total). This gives the probability of a Type I error of 5% as before.

The critical value of the test therefore becomes $z^* = 1.96$, the value which cuts off 2.5% in each tail of the standard Normal distribution. Only if the test statistic falls

Fig. 6.3 *A two tail hypothesis test*

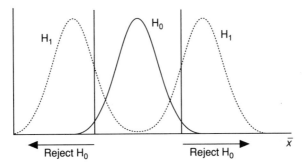

Reject H$_0$ Reject H$_0$

into one of the rejection regions beyond 1.96 standard errors from the mean is H$_0$ rejected.

The test statistic is the same as in the previous example, $z = -1.82$ so that the null hypothesis cannot be rejected in this case. To recap, the five steps of the test are:

(1) H$_0$: $\mu = 5,000$
    H$_1$: $\mu \neq 5,000$
(2) Choose the significance level: $\alpha = 0.05$.
(3) Look up the critical value: $z^* = 1.96$.
(4) Evaluate the test statistic:

$$z = \frac{-100}{\sqrt{280^2/26}} = -1.82$$

(5) Compare test statistic and critical values: if $z < -z^*$ or $z > z^*$ reject H$_0$ in favour of H$_1$. In this case $-1.82 > -1.96$ so H$_0$ cannot be rejected with 95% confidence.

One and two tail tests therefore differ only at steps 1 and 3. Note that we have come to different conclusions according to whether a one or two tail test was used, with the same sample evidence. There is nothing wrong with this, however, for there are different interpretations of the two results. If the investor always uses his rule, he will miss out on 5% of good investment opportunities, when sales are (by chance) low. He will never miss out on a good opportunity because the investment appears too good (i.e. sales by chance are very high). For the accountant, 5% of the firms with sales averaging £5,000 will not be advertised as such, *either* because sales appear too low *or* because they appear too high.

It is tempting on occasion to use a one tail test because of the sample evidence. For example, the accountant might look at the sample evidence above and decide that the franchise operation can only have true sales less than or equal to 5,000. Therefore she uses a one tail test. This is a dangerous practice, since the sample evidence is used to help formulate the hypothesis, which is then tested on that same evidence. This is going round in circles; the hypothesis should be chosen *independently* of the evidence which is then used to test it. Presumably the accountant would also use a one tail test (with H$_1$: $\mu > 5,000$ as the alternative hypothesis) if she noticed that the sample mean were *above* the hypothesised value. In effect therefore she would be using the 10% significance level, not the 5% level, since there would be 5% in each tail of the distribution. She would make a Type I error on 10% of all occasions rather than 5%.

It is acceptable to use a one tail test when you have *independent* information about what the alternative hypothesis should be, or you are not concerned about one side of the distribution (like the investor) and can effectively add that in to the null hypothesis. Otherwise, it is safer to use a two tail test.

The choice of significance level

We justified the choice of the 5% significance level by reference to convention. This is usually a poor argument for anything, but it does have some justification. In an ideal world we would have precisely specified null *and* alternative hypotheses (e.g. we would test H_0: $\mu = 5,000$ against H_1: $\mu = 4,500$, these being the only possibilities). Then we could calculate the probabilities of both Type I *and* Type II errors, for any given decision rule. We could then choose the optimal decision rule, which gave the best compromise between the two types of error. This is reflected in a court of law. In criminal cases, the jury must be convinced of the prosecution's case beyond reasonable doubt, because of the cost of committing a Type I error. In a civil case (libel, for example) the jury need only be convinced *on the balance of probabilities*. In a civil case, the costs of Type I and Type II error are more evenly balanced and so the burden of proof is lessened.

However in practice we usually do not have the luxury of two well specified hypotheses. As in the example, the null hypothesis is precisely specified (it has to be or the test could not be carried out) but the alternative hypothesis is imprecise (composite). Statistical inference is often used not so much as an aid to decision-making but to provide evidence for or against a particular theory, to alter one's degree of belief in the truth of the theory. For example, an economic theory might assert that rising prices are caused by rising wages (the cost-push theory of inflation). The null and alternative hypotheses would be:

H_0 : there is no connection between rising wages and rising prices
H_1 : there is some connection between rising wages and rising prices

(Note that the null has 'no' connection. 'Some' connection is too vague to be the null hypothesis.) Data could be gathered to test this hypothesis (the appropriate methods will be discussed in the chapter on correlation and regression). But what 'decision' rests upon the result of this test? It might be thought that government might make a decision to impose a prices and incomes policy, but if every academic study of inflation led to the imposition or abandonment of a prices and incomes policy there would have been an awful lot of policies! (In fact there *were* a lot of such policies, but not as many as the number of studies of inflation.) No single study is decisive ('more research is needed' is a very common phrase) but each does influence the climate of opinion which may eventually lead to a policy decision. But if a hypothesis test is designed to influence opinion, how is the significance level to be chosen?

It is difficult to trade-off the costs of Type I and Type II errors and the probability of making those errors. A Type I error in this case means concluding that rising wages do cause rising prices when in fact they do not. So what would be the cost of this error, i.e. imposing a prices and incomes policy when in fact it is not needed? It is extremely difficult, if not impossible, to put a figure on it. It would depend on what type of prices and incomes policy were imposed – would wages be frozen or allowed to rise with productivity, how fast would prices be allowed to rise, would company dividends be frozen? The costs of the Type II error would also be problematic (not imposing a needed prices and incomes policy), for they would depend, amongst other things, on what alternative policies might be adopted.

The 5% significance level really does depend upon convention, therefore it cannot be justified by reference to the relative costs of Type I and Type II errors (it is too much to believe that everyone does consider these costs and independently arrives at the conclusion that 5% is the appropriate significance level!). However, the 5% convention does impose some sort of discipline upon research; it sets some kind of standard which all theories (hypotheses) should be measured against. Beware the researcher who reports that a particular hypothesis is rejected at the 8% significance level; it is likely that the significance level was chosen so that the hypothesis could be rejected, which is what the researcher was hoping for in the first place!

The Prob-value approach

Suppose a result is significant at the 4.95% level (i.e. it just meets the 5% convention) and the null hypothesis is rejected. A *very* slight change in the sample data could have meant the result being significant at only the 5.05% level, and the null hypothesis not being rejected. Would we really be happy to alter our belief completely on such fragile results? Most researchers (but not all!) would be cautious if their results were only just significant (or fell just short of significance).

This suggests an alternative approach: the significance level of the test statistic could be reported and the reader could make his own judgements about it. This is known as the **Prob-value** approach, the Prob-value being the significance level of the calculated test statistic. For example, the calculated test statistic for the investor problem was $z = -1.82$ and the associated Prob-value is obtained from Table A2 as 3.44%, i.e. -1.82 cuts off 3.44% in one tail of the standard Normal distribution. This means that the null hypothesis can be rejected at the 3.44% significance level or, alternatively expressed, with 96.56% confidence.

Notice that Table A2 gives the Prob-value for a one tail test; for a two tail test the Prob-value should be doubled. Thus for the accountant, using the two tail test, the significance level is 6.88% and this is the level at which the null hypothesis can be rejected. Alternatively we could say we reject the null with 93.12% confidence. This does not meet the standard 5% criterion (for the significance level) which is most often used.

Significance, effect size and power

Researchers usually look for 'significant' results. Academic papers report that 'the results are significant' or that 'the coefficient is significantly different from zero at the 5% significance level'. It is vital to realise that the word 'significant' is used here in the *statistical* sense and not in its everyday sense of being *important*. Something can be statistically significant yet still unimportant.

Suppose that we have some more data about the business examined earlier. Data for 100 franchises have been uncovered, revealing an average weekly turnover of £4,975 with standard deviation £143. Can we reject the hypothesis that the average weekly turnover is £5,000? The test statistic is

$$z = \frac{4,975 - 5,000}{\sqrt{143^2 / 100}} = -1.75$$

Since this is less than $-z^* = -1.64$ the null is rejected with 95% confidence. True average weekly turnover is less than £5,000. However, the difference is only £25 per week, which is 0.5% of £5,000. Common sense would suggest that the difference may be unimportant, even if it is significant in the statistical sense. One should not interpret statistical results in terms of significance alone, therefore; one should also look at the size of the difference (sometimes known as the **effect size**) and ask whether it is important or not.

This problem with hypothesis testing paradoxically gets worse as the sample size increases. For example, if 250 observations reveal average sales of 4,985 with standard deviation 143, the null would (just) be rejected at 5% significance. In fact, given a large enough sample size we can virtually guarantee to reject the null hypothesis even before we have gathered the data. This can be seen from equation (6.4) for the z-score test statistic: as n gets larger, the test statistic also inevitably gets larger.

A related way of considering the effect of increasing sample size is via the concept of the **power** of a test. This is defined as

(6.5)   **Power** of a test $= 1 - \Pr(\text{Type II error}) = 1 - \beta$

where β is the symbol conventionally used to indicate the probability of a Type II error. Since a Type II error is defined as not rejecting H_0 when false (equivalent to rejecting H_1 when true), power is the probability of rejecting H_0 when false (if H_0 is false, it must be *either* accepted *or* rejected; hence these probabilities sum to one). This is one of the correct decisions identified earlier, associated with the lower right-hand box in Fig. 6.1. The power of a test is therefore given by the area under the H_1 distribution, to the left of the decision line, as illustrated in Fig. 6.4 (for a one tail test).

It is generally desirable to maximise the power of a test, as long as the probability of a Type I error is not raised in the process. There are essentially three ways of doing this:

- Avoid situations where the null and alternative hypotheses are very similar, i.e. the hypothesised means are not far apart (a small effect size).
- Use a large sample size. This reduces the sampling variance of $\bar{x}$ (under both H_0 and H_1) so the two distributions become more distinct.
- Use good sampling methods which have small sampling variances. This has a similar effect to increasing the sample size.

Unfortunately, in economics and business the data are very often given in advance and there is little or no control possible over the sampling procedures. This leads to a neglect of consideration of power, unlike in psychology, for example, where the experiment can often be designed by the researcher. The gathering of sample data will be covered in detail in Chapter 7.

Other hypothesis tests

We now proceed to consider a number of different types of hypothesis test, all involving the same principles but differing in detail. This is similar to the exposition

Fig. 6.4 *The power of a test*

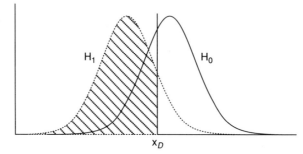

in the last chapter covering, in turn, tests of a proportion, tests of the difference of two means and proportions, and finally problems involving small sample sizes.

Testing a proportion

A car manufacturer claims that no more than 10% of its cars should need repairs in the first three years of their life. A random sample of 50 three-year-old cars found that eight had required attention. Does this contradict the maker's claim?

This problem can be handled in a very similar way to the methods used for a mean. The key, once again, is to recognise the sample proportion as a random variable with an associated probability distribution. From Chapter 5 (equation (5.9)), the sampling distribution of the sample proportion in large samples is given by

$$(6.6) \quad p \sim N\left(\pi, \frac{\pi(1-\pi)}{n}\right)$$

In this case $\pi = 0.10$ (under the null hypothesis, the maker's claim). The sample data are

$p = 8/50 = 0.16$
$n = 50$

The hypothesis test is set out along the same lines as for a sample mean:

(1) $H_0 : \pi = 0.10$
  $H_1 : \pi > 0.10$ (the only concern is the manufacturer not matching his claim).
(2) Significance level: $\alpha = 0.05$.
(3) The critical value of the one tail test at the 5% significance level is $z^* = 1.64$, obtained from the standard Normal table.
(4) The test statistic is

$$z = \frac{p - \pi}{\sqrt{\frac{\pi(1-\pi)}{n}}} = \frac{0.16 - 0.10}{\sqrt{\frac{0.1 \times 0.9}{50}}} = 1.41$$

(5) Since the test statistic is less than the critical value, it falls into the non-rejection region. The null hypothesis is not rejected by the data. The manufacturer's claim is not unreasonable.

Note that for this problem, the rejection region lies in the *upper* tail of the distribution because of the 'greater than' inequality in the alternative hypothesis. The null hypothesis is therefore rejected in this case if $z > z^*$.

Testing the difference of two means

Suppose a car company wishes to compare the performance of its two factories producing an identical model of car. The factories are equipped with the same machinery but their outputs might differ due to managerial ability, labour relations, etc. Senior management wishes to know if there is any difference between the two factories. Output is monitored for 30 days, chosen at random, with the following results:

	Factory 1	Factory 2
Average daily output	420	408
Standard deviation of daily output	25	20

Does this produce sufficient evidence of a real difference between the factories, or does the difference between the samples simply reflect random differences such as minor breakdowns of machinery? The information at our disposal may be summarised as

$\bar{x}_1 = 420$ $\bar{x}_2 = 408$
$s_1 = 25$ $s_2 = 20$
$n_1 = 30$ $n_2 = 30$

The hypothesis test to be conducted concerns the difference between the factories' outputs, so the appropriate random variable to examine is $\bar{x}_1 - \bar{x}_2$. From Chapter 5 (equation (5.12)), this has the following distribution, in large samples:

$$(6.7) \quad \bar{x}_1 - \bar{x}_2 \sim N\left(\mu_1 - \mu_2, \ \frac{\sigma_1^2}{n_1} + \frac{\sigma_2^2}{n_2}\right)$$

The population variances, σ_1^2 and σ_2^2, may be replaced by their sample estimates s_1^2, and s_2^2, if the former are unknown, as here. The hypothesis test is therefore as follows.

(1) $H_0: \mu_1 - \mu_2 = 0$
    $H_1: \mu_1 - \mu_2 \neq 0$

The null hypothesis posits no real difference between the factories. This is a two tail test since there is no *a priori* reason to believe one factory is better than the other, apart from the sample evidence.

(2) Significance level: $\alpha = 1\%$. This is chosen since the management does not want to interfere unless it is really confident of some difference between the factories. In order to favour the null hypothesis, a lower significance level than the conventional 5% is set.

(3) The critical value of the test is $z^* = 2.57$. This cuts off 0.5% in each tail of the standard Normal distribution.

(4) The test statistic is

$$z = \frac{(\bar{x}_1 - \bar{x}_2) - (\mu_1 - \mu_2)}{\sqrt{\dfrac{s_1^2}{n_1} + \dfrac{s_2^2}{n_2}}} = \frac{(420 - 408) - 0}{\sqrt{\dfrac{25^2}{30} + \dfrac{20^2}{30}}} = 2.05$$

Note that this is of the same form as in the single sample cases. The hypothesised value of the difference (zero in this case) is subtracted from the sample difference and this is divided by the standard error of the random variable.

(5) Decision rule: $z < z^*$ so the test statistic falls into the non-rejection region. There does not appear to be a significant difference between the two factories.

A number of remarks about this example should be made. First it should be noted that it is not necessary for the two sample sizes to be equal (although they are in the example). 45 days output from factory 1 and 35 days from factory 2, for example, could have been sampled. Second, the values of s_1^2 and s_2^2 do not have to be equal. They are respectively estimates of σ_1^2 and σ_2^2 and and although the null hypothesis asserts that $\mu_1 = \mu_2$ it does not assert that the variances are equal. Management wants to know if the *average* levels of output are the same; it is not concerned about daily fluctuations in output. A test of the hypothesis of equal variances is set out in Chapter 8.

The final point to consider is whether all the necessary conditions for the correct application of this test have been met. The example noted that the 30 days were chosen at random. If the 30 days sampled were consecutive we might doubt whether the observations were truly independent. Low output on one day (due to a mechanical breakdown, for example) might influence the following day's output (if a special effort were made to catch up on lost production, for example).

Testing the difference of two proportions

In a comparison of two holiday companies' customers, of the 75 who went with Happy Days Tours, 45 said they were satisfied, while 48 of the 90 who went with Fly by Night Holidays were satisfied. Is there a significant difference between the companies?

This problem can be handled by a hypothesis test on the difference of two sample proportions. The procedure is as follows. The sample evidence is

$p_1 = 45/75$ $n_1 = 75$
$p_2 = 48/90$ $n_2 = 90$

The hypothesis test is as follows

(1) $H_0 : \pi_1 - \pi_2 = 0$
     $H_1 : \pi_1 - \pi_2 \neq 0$
(2) Significance level: $\alpha = 5\%$.
(3) Critical value: $z^* = 1.96$.
(4) Test statistic: The distribution of $p_1 - p_2$ is

$$p_1 - p_2 \sim N\left(\pi_1 - \pi_2, \frac{\pi_1(1-\pi_1)}{n_1} + \frac{\pi_2(1-\pi_2)}{n_2} \right)$$

so the test statistic is

$$(6.8) \quad z = \frac{(p_1 - p_2) - (\pi_1 - \pi_2)}{\sqrt{\frac{\pi_1(1-\pi_1)}{n_1} + \frac{\pi_2(1-\pi_2)}{n_2}}}$$

However, π_1 and π_2 in the denominator of equation (6.8) have to be replaced by estimates from the samples. They cannot simply be replaced by p_1 and p_2 because these are unequal; to do so would contradict the null hypothesis that they *are* equal. Since the null hypothesis is assumed to be true (for the moment), it doesn't make sense to use a test statistic which explicitly supposes the null hypothesis to be false. Therefore π_1 and π_2 are replaced by an estimate of their common value which is denoted $\hat{\pi}$ and whose formula is

$$(6.9) \quad \hat{\pi} = \frac{n_1 p_1 + n_2 p_2}{n_1 + n_2}$$

This yields

$$\hat{\pi} = \frac{75 \times 0.6 + 90 \times 0.533}{75 + 90} = 0.564$$

This in fact is just the proportion of all customers who were satisfied, 93 out of 165. The test statistic therefore becomes

$$z = \frac{0.6 - 0.533 - 0}{\sqrt{\dfrac{0.564 \times (1 - 0.564)}{75} + \dfrac{0.564 \times (1 - 0.564)}{90}}} = 0.86$$

(5) The test statistic is less than the critical value so the null hypothesis cannot be rejected with 95% confidence. There is not sufficient evidence to demonstrate a difference between the two companies' performance.

Hypothesis tests with small samples

As with estimation, slightly different methods have to be employed when the sample size is small ($n < 25$) and the population variance is unknown. When both of these conditions are satisfied the t distribution must be used rather than the Normal, so a t-test is conducted rather than a z-test. This means consulting tables of the t distribution to obtain the critical value of a test, but otherwise the methods are similar. These methods will be applied to hypotheses about sample means only, since they are inappropriate for tests of a sample proportion, as was the case in estimation.

Testing the sample mean

A large chain of supermarkets sells 5,000 packets of cereal in each of its stores each month. It decides to test-market a different brand of cereal in 15 of its stores. After a month the 15 stores have sold an average of 5,200 packets each, with a standard deviation of 500 packets. Should all supermarkets switch to selling the new brand?

The sample information is

$$\bar{x} = 5{,}200, \ s = 500, \ n = 15$$

From Chapter 5 the distribution of the sample mean from a small sample when the population variance is unknown is based upon

$$(6.10) \quad \frac{\bar{x} - \mu}{\sqrt{s^2 / n}} \sim t_v$$

with $v = n - 1$ degrees of freedom. The hypothesis test is based on this formula and is conducted as follows:

(1) H_0: $\mu = 5000$
    H_1: $\mu > 5000$ (only an improvement in sales is relevant).
(2) Significance level: $\alpha = 1\%$ (chosen because the cost of changing brands is high).
(3) The critical value of the t distribution for a one tail test at the 1% significance level with $v = n - 1 = 14$ degrees of freedom is $t^* = 2.62$.
(4) The test statistic is

$$t = \frac{\bar{x} - \mu}{\sqrt{s^2/n}} = \frac{5{,}200 - 5{,}000}{\sqrt{500^2/15}} = 1.55$$

(5) The null hypothesis is not rejected since the test statistic, 1.55, is less than the critical value, 2.62. It would probably be unwise to switch over to the new brand of cereals.

Testing the difference of two means

A survey of 20 British companies found an average annual expenditure on research and development of £3.7m with a standard deviation of £0.6m. A survey of 15 similar German companies found an average expenditure on research and development of £4.2m with standard deviation £0.9m. Does this evidence lend support to the view often expressed that Britain does not invest enough in research and development?

This is a hypothesis about the difference of two means, based on small sample sizes. The test statistic is again based on the t distribution, i.e.

(6.11) $$\frac{\bar{x}_1 - \bar{x}_2 - (\mu_1 - \mu_2)}{\sqrt{\frac{S^2}{n_1} + \frac{S^2}{n_2}}} \sim t_v$$

where S^2 is the pooled variance (as given in equation (5.23)) and the degrees of freedom are given by $v = n_1 + n_2 - 2$.

The hypothesis test procedure is as follows:

(1) $H_0: \mu_1 - \mu_2 = 0$
    $H_1: \mu_1 - \mu_2 < 0$
(2) Significance level: $\alpha = 5\%$.
(3) The critical value of the t distribution at the 5% significance level for a one tail test with $v = n_1 + n_2 - 2 = 33$ degrees of freedom is approximately $t^* = 1.70$.
(4) The test statistic is based on equation (6.11):

$$t = \frac{\bar{x}_1 - \bar{x}_2 - (\mu_1 - \mu_2)}{\sqrt{\frac{S^2}{n_1} + \frac{S^2}{n_2}}} = \frac{3.7 - 4.2 - 0}{\sqrt{\frac{0.55}{20} + \frac{0.55}{15}}} = -1.97$$

where S^2 is the pooled variance, calculated by

$$S^2 = \frac{(n_1 - 1)s_1^2 + (n_2 - 1)s_1^2}{n_1 + n_2 - 2} = \frac{19 \times 0.6^2 + 14 \times 0.9^2}{33} = 0.55$$

(5) The test statistic falls in the rejection region, $t < -t^*$, so the null hypothesis is rejected. The data do support the view that Britain spends less on R & D than Germany.

Are the test procedures valid?

A variety of assumptions underlie each of the tests which we have applied above and it is worth considering in a little more detail whether these assumptions are justified. This will demonstrate that one should not rely upon the statistical tests alone; it is important to retain one's sense of judgement.

The first test concerned the weekly turnover of a series of franchise operations. To justify the use of the Normal distribution underlying the test, the sample observations must be independently drawn. The random errors around the true mean turnover figure should be independent of each other. This might not be the case if, for example, similar events could affect the turnover figures of all franchises.

If one were using time-series data, as in the car factory comparison, similar issues arise. Do the thirty days represent independent observations or might there be an autocorrelation problem (e.g. if the sample days were close together in time)? Suppose that factory 2 suffered a breakdown of some kind which took three days to fix. Output would be reduced on three successive days and factory 2 would almost inevitably appear less efficient than factory 1. The fact that the standard deviation for factory 2 is higher than for factory 1 suggests this could have occurred. A look at the individual sample observations might be worthwhile, therefore. It would have been altogether better if the samples had been collected on randomly chosen days over a longer time period to reduce the danger of this type of problem.

If the two factories both obtain their supplies from a common, but limited, source then the output of one factory might not be independent of the output of the other. A high output of one factory would tend to be associated with a low output from the other, which has little to do with their relative efficiencies. This might leave the average difference in output unchanged but might increase the variance substantially (either a very high positive value of $\bar{x}_1 - \bar{x}_2$ or a very high negative value is obtained). This would lead to a low value of the test statistic and the conclusion of no difference in output. Any real difference in efficiency is masked by the common supplier problem. If the two samples are not independent then the distribution of $\bar{x}_1 - \bar{x}_2$ may not be Normal.

Hypothesis tests and confidence intervals

Formally, two tail hypothesis tests and confidence intervals are equivalent. Any value which lies within the 95% confidence interval around the sample mean cannot be rejected as the 'true' value using the 5% significance level in a hypothesis test. For example, our by now familiar accountant could construct a confidence interval for the firm's sales. This yields the 95% confidence interval

(6.12) [4,792, 5,008]

Notice that the hypothesised value of 5,000 is within this interval and that it was not rejected by the hypothesis test carried out earlier. As long as the same confidence level is used for both procedures, they are equivalent.

Having said this, their interpretation is different. The hypothesis test forces us into the reject/do not reject dichotomy, which is rather a stark choice. We have seen how it becomes more likely that the null hypothesis is rejected as the sample size increases. This problem does not occur with estimation. As the sample size increases the confidence interval gets narrower (around the unbiased point estimate) which is entirely beneficial. The estimation approach also tends to emphasise importance over significance in most people's minds. With a hypothesis test one might know that turnover is significantly different from 5,000 without knowing how far from 5,000 it actually is.

One some occasions a confidence interval is inferior to a hypothesis test, however. Consider the following case. In the UK only 17 out of 465 judges are women (3.7%). The Equal Opportunities Commission commented that since the appointment system is so secretive it is impossible to tell if there is discrimination or not. What can the statistician say about this? No discrimination (in its broadest sense) would mean half of all judges would be women. Thus the hypotheses are

$H_0 : \pi = 0.5$ (no discrimination)
$H_1 : \pi < 0.5$ (discrimination against women)

The sample data are $p = 0.037$, $n = 465$. The z score is

$$z = \frac{p - \pi}{\sqrt{\dfrac{\pi(1-\pi)}{n}}} = \frac{0.037 - 0.5}{\sqrt{\dfrac{0.5 \times 0.5}{465}}} = -19.97$$

This is clearly significant (*and* 3.7% is a long way from 50%!) so the null hypothesis is rejected. There is some form of discrimination somewhere against women (unless women choose not to be judges). But a confidence interval estimate of the 'true' proportion of female judges would be meaningless. To what population is this 'true' proportion related?

The lesson from all this is that there exist differences between confidence intervals and hypothesis tests, despite their formal similarity. Which technique is more appropriate is a matter of judgement for the researcher. With hypothesis testing, the rejection of the null hypothesis at some significance level might actually mean a small (and unimportant) deviation from the hypothesised value. It should be remembered that the rejection of the null hypothesis based on a large sample of data is also consistent with the true value and hypothesised value being quite close together.

Independent and dependent samples

The following example illustrates the differences between **independent samples** (as encountered so far) and **dependent samples** where slightly different methods of analysis are required. The example also illustrates how a particular problem can often be analysed by a variety of statistical methods.

A company introduces a training programme to raise the productivity of its clerical workers, which is measured by the number of invoices processed per day. The company wants to know if the training programme is effective. How should it monitor the programme? There is a variety of ways of going about the task, as follows:

- Take two (random) samples of workers, one trained and one not trained, and compare their productivity.
- Take a sample of workers and compare their productivity before and after training.
- Take two samples of workers, one to be trained and the other not. Compare the improvement of the trained workers with any change in the other group's performance over the same time period.

We shall go through each method in turn, pointing out any possible difficulties.

Two independent samples

Suppose a group of ten workers is trained and compared to a group of ten non-trained workers, with the following data being relevant:

$\bar{x}_T = 25.5$	$\bar{x}_N = 21.00$
$s_T = 2.55$	$s_N = 2.91$
$n_T = 10$	$n_N = 10$

Thus trained workers process 25.5 invoices per day compared to only 21 by non-trained workers. The question is whether this is significant, given that the sample sizes are quite small.

The appropriate test here is a t-test of the difference of two sample means, as follows:

$H_0: \mu_T - \mu_N = 0$
$H_1: \mu_T - \mu_N > 0$

$$t = \frac{25.5 - 21.0}{\sqrt{\dfrac{7.49}{10} + \dfrac{7.49}{10}}} = 3.68$$

(7.49 is S^2, the pooled variance). The t statistic leads to rejection of the null hypothesis; the training programme does seem to be effective.

One problem with this test is that the two samples might not be truly random and thus not properly reflect the effect of the training programme. Poor workers might have been reluctant (and thus refused) to take part in training, departmental managers might have selected better workers for training as some kind of reward, or better workers may have simply volunteered. In a well-designed experiment this should not be allowed to happen, of course, but this does not rule out the possibility. There is also the 5% (significance level) chance of unrepresentative samples being selected and a Type I error occurring.

Paired samples

This is the situation where a sample of workers is tested before and after training. The sample data are as follows:

Worker	1	2	3	4	5	6	7	8	9	10
Before	21	24	23	25	28	17	24	22	24	27
After	23	27	24	28	29	21	24	25	26	28

In this case, the observations in the two samples are paired and this has implications for the method of analysis. One could proceed by assuming these are two independent samples and conduct a t-test. The summary data and results are:

$\bar{x}_B = 23.50$ $\bar{x}_A = 25.5$
$s_B = 3.10$ $s_A = 2.55$
$n_B = 10$ $n_A = 10$

The resulting test statistic is $t_{18} = 1.58$ which is not significant at the 5% level.

There are two problems with this test and its result. First, the two samples are not truly independent, since the before and after measurements refer to the same group of workers. Secondly, nine out of ten workers in the sample have shown an improvement, which is odd in view of the result found above, of no significant improvement. If the training programme really has no effect, then the probability of a single worker showing an improvement is $\frac{1}{2}$. The probability of nine or more workers showing an improvement is, by the Binomial method, $(\frac{1}{2})^{10} \times 10C9 + (\frac{1}{2})^{10}$, which is about one in a hundred. A very unlikely event seems to have occurred.

The test used above is inappropriate because it does not make full use of the information in the sample. It does not reflect the fact, for example, that the before and after scores 21 and 23 relate to the same worker. The Binomial calculation above does reflect this fact. A re-ordering of the data would not affect the t-test result, but would affect the Binomial, since a different number of workers would now show an improvement. Of course the Binomial does not use all the sample information either – it dispenses with the actual productivity data for each worker and replaces it with 'improvement' or 'no improvement'. It disregards the amount of improvement for each worker.

The best use of the sample data comes by measuring the improvement for each worker, as follows (if a worker had deteriorated, this would be reflected by a negative number):

Worker	1	2	3	4	5	6	7	8	9	10
Improvement	2	3	1	3	1	4	0	3	2	1

These new data can be treated by single sample methods, and account is taken both of the actual data values and of the fact that the original samples were dependent (re-ordering of the data would produce different improvement figures). The summary statistics of the new data are as follows:

$\bar{x} = 2.00, s = 1.247, n = 10$

The null hypothesis of no improvement can now be tested as follows:

$H_0: \mu = 0$
$H_1: \mu > 0$

$$t = \frac{2.0 - 0}{\sqrt{\dfrac{1.247^2}{10}}} = 5.07$$

This is significant at the 5% level so the null hypothesis of no improvement is rejected. The correct analysis of the sample data has thus reversed the previous conclusion.

Matters do not end here, however. Although we have discovered an improvement, this might be due to other factors apart from the training programme. For example, if the before and after measurements were taken on different days of the week (that Monday morning feeling . . .), or if one of the days were sunnier, making people feel happier and therefore more productive, this would bias the results. These may seem trivial examples but these effects do exist, for example the 'Friday afternoon car', which has more faults than the average.

The way to solve this problem is to use a control group, so called because extraneous factors are controlled for, in order to isolate the effects of the factor under investigation. In this case, the productivity of the control group would be measured (twice) at the same times as that of the training group, though no training would be given to them. Suppose that the average improvement of the control group were 0.5 invoices per day with standard deviation 1.0 (again for a group of ten). This can be compared with the improvement of the training group via the two sample t-test, giving

$$t = \frac{2.0 - 0.5}{\sqrt{\dfrac{1.13^2}{10} + \dfrac{1.13^2}{10}}} = 2.97$$

(1.13^2 is the pooled variance). This confirms the finding that the training programme is of value.

Discussion of hypothesis testing

The above exposition has served to illustrate how to carry out a hypothesis test and the rationale behind it. However, the methodology has been subject to criticism and it is important to understand this since it gives a greater insight into the meaning of the results of a hypothesis test.

In the previous examples the problem has often been posed as a decision-making one, yet we noted that in many instances no decision is actually taken and therefore it is difficult to justify a particular significance level. Bayesian statisticians would argue that their methods do not suffer from this problem, since the result of their analysis (termed a posterior probability) gives the degree of belief which the researcher has in the truth of the null hypothesis. However, this posterior probability does in part depend upon the prior probability (i.e. before the statistical analysis) that the researcher attaches to the null hypothesis. As noted in Chapter 3, the derivation of the prior probabilities can be difficult.

In practice, most people do not regard the results of a hypothesis test as all-or-nothing proof, but interpret the result on the basis of the quality of the data, the care the researcher has taken in analysing the data, personal experience, and a multitude of other factors. Both schools of thought, classical and Bayesian, introduce subjectivity into the analysis and interpretation of data; classical statisticians in the choice of the significance level (and choice of one or two tail test), Bayesians in their choice of prior probabilities. It is not clear which method is superior, but classical methods have the advantage of being simpler.

Another criticism of hypothesis testing is that it is based on weak methodological foundations. The philosopher Karl Popper argued that theories should be rigorously tested against the evidence, and that strenuous efforts should be made to try to falsify the theory or hypothesis. This methodology is not strictly followed in hypothesis testing, where the researcher's favoured hypothesis is usually the alternative. A conclusion in favour of the alternative hypothesis is arrived at by default, because of the failure of the null hypothesis to survive the evidence.

Consider the researcher who believes that health standards have changed in the last decade. This may be tested by gathering data on health and testing the null hypothesis of no change in health standards against the alternative hypothesis of some change. The researcher's theory thus becomes the alternative hypothesis and is never actually tested against the data. No attempt is made to falsify the (alternative) hypothesis; it gets accepted by default if the null hypothesis falls. *Only* the null hypothesis ever gets tested.

A further problem is the asymmetry between the null and alternative hypotheses. The null hypothesis is that there is *exactly* no change in health standards whereas the alternative hypothesis contains all other possibilities, from a large deterioration to a large improvement. The dice seem loaded against the null hypothesis. Indeed, as noted earlier, if a large enough sample is taken the null hypothesis is almost certain to be rejected, because there is bound to have been *some* change, however small. The large sample size leads to a small standard error (σ^2/n) and thus a large z-score. This suggests that the significance level of a test should decrease as the sample size increases.

These particular problems are avoided by the technique of estimation, which measures the size of the change and focuses attention upon that, rather than upon some accept/reject decision. As the sample size gets larger, the confidence interval narrows and an improved measure of the true change in health standards is obtained. Zero (i.e. no change in health standards) might be in the confidence interval or it might not; it is not the central issue. We might say that an estimate tells us what the value of a population parameter *is*, while a hypothesis test tells us what it is *not*. Thus the techniques of estimation and hypothesis testing put different emphasis upon interpretation of the results, even though they are formally identical.

EXERCISES

Exercise 1

Answer true or false, with reasons if necessary.

(a) There is no way of reducing the probability of a Type I error without simultaneously increasing the probability of a Type II error.

(b) The probability of a Type I error is associated with an area under the distribution of $\bar{x}$ assuming the null hypothesis to be true.

(c) It is always desirable to minimise the probability of a Type I error.

(d) A larger sample, *ceteris paribus*, will increase the power of a test.

(e) The significance level is the probability of a Type II error.

(f) The confidence level is the probability of a Type II error.

Exercise 2

Consider the investor in the text, seeking out companies with weekly turnover of at least £5,000. He applies a one tail hypothesis test to each firm, using the 5% significance level. State whether each of the following statements is true or false (or not known) and explain why.

(a) 5% of his investments are in companies with less than £5,000 turnover.

(b) 5% of the companies he *fails* to invest in have turnover greater than £5,000 per week.

(c) He invests in 95% of all companies with turnover of £5,000 or over.

Exercise 3

A coin which is either fair or has two heads is to be tossed twice. You decide on the following decision rule: if two heads occur you will conclude it is a two-headed coin, otherwise you will presume it is fair. Write down the null and alternative hypotheses and calculate the probabilities of Type I and Type II errors.

Exercise 4

In comparing two medical treatments for a disease, the null hypothesis is that the two treatments are equally effective. Why does making a Type I error not matter? What significance level for the test should be set as a result?

Exercise 5

A firm receives components from a supplier, which it uses in its own production. The components are delivered in batches of 2,000. The supplier claims that there are only 1% defective components on average from its production. However, production occasionally gets out of control and a batch is produced with 10% defective components. The firm wishes to intercept these low quality batches, so a sample of size 50 is taken from each batch and tested. If two or more defectives are found in the sample then the batch is rejected.

(a) Describe the two types of error the firm might make in assessing batches of components.

(b) Calculate the probability of each type of error given the data above.

(c) If instead, samples of size 30 were taken and the batch rejected if one or more rejects were found, how would the error probabilities be altered?

(d) The firm can alter the two error probabilities by choice of sample size and rejection criteria. How should it set the relative sizes of the error probabilities

   (i)   if the product might affect consumer safety?

   (ii) if there are many competitive suppliers of components?

   (iii) if the costs of replacement under guarantee are high?

Exercise 6

Computer diskettes which do not meet the quality required for high density (1.44 Mb) diskettes are sold as double density diskettes (720 kb) for 80 pence each. High density diskettes are sold for £1.20 each. A firm samples 30 diskettes from each batch of 1,000 and if any fail the quality test the whole batch is sold as double density diskettes. What are the types of error possible and what is the cost to the firm of a type I error?

Exercise 7

Testing the null hypothesis that $\mu = 10$ against $\mu > 10$, a researcher obtains a sample mean of 12 with standard deviation 6 from a sample of 30 observations. Calculate the z-score and the associated prob–value for this test.

Exercise 8

Given the sample data $\bar{x} = 45$, $s = 16$, $n = 50$, at what level of confidence can you reject H_0: $\mu = 40$ against a two–sided alternative?

Exercise 9

What is the power of the test carried out in exercise 3?

Exercise 10

Given the two hypotheses

H_0: $\mu = 400$
H_1: $\mu = 415$

and $\sigma^2 = 1000$ (for both hypotheses),

(a) Draw the distribution of $\bar{x}$ under both hypotheses.

(b) If the decision rule is chosen to be: reject H_0 if $\bar{x} \geq 410$ from a sample of size 40, find the probability of a Type II error and the power of the test.

(c) What happens to these answers as the sample size is increased? Draw a diagram to illustrate.

Exercise 11

Given the following sample data:

$$\bar{x} = 15 \quad s^2 = 270 \quad n = 30$$

test the null hypothesis that the true mean is equal to 12, against a two-sided alternative hypothesis. Draw the distribution of $\bar{x}$ under the null hypothesis and indicate the rejection regions for this test.

Exercise 12

From experience it is known that a certain brand of tyre lasts, on average, 15,000 miles with standard deviation 1,250. A new compound is tried and a sample of 120 tyres yields an average life of 15,150 miles. Are the new tyres an improvement? Use the 5% significance level.

Exercise 13

Test $H_0: \pi = 0.5$ against $H_0: \pi \neq 0.5$ using $p = 0.45$ from a sample of size $n = 35$.

Exercise 14

Test the hypothesis that 10% of your class or lecture group are left-handed.

Exercise 15

Given the following data from two independent samples:

$$\bar{x}_1 = 115 \qquad \bar{x}_2 = 105$$
$$s_1 = 21 \qquad s_2 = 23$$
$$n_1 = 49 \qquad n_2 = 63$$

test the hypothesis of no difference between the population means against the alternative that the mean of population 1 is greater than the mean of population 2.

Exercise 16

A transport company wants to compare the fuel efficiencies of the two types of lorry it operates. It obtains data from samples of the two types of lorry, with the following results:

Type	Average mpg	Std. devn.	Sample size
A	31.0	7.6	33
B	32.2	6.8	40

Test the hypothesis that there is no difference in fuel efficiency, using the 99% confidence level.

Exercise 17

A random sample of 180 men who took the driving test found that 103 passed. A similar sample of 225 women found that 105 passed. Test whether pass rates are the same for men and women.

Exercise 18

(a) A pharmaceutical company testing a new type of pain reliever administered the drug to 30 volunteers experiencing pain. 16 of them said that it eased their pain.

Does this evidence support the claim that the drug is effective in combating pain?

(b) A second group of 40 volunteers were given a placebo instead of the drug. Thirteen of them reported a reduction in pain. Does this new evidence cast doubt upon your previous conclusion?

Exercise 19

(a) A random sample of 20 observations yielded a mean of 40 and standard deviation 10. Test the hypothesis that $\mu = 45$ against the alternative that it is not. Use the 5% significance level.

(b) What assumption are you implicitly making in carrying out this test?

Exercise 20

A photo processing company sets a quality standard of no more than 10 complaints per week on average. A random sample of 8 weeks showed an average of 13.6 complaints, with standard deviation 6.3. Is the firm achieving its quality objective?

Exercise 21

Two samples are drawn. The first has a mean of 150, variance 50 and sample size 12. The second has mean 130, variance 30 and sample size 15. Test the hypothesis that they are drawn from populations with the same mean.

Exercise 22

(a) A consumer organisation is testing two different brands of battery. A sample of 15 of brand A shows an average useful life of 410 hours with a standard deviation of 20 hours. For brand B, a sample of 20 gave an average useful life of 391 hours with standard deviation 26 hours. Test whether there is any significant difference in battery life.

(b) What assumptions are being made about the populations in carrying out this test?

Exercise 23

The output of a group of 11 workers before and after an improvement in the lighting in their factory is as follows:

Before	52	60	58	58	53	51	52	59	60	53	55
After	56	62	63	50	55	56	55	59	61	58	56

Test whether there is a significant improvement in performance

(a) assuming these are independent samples

(b) assuming they are dependent.

Exercise 24

Another group of workers were tested at the same times, although their department *also* introduced rest breaks into the working day.

Before	51	59	51	53	58	58	52	55	61	54	55
After	54	63	55	57	63	63	58	60	66	57	59

Does the introduction of rest days alone appear to improve performance?

Exercise 25

Discuss in general terms how you might 'test' the following:

(a) astrology

(b) extra-sensory perception

(c) the proposition that company takeovers increase profits.

Exercise 26

Project: Can your class tell the difference between tap water and bottled water? Set up an experiment as follows: fill r glasses with tap water and $n - r$ glasses with bottled water. The subject has to guess which is which. If she gets more than p correct, you conclude she can tell the difference. Write up a report of the experiment including:

(a) a description of the experimental procedure,

(b) your choice of n, r, and p, with reasons,

(c) the power of your test,

(d) your conclusions.

Exercise 27

Computer project: Use the $=RAND()$ function in your spreadsheet to create 100 samples of size 25 (which are effectively all from the same population). Compute the mean and standard deviation of each sample. Calculate the z-score for each sample, using a hypothesised mean of 0.5 (since the $=RAND()$ function chooses a random number in the range 0 to 1).

(a) How many of the z-scores would you expect to exceed 1.96 in absolute value? Explain why.

(b) How many do exceed this? Is this in line with your prediction?

(c) Graph the sample means and comment upon the shape of the distribution. Shade in the area of the graph beyond $z = \pm 1.96$.

Summary of test statistics
Large samples

This section collects together all the test statistics formulae for easy reference.

1. The mean:

$$z = \frac{\bar{x} - \mu}{\sqrt{\sigma^2 / n}} \text{ or } z = \frac{\bar{x} - \mu}{\sqrt{s^2 / n}}$$

(2) The proportion:

$$z = \frac{p - \pi}{\sqrt{\frac{\pi(1 - \pi)}{n}}}$$

(3) The difference of two means:

$$z = \frac{\left(\bar{x}_1 - \bar{x}_2\right) - \left(\mu_1 - \mu_2\right)}{\sqrt{\dfrac{\sigma_1^2}{n_1} + \dfrac{\sigma_2^2}{n_2}}} \quad \text{or} \quad z = \frac{\left(\bar{x}_1 - \bar{x}_2\right) - \left(\mu_1 - \mu_2\right)}{\sqrt{\dfrac{s_1^2}{n_1} + \dfrac{s_2^2}{n_2}}}$$

(4) The difference of two proportions:

$$z = \frac{\left(p_1 - p_2\right) - \left(\pi_1 - \pi_2\right)}{\sqrt{\dfrac{\hat{\pi}\left(1 - \hat{\pi}\right)}{n_1} + \dfrac{\hat{\pi}\left(1 - \hat{\pi}\right)}{n_2}}} \quad \text{where} \quad \hat{\pi} = \frac{n_1 p_1 + n_2 p_2}{n_1 + n_2}$$

Small samples with population variance unknown

(5) The mean:

$$t = \frac{\bar{x} - \mu}{\sqrt{s^2 / n}}$$

where the degrees of freedom are given by $v = n - 1$.

(6) The difference of two means:

$$t = \frac{\bar{x}_1 - \bar{x}_2 - \left(\mu_1 - \mu_2\right)}{\sqrt{\dfrac{S^2}{n_1} + \dfrac{S^2}{n_2}}} \quad \text{where} \quad S^2 = \frac{\left(n_1 - 1\right)s_1^2 + \left(n_2 - 1\right)s_2^2}{n_1 + n_2 - 2}$$

is the pooled variance and the degrees of freedom are given by $v = n_1 + n_2 - 2$.

7

DATA COLLECTION AND SAMPLING METHODS

Introduction

In this chapter we do two things:

- provide some simple advice about using **secondary data sources**, and
- give an introductory account of **sampling methods**.

When conducting statistical research, there are two ways of proceeding:

(1) use secondary data sources, such as the UN Yearbook, or
(2) collect sample data personally, a **primary data source**.

(There is a third and better way, which is to employ a research assistant.) Using secondary data sources sounds simple, but it is easy to waste valuable time by making elementary errors. The first part of this chapter provides some simple advice to help you avoid such mistakes.

Much of this text has been concerned with the analysis of sample evidence and the inferences that can be drawn from it. It has been stressed that this evidence must come from randomly drawn samples and, although the notion of randomness was discussed in Chapter 4, the precise nature of a random sample has not been set out.

The second part of this chapter is therefore concerned with the problems of collecting sample survey data prior to its analysis. The decision to collect the data personally depends upon the type of problem faced, the current availability of data relating to the problem and the time and cost needed to conduct a survey. It should not be forgotten that the first question that needs answering is whether the answer obtained is worth the cost of finding it. It is probably not worthwhile for the government to spend £50,000 to find out how many biscuits people eat, on average (this is not to say this hasn't been done . . .). The sampling procedure is always subject to some limit on cost, therefore, and the researcher is trying to obtain the best value for money.

Using secondary data sources

Much of the research in economics is based on **secondary data sources**, i.e. data which the researcher did not collect herself. The data may be in the form of official statistics such as those published in *Economic Trends* or they may come from unofficial surveys. In either case one has to use the data as presented; there is no control over sampling procedures.

It may seem easy enough to look up some figures in a publication, but there are a number of pitfalls for the unwary. The following advice comes from experience, some of it painful, and it may help you to avoid wasting time and effort.

Make sure you collect the right data

This may seem obvious, but most variables can be measured in a variety of different ways. Suppose you want to measure the cost of labour (over time) to firms. Should you use the wage rate or earnings? The latter includes payment for extra hours such as overtime payments and reflects general changes in the length of the working week. Is the wage measured per hour or per week? Does it include part-time workers? If so, a trend in the proportion of part-timers will bias the wage series. Does the series cover all workers, men only, or women only? Again, changes in the composition will influence the wage series. What about tax and social security costs? Are they included? There are many questions one could ask.

One needs to have a clear idea therefore of the precise variable one needs to collect. This will presumably depend upon the issue in question. Economic theory might provide some guidance: for instance, theory suggests that firms care about *real* wage rates (i.e. after taking account of inflation) so this is what one should measure. Check the definition of any series you collect (this is often at the back of the publication, or in a separate supplement giving explanatory notes and definitions). Make sure that the definition has not changed over the time period you require: the definition of unemployment used in the UK changed about twenty times in the 1980s, generally with the effect of reducing *measured* unemployment, even if actual unemployment was unaffected. In the UK the geographical coverage of data may vary: one series may relate to the UK, another to Great Britain and yet another to England and Wales. Care should obviously be taken if one is trying to compare such series.

Try to get the most up-to-date figures

Many macroeconomic series are revised as more information becomes available. The balance of payments serves as a good example. The first edition of this book showed the balance of payments (current balance, in £m. for the UK) for 1970, as published in successive years, as follows:

1971	1972	1973	1974	1975	1976	1977	1978	. . .	1986
579	681	692	707	735	733	695	731	. . .	795

The difference between the largest and smallest figures is of the order of 37%, a wide range. The latest figure for 1970 (from the 1993 edition of *Economic Trends Annual Supplement*) gives £821m. which is 42% higher than the initial estimate. Most series are better than this. The balance of payments is hard to measure because it is the small difference between two large numbers, exports and imports. A 5% increase in measured exports and a 5% decrease in measured imports could thus change the measured balance by 100% or more.

One should always try to get the most up-to-date figures, therefore, which often means working *backwards* through data publications, i.e. use the current issue first and get data back as far as is available, then get the previous issue to go back a little further, etc. This can be tedious but it will also give some idea of the reliability of the data from the size of data revisions.

Keep a record of your data sources

You should always keep *precise* details of where you obtained each item of data. If you need to go back to the original publication (to check on the definition of a series, for example) you will then be able to find it easily. It is easy to spend hours (if not *days*) trying to find the source of some interesting numbers that you wish to update. 'Precise details' means the name of the publication, issue number or date, and table or page number. It also helps to keep the library reference number of the publication if it is obscure. It is best to take a photocopy of the data (but check copyright restrictions) rather than just copy it down, if possible.

Keeping data in *Excel* or another spreadsheet

Spreadsheets are ideal for keeping your data. It is often a good idea to keep the data all together in one worksheet and extract portions of them as necessary and analyse them in another worksheet. Alternatively, it is usually quite easy to transfer data from the spreadsheet to another program (e.g. *Minitab* or *SPSS*) for more sophisticated analysis. In most spreadsheets you can attach a note to any cell, so you can use this to keep a record of the source of each observation, changes of definition, etc. Thus you can retain all the information about your data together in one place.

Electronic sources of data

A short-cut way of obtaining data is to use *electronic* data sources. A lot of data can now be obtained either on-line or on diskette, which has a number of advantages. First, it saves a lot of time. Secondly, it avoids errors during input. Thirdly, the data should have all the latest revisions and a consistent series over time can be obtained. Some data can be obtained free but other data, particularly if it has commercial value, must be paid for. There may also be restrictions on access to or use of the data, which should be observed. Some useful sources of electronic data are:

(1) The CSO databank – contains most macroeconomic data series for the UK, both annual and quarterly (and sometimes monthly), back to about 1948. These data are available both on-line and on disk. See *Economic Trends Annual Supplement* or other UK government statistical publications for further details.

(2) The 'Heston–Summers' dataset contains a wide range of mainly macroeconomic variables for 138 countries, going back to 1950. Particular care has been taken to ensure that the data are as comparable as possible across countries. Further information can be found in R. Summers and A. Heston, The Penn World Table (Mark 5): an expanded set of international comparisons, 1950–1987, *Quarterly Journal of Economics*, pp. 1–41 (May 1991). The data are available on disk or via the Internet (ask your computing service about this).

(3) A useful guide to on-line sources is by Bill Goffe, Resources for economists on the Internet, *Journal of Economic Perspectives*, Summer 1994. This article can also be obtained over the Internet. The Internet is a world-wide computer network on which a vast amount of information is available. The major difficulty appears to be finding the information you want amongst the vast amount available.

Collecting primary data

Primary data are data that you have collected yourself from original sources, often by means of a sample survey. This has the advantage that you can design the questionnaire to include the questions of interest to you and you have total control over all aspects of data collection. You can also choose the size of the sample (as long as you have sufficient funds available) so as to achieve the desired width of any confidence intervals.

Almost all surveys rely upon some method of sampling, whether random or not. The probability distributions which have been used in previous chapters as the basis of the techniques of estimation and hypothesis testing rely upon the samples having been drawn at random from the population. If this is not the case, then the formulae for confidence intervals, hypothesis tests, etc. are incorrect and not strictly applicable (they may be reasonable approximations but it is difficult to know how reasonable). In addition, the results about the bias and precision of estimators will be incorrect. For example, suppose an estimate of the average expenditure on repairs and maintenance by car owners is obtained from a sample survey. A poor estimate would arise if only Rolls-Royce owners were sampled, since they are not representative of the population as a whole. The precision of the estimator (the sample mean, $\bar{x}$) is likely to be poor because the mean of the sample could either be very low (Rolls-Royce cars are very reliable so rarely need repairs) or very high (if they do break down the high quality of the car necessitates a costly repair). This means the confidence interval estimate will be very wide and thus imprecise. It is not immediately obvious if the estimator would be biased upwards or downwards.

Thus some form of random sampling method is needed to be able to use the theory of the probability distributions of random variables. Nor should it be believed that the theory of random sampling can be ignored if a very large sample is taken, as the following cautionary tale shows. In 1936 the *Literary Digest* tried to predict the result of the forthcoming US election by sending out 10 million mail questionnaires. Two million were returned, but even with this enormous sample size Roosevelt's vote was incorrectly estimated by a margin of 19 percentage points. The problem is that those who respond to questionnaires are not a random sample of those who receive them.

The meaning of random sampling

The definition of random sampling is that every element of the population should have a known, non-zero probability of being included in the sample. The problem with the sample of cars used above was that Ford cars (for example) had a zero probability of being included. Many sampling procedures give an equal probability of being selected to each member of the population but this is not an essential requirement. It is possible to adjust the sample data to take account of unequal probabilities of selection. If, for example, Rolls-Royce had a much greater chance of being included than Ford, then the estimate of the population mean would be calculated as a weighted average of the sample observations, with greater weight being given to 'Ford' observations than to 'Rolls-Royce' observations. A very simple illustration of this is given below. Suppose that for the population we have the following data:

	Rolls-Royce	Ford
Number in population	20,000	2,000,000
Annual repair bill	£1,000	£200

Then the average repair bill is

$$\mu = \frac{20,000 \times 1,000 + 2,000,000 \times 200}{2,020,000} = 207.92$$

Suppose the sample data are as follows:

	Rolls-Royce	Ford
Number in sample	20	40
Probability of selection	1/1,000	1/50,000
Repair bill	£990	£205

To calculate the average repair bill from the sample data we use a weighted average, using the relative population sizes as weights, not the sample sizes:

$$\bar{x} = \frac{20,000 \times 990 + 2,000,000 \times 205}{2,020,000} = 212.77$$

If the sample sizes were used as weights the average would come out at £466.67, which is substantially incorrect.

As long as the probability of being in the sample is known (and hence the relative population sizes known), the weight can be derived; but if the probability is zero this procedure breaks down.

Other theoretical assumptions necessary for deriving the probability distribution of the sample mean or proportion are that the population is of infinite size and that each observation is independently drawn. In practice the former condition is never satisfied since no population is of infinite size, but most populations are large enough that it does not matter. For each observation to be independently drawn (i.e. the fact of one observation being drawn does not alter the probability of others in the sample being drawn) strictly requires that sampling be done with replacement, i.e. each observation drawn is returned to the population before the next observation is drawn. Again in practice this is often not the case, sampling being done without replacement, but again this is of negligible practical importance.

On occasion the population is quite small and the sample constitutes a substantial fraction of it. In these circumstances the **finite population correction (fpc)** should be applied to the formula for the variance of $\bar{x}$, the fpc being given by

(7.1) $\text{fpc} = (1 - n/N)$

where N is the population size and n the sample size. The table below illustrates its usage:

Variance of $\bar{x}$ from infinite population	Variance of $\bar{x}$ from finite population	Example values of *fpc*			
		$n = 20$ $N = 50$	25 100	50 1,000	100 10,000
σ^2/n	$\sigma^2/n \times (1-n/N)$	0.60	0.75	0.95	0.99

The finite population correction serves to narrow the confidence interval because a sample size of (say) 25 reveals more about a population of 100 than about a population of 100,000, so there is less uncertainty about population parameters. When the sample size constitutes only a small fraction of the population (e.g. 5% or less) the finite population correction can be ignored in practice. If the whole population is sampled ($n = N$) then the variance becomes zero and there is no uncertainty about the population mean.

A further important aspect of random sampling occurs when there are two samples to be analysed, when it is important that the two samples are independently drawn. This means that the drawing of the first sample does not influence the drawing of the second sample. This is a necessary condition for the derivation of the probability distribution of the difference between the sample means (or proportions).

Types of random sample

The meaning and importance of randomness in the context of sampling has been explained. However, there are various different types of sampling, all of them random, but which have different statistical properties. Some methods lead to greater precision of the estimates, while others can lead to considerable cost savings in the collection of the sample data, but at the cost of lower precision. The aim of sampling is usually to obtain the most precise estimates of the parameter in question, but the best method of sampling will depend on the circumstances of each case. If it is costly to sample individuals, a sampling method which lowers cost may allow a much larger sample size to be drawn and thus good (precise) estimates to be obtained, even though the method is inherently not very precise. These issues are examined in more detail below, as a number of different sampling methods are examined.

Simple random sampling

This type of sampling has the property that every possible sample that could be obtained from the population has an equal chance of being selected. It is also the case that each element of the population has an equal probability of being included in the sample, but this is not the defining characteristic of simple random sampling. As will be shown below, there are sampling methods where every member of the population has an equal chance of being selected, but some samples (i.e. certain combinations of population members) can never be selected.

The statistical methods in this book are based upon the assumption of simple random sampling from the population. It leads to the most straightforward formulae for estimation of the population parameters. Although many statistical surveys are not based upon simple random sampling, the use of statistical tests based on simple random sampling is justified since the sampling process is often hypothetical. For example, if one were to compare annual growth rates of two countries over a 30-year period, a z-test on the difference of two sample means (i.e. the average annual growth rate in each country) would be conducted. In a sense the data are not a sample since they are the only possible data for those two countries over that time period. Why not just regard the data as constituting the whole population, therefore? Then it would just be a case of finding which country had the higher growth rate; there would be no uncertainty about it.

The alternative way of looking at the data would be to suppose that there exists some hypothetical population of annual growth rates and that the data for the two countries were drawn by (simple) random sampling from this population. Is this story consistent with the data available? In other words, could the data we have simply arise by chance? If the answer to this is no (i.e. the z-score exceeds the critical value) then there is something causing a difference between the two countries (it is not yet known what that something is, but this will be dealt with in later chapters). In this case it is reasonable to assume that all possible samples have an equal chance of selection, i.e. that simple random sampling takes place. Since the population is hypothetical one might as well suppose it to have an infinite number of members, again required by sampling theory.

Stratified sampling

Returning to the practical business of sampling, one problem with simple random sampling is that it is possible to collect 'bad' samples, i.e. those which are unrepresentative of the population. An example of this is the 'basketball player' problem. i.e. in trying to estimate the average height of the population, the sample (by sheer bad luck) contains a lot of basketball players. One way round this problem is to ensure that the proportion of basketball players in the sample accurately reflects the proportion of basketball players in the population (i.e. very small!). The way to do this is to divide up the population into 'strata' and then to ensure that each stratum is properly represented in the sample. This is best illustrated by means of an example.

A survey of newspaper readership, which is thought to be associated with social class, is to be carried out. People higher up the social scale are more likely to read a newspaper and to read different newspapers from those at the bottom of the social scale. Suppose the population is made up of three social classes, *A* (highest), *B* and *C* as follows:

Percentage of population in social class		
A	*B*	*C*
20%	50%	30%

Suppose a sample of size 100 is taken. With luck it would contain 20 people from class *A*, 50 from *B* and 30 from *C* and thus would be representative of the population as a whole. But if, by bad luck (or bad sampling), all 100 people in the sample were from class *A*, poor results would be obtained since newspaper readership differs between social classes.

To avoid this type of problem a stratified sample is taken, which ensures that all social classes are represented in the sample. This means that the survey would have to ask people about their social class as well as their reading habits. The simplest form of stratified sampling is equiproportionate sampling, whereby a stratum which constitutes (say) 20% of the population also makes up 20% of the sample. For the example above the sample would be made up as follows:

Class	*A*	*B*	*C*	Total
Number in sample	20	50	30	100

It should be clear why stratified sampling constitutes an improvement over simple random sampling, since it rules out 'bad' samples, i.e. those not representative of the population. It is simply impossible to get a sample consisting completely of social class *A*, or *B*, or *C*. In fact, it is impossible to get a sample in anything but the proportions 20:50:30, as in the population; this is ensured by the method of collecting the sample.

It is easy to see when stratification leads to large improvements over simple random sampling. If there were no difference between strata (social classes) in reading habits then there would be no gain from stratification. If reading habits were the same regardless of social class there would be no point in dividing up the population by social class. On the other hand, if there were large differences between strata, but within strata reading habits were similar, then the gains to stratification would be large.

Stratification is beneficial therefore when

- the between-strata differences are large and
- the within-strata differences are small.

These benefits take the form of greater precision of the estimates, i.e. narrower confidence intervals.[1] The greater precision arises because stratified sampling makes use of supplementary information – i.e. the proportion of the population in each social class. Simple random sampling does not make use of this. Obviously therefore, if those proportions of the population are unknown, stratified sampling cannot be carried out. However, even if the proportions are only known approximately there could be a gain in precision.

In this example social class is a stratification factor, i.e. a variable which is used to divide the population into strata. Other factors could of course be used, such as income or even height. A good stratification factor is one which is related to the subject of investigation. Income would probably be a good stratification factor, therefore, since it is related to reading habits, but height is not since there is probably little difference between tall and short people in the newspaper they read. What is a good stratification factor obviously depends upon the subject of study. A bed manufacturer might well find height to be a good stratification factor if conducting an enquiry into preferences about the size of beds. Although good stratification factors improve the precision of estimates, bad factors do not make them worse; there will simply be no gain over simple random sampling. It would be as if there were no differences between the social classes in reading habits, so that ensuring the right proportions in the sample is irrelevant, but it has no detrimental effects.

Proportional allocation of sample observations to the different strata (as done above) is the simplest method but is not necessarily the best. For the optimal allocation there should generally be a divergence from proportional allocation, and the sample should have more observations in a particular stratum (relative to proportional allocation):

- the more heterogeneous the stratum, and
- the cheaper it is to sample the stratum.

Starting from the 20:50:30 proportional allocation derived earlier, suppose that members of class A all read the same newspaper, but those of class C read a variety of titles. Then the representation of class C in the sample should be increased, and that of A reduced. If it really were true that everyone in class A read the same paper then one observation from that class would be sufficient to yield all there is to know about it. Furthermore, if it is cheaper to sample class C, perhaps because they are geographically more concentrated than class A, then again the representation of class C in the sample should be increased. This is because, for a given budget, it will allow a larger total sample size.

Cluster sampling

A third form of sampling is cluster sampling which, although intrinsically inefficient, can be much cheaper than other forms of sampling, allowing a larger sample size to

---

[1]   The formulae for calculating confidence intervals with stratified sampling are not given here, since they merit a whole book to themselves. The interested reader should consult C. A. Moser and G. Kalton, *Survey Methods in Social Investigation*, Heinemann, 1971.

be collected. Drawing a simple, or stratified, random sample of size 100 from the whole of Britain would be very expensive to collect since the sample observations would be geographically very spread out. Interviewers would have to make many long and expensive journeys simply to collect one or two observations. To avoid this, the population can be divided into 'clusters' (for example, regions or local authorities) and one or more of these clusters are then randomly chosen. Sampling takes place only within the selected clusters, is therefore geographically concentrated, and the cost of sampling falls, allowing a larger sample to be collected.

Within each cluster one can have either a 100% sample or a lower sampling fraction, which is called multi-stage sampling (this is explained further below). Cluster sampling gives unbiased estimates of population parameters but, for a given sample size, these are less precise than the results from simple or stratified sampling. This arises in particular when the clusters are very different from each other, but fairly homogeneous within themselves. In this case, once a cluster is chosen, if it is unrepresentative of the population, a poor (inaccurate) estimate of the population parameter is inevitable. The ideal circumstances for cluster sampling are when all clusters are identical, since in that case examining one cluster is as good as examining the whole population.

Dividing up the population into clusters and dividing it into strata are similar procedures, but the difference is that sampling is from one or at most a few clusters, but from all strata. This is reflected in the characteristics which make for good sampling. In the case of stratified sampling, it is beneficial if the between–strata differences are large and the within–strata differences small. For cluster sampling this is reversed: it is desirable to have small between–cluster differences but heterogeneity within clusters. Cluster sampling is less efficient (precise) for a given sample size, but is cheaper so can offset this disadvantage with a larger sample size. In general, cluster sampling needs a much larger sample to be effective, so is only worthwhile where there are significant gains in cost.

Multi-stage sampling

Multi-stage sampling was referred to in the previous section and is commonly found in practice. It may consist of a mixture of simple, stratified and cluster sampling at the various stages of sampling. Consider the problem of selecting a random sample of 1,000 people from a population of 25 million to find out about voting intentions. A simple random sample would be extremely expensive to collect, for the reasons given above, so an alternative method must be found. Suppose further that it is suspected that voting intentions differ according to whether one lives in the north or south of the country and whether one is a home owner or renter. How is the sample to be selected? The following would be one appropriate method.

First the country is divided up into clusters of counties or regions, and a random sample of these taken, say one in five. This would be the first way of reducing the cost of selection, since only one-fifth of all counties now need to be visited. This one in five sample would be stratified to ensure that north and south were both appropriately represented. To ensure that each voter has an equal chance of being in the sample, the probability of a county being drawn should be proportional to its adult population. Thus a county with twice the population of another should have twice the probability of being in the sample.

Having selected the counties, the second stage would be to select a random sample of local authorities within each selected county. This might be a one in ten sample from each county and would be a simple random sample within each cluster. Finally a selection of voters from within each local authority would be taken, stratified according to tenure. This might be a one in 500 sample. The sampling fractions would therefore be

$$\frac{1}{5} \times \frac{1}{10} \times \frac{1}{500} = \frac{1}{25,000}$$

So from the population of 25 million voters a sample of 1,000 would be collected. For different population sizes the sampling fractions could be adjusted so as to achieve the goal of a sample size of 1,000.

The sampling procedure is a mixture of simple, stratified and cluster sampling. The two stages of cluster sampling allow the selection of 50 local authorities for study and so costs are reduced. The north and south of the country are both adequately represented and housing tenures are also correctly represented in the sample by the stratification at the final stage. The resulting confidence intervals will be difficult to calculate but should give an improvement over the method of simple random sampling.

Quota sampling

Quota sampling is a non-random method of sampling and therefore it is impossible to use sampling theory to calculate confidence intervals from the sample data, or to find whether or not the sample will give biased results. However, it is by far the cheapest method of sampling and so allows much larger sample sizes. As shown above, large sample sizes can still give biased results if sampling is non-random; but in some cases the budget is too small to afford even the smallest properly conducted random sample, so a quota sample is the only alternative.

Even with quota sampling, where the interviewer is simply told to go out and obtain (say) 1,000 observations, it is worth making some crude attempt at stratification. The problem with human interviewers is that they are notoriously non-random, so that when they are instructed to interview every tenth person they see (a reasonably random method), if that person turns out to be a shabbily dressed tramp slightly the worse for drink, they are quite likely to select the eleventh person instead. Shabbily dressed tramps, slightly the worse for drink, are therefore under-represented in the sample. To combat this sort of problem the interviewers are given quotas to fulfil, e.g. twenty men and twenty women, ten old age pensioners, one shabbily dressed tramp, etc., so that the sample will at least broadly reflect the population under study and give reasonable results.

It is difficult to know how accurate quota samples are, since it is rare for their results to be checked against proper random samples or against the population itself. Probably the most common quota samples relate to voting intentions and so can be checked against actual election results. The 1992 UK general election provides an interesting illustration. The opinion polls predicted a fairly substantial Labour victory but the outcome was a narrow Conservative majority. An enquiry concluded that the erroneous forecast occurred because a substantial number of voters changed their minds at the last moment and that there was 'differential turn-out', i.e. Conservative supporters were more likely to vote than Labour ones. Presumably, future opinion polls will try to take this into account.

Calculating the required sample size

Before collecting sample data it is obviously necessary to know how large the sample size has to be. The required sample size will depend upon two factors:

- the desired level of precision of the estimate, and
- the funds available to carry out the survey.

The greater the precision required the larger the sample size needs to be, other things being equal. But a larger sample will obviously cost more to collect and this might conflict with a limited amount of funds available. There is a trade-off therefore between the two desirable objectives of high precision and low cost. The following example shows how these two objectives conflict.

A firm producing sweets wishes to find out the average amount of pocket money children receive per week. It wants to be 99% confident that the estimate is within 20 pence of the correct value. How large a sample is needed?

The problem is one of estimating a confidence interval, turned on its head. Instead of having the sample information $\bar{x}$, s and n, and calculating the confidence interval for μ, the desired width of the confidence interval is given and it is necessary to find the sample size n which will ensure this. The formula for the 99% confidence interval, assuming a Normal rather than t distribution (i.e. it is assumed that the required sample size will be large), is

$$(7.2) \quad \left[\bar{x} - 2.58 \times \sqrt{s^2 / n}, \ \bar{x} + 2.58 \times \sqrt{s^2 / n} \right]$$

Diagrammatically this can be represented as in Fig. 7.1.

The firm wants the distance between $\bar{x}$ and μ to be no more than 20 pence in either direction, which means that the confidence interval must be 40 pence wide. The value of n which makes the confidence interval 40 pence wide has to be found. This can be done by solving the equation

$$20 = 2.58 \times \sqrt{s^2 / n}$$

and hence by rearranging:

$$(7.3) \quad n = \frac{2.58^2 \times s^2}{20^2}$$

All that is now required to solve the problem is the value of s^2, the sample variance;

Fig. 7.1 *The desired width of the confidence interval*

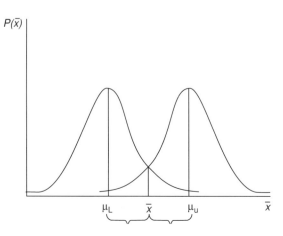

but since the sample hasn't yet been taken this is not available. There are a number of ways of trying to get round this problem:

- using the results of existing surveys if available
- conducting a small, preliminary, survey
- guessing

These may not seem very satisfactory (particularly the last), but something has to be done and some intelligent guesswork should give a reasonable estimate of s^2. Suppose, for example, that a survey of children's *spending* taken five years previously showed a standard deviation of 30p. It might be reasonable to expect that the standard deviation of spending would be similar to the standard deviation of income, so 30p (updated for inflation) can be used as an estimate of the standard deviation. Suppose that five years' inflation turns the 30p into 50p. Using $s = 50$ we obtain

$$n = \frac{2.58^2 \times 50^2}{20^2} = 41.6$$

giving a required sample size of 42 (the sample size has to be an integer). This is a large ($n \geq 25$) sample size so the use of the Normal distribution was justified.

Is the firm willing to pay for such a large sample? Suppose it was willing to pay out £1,000 in total for the survey, which cost £600 to set up and then £6 per person sampled. The total cost would be £600 + 42 × 6 = £852 which is within the firm's budget. If the firm wished to spend less than this, it would have to accept a smaller sample size and thus a lower precision or a lower level of confidence. For example, if only a 95% confidence level were required, the appropriate z-score would be 1.96, yielding

$$n = \frac{1.96^2 \times 50^2}{20^2} = 24.01$$

A sample size of 24 would only cost £600 + 6 × 24 = £804. (At this sample size the assumption that $\bar{x}$ follows a Normal distribution becomes less tenable, so the results should be treated with caution. Use of the t distribution is tricky, because the appropriate t value depends upon the number of degrees of freedom which in turn depends on sample size, which is what is being looked for!)

The general formula for finding the required sample size is

$$(7.4) \quad n = \frac{z_\alpha^2 \times s^2}{p^2}$$

where z_α is the z-score appropriate for the $(100 - \alpha)$% confidence level and p is the desired accuracy (20 pence in this case).

Collecting the sample
The sampling frame

We now move on to the fine detail of how to select the individual observations which make up the sample. In order to do this it is necessary to have some sort of sampling frame, i.e. a list of all the members of the population from which the sample is to be drawn. This can be a problem if the population is extremely large, for example the population of a country, since it is difficult to manipulate so much information (cutting up 50 million pieces of paper to put into a hat for a random draw is a tedious business). Alternatively the list might not even exist or, if it does, not be in one place convenient for consultation and use. In this case there is often an advantage to multistage sampling, for the selection of regions or even local authorities is fairly straightforward and not too time consuming. Once at this lower level the sampling frame is more manipulable (each local authority has an electoral register, for example) and individual observations can be relatively easily chosen. Thus it is not always necessary to have a complete sampling frame for the entire population.

Choosing from the sampling frame

There is a variety of methods available for selecting a sample of (say) 1,000 observations from a sampling frame of (say) 25,000 names, varying from the manual to the electronic. The oldest method is to cut up 25,000 pieces of paper, put them in a (large) hat, shake it (to randomise) and pick out 1,000. This is fairly time consuming, however, and has some pitfalls – if the pieces are not all cut to the same size is the probability of selection the same? It is much better if the population in the sampling frame is numbered in some way, for then one only has to select random numbers. This can be done by using a table of random numbers (see Table A1, for example), or a computer. The use of random number tables is an important feature of statistics and in 1955 the Rand Corporation produced a book entitled *A Million Random Digits with 100,000 Normal Deviates*. This book, as the title suggests, contained nothing but pages of random numbers which allowed researchers to collect random samples. Interestingly, the authors did not bother to fully proof read the text, since a few (random) errors here and there wouldn't matter! These numbers were calculated electronically and nowadays every computer has a facility for rapidly choosing a set of random numbers. (It is an interesting question how a computer, which follows rigid rules of behaviour, can select random numbers which, by definition, are unpredictable by any rule.)

A further alternative, if a 1 in 25 sample is required, is to select a random starting point between 1 and 25 and then select every subsequent 25th observation (e.g. the 3rd, 28th, 53rd, etc.). This is a satisfactory procedure if the sampling frame is randomly sorted to start with, but otherwise there can be problems. For example, if the list is sorted by income (poorest first), a low starting value will almost certainly give an underestimate of the population mean. If all the numbers were randomly selected, this 'error' in the starting value will not be important.

Interviewing techniques

Good training of interviewers is vitally important to the results of a survey. It is very easy to lead an interviewee into a particular answer to a question. Consider the following two sets of questions:

A.
1. Do you know how many people were killed by the Atomic bomb at Hiroshima?
2. Do you think nuclear weapons should be banned?

B.
1. Do you believe in nuclear deterrence?
2. Do you think nuclear weapons should be banned?

*A*2 is almost certain to get a higher 'yes' response than *B*2. Even a different ordering of the questions can have an effect upon the answers (consider asking *A*2 before *A*1). The construction of the questionnaire has to be done with care, therefore. The manner in which the questions are asked is also important, since it can often suggest the answer. Good interviewers are trained to avoid these problems by sticking precisely to the wording of the question and not to suggest an expected answer.

Even when these procedures are adhered to there can be various types of response bias. The first problem is of non-response, due to the subject not being at home when the interviewer calls. There might be a temptation to remove that person from the sample and call on someone else, but this should be resisted. There could well be important differences between those who are at home all day and those who are not, especially if the survey concerns employment or spending patterns, for example. Continued efforts should be made to contact the subject. One should be wary of surveys which have low response rates, particularly where it is suspected that the non-response is in some way systematic and related to the goal of the survey.

A second problem is that subjects may not answer the question truthfully for one reason or another, sometimes inadvertently. An interesting example of this occurred in the survey into sexual behaviour carried out in Britain in 1992 (see *Nature*, 3 December 1992). Amongst other things, this found the following:

• The average number of heterosexual partners during a woman's lifetime is 3.4.
• The average number of heterosexual partners during a man's lifetime is 9.9.

This may be in line with one's beliefs about behaviour, but in fact the figures must be wrong. The *total* number of partners of all women must by definition equal the *total* number for all men. Since there are approximately equal numbers of males and females in the UK the averages must therefore be about the same. So how do the above figures come about?

It is too much to believe that international trade holds the answer. It seems unlikely that British men are so much more attractive to foreign women than British women are to foreign men. Nor is an unrepresentative sample likely. It was carefully chosen and quite large (around 20,000). The answer would appear to be that some people are lying. Either women are being excessively modest or (more likely?) men are boasting. Perhaps the answer is to divide by three whenever a man talks about his sexual exploits!

Case study: the Family Expenditure Survey
Introduction

The Family Expenditure Survey (FES) is an example of a large government survey which examines households' expenditure patterns and income receipts. It is worth having a brief look at it, therefore, to see how the principles of sampling techniques outlined in this chapter are put into practice. The FES is used for many different purposes, including the calculation of weights to be used in the UK Retail Price Index, and the assessment of the effects of changes in taxes and state benefits upon different households.

Choosing the sample

The sample design is known as a **three stage, rotating, stratified, random sample**. This is obviously quite complex so will be examined stage by stage.

Stage 1: The country is first divided into 168 strata, each stratum made up of a number of local authorities sharing similar characteristics. The characteristics used as stratification factors are

• geographic area
• urban or rural character (based on a measure of population density)
• prosperity (based on a measure of property values).

A stratum might therefore be made up of local authorities in the South West region, of medium population density and high prosperity.

In each quarter of the year, one local authority from each stratum is chosen at random, the probability of selection being proportional to population. Once an authority has been chosen, it remains in the sample for one year (four quarters) before being replaced. Only a quarter of the authorities in the sample are replaced in any quarter, which gives the sample its 'rotating' characteristic. Each quarter some authorities are discarded, some kept and some new ones brought in.

Stage 2: From each local authority selected, four wards (smaller administrative units) are selected, one to be used in each of the four quarters for which the local authority appears in the sample.

Stage 3: Finally, within each ward, 16 addresses are chosen at random, and these constitute the sample.

Altogether this means that 10,752 ($168 \times 4 \times 16$) households are chosen each year to make up the sample.

The sampling frame

The register of electors in each ward is used as the sampling frame, which contains the names and addresses of everyone living in the ward. It is reasonably accurate and up to date, but is under-representative of those who have no permanent home or who move frequently (e.g. tramps, students, etc.). The fact that many people took themselves off the register in the early 1990s in order to avoid paying the Community Charge could have an effect upon the qualities of the sample. The addresses are chosen from the register by interval sampling from a random starting point.

The response rate is usually about 70%, meaning that the actual sample consists of about 7,000 households each year. Given the complexity of the information gathered, this is a remarkably good figure.

Collection of information

The data are collected by interview, and by asking participants to keep a diary in which they record everything they purchase over a two week period. Highly skilled interviewers are required to ensure accuracy and compliance with the survey, and each participating family is visited serveral times. As a small inducement to co-operate, each member of the family is paid a small sum of money (it is to be hoped that the anticipation of this does not distort their expenditure patterns!).

Sampling errors

Given the complicated survey design it is difficult to calculate sampling errors exactly. The multistage design of the sample actually tends to increase the sampling error relative to a simple random sample, but of course this is offset by cost savings which allow a greatly increased sample size. Overall, the results of the survey are of good quality, and can be verified by comparison with other statistics, such as retail sales, for example.

EXERCISES

Exercise 1

What issues of definition arise in trying to measure 'output'?

Exercise 2   What issues of definition arise in trying to measure 'unemployment'?

Exercise 3   Find the gross domestic product for both the UK and the US for the period 1985–93. Obtain both series in constant prices.

Exercise 4   Find figures for the monetary aggregate M0 for the years 1985–92 in the UK, in nominal terms.

Exercise 5   A firm wishes to know the average weekly expenditure on food by households to within £2, with 95% confidence. If the variance of food expenditure is thought to be about 400, what sample size does the firm need to achieve its aim?

Exercise 6   A firm has £10,000 to spend on a survey. It wishes to know the average expenditure on gas by businesses to within £30 with 99% confidence. The variance of expenditure is believed to be about 40,000. The survey costs £7,000 to set up and then £15 to survey each firm. Can the firm achieve its aim with the budget available?

Exercise 7   *Project 1*: Visit your college library to collect data to answer the following question: Has females' remuneration risen relative to men's over the past ten years? You should write a short report on your findings. This should include a section describing the data collection process, including any problems encountered and decisions you had to make. Compare your results with those of other students.

Exercise 8   *Project 2*: Do a survey to find the average age of cars parked on your college campus. The prefix on the registration plate gives the year (L: August 1993 to July 1994; M: Aug 1994 to July 1995, etc; precise details can be obtained in various guides to used car prices). You might need stratified sampling (e.g. if administrators have newer cars than faculty and students, for example). You could extend the analysis by comparing the results with a public car park. You should write a brief report outlining your survey methods and the results you obtain. If several students do such a survey you could compare results.

References
W.F.F. Kemsley, R.U. Redpath and M. Holmes, *The Family Expenditure Survey Handbook*, Office of Population Censuses and Surveys, Social Survey Division, HMSO, 1980.

Rand Corporation, *A Million Random Digits with 100,000 Normal Deviates*, The Glencoe Press, 1955.

8

THE χ^2 AND F DISTRIBUTION

Introduction

The final two distributions to be studied are the χ^2 (pronounced 'kye-squared') and F distributions. Both of these distributions have a variety of uses, which are illustrated in this chapter. These distributions allow us to extend some of the estimation and testing procedures covered in Chapters 5 and 6. The χ^2 distribution allows us to establish confidence interval estimates for a variance, just as the Normal and t distributions were used in the case of a mean. Further, just as the Binomial distribution was used to examine situations where the result of an experiment could be either 'success' or 'failure', the χ^2 distribution allows us to analyse situations where there are more than two categories of outcome. The F distribution enables us to conduct hypotheses tests regarding the equality of two variances and also to make comparisons between the means of multiple samples, not just two. The F distribution is also used in Chapters 9 and 10 on regression analysis.

The χ^2 distribution

The χ^2 distribution has a number of uses. In this chapter we make use of it in three ways:

- To calculate a confidence interval estimate of the population variance.
- To compare actual observations on a variable with the (theoretically) expected values.
- To test for association between two variables in a contingency table.

The use of the distribution is in many ways similar to the Normal or t distributions already encountered. Once again, it is actually a family of distributions depending upon one parameter, the degrees of freedom, similar to the t distribution. Some typical χ^2 distributions are drawn in Fig. 8.1 for different values of the parameter. Note the distribution has the following characteristics:

Fig. 8.1 *The χ^2 distribution with different degrees of freedom*

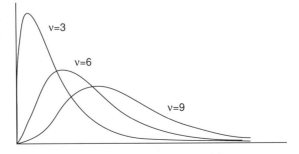

- It is always non-negative.
- It is skewed to the right.
- It becomes more symmetric as the number of degrees of freedom increases.

Confidence intervals are constructed in the usual way, by finding the critical values of the distribution (given in Table A4) which cut off an area $\alpha/2$ in each tail of the distribution. For hypothesis tests, a rejection region is defined which cuts off an area α in either one or both tails of the distribution, whichever is appropriate. The following examples make this clearer.

Estimating a variance

The sample variance is also a random variable like the mean; it takes on different values from sample to sample. We can therefore ask the usual question: given a sample variance, what can we infer about the true value?

To give an example, we use the data on spending by Labour boroughs in the example of Chapter 5. The sample standard deviation was 25 (so the sample variance is 625), based on a sample of 20 observations, around a sample mean of 175. What can we say about the true variance and standard deviation?

We work in terms of variances, taking the square root when we need to refer to the standard deviation. First of all, the sample variance is an unbiased estimator of the population variance, so we may use this as our point estimate, which is therefore 625. To construct the confidence iterval around this we need to know about the distribution of s^2. This does not have a convenient distribution, so we transform it to

$$(8.1) \quad \frac{(n-1)s^2}{\sigma^2}$$

which has a χ^2 distribution with $v = n - 1$ degrees of freedom.

To construct the 95% confidence interval around the point estimate we proceed as follows. First, we find the critical values of the χ^2 distribution which cut off 2.5% in each tail. These are no longer symmetric around zero as was the case with the standard Normal and t distributions. Table 8.1 shows an excerpt from the χ^2 table which is given in full in appendix Table A4 in the Appendix at the end of the book.

Like the t distribution, the first column gives the degrees of freedom, so we require the row corresponding to $v = n - 1 = 19$.

Table 8.1   Excerpt from Table A4 – the χ^2 distribution

v	0.99	0.975	...	0.10	0.05	0.025	0.01
1	0.0002	0.0010	...	2.7055	3.8415	5.0239	6.6349
2	0.0201	0.0506	...	4.6052	5.9915	7.3778	9.2104
⋮	⋮	⋮	...	⋮	⋮	⋮	⋮
18	7.0149	8.2307	...	25.9894	28.8693	31.5264	34.8052
19	7.6327	8.9065	...	27.2036	30.1435	32.8523	36.1908
20	8.2604	9.5908	...	28.4120	31.4104	34.1696	37.5663

Note: The two critical values are found at the intersections of the shaded row and columns. Alternatively you can use *Excel*. The formula =*CHIINV*(0.975, 19) gives the left-hand critical value, 8.91; similarly, =*CHIINV*(0.025, 19) gives the answer 32.85, the right-hand critical value.

- For the *left-hand* critical value (cutting off 2.5% in the left-hand tail) we look at the column headed '0.975', representing 97.5% in the right-hand tail. This critical value is 8.91.
- For the *right-hand* critical value we look up the column headed '0.025' (2.5% in the right-hand tail), giving 32.85.

We can therefore be 95% confident that $(n-1)s^2/\sigma^2$ lies between these two values, i.e.

$$(8.2) \qquad \left[8.91 \le \frac{(n-1)s^2}{\sigma^2} \le 32.85 \right]$$

We now need to rearrange equation (8.2) so that σ^2 lies between the two inequality signs. Rearranging yields

$$(8.3) \qquad \left[\frac{(n-1)s^2}{32.85} \le \sigma^2 \le \frac{(n-1)s^2}{8.91} \right]$$

and evaluating this expression leads to the 95% confidence interval for σ^2 which is

$$\left[\frac{19 \times 625}{32.85} \le \sigma^2 \le \frac{19 \times 625}{8.91} \right] = \left[361.5,\ 1332.8 \right]$$

Note that the point estimate, 625, is no longer at the centre of the interval but is closer to the lower limit. This is a consequence of the skewness of the χ^2 distribution.

The point and interval estimates of the standard deviation are simply obtained as the square roots of the values for the variance. Thus we have a point estimate of 25 and an interval estimate of [19.01, 36.51].

Comparing actual and expected values

A second use of the χ^2 distribution is to compare a set of observed values to expected values, the latter calculated on the basis of some null hypothesis to be tested. If the observed and expected values differ significantly, as judged by the χ^2 test (the test statistic falls into the rejection region of the χ^2 distribution), then the null hypothesis is rejected.

This can be illustrated with a very simple example. Suppose that throwing a die 72 times yields the following data:

Score on die	1	2	3	4	5	6
Frequency	6	15	15	7	15	14

Are these data consistent with the die being unbiased? A crude examination of the data suggests a slight bias against 1 and 4, but is this truly bias or just a random fluctuation quite common in this type of experiment? First the null and alternative hypotheses are set up:

H_0: the die is unbiased
H_1: the die is biased

Note that the null hypothesis should be constructed in such a way as to permit the calculation of the expected outcomes of the experiment. Thus the null and alternative hypotheses could not be reversed in this case, since 'the die is biased' is a vague statement (exactly how biased, for example?) and would not permit the calculation of the expected outcomes of the experiment.

On the basis of the null hypothesis, the expected values are based on the **uniform distribution**, i.e. each number should come up an equal number of times. The expected values are therefore 12 (= 72/6) for each number on the die.

This gives the data shown in Table 8.2 (ignore columns 4–6 for the moment). The χ^2 test statistic is now constructed using the formula

$$(8.4) \quad \chi^2 = \sum \frac{(O - E)^2}{E}$$

which has a χ^2 distribution with $v = k - 1$ degrees of freedom (k is the number of classes, here six). The calculation of the test statistic is shown in columns 4–6 of Table 8.2, and is quite straightforward, yielding a value of the test statistic of $\chi^2 = 7.66$, to be compared to the critical value of the distribution, for $6 - 1 = 5$ degrees of freedom.

Table 8.2   Calculation of the χ^2 statistic for the die problem

Score	Observed frequency (O)	Expected frequency (E)	$O - E$	$(O - E)^2$	$\frac{(O - E)^2}{E}$
1	6	12	−6	36	3.00
2	15	12	3	9	0.75
3	15	12	3	9	0.75
4	7	12	−5	25	2.08
5	15	12	3	9	0.75
6	14	12	2	4	0.33
Totals	72	72	0		7.66

Trap!

In my experience many students misinterpret formula (8.4) and use

$$\chi^2 = \frac{\sum (O - E)^2}{\sum E}$$

instead. This is not the same as the correct formula and gives the wrong answer! Check that you recognise the difference between the two and that you always use the correct version.

Large values of this test statistic mean that observed and expected values do not match very well, and therefore lead to rejection of the null hypothesis upon which the expected values were calculated. The rejection region is in the *right-hand tail* of the distribution, therefore. Thus if the calculated test statistic exceeds the critical value of the χ^2 distribution then the null hypothesis is rejected. This is illustrated in Fig. 8.2.

The critical value of the χ^2 distribution in this case ($v = 5$, 5% significance level) is 11.1, found from Table A4. Note that we require 5% of the distribution in the right-hand tail to establish the rejection region. Since the test statistic is less than the critical value the null hypothesis is not rejected. The differences between scores are due to sampling error rather than to bias in the die.

An important point to note is that the value of the test statistic is sensitive to the total frequency (72 in this case). Therefore the test should not be carried out on the *proportion* of occasions on which each number comes up (the expected values would all be 12/72, and the observed values 8/72, 13/72, etc.), since information about the 'sample size' (number of rolls of the die) would be lost. As with all sampling experiments, the inferences that can be drawn depend upon the sample size, with larger sample sizes giving more reliable results, so care must be taken to retain information about sample size in the calculations. If the test had been incorrectly conducted in terms of proportions, all O and E values would have been divided by 72, and this would have reduced the test statistic by a factor of 72 (check the formula to confirm this), reducing it to 0.14, nowhere near significance. It would be surprising if any data would yield significance given this degree of maltreatment!

A second, more realistic, example will now be examined to reinforce the message about the use of the χ^2 distribution and to show how the expected values might be generated in different ways. This example looks at road accident figures to see if there is any variation through the year. Quarterly data on the number of people killed on British roads are used, and the null hypothesis is that the number does not vary seasonally.

H$_0$: there is no difference in fatal accidents between quarters
H$_1$: there is some difference in fatal accidents between quarters

Such a study might be carried out by government, for example, to try to find the best means of reducing road accidents.

In *Key Data 1994/5*, Table 11.4 (published by the Central Statistical Office), the figures shown in Table 8.3 are found. Under the null hypothesis the total number of deaths (3,819) would be evenly split between the four quarters, yielding Table 8.4 and the calculation that follows.

Fig. 8.2 *The rejection region for the χ^2 test*

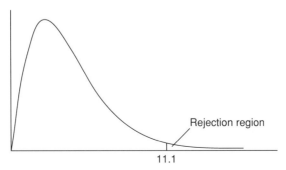

Rejection region

11.1

Table 8.3   Road casualties in the UK 1993

Quarter	I	II	III	IV	Total
Casualties	837	889	951	1,142	3,819

Table 8.4   Calculation of the χ^2 statistic for road deaths

Quarter	Observed deaths	Expected deaths	$O - E$	$(O - E)^2$	$\dfrac{(O - E)^2}{E}$
I	837	954.75	−117.75	13,865.06	14.52
II	889	954.75	−65.75	4,323.06	4.53
III	951	954.75	−3.75	14.06	0.01
IV	1,142	954.75	187.25	35,062.56	36.72
Totals	3,819	3,819	0		55.79

The calculated value of the test statistic is 55.79, given at the foot of the final column. The number of degrees of freedom is $v = k - 1 = 3$, so the critical value at the 5% significance level is 7.82. Since the test statistic exceeds this the null hypothesis is rejected; there is a difference between seasons in the accident rate.

The reason for this difference might be the increased hours of darkness during winter months, leading to more accidents. This particular hypothesis can be tested using the same data, but combining quarters I and IV (to represent winter) and quarters II and III (summer). The null hypothesis is of no difference between summer and winter, and the calculation is set out in Table 8.5. The χ^2 test statistic is reduced, but still exceeds the new critical value ($v = 1$, 5% significance level) of 3.84, so the null hypothesis is rejected.

Another point which the example brings out is that the data can be examined in a number of ways using the χ^2 technique. Some of the classes were combined to test a slightly different hypothesis from the original one. This is a quite acceptable technique but should be used with caution. In any set of data (even totally random data) there is bound to be *some* way of dividing it up such that there are significant differences between the divisions. The point, however, is whether there is any meaning to the division. In the above example the amalgamation of the quarters into summer and winter has some intuitive meaning and we have good reason to believe that there might be differences between them. Driving during the hours of darkness might be

Table 8.5   Seasonal variation in road deaths

Season	Observed deaths	Expected deaths	$O - E$	$(O - E)^2$	$\dfrac{(O - E)^2}{E}$
Summer	1,840	1,909.5	−69.5	4,830.25	2.52959
Winter	1,979	1,909.5	69.5	4,830.25	2.52959
Totals	3,819	3,819	0		5.05918

more dangerous and might have had some relevance to accident prevention policy (e.g. an advertising campaign to persuade people to check that their lights work correctly).

If quarters I and III were combined, and II and IV combined, the χ^2 test statistic might be significant (it is, even more so than for the summer–winter division) but does this signify anything? An advertising campaign to tell people to drive more carefully in quarters II and IV is likely to leave motorists somewhat bemused, and is unlikely to be successful. The point, as usual, is that it is no good looking at data in a vacuum and simply hoping that it will 'tell you something'.

There is one further point to make about carrying out a χ^2 test, and this involves circumstances where classes *must* be combined. The theoretical χ^2 distribution from which the critical value is obtained is a continuous distribution, yet the calculation of the test statistic comes from data which are divided up into a discrete number of classes. The calculated test statistic is therefore only an approximation to a true χ^2 variable, but this approximation is good enough as long as each expected (not observed) value is greater than or equal to five. It does not matter what the observed values are. In other circumstances, the class (or classes) with expected values less than five must be combined with other classes until all expected values are at least five. An example of this will be given below.

In all cases of χ^2 testing the most important part of the analysis is the calculation of the expected values (the rest of the analysis is mechanical). Therefore it is always worth devoting most of the time to this part of the exercise. The expected values are of course calculated on the basis of the null hypothesis being true, so different null hypotheses will give different expected values. Consider again the case of road fatalities. Although the null hypothesis ('no differences in fatal accidents between quarters') seems clear enough, it could mean different things. Here it was taken to mean an equal number of deaths in each quarter; but another interpretation is an equal number of deaths per car kilometre travelled in each quarter; in other words accidents might be higher in a given quarter simply because there are more journeys in that quarter (during holiday periods, for example). Table 8.6 gives an index of vehicle kilometres travelled on British roads.

The pattern of fatalities might follow the pattern of road usage – the first quarter of the year has the fewest fatalities and also the least travel. This may be tested by basing the expected values on the quantities of vehicle kilometres travelled: the 3,819 total casualties are allocated to the four quarters in the ratios 150:168:176:164. This is shown in Table 8.7, along with the calculation of the χ^2 statistic.

The χ^2 test statistic is 51.7, well in excess of the critical value. This indicates that there are significant difference between the quarters, even after accounting for different amounts of traffic. In fact, the statistic is little changed from before, suggesting either that traffic flows do not affect accident probabilities or that the flows do not actually vary very much.

Table 8.6 Index of road traffic 1993

	Q1	Q2	Q3	Q4	Total
Index	150	168	176	164	658

Table 8.7

Quarter	Observed deaths	Expected deaths	$O-E$	$(O-E)^2$	$\dfrac{(O-E)^2}{E}$
I	837	870.6	−33.6	1,128.5	1.3
II	889	975.1	−86.1	7,407.0	7.6
III	951	1,021.5	−70.5	4,969.6	4.9
IV	1,142	951.8	190.2	36,157.8	38.0
Totals	3,819	3,819			51.7

Note: The first expected value is calculated as $3{,}819 \times 150 \div 658 = 870.6$, the second as $3{,}819 \times 168 \div 658 = 975.1$ and so on.

Contingency tables

It is common to have data presented in the form set out in Table 8.8, in what is known as a **contingency table**. This provides a two-way classification of observations on voting intentions by social class, in contrast to the previous one-way classification of road accidents.

The interesting question that arises from these data is whether there is any association between people's voting behaviour and their social class. Are manual workers more likely to vote for the Labour party than for the Conservative party? The table would appear to indicate support for this view, but is this truly the case for the whole population or is this just an unrepresentative sample?

This sort of problem is also amenable to analysis by a χ^2 test. The data presented in the table represent the observed values, so expected values need to be calculated and then compared to them using the χ^2 test. The first task is to formulate a null hypothesis, on which to base the calculation of the expected values, and an alternative hypothesis. These are

H_0: there is no association between social class and voting behaviour
H_1: there is some association between social class and voting behaviour

As always, the null hypothesis has to be precise, so that expected values can be calculated. In this case it is the precise statement that there is no association between the two variables.

Constructing the expected values

If H_0 is true and there is no association, we would expect the proportions voting Labour, Conservative and Liberal Democrat to be the same in each social class. Further, the parties would be identical in the proportions of their support coming from social classes A, B, and C. This means that, since the whole sample of 200 splits

Table 8.8 Data on voting intentions by social class

Social class	Labour	Conservative	Liberal Democrat	Total
A	10	15	15	40
B	40	35	25	100
C	30	20	10	60
Totals	80	70	50	200

80:70:50 for the Labour, Conservative and Liberal Democrat parties, each social class should split the same way. Thus of the 40 people of class A, 80/200 of them should vote Labour, 70/200 Conservative and 50/200 Liberal Democrat. This yields:

Split of social class A:

Labour	$40 \times 80/200 = 16$
Conservative	$40 \times 70/200 = 14$
Liberal Democrat	$40 \times 50/200 = 10$

For class B:

Labour	$100 \times 80/200 = 40$
Conservative	$100 \times 70/200 = 35$
Liberal Democrat	$100 \times 50/20 = 25$

And for C the 60 votes are split Labour 24, Conservative 21 and Liberal Democrat 15.

Both observed and expected values are presented in Table 8.9 (expected values are in brackets). Notice that both the observed and expected values sum to the appropriate row and column totals. It can be seen that, compared with the 'no association' position, Labour gets too few votes from Class A and the Liberal Democrats too many. However, Labour gets disproportionately many class C votes, the Liberal Democrats too few. The Conservatives' observed and expected values are almost identical, indicating that the propensities to vote Conservative are the same in all social classes.

A quick way to calculate the expected value in any cell is to multiply the appropriate row total by column total and divide through by the grand total (200). For example, to get the expected value for the class A/Labour cell:

$$Expected \ \ value = \frac{row \ total \times column \ \ total}{grand \ \ total} = \frac{40 \times 80}{200} = 16$$

In carrying out the analysis care should again be taken to ensure that information is retained about the sample size, i.e. the numbers in the table should be actual numbers and not percentages or proportions. This can be checked by ensuring that the grand total is always the same as the sample size.

As was the case before, the χ^2 test is only valid if the expected value in each cell is

Table 8.9 Observed and expected values (latter in brackets)

Social class	Labour	Conservative	Liberal Democrat	Total
A	10 (16)	15 (14)	15 (10)	40
B	40 (40)	35 (35)	25 (25)	100
C	30 (24)	20 (21)	10 (15)	60
Totals	80	70	50	200

not less than five. In the event of one of the expected values being less than five, some of the rows or columns have to be combined. How to do this is a matter of choice and depends upon the aims of the research. Suppose for example that the expected value of class C voting Liberal Democrat were less than five. There are four options open:

(1) Combine the Liberal Democrat column with the Labour column.
(2) Combine the Liberal Democrat column with the Conservative column.
(3) Combine the class C row with the class A row.
(4) Combine the class C row with the class B row.

Whether rows or columns are combined depends upon whether interest centres upon differences between parties or differences between classes. If the main interest is the difference between class A and the others, option (4) should be chosen. If it is felt that the Liberal Democrat and Conservative parties are similar, option (2) would be preferred, and so on. If there are several expected values less than five, rows and columns must be combined until all are eliminated.

The χ^2 test on a contingency table is similar to the one carried out before, the formula being the same:

$$(8.5) \quad \chi^2 = \sum \frac{(O-E)^2}{E}$$

with the number of degrees of freedom given by $v = (r - 1) \times (c - 1)$ where r is the number of rows in the table and c is the number of columns. In this case $r = 3$ and $c = 3$ so

$$v = (3 - 1) \times (3 - 1) = 4$$

The reason why there are only four degrees of freedom is that once any four cells of the contingency table have been filled, the other five are constrained by the row and column totals. The number of 'free' cells can always be calculated as the number of rows less one, times the number of columns less one, as given above.

Calculation of the test statistic

The evaluation of the test statistic then proceeds as follows, cell by cell:

$$\frac{(10-16)^2}{16} + \frac{(15-14)^2}{14} + \frac{(15-10)^2}{10}$$
$$+ \frac{(40-40)^2}{40} + \frac{(35-35)^2}{35} + \frac{(25-25)^2}{25}$$
$$+ \frac{(30-24)^2}{24} + \frac{(20-21)^2}{21} + \frac{(10-15)^2}{15}$$
$$= 2.25 + 0.07 + 2.50$$
$$+ 0 + 0 + 0$$
$$+ 1.5 + 0.05 + 1.67$$
$$= 8.04$$

This must be compared with the critical value from the χ^2 distribution with four degrees of freedom. At the 5% significance level this is 9.50 (from Table A4).

Since $8.04 < 9.50$ the test statistic is smaller than the critical value, so the null hypothesis cannot be rejected. The evidence is not strong enough to support an association between social class and voting intention. We cannot reject the null of the lack of any association with 95% confidence.

Oops!

A leading firm of chartered accountants produced a report for the UK government on education funding. One question it asked of schools was: Is the school budget sufficient to provide help to pupils with special needs? This produced the following table:

	Primary schools	Secondary schools
Yes	34%	45%
No	63%	50%
No response	3%	5%
Totals	100%	100%
$n=$	137	159
$\chi^2 = 3.50$ n.s.		

Their analysis produces the conclusion that there is no significant difference between primary and secondary schools. But the χ^2 statistic is based on the percentage figures! Using frequencies (which can be calculated from the sample size figures) gives a correct χ^2 figure of 5.05. Fortunately for the accountants, this is still not significant.

The *F* distribution

The second distribution we encounter in this chapter is the F distribution. It has a variety of uses in statistics; in this section we look at two of these: testing for the equality of two variances and conducting an **analysis of variance** (ANOVA) test. Both of these are variants on the hypothesis test procedures which should by now be familiar. The F distribution will also be encountered in later chapters on regression analysis.

The F family of distributions resembles the χ^2 distribution in shape: it is always non-negative and is skewed to the right. It has two sets of degrees of freedom (these are its parameters) and these determine its precise shape. Typical F distributions are shown in Fig. 8.3.

As usual, for a hypothesis test we define an area in one or both tails of the distribution to be the rejection region. If a test statistic falls into the rejection region then the null hypothesis upon which the test statistic was based is rejected. Once again, examples will clarify the principles.

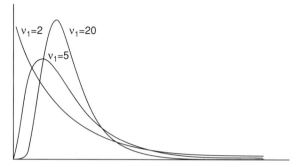

Fig. 8.3 *The F distribution, for different* v_1 *(*$v_2 = 25$*)*

Testing the equality of two variances

Just as one can conduct a hypothesis test on a mean, so it is possible to test the variance. It is unusual to want to conduct a test of a specific value of a variance, since we usually have little intuitive idea what the variance should be in most circumstances. A more likely circumstance is a test of the equality of two variances (across two samples). In Chapter 6 two car factories were tested for the equality of output *levels*. One can also test whether the *variance* of output differs or not. A more consistent output (lower variance) from a factory might be beneficial to the firm, e.g. dealers can be reassured that they are more likely to be able to obtain models when they require them. In the example in Chapter 6, one factory had a standard deviation of daily output of 25, the second of 20, both from samples of size 30 (i.e. 30 days' output was sampled at each factory). We can test whether the difference between these figures is significant or not.

Such a test is set up as follows. It is known as a **variance ratio test** for reasons which will become apparent.

The null and alternative hypotheses are

$$H_0: \sigma_1^2 = \sigma_2^2$$
$$H_1: \sigma_1^2 \neq \sigma_2^2$$

or, equivalently

$$(8.6) \quad H_0: \sigma_1^2 / \sigma_2^2 = 1$$
$$\qquad H_1: \sigma_1^2 / \sigma_2^2 \neq 1$$

It is appropriate to write the hypotheses in the form shown in (8.6) since the random variable we shall use is the ratio of sample variances, s_1^2 / s_2^2. This is a random variable which follows an F distribution with $v_1 = n_1 - 1$, $v_2 = n_2 - 1$ degrees of freedom. Thus we write:

$$(8.7) \quad \frac{s_1^2}{s_2^2} \sim F_{n_1 - 1, n_2 - 1}$$

The F distribution thus has two parameters, the two sets of degrees of freedom, one (v_1) associated with the numerator, the other (v_2), associated with the denominator. In each case, the degrees of freedom are given by the sample size minus one.

Note that s_1^2 / s_2^2 is also an F distribution (i.e. it doesn't matter which variance goes into the numerator) but with the degrees of freedom reversed, $v_1 = n_2 - 1$, $v_2 = n_1 - 1$.

The sample data are:

$$s_1 = 25, s_2 = 20$$
$$n_1 = 30, n_2 = 30$$

The test statistic is simply the ratio of sample variances. In calculation it is *much* more convenient if the larger of the two variances is made the numerator of the test statistic. Therefore we have the following test statistic:

$$(8.8) \quad F = \frac{25^2}{20^2} = 1.5625$$

This must be compared to the critical value of the F distribution with $v_1 = 29$, $v_2 = 29$ degrees of freedom.

The rejection regions for the test are the two tails of the distribution, cutting off 2.5% in each tail. Since we have placed the larger variance in the denominator, only large values of F reject the null hypothesis so we need only consult the upper critical value of the F distribution, i.e. that value which cuts off the top 2.5% of the distribution. (This is the advantage of putting the larger variance in the numerator of the test statistic.)

Table 8.10 shows an excerpt from the F distribution. The degrees of freedom for the test are given along the top row (v_1) and down the first column (v_2). The numbers in the table give the critical values cutting off the top 2.5% of the distribution. The critical value in this case is 2.09, at the intersection of the row corresponding to $v_2 = 29$ and the column corresponding to $v_1 = 30$ ($v_1 = 29$ is not given so 30 is used instead; this gives a very close approximation to the correct critical value). Since the test statistic does not exceed the critical value, the null hypothesis of equal variances cannot be rejected with 95% confidence.

In Chapter 6 we learned how to test the hypothesis that the means of two samples are the same, using a z- or t-test, depending upon the sample size. This type of hypothesis test can be generalised to more than two samples using a technique called **analysis of variance** (ANOVA), based on the F distribution. Although it is called analysis of variance, it actually tests differences in means. Using this technique we

Table 8.10   Excerpt from the F distribution: upper 2.5% points

v_2 \ v_1	1	2	3	...	20	24	30	40
1	647.7931	799.4822	864.1509	...	993.0809	997.2719	1,001.4046	1,005.5955
2	38.5062	39.0000	39.1656	...	39.4475	39.4566	39.4648	39.4730
3	17.4434	16.0442	15.4391	...	14.1674	14.1242	14.0806	14.0365
⋮	⋮	⋮	⋮	...	⋮	⋮	⋮	⋮
28	5.6096	4.2205	3.6264	...	2.2324	2.1735	2.1121	2.0477
29	5.5878	4.2006	3.6072	...	2.2131	2.1540	2.0923	2.0276
30	5.5675	4.1821	3.5893	...	2.1952	2.1359	2.0739	2.0089
40	5.4239	4.0510	3.4633	...	2.0677	2.0069	1.9429	1.8752

Note: The critical value lies at the intersection of the shaded row and column. Alternatively, use *Excel* or another computer package to give the answer. In *Excel*, the formula $=FINV(0.025, 29, 29)$ will give the answer 2.09, the upper 2.5% critical value of the F distribution with $v_1 = 29$, $v_2 = 29$ degrees of freedom.

can test the hypothesis that the means of *all* the samples are equal, versus the alternative hypothesis that at least one of them is different from the others. To illustrate the technique we shall extend the example in Chapter 6 where two different car factories' outputs were compared.

The assumptions underlying the analysis of variance technique are essentially the same as those used in the *t*-test when comparing two different means. We assume that the samples are randomly and independently drawn from Normally distributed populations which have equal variances.

Suppose there are three factories, whose outputs have been sampled, with the results shown in Table 8.11. We wish to answer the question whether this is evidence of different outputs from the three factories, or simply random variations around a (common) average output level. The null and alternative hypotheses are therefore:

H_0: $\mu_1 = \mu_2 = \mu_3$
H_1: at least one mean is different from the others

This is the simplest type of ANOVA, known as **one-way analysis of variance**. In this case there is only one **factor** which affects output – the factory. The factor which may affect output is also known as the **independent variable**. In more complex designs, there can be two or more factors which influence output. The output from the factory is the **dependent** or **response variable** in this case.

Figure 8.4 presents a chart of the output from the three factories, which shows the greatest apparent difference between factories 2 and 3. Their ranges scarcely overlap, which does suggest some genuine difference between them but as yet we cannot be

Table 8.11   Samples of output from three factories

Observation	Factory 1	Factory 2	Factory 3
1	415	385	408
2	430	410	415
3	395	410	418
4	399	403	440
5	408	405	425
6	418	400	
7		399	

Fig. 8.4 *Chart of factory output on sample days*

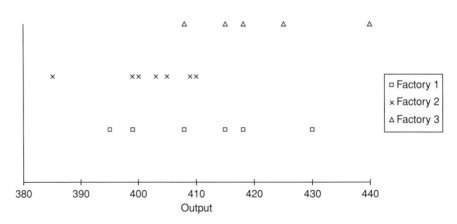

sure that this is not just due to sampling variation. Factory 1 appears to be mid-way between the other two and this must also be included in the analysis.

To decide whether or not to reject H_0 we compare the variance of output *within* factories to the variance of output *between* factories. If the latter is large relative to the former we reject H_0; if it is small we do not reject. For example, if there were little variation between different days' outputs, but they differed substantially between factories, then we would would reject H_0; at the other extreme, if each factory's output varied substantially from one day to another, but the average levels of output were similar, it would be clear that there is no difference between them. In this case we would conclude that the variations were due to other random factors, not the factories.

To formalise this we break down the **total variance** of all the observations into

(1) the variance due to differences **between** factories, and
(2) the variance due to differences **within** factories (also known as the **error** variance).

Initially we work with **sums of squares** rather than variances. Recall from Chapter 1 that the sample variance is given by

$$(8.9) \quad s^2 = \frac{\sum \left(x - \bar{x} \right)^2}{n - 1}$$

The numerator of this expression gives the sum of squares, i.e. the sum of squared deviations from the mean. In the factory example, we calculate the **total sum of squares** by the formula:

$$(8.10) \quad \text{Total sum of squares} = \sum_{j=1}^{ni} \sum_{i=1}^{k} \left(x_{ij} - \bar{x} \right)^2$$

where x_{ij} is the output from factory i on day j. The index i runs from 1 to 3 in this case (there are three **classes** or **groups** for this factor) and the index j (indexing the observations) goes from 1 to 6, 7, or 5 (for factories 1, 2 and 3 respectively). There are n_i observations for factor i. Equation (8.10) involves a double summation because we first have to sum over the factors i and then over observations j for each factor. Don't be put off, though; it is just a different way of summing all the squared deviations from the mean. $\bar{x}$ is the mean of *all* the observations in the sample, which is called the **grand average**.

An alternative formula for the total sum of squares is

$$(8.11) \quad \text{Total sum of squares} = \sum_{j=1}^{ni} \sum_{i=1}^{k} x_{ij}^2 - n\bar{x}^2$$

where n is the total number of observations (18 in this case).

The **between sum of squares** is based upon the averages for each factor and measures how they deviate from the grand average $\bar{x}$. If we denote the mean output for factor i by $\bar{x}_i$ then the between sum of squares is given by

$$(8.12) \quad \text{Between sum of squares} = \sum_{j} \sum_{i} \left(\bar{x}_i - \bar{x} \right)^2$$

The term $\bar{x}_i - \bar{x}$ measures the deviations of the class averages from the grand average, and these are first squared and then summed. Again, an alternative formula is often more convenient in calculation:

$$(8.13) \quad \text{Between sum of squares} = \sum_i n_i \bar{x}_i^2 - n\bar{x}^2$$

The **within sum of squares** is the difference between the total and between sums of squares so does not need separate calculation. This is based upon the following identity:

$$(8.14) \quad \begin{array}{ccccc} \text{Total sum} & = & \text{Between sum} & + & \text{Within sum} \\ \text{of squares} & & \text{of squares} & & \text{of squares} \end{array}$$

For completeness and if needed, the formula for the within sum of squares is

$$(8.15) \quad \text{Within sum of squares} = \sum_j \sum_i \left(x_{ij} - \bar{x}_i \right)^2$$

The term $x_{ij} - \bar{x}_i$ measures the deviations of the observations from the class mean and so the within sum of squares gives a measure of dispersion within the classes.

We now proceed to calculate these values using the example data.

The Total Sum of Squares
We shall make use of equation (8.11) here. The sum of all 18 observations is 7,382 and hence the grand average is $\bar{x} = 7,382/18 = 410.11$. The sum of the squares of all the observations is 3,030,418 (calculation not shown). Hence the total sum of squares is given by

$$(8.16) \quad \sum_{j=1}^{n_i} \sum_{i=1}^{k} x_{ij}^2 - n\bar{x}^2 = 3,030,418 - 18 \times 410.11^2 = 2977.778$$

The Between Sum of Squares
The mean output levels for the three factories are 410.83, 401.57 and 421.2 respectively. These are the $\bar{x}_i$ values. Inserting these into equation (8.13) gives the between sum of squares as

$$(8.17) \quad \sum_i n_i \bar{x}_i^2 - n\bar{x}^2 = 6 \times 410.83^2 + 7 \times 401.57^2 + 5 \times 421.2^2 - 18 \times 410.10^2$$

$$= 1,128.430$$

The Within Sum of Squares
This follows simply as $2,977.778 - 1,128.430 = 1,849.348$.

The analysis of variance table

We can summarise these results and add a few more simple calculations in an **analysis of variance table**. This provides all the information needed to conclude the hypothesis test. Figure 8.5 shows such a table, as produced by *Excel*.

The column of the ANOVA table headed '*SS*' gives the sums of squares, which we calculated above. It can be seen that the between group sum of squares makes up a substantial proportion of the total, about 37%, suggesting that the differences

Fig. 8.5 *One-way analysis of variance:* Excel *output*

K28		4.57633064942054

	G	H	I	J	K	L	M
13							
14	Anova: Single-Factor						
15							
16	Summary						
17							
18	*Groups*	*Count*	*Sum*	*Average*	*Variance*		
19							
20	factory 1	6	2465	410.833	166.967		
21	factory 2	7	2811	401.571	70.619		
22	factory 3	5	2106	421.200	147.700		
23							
24	ANOVA						
25							
26	Source of Variation						
27		*SS*	*df*	*MS*	*F*	*P-value*	*F crit*
28	Between Groups	1128.430	2	564.215	4.576	0.028	3.682
29	Within Groups	1849.348	15	123.290			
30							
31	Total	2977.7778	17				

Note: *Excel*, like many other statistical packages, performs all the ANOVA calculations automatically, based on the data in the spreadsheet. There is no need to evaluate any formulae, so you can concentrate on the interpretation of the results.

between factories (referred to as 'groups' by *Excel*) do make a substantial contribution to the total variation in output.

The '*df*' column gives the degrees of freedom associated with each sum of squares. These degrees of freedom are given by

Between sum of squares	$k - 1$	(k is the number of factors)
Within sum of squares	$n - k$	
Total sum of squares	$n - 1$	

The '*MS*' ('mean square') column divides the sums of squares by their degrees of freedom and the F column gives the F statistic, which is the ratio of the two values in the *MS* column, i.e. $4.58 = 564.22/123.29$. This is the test statistic for the hypothesis test, which has an F distribution with 2 and 15 degrees of freedom. The test statistic is thus the ratio of the between sum of squares to the within sum of squares, each divided by their degrees of freedom, i.e.

$$F = \frac{\text{Between sum of squares}/(k-1)}{\text{Within sum of squares}/(n-k)}$$

Excel helpfully gives the critical value of the test (at the 5% significance level) in the final column, 3.68. This is the value which cuts off 5% in the upper tail of the F distribution with 2 and 15 degrees of freedom. Since the test statistic is larger than the critical value, the null hypothesis is rejected with 95% confidence. In other words we can be 95% confident that the observed differences between the factories are not simply due to chance variation but represent some underlying differences.

The test has found that the between sum of squares is 'large' relative to the within sum of squares, too large to be due simply to random variation, and this is why the null hypothesis of equal outputs is rejected. The rejection region for the test consists of the *upper* tail only of the F distribution; small values of the test statistic would indicate small differences between factories and hence non-rejection of H_0.

This simple example involves only three groups, but the extension to four or more follows the same principles, with different values of k in the formulae, and is fairly straightforward. Also, we have covered only the simplest type of ANOVA, with a one-way classification. More complex experimental designs are possible, with a two-way classification, for example, where there are two independent factors affecting the dependent variable. This is not covered in this book, although Chapter 10 on the subject of multiple regression does examine a method of modelling situations where two or more explanatory variables influence a dependent variable.

EXERCISES

Exercise 1

A sample of 40 observations has a standard deviation of 20. Estimate the 95% confidence interval for the standard deviation of the population.

Exercise 2

Using the data $n = 70$, $s = 15$, construct a 99% confidence interval for the true standard deviation.

Exercise 3

Use the data in Table 8.3 to see if there is a significant difference between road casualties in quarters I and III on the one hand and quarters II and IV on the other.

Exercise 4

A survey of 64 families with five children found the following gender distribution:

Number of boys	0	1	2	3	4	5
Number of families	1	8	28	19	4	4

Exercise 4

Test whether the distribution can be adequately modelled by the Binomial distribution.

Exercise 5

Four different holiday firms which all carried equal numbers of holiday-makers reported the following numbers who expressed satisfaction with their holiday:

Firm	A	B	C	D
Number satisfied	576	558	580	546

Is there any significant difference between the firms? If told that the four firms carried 600 holiday-makers each, would you modify your conclusion? What do you conclude about your first answer?

Exercise 6

A company wishes to see whether there are any differences between its departments in staff turnover. Looking at their records for the past year the company finds the following data:

Department	Personnel	Marketing	Admin.	Accounts
Number in post at start of year	23	16	108	57
Number leaving	3	4	20	13

Do the data provide evidence of a difference in staff turnover between the various departments?

Exercise 7

A survey of 100 firms found the following evidence regarding profitability and market share:

Profitability	<15%	Market share 15–30%	>30%
Low	18	7	8
Medium	13	11	8
High	8	12	15

Is there evidence that market share and profitability are associated?

Exercise 8

The following data show the percentages of firms using computers in different aspects of their business.

Firm size	Admin.	Computers used in Design	Manufacture	Total numbers of firms
Small	60%	24%	20%	450
Medium	65%	30%	28%	140
Large	90%	44%	50%	45

Is there an association between the size of firm and its use of computers?

Exercise 9

(a) Do the accountants' job properly for them (see the *Oops!* box in the text).

(b) It might be justifiable to omit the 'no responses' entirely from the calculation. What happens if you do this?

Exercise 10

A roadside survey of the road-worthiness of vehicles obtained the following results

	Road-worthy	Not road-worthy
Private cars	114	30
Company cars	84	24
Vans	36	12
Lorries	44	20
Buses	36	12

Is there any association between the type of vehicle and the likelihood of it being unfit for the road?

Exercise 11

Given the following data on two sample variances, test whether there is any significant difference. Use the 1% significance level.

$s_1^2 = 55 \qquad s_2^2 = 48$

$n_1 = 25 \qquad n_2 = 30$

Exercise 12

An example in Chapter 6 compared R & D expenditure in Britain and Germany. The sample data were

$\bar{x}_1 = 3.7 \qquad \bar{x}_2 = 4.2$

$s_1 = 0.6 \qquad s_2 = 0.9$

$n_1 = 20 \qquad n_2 = 15$

Is there evidence, at the 5% significance level, of difference in the variances of R & D expenditure between the two countries? What are the implications, if any, for the test carried out on the difference of the two means, in Chapter 6?

Exercise 13

Groups of children from four different classes in a school were randomly selected and sat a test, with the following test scores:

	Pupil						
Class	1	2	3	4	5	6	7
A	42	63	73	55	66	48	59
B	39	47	47	61	44	50	52
C	71	65	33	49	61		
D	49	51	62	48	63	54	

(a) Test whether there is any difference between the classes, using the 95% confidence level for the test.

(b) How would you interpret a 'significant' result from such a test?

Exercise 14

Lottery tickets are sold in different outlets: supermarkets, smaller shops and outdoor kiosks. Sales were sampled from several of each of these, with the following results:

Supermarkets	355	251	408	302
Small shops	288	257	225	299
Kiosks	155	352	240	

Does the evidence indicate a significant difference in sales. Use the 5% significance level.

Exercise 15

Project: Conduct a survey among fellow students to examine whether there is any association between:

(a) gender and political preference, or

(b) subject studied and political preference, or

(c) star sign and personality (introvert/extrovert – self assessed: I am told that Aries, Cancer, Capricorn, Gemini, Leo and Scorpio are associated with an extrovert personality), or

(d) any other two categories of interest.

Exercise 16

Computer project: Use your spreadsheet or other computer program to generate 100 random integers in the range 0 to 9. Draw up a frequency table and use a χ^2 test to examine whether there is any bias towards any particular integer. Compare your results with those of others in your class.

Appendix: Use of χ^2 and F distribution tables

Tables of the χ^2 distribution

Table A4 presents critical values of the χ^2 distribution for a selection of significance levels and for different degrees of freedom. As an example, to find the critical value of the χ^2 distribution at the 5% significance level, for $v = 20$ degrees of freedom, the cell entry in the column labelled '0.05' and the row labelled '20' is consulted. The critical value is 31.4. A test statistic greater than this value implies rejection of the null hypothesis at the 5% significance level.

Tables of the F distribution

Table A5 presents critical values of the F distribution. Since there are two sets of degrees of freedom to be taken into account, a separate table is required for each significance level. Four sets of tables are provided, giving critical values cutting off the top 5%, 2.5%, 1% and 0.5% of the distribution (Tables A5(a), A5(b), A5(c) and A5(d) respectively). These allow both one and two tail tests at the 5% and 1% significance levels to be conducted. Its use is illustrated by example.

Two tail test
To find the critical values of the F distribution at the 5% significance level for degrees of freedom v_1 (numerator) = 10, v_2 = 20. The critical values in this case cut off the extreme 2.5% of the distribution in each tail, and are found in Table A5(b):

Right-hand critical value: this is found from the cell of the table corresponding to the column $v_1 = 10$ and row $v_2 = 20$. Its value is 2.77.
Left-hand critical value: this cannot be obtained directly from the tables, which only gives right-hand values. However, it is obtained indirectly as follows:

(a) Find the right-hand critical value for $v_1 = 20$, $v_2 = 10$ (note reversal of degrees of freedom). This gives 3.42.

(b) Take the reciprocal to obtain the desired left-hand critical value. This gives $1/3.42 = 0.29$.

The rejection region thus consists of values of the test statistic less than 0.29 and greater than 2.77.

One tail test
To find the critical value at the 5% significance level for $v_1 = 15$, $v_2 = 25$. As long as

the test statistic has been calculated with the larger variance in the numerator, the critical value is in the right-hand tail of the distribution and can be obtained directly from Table A5(a). For $v_1 = 15$, $v_2 = 25$ the value is 2.09. The null hypothesis is rejected, therefore, if the test statistic is greater than 2.09.

9

CORRELATION AND REGRESSION

Introduction

Correlation and regression are techniques for investigating the statistical relationship between two, or more, variables. In Chapter 1 we examined the relationship between investment and GDP using graphical methods (the XY chart). Although visually helpful, this did not provide any precise measurement of the strength of the relationship. In Chapter 8 the χ^2 test did provide a test of the significance of the association between two category-based variables, but this test cannot be applied to variables measured on a ratio scale. Correlation and regression fill in these gaps: the strength of the relationship between two (or more) ratio scale variables can be measured and the significance tested.

Correlation and regression are the techniques most often used by economists and forecasters. They can be used to answer such questions as

- Is there a link between the money supply and the price level?
- Do bigger firms produce at lower cost than smaller firms?
- Does instability in a country's export performance hinder its growth?

Each of these questions is about economics or business as much as about statistics. The statistical analysis is part of a wider investigation into the problem; it cannot provide a complete answer to the problem but, used sensibly, is a vital input. Correlation and regression techniques may be applied to time-series or cross-section data. The methods of analysis are similar in each case, though there are differences of approach and interpretation which are highlighted in this chapter and the next.

This chapter begins with the topic of correlation and simple (i.e. two variable) regression, using as an example the determinants of the birth rate in developing countries. In Chapter 10, multiple regression is examined, where a single dependent variable is explained by more than one explanatory variable. This is illustrated using time-series data pertaining to imports into the UK. This shows how a small research project can be undertaken, avoiding the many possible pitfalls along the way. Finally, a variety of useful additional techniques, tips and traps is set out, to help you understand and overcome a number of problems that can arise in regression analysis.

What determines the birth rate in developing countries?

This example follows the analysis in Michael Todaro's book, *Economic Development in the Third World* (3rd edn, pp. 197–200) where he tries to establish which of three variables (GNP per capita, the growth rate per capita, or income inequality) is most important in determining a country's birth rate. The analysis is instructive as an example of correlation and regression techniques in a number of ways. First, the question is an important one; as I write, the UN International Conference on Population and Development is discussing the issue in Cairo. It is felt by many that reducing the birth rate is a vital factor in economic development (birth rates in developed countries average around 12 per 1000 population, in developing countries around 30). Secondly, Todaro gets the statistical analysis wrong (it's always best to learn from others' mistakes).

The data used by Todaro are shown in Table 9.1 for a sample of 12 developing countries. Two points need to be made initially. First, the sample only includes developing countries, so the results will not give an all-embracing explanation of the birth rate. Different factors might be relevant to developed countries, for example. Secondly, there is the important question of why these particular countries were chosen as the sample and others ignored. The choice of country was in fact limited by data availability, and one should ask whether countries with data available are likely to be representative of all countries. Data were in fact available for more than 12 countries, so Todaro was selective. You are asked to explore the implications of this in some of the exercises.

The variables are defined as follows:

Birth rate: the number of births per 1000 population in 1981.
GNP per capita: 1981 gross national product p.c., in US dollars.
Growth rate: the growth rate of GNP p.c. per annum, 1961–81.
Income ratio: the ratio of the income share of the richest 20% to that of the poorest 40%.

We leave aside the concerns about the sample until later and concentrate now on analysing the figures. The first thing it is useful to do is to graph the variables to see if anything useful is revealed. *XY* graphs are the most suitable in this case and they are shown in Fig. 9.1.

From these we see a reasonably tidy relationship between the birth rate and the growth rate, with a negative slope; there is a looser relationship with the income ratio, with a positive slope; and there is little discernible pattern (apart from a flat line) in the graph of birth rate against GNP. Todaro asserts that the best relationship is between the birth rate and income inequality. He rejects the growth rate as an important determinant of the birth rate because of the four countries at the top of the

Table 9.1   Todaro's data on birth rate, GNP, growth and inequality

Country	Birth rate	1981 GNP p.c.	GNP growth	Income ratio
Brazil	30	2,200	5.1	9.5
Colombia	29	1,380	3.2	6.8
Costa Rica	30	1,430	3.0	4.6
India	35	260	1.4	3.1
Mexico	36	2,250	3.8	5.0
Peru	36	1,170	1.0	8.7
Philippines	34	790	2.8	3.8
Senegal	48	430	−0.3	6.4
South Korea	24	1,700	6.9	2.7
Sri Lanka	27	300	2.5	2.3
Taiwan	21	1,170	6.2	3.8
Thailand	30	770	4.6	3.3

Fig. 9.1 *Graphs of the birth rate against (a) GNP, (b) growth, and (c) income ratio*

(a)

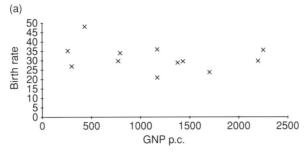

(b)

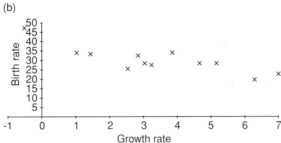

(c)

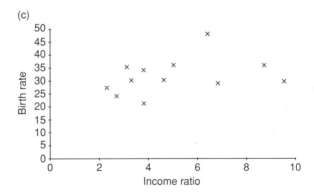

chart, which have very different growth rates, yet similar birth rates. In the following sections we shall see whether Todaro's conclusions are justified.

Correlation

The relationships graphed in Fig. 9.1 can be summarised numerically by measuring the **correlation coefficient** between any pair of variables. We illustrate this by calculating the correlation coefficient between the birth rate (B) and growth (G), though we also present the results for the other cases.

The different types of relationship between any two variables, X and Y, may be summarised as follows:

- High values of X tend to be associated with low values of Y and vice-versa. This is termed *negative correlation*, and appears to be the case for B and G.
- High (low) values of X tend to be associated with high (low) values of Y. This is *positive correlation* and reflects (rather weakly) the relationship between B and the income ratio (IR).
- No relationship between X and Y exists. High (low) values of X are associated

about equally with high and low values of Y. This is *zero*, or the absence of, *correlation*. There appears to be little correlation between the birth rate and per capita GNP.

It should be noted that positive correlation does not mean that high values of X are *always* associated with high values of Y, but usually they are. It is also the case that correlation only represents a *linear* relationship between the two variables. As a counter-example, consider the backward bending labour supply curve, as suggested by economic theory (higher wages initially encourage extra work effort, but above a certain point the benefit of higher wage rates is taken in the form of more leisure). The relationship is non-linear and the measured degree of correlation between wages and hours of work is likely to be low, even though the former obviously influences the latter.

The sample correlation coefficient, r, is a numerical statistic which distinguishes between the types of cases shown in Fig. 9.1. It has the following properties:

- It always lies between -1 and $+1$.
- A positive value of r indicates positive correlation, a higher value indicating a stronger correlation between X and Y. $r = 1$ indicates perfect positive correlation and means that all the observations lie on a straight line with positive slope, as Fig. 9.2 illustrates.
- A negative value of r indicates negative correlation. Similar to the above, a larger negative value indicates stronger negative correlation and $r = -1$ signifies perfect negative correlation.
- A value of $r = 0$ (or close to it) indicates a lack of correlation between X and Y.
- The relationship is symmetric, i.e. the correlation between X and Y is the same as between Y and X. It does not matter which variable is labelled Y and which is labelled X.

The formula for calculating the correlation coefficient is given in equation (9.1):

The formula for r can be written in a variety of different ways. The one given here is the most convenient for calculation.

$$(9.1) \quad r = \frac{n\sum XY - \sum X \sum Y}{\sqrt{\left(n\sum X^2 - \left(\sum X\right)^2\right)\left(n\sum Y^2 - \left(\sum Y\right)^2\right)}}$$

The calculation of r for the relationship between birth rate (Y) and growth (X) is shown in Table 9.2 and equation (9.2). From the totals in Table 9.2 we calculate:

$$(9.2) \quad r = \frac{12 \times 1{,}139.7 - 40.2 \times 380}{\sqrt{\left(12 \times 184.04 - 40.2^2\right)\left(12 \times 12{,}564 - 380^2\right)}} = -0.824$$

Fig. 9.2 *Perfect positive correlation*

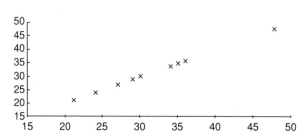

Table 9.2   Factors used in the calculation of the correlation coefficient, r

Country	Birth rate Y	GNP growth X	Y^2	X^2	XY
Brazil	30	5.1	900	26.01	153.0
Colombia	29	3.2	841	10.24	92.8
Costa Rica	30	3.0	900	9.00	90.0
India	35	1.4	1,225	1.96	49.0
Mexico	36	3.8	1,296	14.44	136.8
Peru	36	1.0	1,296	1.00	36.0
Philippines	34	2.8	1,156	7.84	95.2
Senegal	48	−0.3	2,304	0.09	−14.4
South Korea	24	6.9	576	47.61	165.6
Sri Lanka	27	2.5	729	6.25	67.5
Taiwan	21	6.2	441	38.44	130.2
Thailand	30	4.6	900	21.16	138.0
Totals	380	40.2	12,564	184.04	1,139.7

Note: In addition to the X and Y variables in the first two columns, three other columns are needed, for X^2, Y^2 and XY values.

This result indicates a fairly strong negative correlation between the birth rate and growth. Countries which have higher economic growth rates also tend to have lower birth rates. The result of calculating the correlation coefficient for the case of the birth rate and the income ratio is $r = 0.35$, which is positive as expected. Greater inequality (higher IR) is associated with a higher birth rate, though the degree of correlation is not particularly strong and less than the correlation with the growth rate. Between the birth rate and GNP per capita the value of r is only -0.26 indicating only a modest degree of correlation. All of this begins to cast doubt upon Todaro's interpretation of the data.

Are the results significant?

These results come from a (small) sample, one of many that could have been collected. Once again we can ask the question, what can we infer about the population (of all developing countries) from the sample? *Assuming* the sample was drawn at random (which may not be justified) we can use the principles of hypothesis testing introduced in Chapter 6. As usual, there are two possibilities:

(1)   The truth is that there is no correlation (in the population) and that our sample exhibits such a large (absolute) value by chance.
(2)   There really is a correlation between the birth rate and the growth rate and the sample correctly reflects this.

Denoting the true but unknown population correlation coefficient by ρ (the Greek letter 'rho') the possibilities can be expressed in terms of a hypothesis test:

$H_0: \rho = 0$
$H_1: \rho \neq 0$

The test statistic in this case is

$$(9.3) \quad t = \frac{r\sqrt{n-2}}{\sqrt{1-r^2}}$$

which has a t distribution with $n-2$ degrees of freedom. The five steps of the test procedure are therefore:

(1) Write down the null and alternative hypotheses (shown above).
(2) Choose the significance level of the test: 5% by convention.
(3) Look up the critical value of the test for $n-2 = 10$ degrees of freedom: $t^*_{10} = 2.228$ for a two tail test.
(4) Calculate the test statistic using equation (9.3):

$$t = \frac{-0.824\sqrt{12-2}}{\sqrt{1-\left(-0.824\right)^2}} = -4.59$$

(5) Compare the test statistic with the critical value. In this case $t < -t^*_{10}$ so H_0 is rejected. There is a less than 5% chance of the sample evidence occurring if the null hypothesis were true, so the latter is rejected. There does appear to be a genuine association between the birth rate and the growth rate.

Performing similar calculations (which you should check) for the income ratio and for GNP reveals that in both cases the null hypothesis cannot be rejected at the 5% significance level. The observed associations could well have arisen by chance.

Correlation and causality

It is important to test the significance of any result because almost every pair of variables will have a non-zero correlation coefficient, even if they are totally unconnected (the chance of the sample correlation coefficient being *exactly* zero is very, very small). Therefore it is important to distinguish between correlation coefficients which are significant and those which are not, using the t test just outlined. But even when the result is significant one should beware of the danger of 'spurious' correlation. Many variables which clearly cannot be related turn out to be significantly correlated with each other. One now famous example is between the price level and cumulative rainfall. Since they both rise year after year it is easy to see why they are correlated, yet it is hard to think of a plausible reason why they should be causally related to each other.

Apart from spurious correlation there are four possible reasons for a non-zero value of r:

(1) X influences Y.
(2) Y influences X.
(3) X and Y jointly influence each other.
(4) Another variable, Z, influences both X and Y.

Correlation alone does not allow us to distinguish between these alternatives. For example, wages (X) and prices (Y) are highly correlated. Some people believe this is due to cost–push inflation, i.e. that wage rises lead to price rises. This is case (1) above. Others believe that wages rise to keep up with the cost of living (i.e. rising prices), which is (2). Perhaps a more convincing explanation is (3), a wage–price spiral where each feeds upon the other. Others would suggest that it is the growth of the money supply, Z, which allows both wages and prices to rise. To distinguish between these alternatives is important for the control of inflation, but correlation alone does not allow that distinction to be made.

Correlation is best used therefore as a suggestive and descriptive piece of analysis, rather than a technique which gives definitive answers. It is often a preparatory piece of analysis, which gives some clues to what the data might yield, to be followed by more sophisticated techniques such as regression.

The coefficient of rank correlation

If the data are presented in the form of ranks, instead of the actual values, the technique of *rank correlation* can be used. Table 9.3 presents the data for birth and growth rates in the form of ranks.

Where two or more observations are the same, as are the birth rates of Mexico and Peru, then they are given the same rank, which is the average of the relevant ranking values. For example, both countries are given the rank of 2.5, which is the average of 2 and 3. Similarly, Brazil, Costa Rica and Thailand are all given the rank of 7, which is the average of 6, 7 and 8. The next country, Colombia, is then given the rank of 9.

It is preferable to use the actual data when available, since it contains more information, i.e. *by how much* countries' birth and growth rates differ. However, when only the ranks are known then *Spearman's rank correlation coefficient*, r_s, can be used instead. This statistic may be quickly calculated using formula (9.4):[1]

$$(9.4) \quad r_s = 1 - \frac{6 \times \sum d^2}{n\left(n^2 - 1\right)}$$

Table 9.3 Calculation of Spearman's rank correlation coefficient

	Birth rate Y	Growth rate X	Rank Y	Rank X	Difference d	d^2
Brazil	30	5.1	7	3	4	16
Colombia	29	3.2	9	6	3	9
Costa Rica	30	3.0	7	7	0	0
India	35	1.4	4	10	−6	36
Mexico	36	3.8	2.5	5	−2.5	6.25
Peru	36	1.0	2.5	11	−8.5	72.25
Philippines	34	2.8	5	8	−3	9
Senegal	48	−0.3	1	12	−11	121
South Korea	24	6.9	11	1	10	100
Sri Lanka	27	2.5	10	9	1	1
Taiwan	21	6.2	12	2	10	100
Thailand	30	4.6	7	4	3	9
Totals	380	40.2				479.5

Note: The country with the highest growth rate (South Korea) is ranked 1 for variable X; Taiwan, the next fastest growth nation, is ranked 2, etc. For the birth rate, Senegal is ranked 1, having the highest birth rate, 48. Taiwan has the lowest birth rate and so is ranked 12 for variable Y.

[1] You can also use formula (9.1) on the ranks, but (9.4) is easier.

where d is the difference in the ranks. The differences and their squared values are shown in the final columns of Table 9.3 and from these we obtain

$$(9.5) \quad r_s = 1 - \frac{6 \times 479.5}{12 \times \left(12^2 - 1\right)} = -0.676$$

This indicates a negative rank correlation between the two variables, as with the standard correlation coefficient, but with a smaller absolute value.

To test the significance of the result a hypothesis test can be performed on the value of ρ_s, the corresponding population parameter.

$H_0: \rho_s = 0$
$H_1: \rho_s \neq 0$

This time the t distribution cannot be used, but prepared tables of the critical values of ρ_s may be consulted, which are given in Table A6, and an excerpt is given in Table 9.4 .

The null hypothesis is rejected if the test statistic falls outside the range $[-0.591, 0.591]$, which it does in this case. Thus the null can be rejected with 95% confidence; the data do support the hypothesis of a relationship between the birth rate and growth. This critical value shown in the table is for a two tail test. For a one tail test, the significance level given in the top row of the table should be halved.

Regression analysis

Regression analysis is a more sophisticated way of examining the relationship between two (or more) variables. The major differences between correlation and regression are the following:

- Regression can investigate the relationships between two *or more* variables.
- A *direction* of causality is asserted, from the explanatory variable (or variables) to the dependent variable.
- The *influence* of each explanatory variable upon the dependent variable is measured.
- The *significance* of each explanatory variable can be ascertained.

Thus regression permits answers to such questions as:

Does the growth rate influence a country's birth rate?
If the growth rate increases, by how much might a country's birth rate be expected to fall?
Are other variables important in determining the birth rate?

Table 9.4 Excerpt from Table A6: Critical values of the rank correlation coefficient

n	10%	5%	2%	1%
5	0.900			
6	0.829	0.886	0.943	
⋮	⋮	⋮	⋮	⋮
11	0.523	0.623	0.763	0.794
12	0.497	0.591	0.703	0.780
13	0.475	0.566	0.673	0.746

Note: The critical value is given at the intersection of the shaded row and column.

In this example we assert that the direction of causality is from the growth rate (X) to the birth rate (Y) and not vice-versa. The growth rate is therefore the explanatory variable (also referred to as the **independent** or **exogenous** variable) and the birth rate is the dependent variable (also called the **explained** or **endogenous** variable).

Regression analysis describes this causal relationship by fitting a straight line drawn through the data, which best summarises them. It is sometimes called 'the line of best fit' for this reason. This is illustrated in Fig. 9.3 for the birth rate and growth rate data.

Note that (by convention) the explanatory variable is placed on the horizontal axis, the explained on the vertical. This regression line is downward sloping (its derivation will be explained shortly) for the same reason that the correlation coefficient is negative, i.e. high values of Y are generally associated with low values of X and vice-versa.

Since the regression line summarises knowledge of the relationship between X and Y, it can be used to predict the value of Y given any particular value of X. In Fig. 9.3 the value of $X = 3$ (the observation for Costa Rica) is related via the regression line to a value of Y (denoted by $\hat{Y}$) of 32.6. This predicted value is close (but not identical) to the actual birth rate of 30. The difference reflects the absence of perfect correlation between the two variables.

The difference between the actual value, Y, and the predicted value, $\hat{Y}$, is called the **error** or **residual**. It is labelled e in Figure 9.3. Why should such errors occur? The relationship is never going to be an exact one for a variety of reasons. There are bound to be other factors besides growth which affect the birth rate (e.g. the education of women) and these effects are all subsumed into the error term. There might additionally be simple measurement error (of Y) and, of course, people do act in a somewhat random fashion rather than follow rigid rules of behaviour.

All of these factors fall into the error term and this means that the observations lie around the regression line rather than on it. If there are many of these factors, none of which is predominant, and they are independent of each other, then these errors may be assumed to be Normally distributed about the regression line.

Why not include these factors explicitly? On the face of it this would seem to be an improvement, making the model more realistic. However, the costs of doing this are that the model becomes more complex, calculation becomes more difficult (not so

Fig. 9.3 *The line of best fit*

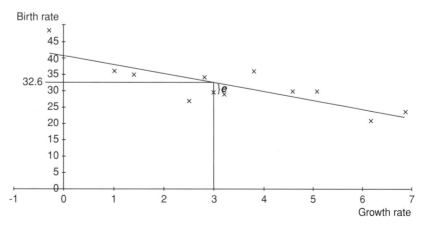

important now with computers) and it is generally more difficult for the reader (or researcher) to interpret what is going on. If the main interest is the relationship between the birth rate and growth, why complicate the model unduly? There is a virtue in simplicity, as long as the simplified model still gives an undistorted view of the relationship. In Chapter 10 on multiple regression the trade-off between simplicity and realism will be further discussed, particularly with reference to the problems which can arise if relevant explanatory variables are omitted from the analysis.

Calculation of the regression line

The equation of the sample regression line may be written

(9.6) $\hat{Y}_i = a + bX_i$

where
$\hat{Y}_i$ is the predicted value of Y for observation (country) i
X_i is the value of the explanatory variable for observation i, and
a, b are fixed coefficients to be estimated; a measures the intercept of the regression line on the Y axis, b measures its slope.

This is illustrated in Fig. 9.4.

The first task of regression analysis is to find the values of a and b so that the regression line may be drawn. To do this we proceed as follows. The difference between the actual value Y_i, and its predicted value, $\hat{Y}_i$, is e_i, the error. Thus

(9.7) $Y_i = \hat{Y}_i + e_i$

Substituting equation (9.6) into equation (9.7) the regression equation can be written

(9.8) $Y_i = a + bX_i + e_i$

Equation (9.8) shows that observed birth rates are made up of two components:

(1) that part explained by the growth rate, $a + bX_i$, and
(2) an error component, e_i.

In a good model, part (1) should be large relative to part (2). The line of best fit is therefore found by finding the values of a and b which *minimise the sum of squared errors* from the regression line. For this reason, this method is known as 'the method of least squares' or simply 'ordinary least squares' (OLS). The use of this criterion will be justified later on, but it can be said in passing that the sum of the errors is not minimised because that would not lead to a unique answer for the values a and b. In

Fig. 9.4 *Intercept and slope of the regression line*

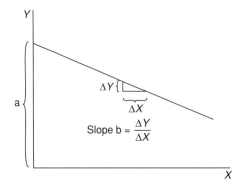

fact there is an infinite number of possible regression lines which all yield a sum of errors equal to zero. Minimising the sum of *squared* errors does yield a unique answer.

The task is therefore to

(9.9)   minimise $\sum e_i^2$

by choice of *a* and *b*.

Rearranging equation (9.8) the error is given by

(9.10) $e_i = Y_i - a - bX_i$

so equation (9.9) becomes

(9.11)   minimise $\sum \left(Y_i - a - bX_i\right)^2$

by choice of *a* and *b*.

Finding the solution to (9.11) requires the use of differential calculus, and is not presented here. The resulting formulae for *a* and *b* are

$$(9.12)\quad b = \frac{n\sum XY - \sum X \sum Y}{n\sum X^2 - \left(\sum X\right)^2}$$

and

$$(9.13)\quad a = \overline{Y} - b\overline{X}$$

where $\overline{X}$ and $\overline{Y}$ are the mean values of X and Y respectively. The values necessary to evaluate equations (9.12) and (9.13) can be obtained from Table 9.2 which was used to calculate the correlation coefficient. These values are repeated for convenience:

$$\sum Y = 380 \qquad \sum Y^2 = 12{,}564$$
$$\sum X = 40.2 \qquad \sum X^2 = 184.04$$
$$\sum XY = 1{,}139.70 \qquad n = 12$$

Using these values we obtain

$$b = \frac{12 \times 1{,}139.70 - 40.2 \times 380}{12 \times 184.04 - 40.2^2} = -2.700$$

and

$$a = \frac{380}{12} - \left(-2.700\right) \times \frac{40.2}{12} = 40.711$$

Thus the regression equation can be written, to two decimal places for clarity, as

$$Y_i = 40.71 - 2.70X_i + e_i$$

Interpretation of the slope and intercept

The most important part of the result is the slope coefficient $b = -2.7$. This implies that an increase in the growth rate of 1% point (e.g. from 2% to 3% p.a.) would lower the birth rate by 2.7, e.g. from 30 births per 1000 population to 27.3. Given that the growth data refer to a 20-year period (1961 to 1981), this increase in the growth rate would have to be sustained over such a time, not an easy task. How big is the effect upon the birth rate? The average birth rate in the sample is 31.67, so a reduction of 2.7 for an average country would be a fall of 8.5% ($2.7/31.67 \times 100$). This is reasonably substantial (though not enough to bring the birth rate down to developed country levels) but would need a substantial, sustained increase in the growth rate to bring it about.

The value of a, the intercept, may be interpreted as the predicted birth rate of a country with zero growth ($X = 0$). This value is fairly close to that of Senegal, which actually had negative growth over the period and whose birth rate was 48, a little higher than the intercept value. Although a has a sensible interpretation in this case, this is not always so. For example, in a regression of the demand for a good on its price, a would represent demand at zero price, which is unlikely ever to be observed.

Measuring the goodness of fit of the regression line

Even if X does not influence Y a regression line can always be calculated, so by itself the meaning of the regression line may be difficult to evaluate. Some way of differentiating between genuine and invalid regressions is therefore needed. Using the income ratio and GNP variables to explain the birth rate gives the following regression equations (calculations not shown):

for the income ratio (IR): $B = 26.44 + 1.045 \text{ IR} + e$
for GNP (GNP): $B = 34.72 - 0.003 \text{ GNP} + e$

How can we decide which of these three is 'best' on the basis of the regression equations alone? From Fig. 9.1 it is evident that some relationships appear stronger than others, yet this is not revealed by the regression equation alone. More information is needed. (You cannot choose the best equation simply by looking at the size of the coefficients. Try to work out why.)

One useful way of differentiating between these cases is on the basis of the 'goodness of fit' of the line, i.e. how close the observations are to the line. This can be measured by the **coefficient of determination** and is denoted R^2. Fig. 9.5 illustrates the principle behind the calculation of R^2.

The figure shows the mean value of $\overline{Y}$, the calculated sample regression line and an arbitrarily chosen sample observation (X_i, Y_i). The difference between Y_i and $\overline{Y}$ (length AC) can be divided up into:

(1) That part 'explained' by the regression line, $\hat{Y}_i - \overline{Y}$ (i.e. explained by the value of X_i). This is length AB.
(2) The error term $e_i = Y_i - \hat{Y}_i$, length BC.

In algebraic terms,

(9.14) $Y_i - \overline{Y} = (Y_i - \hat{Y}_i) + (\hat{Y}_i - \overline{Y})$

A good regression model should 'explain' a large part of the differences between the Y_i values and $\overline{Y}$, i.e. the length $\hat{Y}_i - \overline{Y}$ should be large relative to $Y_i - \hat{Y}_i$. A measure of fit would therefore be $\dfrac{(\hat{Y}_i - \overline{Y})}{(Y_i - \overline{Y})}$. However, this has two drawbacks: it

Fig. 9.5 *The calculation of R^2*

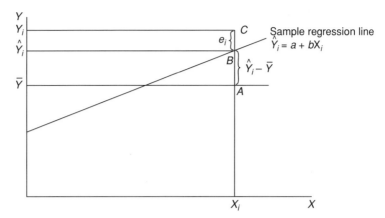

only applies to one observation and often takes a negative value. To get round these problems we square and then sum (over all the observations) each of the terms in equation (9.14), giving

$$\sum\left(Y_i - \overline{Y}\right)^2, \text{ known as the total sum of squares (TSS)}$$

$$\sum\left(\hat{Y}_i - \overline{Y}\right)^2, \text{ the regression sum of squares (RSS), and}$$

$$\sum\left(Y_i - \hat{Y}_i\right)^2, \text{ the error sum of squares (ESS)}$$

The measure of goodness of fit, R^2, is then defined as the ratio of the regression sum of squares to the total sum of squares, i.e.

$$(9.15) \quad R^2 = \frac{\text{RSS}}{\text{TSS}}$$

The better the divergences between Y_i and $\overline{Y}$ are explained by the regression line, the better the goodness of fit, and the higher the calculated value of R^2. Further, it is true that

$$(9.16) \quad \text{TSS} = \text{RSS} + \text{ESS}$$

From equations (9.15) and (9.16) we see that R^2 must lie between 0 and 1 (note that since each term in equation (9.16) is a sum of squares, none of them can be negative). Thus

$$0 \le R^2 \le 1$$

A value of $R^2 = 1$ indicates that all the sample observations lie exactly on the regression line (equivalent to perfect correlation). If $R^2 = 0$ then the regression line is of no use at all – X does not influence Y (linearly) at all, and to try to predict a value of Y_i one might as well use the mean $\overline{Y}$ rather than the value X_i inserted into the sample regression equation.

To calculate R^2, alternative formulae to those above make the task easier. Instead we use:

$$TSS = \sum\left(Y_i - \overline{Y}\right)^2 = \sum Y_i^2 - n\overline{Y}^2 = 12{,}564 - 12 \times 31.66^2 = 530.667$$

$$ESS = \sum\left(Y_i - \hat{Y}_i\right)^2 = \sum Y_i^2 - a\sum Y_i - b\sum X_i Y_i$$

$$= 12{,}564 - 40.711 \times 380 - \left(-2.7\right) \times 1{,}139.70 = 170.754$$

$$RSS = TSS - ESS = 530.667 - 170.754 = 359.913$$

This gives the result

$$R^2 = \frac{RSS}{TSS} = \frac{359.913}{530.667} = 0.678$$

This is interpreted as follows. Countries' birth rates vary around the overall mean value of 31.67. 67.8% of this variation is explained by variation in countries' growth rates. This is quite a respectable figure to obtain, leaving only 32.8% of the variation in Y left to be explained by other factors. The regression seems to make a worthwhile contribution to explaining why birth rates differ.

It turns out that in simple regression (i.e. where there is only one explanatory variable), R^2 is simply the square of the correlation coefficient between X and Y. Thus for the income ratio and for GNP we have:

for IR: $R^2 = 0.35^2 = 0.13$
for GNP: $R^2 = -0.26^2 = 0.07$

This shows, once again, that these other variables are not terribly useful in explaining why birth rates differ. Each of them only explains a small proportion of the variation in Y.

It should be emphasised at this point that R^2 is not the only criterion (or even an adequate one in all cases) for judging the quality of a regression equation and that other statistical measures, set out below, are also required.

Inference in the regression model

So far, regression has been used as a descriptive technique, to measure the relationship between the two variables. We now go on to draw inferences from the analysis about what the *true* regression line might look like. As with correlation, the estimated relationship is in fact a *sample* regression line, based upon data for 12 countries. The estimated coefficients a and b are random variables, since they would differ from sample to sample. What can be inferred about the true (but unknown) regression equation?

The question is best approached by first writing down a true or population regression equation, in a form similar to the sample regression equation:

(9.17) $Y_i = \alpha + \beta X_i + \varepsilon_i$

As usual, Greek letters denote true, or population, values. α and β are thus the population *parameters*, of which a and b are (point) estimates, using the method of least squares. ε is the population error term. If we could observe the individual error terms ε_i then we would be able to get exact values of α and β (even from a sample), rather than just estimates.

Given that a and b are estimates, we can ask about their properties: whether they are unbiased and how precise they are, compared to alternative estimators. Under reasonable assumptions (see Thomas (1993), ch. 1; Maddala (1992), ch. 3) it can be shown that the OLS estimates of the coefficients are unbiased. Thus OLS provides useful point estimates of the parameters (the true values α and β). This is one reason for using the least squares method. It can also be shown that, among the class of linear, unbiased estimators, OLS has the minimum variance, i.e. the method provides the most precise estimates. This is another, powerful justification for the use of OLS. So, just as the sample mean provides a more precise estimate of the population mean than does a single observation, the least squares estimates of α and β are the most precise.

Analysis of the errors
To find confidence intervals for α and β we need to know which statistical distribution we should be using, i.e. the distributions of a and b. These can be derived, based on the assumption that the error term ε in equation (9.17) above is Normally distributed and that the errors are statistically independent of each other. Since we are using cross-section data from countries which are different geographically, politically and socially it seems reasonable to assume the errors are independent.

To check the Normality assumption we graph the residuals calculated from the sample regression line. If the true errors are Normal it seems likely that these residuals should be approximately Normal also. The residuals are calculated according to equation (9.10) above. Table 9.5 shows the calculation of some of these.

These residuals may then be gathered together in a frequency table (as in Chapter 1) and graphed. This is shown in Fig. 9.6.

Although the number of observations is small (and therefore the graph is not a smooth curve) the chart does have the greater weight of frequencies in the centre as one would expect, with less weight as one moves into the tails of the distribution. The assumption that the true error term is Normally distributed does not seem unreasonable.

If the residuals from the sample regression equation appeared distinctly non-Normal (heavily skewed, for example) then one should be wary of constructing confidence intervals using the formulae below. Instead, one might consider transforming the data (see below) before continuing.

If one were using time-series data one should also check the residuals for **autocorrelation** at this point. This occurs when the error in period t is dependent in some way on the error in the previous period(s) and implies that the method of least

Table 9.5 Calculation of residuals

	Actual birth rate	Fitted values	Residuals
Brazil	30	26.9	3.1
Colombia	29	32.1	−3.1
Costa Rica	30	32.6	−2.6
⋮	⋮	⋮	⋮
Sri Lanka	27	34.0	−7.0
Taiwan	21	24.0	−3.0
Thailand	30	28.3	1.7

Note: The fitted values are calculated by substituting the growth rate into the estimated regression equation. Thus for Brazil, for example, $40.712 - 2.7 \times 5.1 = 26.9$.

Fig. 9.6 *Bar chart of residuals from the regression equation*

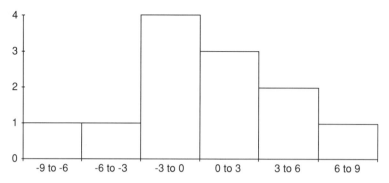

squares may not be the best way of estimating the relationship. In this example we have cross-section data, so it is not appropriate to check for autocorrelation, since the ordering of the data does not matter. The next chapter, on multiple regression, covers this topic.

Confidence interval estimates of α and β

First the sampling variance of b is calculated, then we use it to obtain a confidence interval estimate for β, based around the point estimate. The principle is just the same as for the confidence interval estimate of the sample mean, covered in Chapter 5.

The estimated sampling variance of b, the slope coefficient, is given by

$$(9.18) \quad s_b^2 = \frac{s_e^2}{\sum\left(X_i - \overline{X}\right)^2}$$

where

$$(9.19) \quad s_e^2 = \frac{\sum e_i^2}{n-2} = \frac{\text{ESS}}{n-2}$$

is the estimated variance of the error term, ε. The value of this is

$$(9.20) \quad s_e^2 = \frac{170.754}{10} = 17.0754$$

and so the estimated variance of b is

$$(9.21) \quad s_b^2 = \frac{17.0754}{49.37} = 0.346$$

$(Use \sum\left(X_i - \overline{X}\right)^2 = \sum X^2 - n\overline{X}^2$ in calculating (9.21).) The estimated standard error of b is the square root of (9.21),

$$(9.22) \quad s_b = \sqrt{0.346} = 0.588$$

To construct the confidence interval around the point estimate, $b = -2.7$, the t distribution is used (in regression this applies to all sample sizes, not just small ones). The 95% confidence interval is thus given by

(9.23) $[b - t_v s_b, b + t_v s_b]$

where t_v is the (two-tail) critical value of the t distribution at the appropriate signifi-cance level (5% in this case), with $v = n - 2$ degrees of freedom. The critical value is 2.228. Thus the confidence interval evaluates to:

$$[-2.7 - 2.228 \times 0.588, -2.7 + 2.228 \times 0.588] = [-4.01, -1.39]$$

Thus we can be 95% confident that the true value of β lies within this range. Note that the interval only includes negative values: we can rule out an upward sloping regression line.

For the intercept a, the estimate of the variance is given by

$$(9.24) \quad s_a^2 = s_e^2 \times \left(\frac{1}{n} + \frac{\overline{X}^2}{\sum \left(X_i - \overline{X} \right)^2} \right) = 17.0754 \times \left(\frac{1}{12} + \frac{3.35^2}{49.37} \right) = 5.304$$

and the estimated standard error of a is the square root of this, 2.303. The 95% con-fidence interval for α, again using the t distribution, is

$$[40.71 - 2.228 \times 2.303, 40.71 + 2.228 \times 2.303] = [35.57, 45.84]$$

It is useful (and customary) to write the regression equation with the standard errors below the appropriate coefficient, and also with the value of R^2 given, as follows:

$Y_i = 40.711 - 2.70X_i + e_i$
s.e. (2.30)   (0.59)

$R^2 = 0.678$ $n = 12$

This conveys all the necessary information to the reader at a glance, who can then draw the inferences deemed appropriate. Any desired confidence interval (not just the 95% one) can be quickly calculated with the aid of a set of t-tables.

Testing hypotheses about the coefficients

One might also wish to conduct hypothesis tests upon the coefficients. These tests are quickly and easily conducted given the information above. Consider the following hypothesis:

$H_0 : \beta = 0$
$H_1 : \beta \neq 0$

This null hypothesis is interesting because it implies no influence of X upon Y at all (i.e. the slope of the true regression line is flat and Y_i can be equally well predicted by $\overline{Y}$). The alternative hypothesis asserts that X does in fact influence Y.

The procedure is in principle the same as in Chapter 6 on hypothesis testing. The test statistic is

$$(9.25) \quad t = \frac{b - \beta}{s_b}$$

$$= \frac{-2.7 - 0}{0.588} = -4.59$$

Thus the sample coefficient b differs by 4.59 standard errors from its hypothesised value β. This is compared to the critical value of the t-distribution, using $n-2$ degrees of freedom. Since $t < -t^*_{10} (= -2.228)$, in this case the null hypothesis is rejected with 95% confidence. X does have some influence on Y. Similar tests using the income ratio and GDP to attempt to explain the birth rate show that in neither case is the slope coefficient significantly different from zero, i.e. neither of these variables influences the birth rate.

Rule of thumb for hypothesis tests

A quick and reasonably accurate method for establishing whether a coefficient is significantly different from zero is to see if it is at least twice its standard error. If so, it is significant. This works because the critical value (at 95%) of the t distribution for reasonable sample sizes is about 2.

Sometimes regression results are presented with the t-statistic (as calculated above), rather than the standard error, below each coefficient. This implicitly assumes that the hypothesis of interest is that the coefficient is zero. This is not always appropriate: in the consumption function a test for the marginal propensity to consume being equal to 1 might be of greater relevance, for example. In a demand equation, one might want to test for unit elasticity. For this reason, it is better to present the standard errors rather than the t-statistics.

Testing the significance of R²: the F-test

An equivalent test to the one above is the F-test for the significance of the R^2 statistic. Just as the significance of r was tested using the t distribution, so the significance of R^2 can be tested using the F distribution. The null hypothesis for the test is H_0: $R^2 = 0$, implying once again that X does not influence Y. The test statistic is

$$(9.26)\quad F = \frac{R^2/1}{(1-R^2)/(n-2)}$$

or equivalently

$$(9.27)\quad F = \frac{RSS/1}{ESS/(n-2)}$$

The F statistic is therefore the ratio of the regression sum of squares to the error sum of squares, each divided by their degrees of freedom (for the RSS there is one degree of freedom because of the one explanatory variable, for the ESS there are $n-2$ degrees of freedom). A high value of the F statistic rejects H_0 in favour of the alternative hypothesis, H_1: $R^2 > 0$. Evaluating (9.26) gives

$$(9.28)\quad F = \frac{0.678/1}{(1-0.678)/10} = 21.078$$

The critical value of the F distribution at the 5% significance level, with $v_1 = 1$ and

$v_2 = 10$ is, $F^*_{1,10} = 4.96$. The test statistic exceeds this, so the regression as a whole is significant. It is better to use the regression model to explain birth rate than to use the simpler model which assumes all countries have the same birth rate (the sample average).

In the case of simple regression, with only one explanatory variable, this F-test is equivalent to a t-test of the hypothesis H_0: $\beta = 0$, and also to the test H_0: $\rho = 0$. The F-test statistic is in fact the square of the t-statistic calculated earlier. This just reflects one of the relationships between different statistical distributions, for

$$F_{1, n-2} = t^2_{n-2}$$

so a superfluous test has been conducted. However, in multiple regression with more than one explanatory variable, the relationship no longer holds and the tests do fulfil different roles.

Interpreting computer output

Having shown how to use the appropriate formulae to derive estimates of the parameters, their standard errors and test hypotheses, we now present all these results as they would be generated by a computer software package, in this case *Excel*. This removes all the effort of calculation and allows us to concentrate on more important issues such as the interpretation of the results. Table 9.6 shows the computer output.

The table presents all the results we have already derived, plus a few more.

- The regression coefficients, standard errors and t-ratios are given at the bottom of the table, suitably labelled. The column headed '*P-value*' (also known as the *Prob-value*, as in Chapter 6) gives some additional information – it shows the significance level of the t-statistic. For example, the slope coefficient is significant at the level of 0.1%,[2] i.e. there is this probability of getting such a sample estimate by chance. This is much less than our usual 5% criterion, so we conclude that the sample evidence did not arise by chance.
- The program helpfully calculates the 95% confidence interval for the coefficients also, which were derived above in equation (9.23).
- Moving up the table, there is a section headed '*Analysis of Variance*'. This is similar to the ANOVA covered in Chapter 8. This table provides the sums of squares values (RSS, ESS and TSS, in that order) and their associated degrees of freedom in the '*df*' column. The '*MS*' column calculates the sums of squares each divided by their degrees of freedom, whose ratio gives the F statistic in the next column. This is the value calculated in equation (9.27). The '*Significance F*' value is similar to the *P-value* discussed previously: it shows the level at which the F statistic is significant (0.099% in this case) and saves us looking up the F tables.
- At the top of the table is given the R^2 value and the standard error of the error term, s_e, labelled 'Standard Error', which we have already come across. 'Multiple R' is simply the square root of R^2; 'Adjusted R^2' (sometimes called '*R*-bar squared' and written $\bar{R}^2$) adjusts the R^2 value for the degrees of freedom. This is an alternative measure of fit, which is not affected by the number of explanatory variables, unlike R^2. See Thomas, (1993) ch. 2 for a more detailed explanation.

---

[2] This is the area in *both* tails, so it is for a two tail test.

Table 9.6   Regression analysis output using *Excel*

	A	B	C	D	E	F	G
2	*Regression Statistics*						
3							
4	Multiple R	0.824					
5	R Square	0.678					
6	Adj. R Square	0.646					
7	Standard Error	4.132					
8	Observations	12					
9							
10	*Analysis of Variance*						
11		*df*	*SS*	*MS*	*F*	*Significance F*	
12	Regression	1	359.913	359.913	21.078	0.001	
13	Residual	10	170.754	17.075			
14	Total	11	530.667				
15							
16		*Coefficients*	*Std Err*	*t Statistic*	*P-value*	*Lower 95%*	*Upper 95%*
17							
18	Intercept	40.712	2.303	17.677	0.000	35.580	45.843
19	growth	−2.700	0.588	−4.591	0.001	−4.010	−1.390
20							

Prediction

Earlier we showed that the regression line could be used for prediction, using the figures for Costa Rica. The point estimate of Costa Rica's birth rate is calculated simply by putting its growth rate into the regression equation and assuming a zero value for the error, i.e.

$$\hat{Y} = 40.711 - 2.7 \times 3 + 0 = 32.6$$

This is a point estimate, which is unbiased, around which we can build a confidence interval. There are in fact two confidence intervals we can construct, the first for the position of the *regression line* at $X = 3$, the second for an *individual observation* (on Y) at $X = 3$. Using the 95% confidence level, the first interval is given by the formula

$$(9.29) \quad \left[\hat{Y} - t_{n-2} \times s_e \sqrt{\frac{1}{n} + \frac{\left(X_P - \overline{X}\right)^2}{\sum\left(X - \overline{X}\right)^2}}, \hat{Y} + t_{n-2} \times s_e \sqrt{\frac{1}{n} + \frac{\left(X_P - \overline{X}\right)^2}{\sum\left(X - \overline{X}\right)^2}} \right]$$

where X_P is the value of X for which the prediction is made. $t_{n-2}^{2.5\%}$ denotes the critical value of the t distribution at the 5% significance level (for a two tail test) with $n-2$ degrees of freedom. This evaluates to

$$\left[32.6 - 2.228 \times 4.132 \sqrt{\frac{1}{12} + \frac{\left(3 - 3.35\right)^2}{49.37}}, 32.6 + 2.228 \times 4.132 \sqrt{\frac{1}{12} + \frac{\left(3 - 3.35\right)^2}{49.37}} \right]$$

$$= \left[29.90, 35.30 \right]$$

This means that we predict with 95% confidence that the *average* birth rate of all countries growing at 3% p.a. is between 29.9 and 35.3.

     The second type of interval, for the value of Y itself at $X_P = 3$, is somewhat wider, because there is an additional element of uncertainty: individual countries do not lie on the regression line, but around it. This is referred to as the 95% **prediction interval**. The formula for this interval is

$$(9.30) \quad \left[\hat{Y} - t_{n-2} \times s_e \sqrt{1 + \frac{1}{n} + \frac{\left(X_P - \overline{X}\right)^2}{\sum\left(X - \overline{X}\right)^2}}, \right.$$
$$\left. \hat{Y} + t_{n-2} \times s_e \sqrt{1 + \frac{1}{n} + \frac{\left(X_P - \overline{X}\right)^2}{\sum\left(X - \overline{X}\right)^2}} \right]$$

Note the extra '1' inside the square root sign. When evaluated, this gives a 95% confidence interval of [23.01, 42.19]. Thus we are 95% confident that an individual country growing at 3% p.a. will have a birth rate within this range.

The two intervals are illustrated in Fig. 9.7. Note that the prediction is more precise (the interval is smaller):

- the closer the sample observations lie to the regression line (smaller s_e)
- the greater the spread of sample X values (larger $\Sigma(X - \overline{X})^2$)
- the closer to the mean of X the prediction is made (smaller $X_P - \overline{X}$)
- the larger the sample size.

There is an additional danger of predicting far outside the range of sample X values, if the true regression line is not linear as we have assumed. The linear sample regression line might be close to the true line within the range of sample X values but diverge substantially outside. Figure 9.8 illustrates this point.

In the birth rate sample, we have a fairly wide range of X values; few countries grow more slowly than Senegal or faster than Korea.

Units of measurement

The measurement and interpretation of the regression coefficients depends upon the units in which the variables are measured. For example, suppose we had measured the birth rate in births per *hundred* (not *thousand*) of population; what would be the

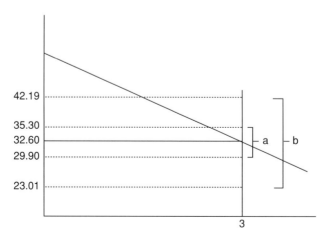

Fig. 9.7 *Confidence and prediction intervals: a = confidence interval, b = prediction interval*

Fig. 9.8 *The danger of prediction outside the range of sample data*

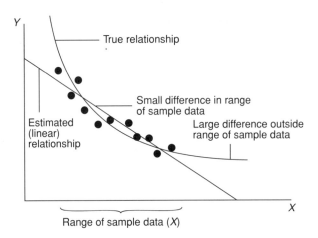

implications? Obviously nothing fundamental is changed; we ought to get the same qualitative result, with the same interpretation. However, the regression coefficients cannot remain the same: if the slope coefficient remained $b = -2.7$, this would mean that an increase in the growth rate of one percentage point reduces the birth rate by 2.7 births *per hundred*, which is clearly wrong. The right answer should be 0.27 births per hundred (equivalent to 2.7 per thousand) so the coefficient should change to $b = -0.27$. Thus, in general, the sizes of the coefficients depend upon the units in which the variables are measured. This is why one cannot judge the importance of a regression equation from the size of the coefficients alone.

It is easiest to understand this in graphical terms. A graph of the data will look exactly the same, except that the scale on the Y axis will change; it will be divided by 10. The intercept of the regression line will therefore change to $a = 4.0711$ and the slope to $b = -0.27$. Thus the regression equation becomes

$$Y_i = 4.0711 - 0.27X_i + e'_i$$

$$(e'_i = e_i/10)$$

Since nothing fundamental has altered, any hypothesis test must yield the same test statistic. Thus t and F statistics are unaltered by changes in the units of measurement, nor is R^2. However, standard errors will be divided by 10 (they have to be to preserve the t statistics; see equation (9.25) for example). Table 9.7 sets out the effects of changes in the units of measurement upon the coefficients and standard errors. In the table it is assumed that the variables have been multiplied by a constant k; in the above case $k = 1/10$ was used.

How to avoid measurement problems: calculating the elasticity

A neat way of avoiding the problems of measurement is to calculate the **elasticity**, i.e. the *proportionate* change in Y divided by the *proportionate* change in X. The proportionate changes are the same whatever units the variables are measured in. The proportionate change in X is given by $\Delta X/X$, where ΔX indicates the *change* in X. Thus the elasticity, η, is given by

$$(9.31) \quad \eta = \frac{\Delta Y / Y}{\Delta X / X} = \frac{\Delta Y}{\Delta X} \times \frac{X}{Y}$$

Table 9.7   The effects of data transformations

Factor (k) multiplying ...		Effect upon			
Y	X	a	s_a	b	s_b
k	1	— all multiplied by k —			
1	k	unchanged		divided by k	
k	k	multiplied by k		unchanged	

The second form of the equation is more useful, since $\Delta Y/\Delta X$ is simply the slope coefficient b. We simply need to multiply this by the ratio X/Y, therefore. But what values should be used for X and Y? The convention is to use the means, so we obtain the following formula for the elasticity, from a linear regression equation:

$$(9.32) \quad \eta = b \times \frac{\overline{X}}{\overline{Y}}$$

This evaluates to $-2.7 \times 3.35/31.67 = -0.29$. This is interpreted as follows: a 1% increase in the growth rate would lead to a 0.29% decrease in the birth rate. Equivalently, and perhaps a little more usefully, a 10% rise in growth (from say 3% to 3.3% p.a.) would lead to a 2.9% decline in the birth rate (e.g. from 30 to 29.13). This result is the same whatever units the variables X and Y are measured in.

Note that this elasticity is measured at the means; it would have a different value at different points along the regression line. Later on we show an alternative method for estimating the elasticity, in this case the elasticity of demand which is familiar in economics.

Non-linear transformations

So far only *linear* regression has been dealt with, that is fitting a straight line to the data. This can sometimes be restrictive, especially when there is good reason to believe that the true relationship is non-linear (e.g. the labour supply curve). Poor results would be obtained by fitting a straight line through the data in Fig. 9.9, yet the shape of the relationship seems clear at a glance.

Fortunately this problem can be solved by transforming the data, so that when graphed a linear relationship between the two variables appears. Then a straight line can be fitted to these transformed data. This is equivalent to fitting a curved line to

Fig. 9.9 *Graph of Y against X*

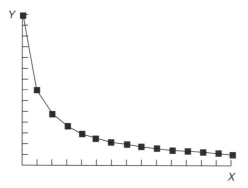

the original data. All that is needed is to find a suitable transformation to 'straighten out' the data. Given the data represented in Fig. 9.9, if Y were graphed against $1/X$ the relationship shown in Fig. 9.10 would appear.

Thus if the regression line

$$(9.33) \quad Y_i = a + b\frac{1}{X_i} + e_i$$

were fitted, this would provide a good representation of the data in Fig. 9.9. The procedure is straightforward. First, calculate the reciprocal of each of the X values and then use these (together with the original data for Y), using exactly the same methods as before. This transformation appears inappropriate for the birth rate data (see Fig. 9.1) but serves as an illustration. The transformed X values are $0.196 (= 1/5.1)$ for Brazil, $0.3125 (=1/3.2)$ for Colombia, etc. The resulting regression equation is

$$(9.34) \quad Y_i = 31.92 - 3.96\frac{1}{X_i} + e_i$$

$$s.e. \quad (1.64) \quad (1.56)$$

$$R^2 = 0.39, \quad F = 6.44, \quad n = 12$$

This appears worse than the original specification so the transformation does not appear to be a good one. Later on, we deal with a different example where a non-linear transformation does improve things.

Table 9.8 presents a number of possible shapes for data, with suggested data transformations which will allow the relationship to be estimated using linear regression. In each case, once the data have been transformed, the methods used above can be applied.

It is sometimes difficult to know which transformation (if any) to apply. Economic theory rarely suggests the form which a relationship should follow, and there are no simple statistical tests for choosing alternative formulations. The choice can sometimes be made after visual inspection of the data, or on the basis of convenience.

Fig. 9.10 *Figure 9.9 transformed: Y against 1/X*

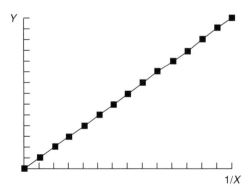

Table 9.8 Data transformations

Name	Graph of relationship	Original relationship	Transformed relationship	Regression
Double log		$Y = aX^b e$	$\ln Y = \ln a + b \ln X + \ln e$	$\ln Y$ on $\ln X$
Reciprocal		$Y = a + b/X + e$	$Y = a + b\dfrac{1}{X} + e$	Y on $\dfrac{1}{X}$
Semi-log		$e^Y = aX^b e$	$Y = \ln a + b \ln X + \ln e$	Y on $\ln X$
Exponential		$Y = e^{a+bX+e}$	$\ln Y = a + bX + e$	$\ln Y$ on X

EXERCISES

Exercise 1

The other data which Todaro might have used to analyse the birth rate were:

	Birth rate	GNP	Growth	Income ratio
Bangladesh	47	140	0.3	2.3
Tanzania	47	280	1.9	3.2
Sierra Leone	46	320	0.4	3.3
Sudan	47	380	−0.3	3.9
Kenya	55	420	2.9	6.8
Indonesia	35	530	4.1	3.4
Panama	30	1,910	3.1	8.6
Chile	25	2,560	0.7	3.8
Venezuela	35	4,220	2.4	5.2
Turkey	33	1,540	3.5	4.9
Malaysia	31	1840	4.3	5.0
Nepal	44	150	0.0	4.7
Malawi	56	200	2.7	2.4
Argentina	20	2,560	1.9	3.6

For *one* of the three possible explanatory variables (in class, different groups could examine each of the variables):

(a) Draw an XY chart of the data and comment upon the result.

(b) Would you expect a line of best fit to have a positive or negative slope? Roughly, what would you expect the slope to be?

(c) What would you expect the correlation coefficient to be?

(d) Calculate the correlation coefficient, and comment.

(e) Test to see if the correlation coefficient is different from zero. Use the 95% confidence level.

(Analysis of this problem continues in exercise 5.)

Exercise 2

The data below show consumption of margarine (in ounces per person per week) and its real price, for the UK.

Year	Consumption	Price	Year	Consumption	Price
1970	2.86	125.6	1980	3.83	104.2
1971	3.15	132.9	1981	4.11	95.5
1972	3.52	126.0	1982	4.33	88.1
1973	3.03	119.6	1983	4.08	88.9
1974	2.60	138.8	1984	4.08	97.3
1975	2.60	141.0	1985	3.76	100.0
1976	3.06	122.3	1986	4.10	86.7
1977	3.48	132.7	1987	3.98	79.8
1978	3.54	126.7	1988	3.78	79.9
1979	3.63	115.7			

(a) Draw an XY plot of the data and comment.

(b) From the chart, would you expect the line of best fit to slope up or down? *In theory*, which way should it slope?

(c) What would you expect the correlation coefficient to be, approximately?

(d) Calculate the correlation coefficient* between margarine consumption and its price.

(e) Is the coefficient significantly different from zero? What is the implication of the result?

* The following totals will reduce the burden of calculation: $\Sigma Y = 67.52$; $\Sigma X = 2{,}101.70$; $\Sigma Y^2 = 245.055$; $\Sigma X^2 = 240{,}149.27$; $\Sigma XY = 7{,}299.638$; Y is consumption, X is price. If you wish, you could calculate a logarithmic correlation. The relevant totals are: $\Sigma y = 23.88$; $\Sigma x = 89.09$; $\Sigma y^2 = 30.45$; $\Sigma x^2 = 418.40$; $\Sigma xy = 111.50$, where $y = \ln Y$ and $x = \ln X$.

(Analysis of this problem continues in exercise 6.)

Exercise 3

What would you expect to be the correlation coefficient between the following variables? Should the variables be measured contemporaneously or might there be a lag in the effect of one upon the other?

(a) nominal consumption and nominal income

(b) GDP and the imports/GDP ratio

(c) investment and the interest rate.

Exercise 4

As exercise 3, for

(a) real consumption and real income

(b) individuals' alcohol and cigarette consumption

(c) UK and US interest rates.

Exercise 5

Using the data from exercise 1, calculate the rank correlation coefficient between the variables and test its significance. How does it compare with the ordinary correlation coefficient?

Exercise 6

Calculate the rank correlation coefficient between price and quantity for the data in exercise 2. How does it compare with the ordinary correlation coefficient?

Exercise 7

(a) For the data in exercise 1, find the estimated regression line and calculate the R^2 statistic. Comment upon the result. How does it compare with Todaro's findings?

(b) Calculate the standard error of the estimate and the standard errors of the coefficients. Is the slope coefficient significantly different from zero? Comment upon the result.

(c) Test the overall significance of the regression equation and comment.

(d) Taking your own results and Todaro's, how confident do you feel that you understand the determinants of the birth rate?

(e) What do you think will be the result of estimating your equation using all 26 countries' data? Try it! What do you conclude?

Exercise 8

(a) For the data given in exercise 2, estimate the sample regression line and calculate the R^2 statistic. Comment upon the results.

(b) Calculate the standard error of the estimate and the standard errors of the coefficients. Is the slope coefficient significantly different from zero? Is demand inelastic?

(c) Test the overall significance of the regression and comment upon your result.

Exercise 9

From your results for the birth rate model, predict the birth rate for a country with *either* (a) GNP equal to $3,000, (b) a growth rate of 3% p.a., or (c) an income ratio of 7. How does your prediction compare with one using Todaro's results? Comment.

Exercise 10

Predict margarine consumption given a price of 70. Use the 99% confidence level.

Exercise 11   *Project*: Update Todaro's study using more recent data.

Exercise 12   Try to build a model of the determinants of infant mortality. You should use cross-section data for 20 countries or more and should include both developing and developed countries in the sample. Write up your findings in a report which includes the following sections: discussion of the problem; data gathering and transformations; estimation of the model; interpretation of results.

References   Maddala, G. S. (1992) *Introduction to Econometrics*, 2nd edition. Macmillan.

Thomas, R. L. (1993) *Introductory Econometrics*, 2nd edition. Longman.

10 MULTIPLE REGRESSION

Introduction

Simple regression is rather restrictive, as it assumes that there is only one explanatory factor affecting the dependent variable, which is unlikely to be true in most situations. Price *and* income affect demand, for example. Multiple regression, the subject of this chapter, overcomes this problem by allowing there to be several explanatory variables (though still only one dependent variable) in a model. The techniques are an extension of those used in simple, or bivariate, regression. Multivariate regression allows more general and more helpful models to be estimated, although this does involve new problems as well as advantages.

The regression relationship now becomes

$$(10.1) \quad Y = b_0 + b_1 X_1 + b_2 X_2 + \ldots + b_k X_k + e$$

where there are k explanatory variables. The principles used in multiple regression are basically the same as in the two variable case: the coefficients $b_0, \ldots, b_k$ are found by minimising the sum of squared errors; a standard error can be calculated for each coefficient; R^2, t-ratios, etc. can be calculated and hypothesis tests performed. However, there are a number of additional issues which arise and these are dealt with in this chapter.

The formulae for calculating coefficients, standard errors, etc. become very complicated in multiple regression and are time-consuming (and error prone) when done by hand. For this reason, these calculations are invariably done by computer nowadays. Therefore the formulae are not given in this book: instead we present the results of computer calculations (which you can replicate) and concentrate on understanding and interpretating the results. This is as it should be; the calculations themselves are the means to an end, not the end in itself.

Using spreadsheet packages

Standard spreadsheet packages such as *Lotus 123* or *Excel* can perform multiple regression analysis and are sufficient for most routine tasks. A regression equation can be calculated via menus and dialogue boxes and no knowledge of the formulae is required. However, when problems such as autocorrelation (see below) are present, specialised packages such as *TSP* or *Microfit* are much easier to use and provide more comprehensive results.

We also introduce a new example in this section, estimating a demand equation for imports into the UK over the period 1973–91. There are a number of reasons for this switch, for we could have continued with the birth rate example (you are asked to do this in the exercises). First, it allows us to work through a small 'research project' from beginning to end, including the gathering of data, data transformations, interpretation of results, etc. Secondly, the example uses time-series data and this allows us to bring out some of the particular issues that arise in such cases. Time-series data do not generally constitute a random sample of observations such as we have dealt with in the rest of this book. This is because the observations are constrained to follow one another in time rather than being randomly chosen. The proper analysis of time-series data goes far beyond the scope of this book; however, students often want or need to analyse such data using elementary techniques. This chapter therefore also emphasises the checking of the adequacy of the regression equation for such data. For a fuller treatment of the issues, the reader should consult a more advanced text such as Maddala (1992) or Thomas (1993).

Principles of multiple regression

We illustrate some of the principles involved in multiple regression using two explanatory variables, X_1 and X_2. Since we are using time-series data we replace the subscript i with a subscript t to denote the individual observations.

The sample regression equation now becomes

(10.1)　　$Y_t = b_0 + b_1 X_{1t} + b_2 X_{2t} + e_t$　　　　　　$t = 1, \ldots, T$

with three coefficients, b_0, b_1 and b_2, to be estimated. Note that b_0 now signifies the constant. Rather than fitting a line through the data, the task is now to fit a *plane* to the data, in three dimensions, as shown in Fig. 10.1.

The plane is drawn sloping down in the direction of X_1 and up in the direction of X_2. The observations are now points dotted about in three-dimensional space (with co-ordinates X_{1t}, X_{2t} and Y_t) and the task of regression analysis is to find the equation of the plane so as to minimise the sum of squares of vertical distances from each

Fig. 10.1 *The regression plane in three dimensions*

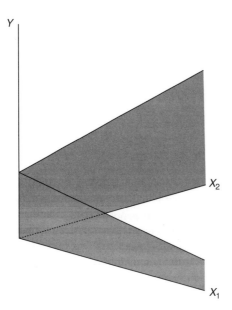

point to the plane. The principle is the same as in simple regression and the regression plane is the one that best summarises the data.

The coefficient b_0 gives the intercept on the Y axis, b_1 is the slope of the plane in the direction of the X_1 axis and b_2 is the slope in the direction of the X_2 axis. Thus b_1 gives the effect upon Y of a unit change in X_1 *assuming X_2 remains constant*. Similarly, b_2 gives the response of Y to a unit change in X_2, given no change in X_1. If X_1 and X_2 both change by 1, then the effect on Y is $b_1 + b_2$. b_1 and b_2 are both estimates of the true parameters β_1 and β_2 and so standard errors and confidence intervals can be calculated, implying that we are not absolutely certain about the true position of the plane. In general, the smaller these standard errors, the better, since it implies less uncertainty about the true relationship between Y and the X variables.

When there are more than two explanatory variables, more than three dimensions are needed to represent the data and a **hyperplane** has to be fitted to the data. The reader will understand that it is difficult to give a visual interpretation of this case.

What determines imports into the UK?

To illustrate multiple regression we suppose that we have the job of finding out what determines the volume of imports into the United Kingdom and whether there are any policy implications of the result. We are given this very open-ended task, which we have to carry through from start to finish. We end up by estimating a demand equation, so the analysis serves as a model for any demand estimation, for example a firm trying to find out about the demand for its product.

How should we set about this task? The project can be broken down into the following steps:

(1) Theoretical considerations: what can economic theory tell us about the problem and how will this affect our estimation procedures?
(2) Data gathering: what data do we need? Are there any definitional problems, for example?
(3) Data transformation: are the data suitable for the task? We might want to transform one or more variables before estimation.
(4) Estimation: this is mainly done automatically, by the computer.
(5) Interpretation of the results: what do the results tell us? Do they appear satisfactory? Do we need to improve the model? Are there any policy conclusions?

Although this appears reasonably clear cut, in practice these steps are often mixed up. A researcher might gather the data, estimate a model and then not be happy with the results. He therefore goes back and gets some different data, perhaps some new variables, or maybe tries a different method of investigation until 'satisfactory' results are obtained. There is usually some element of data 'mining' or 'fishing' involved. These methodological issues are examined in more detail later on.

Theoretical issues

What does economic theory tell us about imports? Like any market, the quantity transacted depends upon supply and demand. Strictly, therefore, we should estimate a **simultaneous equation model** of both the demand and supply equations. Since this is beyond the scope of this book (see Thomas, ch. 8 or Maddala, ch. 9 for analyses of such models) we simplify by assuming that, as Britain is a small economy in the world market, we can buy any quantity of imports that we demand (at the prevailing price). In other words, supply is never a constraint, and Britain's demand never influences the world price. This assumption, which seems reasonable, means that we can concentrate on estimating the demand equation alone.

Secondly, economic theory suggests that demand depends upon income and relative prices, particularly the prices of close substitutes and complements. Furthermore, rational consumers do not suffer from money illusion, so real variables should be used throughout.

Economic theory does *not* tell us some things, however. It does not tell us whether the relationship is linear or not. Nor does it tell us whether demand responds *immediately* to price or income changes, or whether there is a lag. For these questions, the data are more likely to give us the answer.

Data

The raw data are presented in Table 10.1, obtained from official UK statistics. Note that there is some slight rounding of the figures: imports are measured to the nearest £0.1bn (£100m) so there is a possible (rounding) error of up to about 0.1%. This is unlikely to substantially affect our estimates.

The variables are defined as follows:

Imports (variable M): imports of goods and services into the UK, at current prices, in £bn.
Income (*GDP*): UK gross domestic product at factor cost, at current prices, in £bn.
The GDP deflator (P_{GDP}): an index of the ratio of nominal to real GDP. 1985 = 100.
The price of imports (P_M): the unit value index of imports, 1990 = 100
The price of competing products (P): the retail price index (RPI), 1985 = 100.

These variables were chosen from a wide range of possibilities. To take income as an

Table 10.1 Original data for study of imports

Year	Imports (£bn current prices)	GDP (£bn current prices)	GDP deflator	Unit value index	RPI – all items
1973	19.0	65.7	25.2	23.7	25.1
1974	27.1	75.6	29.4	34.6	29.1
1975	28.8	95.6	37.5	39.5	36.1
1976	36.6	112.5	43.0	48.4	42.1
1977	42.4	129.5	48.3	55.9	48.8
1978	45.4	149.5	54.1	58.1	52.8
1979	54.3	173.2	61.0	61.8	59.9
1980	57.6	201.0	72.3	67.8	70.7
1981	60.4	218.8	79.6	73.7	79.1
1982	67.8	238.4	85.2	79.9	85.9
1983	77.6	261.2	90.0	84.2	89.8
1984	92.8	280.7	94.9	91.8	94.3
1985	99.0	307.9	100.0	96.3	100.0
1986	101.2	328.3	102.6	91.9	103.4
1987	111.7	360.7	107.8	94.6	107.7
1988	124.8	401.4	114.8	93.7	113.0
1989	142.8	441.8	123.7	97.7	121.8
1990	148.3	478.9	133.6	100.0	133.3
1991	140.8	494.8	141.8	101.2	141.1
1992	149.2	514.6	147.9	102.1	146.4
1993	167.5	543.8	153.4	110.8	148.7

example, we could use personal disposable income or GDP. Since firms as well as consumers import goods, the wider measure is used. Then there is the question of whether to use GDP or GNP, and whether to measure them at factor cost or market prices. Because there is little difference between these different magnitudes, this is not an important decision in this case. However, in a research project one might have to consider such issues in more detail.

Data transformations   We must transform the variables to real terms before we can estimate our regression equation. The transformed variables are shown in Table 10.2.[1]

These variables are derived as follows:

Real imports (M/P_M): this series is obtained by dividing the nominal series for imports by the unit value index (i.e. the import price index). The series gives imports at 1985 prices (in £bn).

Real income (GDP/P_{GDP}): this is the nominal GDP series divided by the GDP deflator to give GDP at 1985 prices (in £bn).

Real import prices (P_M/P): the unit value index is divided by the RPI to give this series. It is an index number series with $1990 = 100$.

Note that the imports and GDP series use the same price base and that the reference year for the price index is different. It is not essential to use the same base or

Table 10.2 Transformed data

	Real imports M/P_M	Real GDP GDP/P_{GDP}	Real UVI P_M/P
1973	77.2	260.7	125.9
1974	75.4	257.1	158.5
1975	70.2	254.9	145.9
1976	72.8	261.6	153.2
1977	73.0	268.1	152.7
1978	75.2	276.3	146.7
1979	84.6	283.9	137.5
1980	81.8	278.0	127.8
1981	78.9	274.9	124.2
1982	81.7	279.8	124.0
1983	88.8	290.2	125.0
1984	97.3	295.8	129.8
1985	99.0	307.9	128.4
1986	106.0	320.0	118.5
1987	113.7	334.6	117.1
1988	128.3	349.7	110.5
1989	140.8	357.2	106.9
1990	142.8	358.5	100.0
1991	134.0	348.9	95.6
1992	140.7	347.9	93.0
1993	145.6	354.5	99.3

[1] The transformed numbers have been rounded to 1 d.p. Normally one would not round here, but it has been done so that you can replicate the results if you type the transformed values into a computer. Again, this has little effect upon the estimates.

reference year for all the series, though it can be more convenient to do so. When we interpret the results we shall have to take account of the units of measurement.

We should now 'eyeball' the data using appropriate graphical techniques. This will give a broad overview of the characteristics of the data and any unusual or erroneous observations may be spotted. This is an important step in the analysis.

Figure 10.2 shows a time-series plot of the three variables, with the price index measured on the right-hand axis. The graph shows that both imports and GDP increase smoothly over the period, and that there appears to be a fairly close relationship between them. This is confirmed by the XY plot of imports and GDP in Fig. 10.3. Care should be taken in interpreting this since it shows only the *partial* relationship between two of the three variables. However, it does appear to be fairly strong.

The price of imports has declined by about 20% over the period so this might also have contributed to the rise in imports. There is not such an obvious relationship between imports and their price, however. On the basis of the graphs we might expect a positive relation between imports and GDP, and a negative one between imports and their price. Both of these expectations are in line with what economic theory would predict.

Estimation

The model to be estimated is therefore

$$(10.3) \quad \left(\frac{M}{P_M}\right)_t = b_0 + b_1\left(\frac{\text{GDP}}{P_{\text{GDP}}}\right)_t + b_2\left(\frac{P_M}{P}\right)_t + e_t$$

Fig. 10.2 *A time-series plot of imports, GDP and import prices (real terms)*

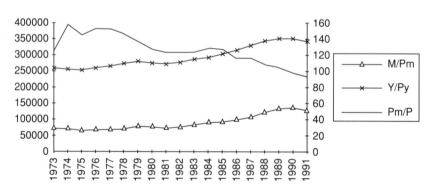

Note: This is a multiple time-series graph as described in Chapter 1.

Fig. 10.3 *XY graph of imports against GDP*

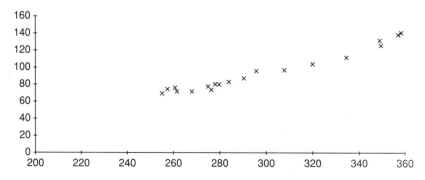

To simplify notation we rewrite this as

(10.4) $m_t = b_0 + b_1 gdp_t + b_2 pm_t + e_t$

The results of estimating this equation are shown in Table 10.3, which shows the output in a slightly different format. This is produced by *Microfit*, a specialised regression package.

The print-out gives all the results we need, which may be summarised as

(10.5) $m_t = -80.2 + 0.63\, gdp_t - 0.09\, pm_t + e_t$
$$\qquad\qquad (0.06) \qquad (0.12)$$
$$R^2 = 0.97, \quad F_{2,16} = 263.6, \quad n = 19$$

How do we judge and interpret these results? As expected, we obtain a positive coefficient on income and a negative one on price. Note that it is difficult to give a sensible interpretation to the constant. The coefficients should be judged in two ways: in terms of their *size* and their *significance*.

Size

As noted earlier, the size of a coefficient depends upon the units of measurement. How 'big' is the coefficient 0.63, for income? This tells us that a rise in GDP, measured in 1985 prices, of £1bn would raise imports, also measured in 1985 prices, by £0.63bn. This is a bit cumbersome. It is better to interpret everything in proportionate terms, and calculate the *elasticity* of imports with respect to income. This is the proportionate change in imports divided by the proportionate change in price:

Table 10.3 Regression results using *Microfit*

Ordinary Least Squares Estimation
****

Dependent variable is IMPORTS
19 observations used for estimation from 1973 to 1991

****

Regressor	Coefficient	Standard Error	T-Ratio [Prob]
CONSTANT	−80.1871	31.0990	−2.5784 [.020]
GDP	.63148	.057960	10.8950 [.000]
PRICE	−.093862	.11688	−.80306 [.434]

****

R-Squared	.97054	F-statistic F(2, 16)	263.554 [.000]
R-Bar-Squared	.96686	S.E. of Regression	4.4865
Residual Sum of Squares	322.0537	Mean of Dependent Variable	95.8684
S.D. of Dependent Variable	24.6440	Maximum of Log-likelihood	−53.8475
DW-statistic	.74229		

Note: The layout of the results is similar to *Excel*. The values in square brackets, labelled [Prob], are the same as *P-values* in *Excel*. The only additional information is the DW-statistic, which is discussed later, and the log-likelihood, which we shall not discuss.

$$(10.6) \quad \eta_{gdp} = \frac{\Delta m/m}{\Delta gdp/gdp}$$

which can be evaluated (see equation (9.32)) as:

$$(10.7) \quad \eta_{gdp} = b_1 \times \frac{\overline{gdp}}{\overline{m}} = 0.63 \times \frac{297.8}{95.9} = 1.96$$

which shows that imports are highly responsive to income. A 3% rise in real GDP (a fairly typical annual figure) leads to an approximate 6% rise in imports, as long as prices do not change at the same time. Thus as income rises, imports rise substantially faster.

A similar calculation for the price variable yields

$$(10.8) \quad \eta_{pm} = -0.09 \times \frac{127.8}{95.9} = -0.13$$

which suggests that imports are inelastic with respect to price. It would take a 10% price rise (relative to domestic prices) to lower import demand by about 1%.

Significance
We can test whether each coefficient is significantly different from zero, i.e. whether the variable truly affects imports or not, using a conventional hypothesis test. For income we have the test statistic

$$t = \frac{b_1 - \beta_1}{S_{b_1}} = \frac{0.63 - 0}{0.058} = 10.90$$

which has a t distribution with $n - k - 1 = 19 - 2 - 1 = 16$ degrees of freedom (k is the number of explanatory variables, two). The critical value for a one tail test at the 95% confidence level is 1.746. Since the test statistic exceeds this we reject H_0: $\beta_1 = 0$ in favour of H_1: $\beta_1 > 0$. Hence income does indeed affect imports; the sample data are unlikely to have arisen purely by chance. Note that this t-ratio is given on the *Microfit* print-out.

For price, the test statistic is

$$t = \frac{-0.094 - 0}{0.117} = -0.80$$

which is greater than -1.746, so does not fall into the rejection region. H_0: $\beta_2 = 0$ cannot be rejected, therefore. So not only is the coefficient on price quantitatively small, it is insignificantly different from zero, i.e. there is a reasonable probability of this result arising simply by chance.

The significance of the regression as a whole

We can test this via an F test as we did for simple regression. This is a test of the hypothesis that *all* the slope coefficients are simultaneously zero (equivalent to the hypothesis that $R^2 = 0$):

H_0: $\beta_1 = \beta_2 = 0$
H_1: $\beta_1 \neq \beta_2 \neq 0$

This tests whether *either* income *or* price affects demand. Since we have already found that income is a significant explanatory variable, via the *t*-test, it would be surprising if this null hypothesis were not rejected. The test statistic is similar to equation (9.27):

$$(10.9) \quad F = \frac{\text{RSS}/k}{\text{ESS}/(n-k-1)}$$

which has an *F* distribution with *k* and $n - k - 1$ degrees of freedom. Substituting in the appropriate values[2] gives

$$F = \frac{10609.83/2}{322.05/16} = 263.55$$

which is in excess of the critical value for the *F* distribution of 3.63 (at 5% significance), so the null hypothesis is rejected, as expected. The actual significance level is given by *Microfit* as 0.000, which indicates that it is less than 0.05%.

Are the results satisfactory?

The results so far *appear* satisfactory: we have found one significant coefficient, the R^2 value is quite high at 97% (although R^2 values tend to be high in time-series regressions) and the result of the *F* test proves the regression is worthwhile. Nevertheless, it is perhaps surprising to find no effect from the price variable; we might as well drop it from the equation and just regress imports on GDP.

A more stringent test is to use the equation for forecasting, since this uses out-of-sample information for the test. So far, the diagnostic tests such as the *F* test are based on the same data that were used for estimation. A more suitable test might be to see if the equation can forecast imports to within (say) 3% of the correct value. Since real imports increased by about 3.1% p.a. on average between 1973 and 1991, a simple forecasting rule would be to increase the current year's figure by 3.1%. The regression model might be compared to this standard.

Forecasts for 1992 and 1993 are obtained by inserting the values of the explanatory variables for these years into the regression equation, giving

1992: $\hat{Y} = -80.19 + 0.63 \times 347.9 - 0.094 \times 93.0 = 130.8$
1992: $\hat{Y} = -80.19 + 0.63 \times 354.5 - 0.094 \times 99.0 = 134.4$

Microfit calculates these forecasts automatically and presents the screen shown in Table 10.4.

The percentage error is about 8% in each year. This is not very good! Both years are under-predicted by a large amount. The simple growth rule would have given predictions of 138.2 and 142.4 which are much closer. *Microfit* also calculates a standard error for each of the forecast errors. Although we do not explain their derivation, their interpretation should be familiar. Since each forecast error is about twice its own standard error, this suggests the forecasts are significantly different from the actual values. More work needs to be done.

[2] Microfit only gives the ESS = 322.05, but we can use TSS = ESS/$(1 - R^2)$ and RSS = TSS − ESS to get the other values.

Table 10.4 Forecasts from *Microfit*

Static Forecasts

****

Based on OLS regression of IMPORTS on:
CONSTANT   GDP   PRICE
19 observations used for estimation from 1973 to 1991

****

Observation	Actual	Prediction	Error	S.D. of Error
1992	140.7000	130.7752	9.9248	5.0769
1993	145.6000	134.3517	11.2483	4.9181

Improving the model

Because the price variable 'doesn't work' we might try its lagged value as an explanatory variable (an alternative would be simply to drop it from the equation, but this is theoretically unsatisfactory; demand equations should have a price variable!). The justification for this change is that importers might be tied in to long term contracts so they cannot alter demand quickly when prices change (stock levels, rather than imports, would change in the short run).[3] Demand might not respond until a year or so has passed. We therefore try the model

$$(10.10) \quad m_t = b_0 + b_1 gdp_t + b_2 pm_{t-1} + e_t$$

which gives the result (output not shown):

$$(10.11) \quad m_t = -62.57 + 0.61\, gdp_t - 0.19\, pm_{t-1} + e_t$$
$$\qquad\qquad\qquad (0.03) \qquad\quad (0.07)$$
$$R^2 = 0.98, \quad F_{2,16} = 362.1, \quad n = 19$$

This is slightly better, since the price variable is now 'significant' (i.e. the *t*-ratio is -2.59 so $H_0: \beta_2 = 0$ is rejected) and its coefficient is much increased. The elasticity remains quite small, however (-0.25), so it still has quantitatively little effect. Note that the coefficient on income changes slightly, though this does not alter any of our conclusions. Forecasting performance is slightly improved, but is still not as good as the simple growth rule:

Year	Actual value	Predicted value	% error
1992	140.7	132.7	6.0%
1993	145.6	137.3	6.1%

As our next move we could try estimating the relationship in (natural) logs. This has the advantages that (a) it utilises a different functional form, which may be more appropriate, and (b) the coefficients are direct estimates of the elasticities, so can be easily interpreted. In view of this second advantage, we might have started the analysis using logs rather than using 'levels' data.

---

[3] Note that this might also justify lags on the income variable.

The data transformed into (natural) logarithms are shown in Table 10.5 (selected years only). We can try estimating with either price or lagged price as the explanatory variable (along with income); the latter turns out better so is reported here in Table 10.6.

We can now see directly that the elasticity with respect to income is 1.8; with respect to (lagged) price it is -0.28, which is 'significant' ($t = -3.87$) but still quite small. The price inelasticity of import demand appears to be a fairly robust result. The forecasting performance of this equation is substantially better:

Year	Actual	Predicted	Difference
1992	4.947	4.908	0.039
1993	4.981	4.949	0.032

Note: Note that these figures are in natural logs, i.e. 4.947 = ln 140.7, etc.

Table 10.5   Data in natural logarithm form

	ln m	ln gdp	ln pm
1973	4.346	5.563	4.835
1974	4.323	5.549	5.066
1975	4.251	5.541	4.983
1976	4.288	5.567	5.032
1977	4.290	5.591	5.028
⋮	⋮	⋮	⋮
1989	4.947	5.878	4.672
1990	4.961	5.882	4.605
1991	4.898	5.855	4.560

Table 10.6   Results of logarithmic regression

Ordinary Least Squares Estimation

****

Dependent variable is LNIMPORT
19 observations used for estimation from 1973 to 1991

****

Regressor	Coefficient	Standard Error	T-Ratio [Prob]
CONSTANT	-4.3412	.74610	-5.8186 [.000]
LNGDP	1.8008	.081021	22.2267 [.000]
LNP(-1)	$-.28278$	.072996	-3.8739 [.001]

****

R-Squared	.98611	F-statistic F(2, 16)	568.0946 [.000]
R-Bar-Squared	.98438	S.E. of Regression	.030176
Residual Sum of Squares	.014569	Mean of Dependent Variable	4.5342
S.D. of Dependent Variable	.24143	Maximum of Log-likelihood	41.1863
DW-statistic	1.4057		

The difference (actual minus predicted) is roughly the percentage error, which is coming down to around 3–4% and beginning to look respectable. This is confirmed if we transform back to non-logarithmic form (using e^x as the inverse transformation):

Year	Actual	Predicted	% error
1992	140.7	135.3	4.0%
1993	145.6	141.1	3.2%

The accuracy of these forecasts can also be tested more formally using a **Chow test** (named after its inventor). The procedure is as follows:

(1) Use the first n_1 observations for estimation, the last n_2 observations for the forecast. In this case we have $n_1 = 19$, $n_2 = 2$.
(2) Estimate the regression equation using the first n_1 observations, as above, and obtain the error sum of squares, ESS_1.
(3) Re-estimate the equation using all $n_1 + n_2$ observations, and obtain the pooled error sum of squares, $\text{ESS}_\text{P.}$
(4) Calculate the F statistic:

$$F = \frac{\left(\text{ESS}_\text{P} - \text{ESS}_1\right)/n_2}{\text{ESS}_1 /\left(n_1 - k - 1\right)}$$

Compare the F statistic with the critical value of the F distribution with n_2, $n_1 - k - 1$ degrees of freedom. If the test statistic exceeds the critical value, the model fails the prediction test. The null hypothesis is that the regression coefficients remain stable between the two sub-periods. The alternative hypothesis is that they differ.

A large value of the test statistic indicates a large divergence between ESS_P and ESS_1 (adjusted for the different sample sizes), suggesting that the model does not fit the two periods equally well.

Evaluating the test (for the log regression), we have $\text{ESS}_1 = 0.014569$ (which can be obtained directly from computer print-out). Estimating using pooled data gives:

$$\ln m_t = -4.12 + 1.80 \ln gdp_t - 0.32 \ln pm_{t-1}$$
$$(0.08) \qquad\quad (0.06)$$
$$R^2 = 0.99, \quad F_{2,16} = 765.2, \quad \text{ESS} = 0.016084$$

so the test statistic is

$$F = \frac{\left(0.016084 - 0.014569\right)/2}{0.014569/16} = 0.83$$

The critical value of the F distribution for 2,16 degrees of freedom is 3.63, so the equation passes the test for parameter stability.

It is noticeable that the predictions are always too low (for all the models); the errors in both years are positive. This suggests a slight 'boom' in imports relative to what one might expect. Perhaps we have omitted an explanatory variable which has changed markedly in 1992–93 or perhaps the errors are not truly random. Alternatively, we could have chosen the wrong functional form for the model. Since we already have an R^2 value of 0.99 we are unlikely to find another variable which adds significantly to the explanatory power of the model. Therefore we shall examine the errors in the model.

Analysis of the errors   This is another important part of the checking procedure, to see if the model is adequate or whether it is mis-specified (e.g. has the wrong functional form, or a missing explanatory variable). If the model is a good one then the error term should contain only random elements and ideally should be unpredictable. If there are any predictable elements to it, then we could use this information to improve our model and forecasts. Unlike forecasting, this is a within-sample procedure.

A complete, formal, treatment of this issue is again beyond the scope of this book (see for example Thomas, ch. 5, or Maddala, chs 5,6 and 12). Instead, we give an outline of how to detect the problems and some simple procedures which might overcome them. At least, if you are aware of the problem you know that you should consult a more advanced text.

First, we could check the errors for Normality by constructing their frequency distribution, as was done in the previous chapter. This is left as an exercise for the reader. Secondly, we can examine the error term for evidence of **autocorrelation**. This was introduced briefly in Chapter 1, so should be familiar. To recapitulate: autocorrelation occurs when one error observation is correlated with an earlier (often the previous) one. It only occurs with time-series data (in cross-section, the ordering of the observations does not matter). Autocorrelation could occur in the import equation because of the 'stickiness' of imports, i.e. if imports are higher than predicted in period t, then they are likely to be high in $t + 1$ also. This could explain the two negative forecasting errors. Alternatively, it could be a sign of the wrong functional form of the equation having been estimated.

Checking for autocorrelation

The errors are obtained by subtracting the fitted values from the actual observations. Using time-series data we have:

$$(10.12) \quad e_t = Y_t - \hat{Y}_t = Y_t - b_0 - b_1 X_{1t} - b_2 X_{2t}$$

The errors obtained from the import demand equation (for the logarithmic model of import demand, X_2 representing lagged price) are shown in Table 10.7 and are graphed in Fig. 10.4.

Table 10.7 Calculation of residuals

Observation	Actual	Predicted	Residual
1973	4.346	4.354	−0.008
1974	4.323	4.285	0.038
1975	4.251	4.204	0.047
1976	4.288	4.275	0.013
1977	4.290	4.305	−0.015
⋮	⋮	⋮	⋮
1989	4.947	4.914	0.033
1990	4.961	4.930	0.031
1991	4.898	4.900	−0.002

Fig. 10.4 *Time-series graph of the errors from the import demand equation*

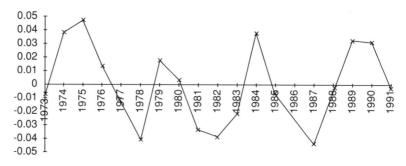

The graph suggests a definite pattern, that of *positive* autocorrelation: positive errors tend to follow positive errors, negative errors generally follow negative ones. In other words, there appears to be a positive correlation between e_t and e_{t-1}. A truly random series would have a low or zero correlation.

This non-randomness can be summarised and tested numerically by the **Durbin–Watson** (DW) statistic (named after its two inventors). This is routinely printed out by specialist software packages (see the *Microfit* print-out earlier) but, unfortunately, not by spreadsheet programs. The statistic is a one-tail test of the null hypothesis of no autocorrelation against the alternative of positive, or of negative, autocorrelation. The test statistic always lies in the range 0–4 and is compared to critical values d_L and d_U (given in Appendix Table A7). The decision rule is best presented graphically, as Fig. 10.5.

Low values of DW (below d_L) suggest positive autocorrelation, high values (above $4 - d_L$) suggest negative autocorrelation, and a value near 2 (between d_U and $4 - d_U$) suggests the problem is absent. There are also two regions where the test is, unfortunately, inconclusive.

The test statistic can be calculated by the formula

> The DW statistic can also be approximated using the correlation coefficient between e_t and e_{t-1}, and then DW $\approx 2 \times (1 - r)$. The approximation gets closer, the larger the sample size. It should be reasonably accurate if you have 20 observations or more.

$$(10.13) \quad DW = \frac{\sum_{t=2}^{n}\left(e_t - e_{t-1}\right)^2}{\sum_{t=1}^{n} e_t^2}$$

This is relatively straightforward using a spreadsheet program. Table 10.8 shows part of the calculation. Hence:

$$DW = \frac{0.02048}{0.01457} = 1.41$$

Fig. 10.5 *The Durbin–Watson test statistic*

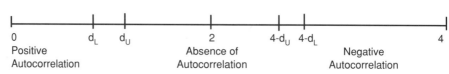

Table 10.8 Calculation of the DW statistic

	e_t	e_{t-1}	$e_t - e_{t-1}$	$(e_t - e_{t-1})^2$	e_t^2
1973	−0.008				
1974	0.038	−0.008	0.045	0.00206	0.00142
1975	0.047	0.038	0.009	8.3E-05	0.0022
1976	0.013	0.047	−0.034	0.00114	0.00017
1977	−0.015	0.013	-0.028	0.00076	0.00021
⋮	⋮	⋮	⋮	⋮	⋮
1989	0.033	−0.005	0.038	0.00147	0.0011
1990	0.031	0.033	−0.002	3.3E-06	0.00099
1991	−0.002	0.031	−0.034	0.00113	4.8E−06
Totals				0.02048	0.01457

The result suggests possible positive autocorrelation[4] of the errors. For $n = 20$ (close enough to $n = 19$) the critical values are $d_L = 1.100$ and $d_U = 1.537$ (using the 95% confidence level, see Table A7) so in this case we have an inconclusive result. It *may* be the case therefore that we could obtain better estimates and predictions by taking further account of the autocorrelated nature of the errors. Note that the original equation estimated (see Table 10.3) had a Durbin–Watson statistic of 0.74, which does suggest positive autocorrelation. Using the lagged price variable yields DW = 0.93, still indicating positive autocorrelation. The switch to the logarithmic form pushes the DW statistic into the inconclusive region and suggests this is a better functional form for the equation.

Autocorrelation can arise if a linear relationship is estimated when the true relationship is non-linear (e.g. in logarithms). In this case, the errors tend to follow a curve (see Fig. 9.7 for an illustration) and positive autocorrelation results. The non-linear transformation (taking logs) resolves the problem.

Spurious regression
There is a danger when using time-series data of getting 'spurious' regressions, similar to the existence of spurious correlations. This danger occurs when the variables used in the analysis are trended (as many economic variables are) so that 'significant' results (e.g. high t-ratios) are obtained even though there is no true underlying relationship. It has been suggested that a low value of the DW statistic (typically, less than the R^2 value) can be a symptom of such a problem. The problem can often be alleviated by removing the trends from the data, as was done with the investment data in Chapter 1, and then re-estimating using the transformed data. For a detailed exposition, see Thomas, ch. 7, or Maddala, ch. 6.

Finding the right model

How do you know that you have found the 'right' model for the data? Can you be confident that another researcher, using the same data, would arrive at the same results? How can you be sure there isn't a relevant explanatory variable out there that you have omitted from your model? Without trying them all it is difficult to be sure. Good modelling is based on theoretical considerations (e.g. models consistent with

---

[4] The correlation between e_t and e_{t-1} is 0.285, yielding an estimate of DW = 1.43.

economic or business principles) and statistical ones (e.g. significant t-ratios). One can identify two different approaches to modelling:

- *General to specific*: this starts off with a comprehensive model, including all the likely explanatory variables, then simplifies it.
- *Specific to general*: this begins with a simple model that is easy to understand, then explanatory variables are added to improve the model's explanatory power.

There is something to be said for both approaches, but it is not guaranteed that the two will end up with the same model. The former approach is usually favoured nowadays; it suffers less from the problem of **omitted variable bias** (OVB, discussed below) and the simplifying procedure is usually less *ad hoc* than that of generalising a simple model. A very general model will almost certainly initially contain a number of irrelevant explanatory variables. However, this is not much of a problem (and less serious than OVB): standard errors on the coefficients tend to be higher than otherwise, but this is remedied once the variables are excluded.

It is rare for either of these approaches to be adopted in its pure, ideal form. For example, in the import demand equation we should have started out with several lags on the price variable, since we cannot be sure how long imports take to adjust to price changes. Therefore we might have started with (assuming a maximum lag of two years is 'reasonable'):

$$(10.14) \quad m_t = b_0 + b_1 gdp_t + b_2 pm_t + b_3 pm_{t-1} + b_4 pm_{t-2} + e_t$$

If b_2 proved to be insignificantly different from zero we would then re-estimate the equation without pm_t and obtain new coefficient estimates. If the new b_4 proved insignificant we would omit pm_{t-2} and re-estimate. This process would continue until all the remaining coefficients had significant t-ratios. We would then have the final, simplified model. At each stage we would omit the variable with the least significant coefficient. Having found the right model we could then test it on new data, to see if it can explain the new observations.

In practice the procedure is not as mechanical (nor as pure) as this and more judgement should be exercised. You may not want to exclude all the price variables from a demand equation even though the t-ratios are small. A coefficient may be large in *size* even though it is not *significant*. 'Not significant' does not mean the same as 'insignificant', rather that there is a lot of uncertainty about its true value. In modelling imports, we used the 1992 and 1993 observations to test the model's forecasts. When it failed, we revised the model and applied the forecast test again. But this is no longer a strictly independent test, since we used the 1992–93 observations to decide upon revision to the model.

To briefly sum up a complex and contentious debate, a good model should be:

- *consistent with theory*: an estimated demand curve should not slope upwards, for example;
- *statistically satisfactory*: there should be good explanatory power (e.g. R^2, F statistics), the coefficients should be statistically significant (t-ratios) and the errors should be random. It should also predict well, using new data (i.e. data not used in the estimation procedure);
- *simple*: although a very complicated model predicts better, it might be difficult for the reader to understand and interpret.

Sometimes these criteria conflict and then the researcher must use her judgement and experience to decide between them.

Simplifying a general model is largely based on hypothesis testing. Usually this means a hypothesis of the form H_0: $\beta = 0$ using a t-test. Sometimes, however, the hypothesis is more complex, as in the following examples:

- You want to test the equality of two coefficients, H_0: $\beta_1 = \beta_2$.
- You want to test if a *group* of coefficients are all zero, H_0: $\beta_1 = \beta_2 = 0$.

A general method for testing these compound hypotheses is to use an F test. We illustrate this by examining whether consumers suffer from money illusion in the import demand equation. We assumed, in line with economic theory, that only relative prices matter and used P_M/P as an explanatory variable. But suppose consumers actually respond differently to changes in P_M and in P? In that case we should enter P_M and P as separate explanatory variables and they would have different coefficients. In other words, we should estimate (using the log form[5]):

$$(10.15) \quad \ln m_t = c_0 + c_1 \ln gdp_t + c_2 \ln P_{Mt-1} + c_3 \ln P_{t-1} + e_t$$

rather than

$$(10.16) \quad \ln m_t = b_0 + b_1 \ln gdp_t + b_2 \ln pm_{t-1} + e_t$$

where P_M is the nominal price of imports and P is the nominal price level. We would expect $c_2 < 0$ and $c_3 > 0$. Note that (10.16) is a *restricted* form of (10.15), with the restriction $c_2 = -c_3$ imposed. A lack of money illusion implies that this restriction should be valid and that (10.16) is the correct form of model.

How can we test this? If the restriction is valid, (10.15) and (10.16) should fit equally well and thus have similar error sums of squares. Conversely, if they have very different ESS values, then we would reject the validity of the restriction. To carry out the test, we therefore do the following:

- Estimate the *unrestricted* model (10.15) and obtain the *unrestricted* ESS from it (ESS_U).
- Estimate the *restricted* model (10.16) and obtain the *restricted* ESS (ESS_R).
- Form the test statistic

$$F = \frac{\left(ESS_R - ESS_U\right)/q}{ESS_U/\left(n-k-1\right)}$$

where q is the number of restrictions (one in this case) and k is the number of explanatory variables in the *unrestricted* model.
- Compare the test statistic with the critical value of the F distribution with q and $n - k - 1$ degrees of freedom. If the test statistic exceeds the critical value, reject the restricted model in favour of the unrestricted one.

We have already estimated the restricted model (equation (10.16)) and from that we obtain $ESS_R = 0.014569$ (see Table 10.6). Estimating the unrestricted model gives

$$(10.17) \quad \ln m_t = -6.77 + 2.02 \ln gdp_t + 0.26 \ln P_{Mt-1} - 0.21 \ln P_{t-1+e_t}$$

with $ESS_U = 0.01187$. The test statistic is therefore

---

5 Note that it is much easier to test the restriction in log form, since p_m and p are entered additively. It would be much harder to do this in levels form.

$$(10.18) \quad F = \frac{(0.014569 - 0.01187)/1}{0.01187/(19 - 3 - 1)} = 3.41$$

The critical value at the 95% confidence level is 4.54, so the restriction is accepted. Consumers use relative, not absolute, prices and economic theory is vindicated! Note the similarity (in absolute terms) of the two price coefficients in (10.17).

This method is quite general: it is possible to test any number of (linear) restrictions by estimating the restricted and unrestricted forms of the equation.

Omitted variable bias   Omitting a relevant explanatory variable from a regression equation can lead to serious problems. Not only is the model inadequate because there is no information about the effect of the omitted variable but, in addition, the coefficients on the variables which *are* included are usually biased. This is called *omitted variable bias* (OVB).

In our model of import demand we found that omitted variable bias was not a serious problem: if we omit the price variable, nothing much happens. The R^2 figure falls slightly and the coefficient on GDP changes marginally. Nevertheless, the change in the coefficient shows the effect of omitting another variable. If the price variable were more important (i.e. it had a bigger influence upon imports) then its exclusion from the model could change the income coefficient substantially.

The direction of OVB depends upon two things: the correlation between the omitted and included explanatory variables and the sign of the coefficient on the omitted variable. Thus if you have to omit what you believe is a relevant explanatory variable (because the observations are unavailable, for example) you might be able to infer the direction of bias on the included variable(s). Table 10.9 summarises the possibilities, where the true model is $Y = b_0 + b_1 X_1 + b_2 X_2 + e$ but the estimated model omits the X_2 variable. Table 10.9 only applies to a single omitted variable; when there are several, matters are more complicated (see Maddala, ch. 4).

In addition to coefficients being biased, their standard errors are biased upwards as well, so that inferences and confidence intervals will be incorrect. The best advice therefore is to ensure you don't omit a relevant variable!

Table 10.9   The effects of omitted variable bias

Sign of omitted coefficient, b_2	Correlation between X_1 and X_2	Direction of bias of b_1	Example values of b_1 — True	Example values of b_1 — Estimated
> 0	> 0	upwards	0.5	0.9
			-0.5	-0.1
> 0	< 0	downwards	0.5	0.1
			-0.5	-0.9
< 0	> 0	downwards	0.5	0.1
			-0.5	-0.9
< 0	< 0	upwards	0.5	0.9
			-0.5	-0.1

Dummy variables, trends and seasonals

A *dummy variable* is one that takes on a restricted range of values, usually just 0 and 1. Despite this simplicity, it can be useful in a number of situations. For example, suppose we suspect that Britain's import demand function shifted after the rise in the oil price in 1979. How could we explore this possibility empirically?

The answer is to construct a variable, D_t, which takes the value 0 for the years 1973–79, and 1 thereafter (i.e. 0, 0, . . ., 0, 1, 1, . . ., 1, the switch occurring in 1979). We then estimate:

(10.19) $m_t = b_0 + b_1 gdp_t + b_2 pm_t + b_3 D_t + e_t$

The coefficient b_3 gives the size of the shift in 1979. The constant for the equation is equal to b_0 for 1973–79, when $D_t = 0$, and equal to $b_0 + b_3$ thereafter, when $D_t = 1$. The sign of b_3 shows the direction of any shift, and one can also test its significance, via the *t*-ratio. If it turns out not to be significant, then there was probably no shift in the relationship.

Dummy variables are quite flexible. We can test if the price elasticity altered in 1979, by estimating:

(10.20) $m_t = b_0 + b_1 gdp_t + b_2 pm_t + b_3 (D_t \times pm_t) + e_t$

The size of the coefficient b_3 shows the extent of the change in price elasticity (assuming the equation is estimated in logs) in 1979. Again, its significance can be tested via a *t*-ratio.

Trap!

There were in fact two oil shocks – in 1973 and 1979. You might therefore want to use a dummy variable {0, 0, . . ., 0, 1, . . ., 1, 2, . . ., 2}, with the first switch in 1973, the second in 1979 (this assumes you have some pre-1973 observations). This is wrong! It implicitly assumes that the two shocks had the same effect upon the dependent variable. The correct technique is to use two dummies, both using only zeroes and ones. The first dummy would switch from 0 to 1 in 1973, the second would switch in 1979. Their individual coefficients would then measure the size of each shock.

Seasonal dummy variables are a way of accounting for seasonal (usually quarterly) effects in a regression model. Suppose we have quarterly data on ice cream sales which we want to explain using a regression model. It is very likely that sales are substantially higher in the third quarter of each year, during July–September. A model which ignores this phenomenon would probably have a low R^2 value and imprecise coefficient estimates. To remedy this we include seasonal dummy variables, S_1–S_4, defined as follows:

$S_1 = 1$ in the first quarter of each year, 0 otherwise (i.e. 1,0,0,0,1,0,0,0,1, . . .)
$S_2 = 1$ in the second quarter of each year, 0 otherwise (i.e. 0,1,0,0,0,1,0,0,0, . . .)
S_3 and S_4 are defined analogously for the third and fourth quarters.

We then estimate

$I_t = b_0 + b_1 P_t + b_2 S_2 + b_3 S_3 + b_4 S_4 + e_t$

where I stands for ice cream sales and P for the price. Note an important point: only three of the seasonal dummies are included. If all four were included, along with a constant, there would be perfect multicollinearity (see below) and it would be impossible to calculate the regression line (the calculation would involve dividing by zero, which is impossible). It does not matter which dummy is omitted, it is simply a matter of convenience. In this case, S_1 is omitted, so the first quarter becomes the *base case*. This means that b_2 measures the difference in sales between the first and second quarters, b_3 is the difference between the first and third quarters, etc.

Note that dummy variables are really a measure of ignorance, not knowledge. They do not tell us *why* the price elasticity changed in 1973 or ice cream sales are higher in summer. In the latter case it would be better to have temperature data to better estimate the demand for ice cream. However, in their absence, seasonal dummies are very useful in improving the fit of the equation and the precision of other coefficient estimates. Note also that this technique implicitly assumes that the seasonal effect is the same in every year, which may not be the case.

A *time trend* is another useful type of dummy variable used with time-series data. It takes the values $\{1, 2, 3, 4, \ldots, T\}$ where there are T observations. It is used as a proxy for a variable which we cannot measure and which we believe increases in a linear fashion. For example, suppose we are trying to model petrol consumption of cars. Price and income would obviously be relevant explanatory variables; but in addition, technical progress has made cars more fuel-efficient over time. It is impossible to measure this accurately, so we use a time trend as an additional regressor. In this case it should have a negative coefficient which would measure the annual reduction in consumption due to more fuel-efficient cars.

Multicollinearity

Sometimes some or all of the explanatory variables are highly correlated (in the sample data) which means that it is difficult to tell *which* of them is influencing the dependent variable. This is known as **multicollinearity**. Since all variables are correlated to some degree, multicollinearity is a problem of degree also. For example, if GDP and import prices both rise over time, it is difficult to tell which of them influences imports. There has to be some independent movement of the explanatory variables for us to be able to disentangle their separate influences.

The symptoms of multicollinearity are:

- high correlation between two or more of the explanatory variables
- high standard errors of the coefficients leading to low t-ratios
- a high value of R^2 in spite of the insignificance of the individual coefficients

In this situation, one might make the mistake of concluding that a variable is insignificant because of a large standard error, when in fact multicollinearity is to blame.

The best cure is to obtain more data which might exhibit more independent variation of the explanatory variables. This is not always possible, however, for example if a sample survey has already been completed. An alternative is to drop one of the correlated variables from the regression equation, though the choice of which to exclude is somewhat arbitrary. Another procedure is to obtain extraneous estimates of the effects of one of the collinear variables (for example from another study). These effects can then be allowed for when estimates of the remaining coefficients are made.

Simultaneity

In the import demand model we asserted that we could safely estimate a single equation and ignore the problem of simultaneity. This is not always possible, however.

For example, the price and quantity of a good consumed are generally simultaneously determined by demand *and* supply equations. In this case we should use a **simultaneous equations model** to avoid obtaining biased estimates of the parameters. This technique is again beyond the scope of this book; see Maddala or Thomas for an exposition if you think you should estimate this type of model.

Measurement error

It is not always possible to measure the variables in a regression equation precisely, so the problem of **measurement error** arises. Either or both the endogenous or exogenous variables could be affected. This is mainly a problem for estimation when the measurement error is systematic rather than random (in which case it disappears into the error term) and can result in biased estimates. If transport costs are left out of the measured price of imported goods, and these costs have declined over time, then there is systematic measurement error in the price variable and possible bias in the coefficient.

Some final advice on regression

- As always, large samples are better than small. Reasonable results were obtained above with only 19 observations, but this is rather a small sample size on which to base solid conclusions.
- Check the data carefully before calculation. This is especially true if a computer is used to analyse the data. If the data are typed in incorrectly, *every* subsequent result will be wrong. A substantial part of any research project should be devoted to verifying the data, checking the definitions of variables, etc. The work is tedious, but important.
- Don't go fishing. Otherwise known as data-mining, this is searching through the data hoping something will turn up. Some idea of what the data is expected to reveal, and why, allows the search to be conducted more effectively. It is easy to see imaginary patterns in data if an aimless search is being conducted. Try looking at the table of random numbers (Table A1), which will probably soon reveal something 'significant', like your telephone number or your credit card number.
- Don't be afraid to start with fairly simple techniques. Draw a graph of demand against price to see what it looks like, if it looks linear or log linear, if there are any outliers (a data error?), if there are seasonal factors, etc. This will give an overview of the problem which can be kept in mind when more refined techniques are used.

EXERCISES

Exercise 1

(a) Using the data in exercise 1 of Chapter 9, estimate a multiple regression model of the birth rate explained by GNP, the growth rate and the income ratio. Comment upon:

  (i) the sizes and signs of the coefficients,

  (ii) the significance of the coefficients,

  (iii) the overall significance of the regression.

(b) How would you simplify the model?

(c) Test for the *joint* significance of the coefficients on growth and the income ratio.

(d) Repeat the above steps for all 26 observations. Comment.

(e) Do you feel your understanding of the birth rate is improved after estimating the multiple regression equation?

(f) What other possible explanatory variables do you think it might be worth investigating?

Exercise 2

The following data show the real price of butter and real incomes, to supplement the data in exercise 2 of Chapter 9.

Year	Price of butter	Real income	Year	Price of butter	Real income
1970	105.5	70.3	1980	119.2	92.1
1971	130.9	71.1	1981	114.2	91.4
1972	131.9	77.1	1982	114.5	90.9
1973	99.5	82.1	1983	110.0	93.3
1974	89.6	81.5	1984	107.9	96.8
1975	92.1	81.9	1985	100.0	100.0
1976	109.1	81.7	1986	104.2	104.5
1977	118.2	79.9	1987	99.8	108.1
1978	123.4	85.8	1988	100.2	114.6
1979	130.6	90.7			

(a) Estimate a multiple regression model of the demand for margarine. Do the coefficients have the expected signs?

(b) Test the significance of the individual coefficients and of the regression as a whole.

(c) Should the model be simplified?

(d) Calculate the elasticity of demand. How does it differ from your earlier answer?

(e) Estimate the cross-price demand elasticity.

(f) Should other variables be added to improve the model, in your view?

Exercise 3

Using the results from exercise 1 forecast the birth rate of a country with the characteristics given in exercise 9 of Chapter 9 (point estimate only).

Exercise 4

Given the following data for 1989 and 1990:

Year	Price of margarine	Price of butter	Real income
1989	79.3	104.3	120.2
1990	79.3	97.0	122.7

(a) Predict the levels of margarine consumption in the two years.

(b) The actual values of consumption for the two years were 3.47 and 3.19. How accurate are your forecasts?

(c) Test for the stability of the coefficients between sample and forecast periods.

Exercise 5   How would you most appropriately measure the following variables:

(a)   social class in a model of alcohol consumption

(b)   crime

(c)   central bank independence from political interference.

Exercise 6   As exercise 5, for

(a)   the output of a car firm, in a production function equation

(b)   potential trade union influence in wage bargaining

(c)   the performance of a school.

Exercise 7   Would it be better to use time-series or cross-section data in the following models?

(a)   The relationship between the exchange rate and the money supply

(b)   The determinants of divorce

(c)   The determinants of hospital costs

Explain your reasoning.

Exercise 8   As exercise 7, for

(a)   Measurement of economies of scale in the production of books

(b)   The determinants of cinema attendances

(c)   The determinants of the consumption of perfume.

Exercise 9   How would you estimate a model explaining the following variables?

(a)   Airline efficiency

(b)   Infant mortality

(c)   Bank profits

You should consider such issues as whether to use time-series or cross-section data; the explanatory variables to use and any measurement problems; any relevant data transformations; the expected results.

Exercise 10   As exercise 9, for

(a)   Investment

(b)   The pattern of UK exports (i.e. which countries they go to)

(c)   Attendance at football matches.

Exercise 11   Dornbusch and Fischer (in R.E. Caves and L.B. Krause, *Britain's Economic Performance*, Brookings, 1980) report the following equation for predicting the UK balance of payments:

$$B = 0.29 + 0.24U + 0.17 \ln Y - 0.004t - 0.10 \ln P - 0.24 \ln C$$
$$t \, (.56) \quad (5.9) \quad (2.5) \qquad (3.8) \qquad (3.2) \qquad (3.9)$$

$R^2 = 0.76$, $s_e = 0.01$, $n = 36$ (quarterly data 1970:1–1978:1) where

> B: the current account of the balance of payments as a percentage of gross domestic product (a balance of payments deficit of 3% of GDP would be recorded as -3.0, for example)
> U: the rate of unemployment
> Y: the OECD index of industrial production
> t: a time trend
> P: the price of materials relative to the GDP deflator (price index)
> C: an index of UK competitiveness (a lower value of the index implies greater competitiveness)
> (ln indicates the natural logarithm of a variable)

(a) Explain why each variable is included in the regression. Do they all have the expected sign for the coefficient?

(b) Which of the following lead to a higher BOP deficit (relative to GDP): (i) higher unemployment; (ii) higher OECD industrial production; (iii) higher material prices; (iv) greater competitiveness?

(c) What is the implied shape of the relationship between B and (i) U, (ii) Y?

(d) Why cannot a double log equation be estimated for this data? What implications does this have for obtaining elasticity estimates? Why are elasticity estimates not very useful in this context?

(e) Given the following values of the explanatory variables, estimate the state of the current account (point estimate): unemployment rate = 10%, OECD index = 110, time trend = 37, materials price index = 100, competitiveness index = 90.

Exercise 12

In a cross-section study of the determinants of economic growth (National Bureau of Economic Research, *Macroeconomic Annual*, 1991), Stanley Fischer obtained the following regression equation:

$$GY = 1.38 - 0.52\ RGDP70 + 2.51\ PRIM70 + 11.16\ INV - 4.75\ INF + 0.17\ SUR$$
$$ (-5.9) \qquad\quad (2.69) \qquad\quad (3.91) \qquad\quad (2.7) \qquad\quad (4.34)$$
$$- 0.33\ DEBT80 - 2.02\ SSA - 1.98\ LAC$$
$$(-0.79) \qquad\quad (-3.71) \qquad\quad (-3.76)$$
$$R^2 = 0.60,\ n = 73$$

where GY: growth per capita 1970–85; $RGDP$: real GDP per capita; $PRIM70$: primary school enrolment rate, 1970; INV: investment/GNP ratio; INF: inflation rate; SUR: budget surplus/GNP ratio; $DEBT80$: foreign debt/GNP ratio; SSA: dummy for sub-Saharan Africa; LAC: dummy for Latin America and the Caribbean.

(a) Explain why each variable is included. Does each have the expected sign on its coefficient? Are there any variables which are left out, in your view?

(b) If a country were to increase its investment ratio by 0.05, by how much would its estimated growth rate increase?

(c) Interpret the coefficient on the inflation variable.

(d) Calculate the F statistic for the overall significance of the regression equation. Is it significant?

(e) What do the SSA and LAC dummy variables tell us?

Exercise 13   *Project*: Build a suitable model to predict car sales in the UK. You should use time-series data (at least 20 annual observations). You should write a report in a similar manner to exercise 11 of Chapter 9.

References   Maddala, G. S. (1992) *Introduction to Econometrics*, 2nd edition. Macmillan.

Thomas, R. L. (1993) *Introductory Econometrics*, 2nd edition. Longman.

11 THE ANALYSIS OF TIME SERIES

Introduction

'The headline total of jobless, including school leavers, rose last month by 12,400 to 3,229,167. But, bucking the seasonal trend, the underlying total fell by 28,400 to 3,116,400 adults.'

– Guardian, 16 January 1987

One often reads such a statement in the newspapers, which seems to imply unemployment both rising and falling at the same time. What is the meaning of the figures? The answer is that the actual number of people unemployed rose in December; but unemployment always rises in December, and this year's rise isn't as large as it usually is. It is therefore said that the seasonally adjusted figure (i.e. adjusted for the usual rise in December) has fallen. The bad news isn't as bad as expected, so it's really quite good.

Seasonal adjustment is one part of what is known as time-series analysis (since it applies to time-series, not cross-section, data). Time-series analysis consists of a set of techniques for decomposing time-series data into its constituent parts: the trend, cycle, seasonal and random components. The technique of seasonal adjustment can be used to

- interpret data as they arise, as in the case of the unemployment data above;
- forecast the future course of the series. Since unemployment usually rises in December, this fact can help forecast unemployment for that month.

There is in fact a variety of methods of analysing time-series data; this chapter looks at the more straightforward methods. Although the methods differ, they tend to give similar answers, so the precise method used may not be that important. Seasonal adjustment does not explain *why* a series varies seasonally and analysis of the reasons may also be useful for forecasting purposes.

Decomposing a time series

Unemployment data will be used to illustrate the methods involved in time-series analysis. Exactly the same sort of analysis could be carried out for any time-series data, common examples being monthly sales data for a firm or quarterly data on the money supply.

Table 11.1 presents the monthly unemployment figures for the period January 1991 to December 1993, and Fig. 11.1 shows a plot of the data. The chart shows an upward trend to unemployment, levelling off towards the end of the period. Around this trend there also appears to be a cyclical element.

Any time series such as this is made up of two types of elements:

Table 11.1   Unemployment in the UK, January 1991 to December 1993 (000s)

	1991	1992	1993
January	1,959.7	2,673.9	3,062.1
February	2,045.4	2,710.5	3,042.6
March	2,142.1	2,707.5	2,996.7
April	2,198.5	2,736.5	3,000.5
May	2,213.8	2,707.9	2,916.6
June	2,241.0	2,678.2	2,865.0
July	2,367.5	2,774.0	2,929.3
August	2,435.1	2,845.5	2,960.0
September	2,450.7	2,847.4	2,912.1
October	2,426.0	2,814.4	2,793.6
November	2,471.8	2,864.1	2,769.4
December	2,551.7	2,983.3	2,782.7

Fig. 11.1 *Monthly unemployment in the UK, January 1991 to December 1993*

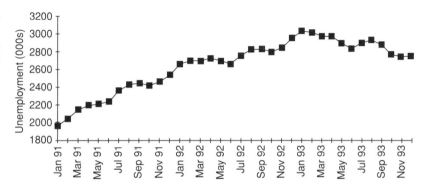

(1) systematic components, such as a trend, cycle and seasonals, and

(2) random elements, which are by definition unpredictable.

It would be difficult to analyse a series which is completely random. A look at the unemployment data, however, suggests that the series is definitely non-random – there is evidence of an upward trend and there does appear to be a seasonal component. The latter can be seen in Figure 11.2 which superimposes the three years' figures.

The series show a dip in the month of June, followed by a rise and then another dip in September before rising again towards the end of the year.

If one wished to predict unemployment in June 1994, the trend would be projected forward and account taken of the fact that unemployment tends to dip below the trend in June. Time-series analysis provides the quantitative tools for this type of task.

A time series can be decomposed into four components, three of them systematic and one random. These are:

(1) A **trend**: many economic variables are trended over time, as noted in Chapter 1 (the investment series).

(2) A **cycle**: most economies tend to progress unevenly, mixing periods of rapid growth with periods of relative stagnation. This business cycle can vary in length, which makes it difficult to analyse, so it is often ignored.

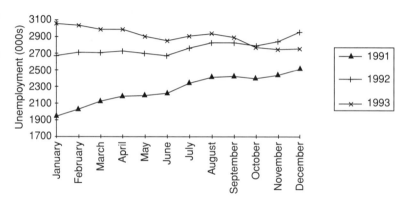

Fig. 11.2 *Monthly unemployment in the UK, 1991–93, series superimposed*

(3) A **seasonal component**: this is a regular, short term (one year) cycle. Sales of ice cream vary seasonally, for obvious reasons. Since it is a regular cycle, it is relatively easy to isolate.

(4) A **random component**: this is what is left over after the above factors have been taken into account. By definition it cannot be predicted.

These four elements can be combined in either an **additive** or a **multiplicative** model. The additive model of unemployment is

(11.1) $X = T + C + S + R$

where X represents unemployment, T the trend component, C the cycle, S the seasonal component and R the random element.

The multiplicative model is

(11.2) $X = T \times C \times S \times R$

There is little to choose between the two alternatives; the multiplicative formulation will be used in the rest of this chapter.

The analysis of unemployment proceeds as follows.

(1) First the trend is isolated from the original data by the method of **moving averages**.

(2) Second, the actual employment figures are compared to the trend to see which months tend to have unemployment above trend. This allows **seasonal factors** to be extracted from the data.

(3) Finally, the seasonal factors are used to **seasonally adjust** the data, so that the underlying movement in the figures can be observed.

Isolating the trend

There is a variety of methods for isolating the trend from time-series data. The method used here is that of moving averages, which is one of several methods of **smoothing** the data. These smoothing methods iron out the short term fluctuations in the data by averaging successive observations. For example, to calculate the **three-month moving average** figure for the month of July, one would take the average of the unemployment figures for June, July and August. The three-month moving average for August would be the average of the July, August and September figures. The figures are therefore as follows (for 1991):

$$\text{July} \quad \frac{2,241.0 + 2,367.5 + 2,435.1}{3} = 2,347.9$$

$$\text{August} \quad \frac{2,367.5 + 2,435.1 + 2,450.7}{3} = 2,417.8$$

Note that two values (2,367.5 and 2,435.1) are common to the two calculations, so that the two averages tend to be similar and the data series is smoothed out.

The choice of the three-month moving average was arbitrary; it could just as easily have been a four, five or twelve-month moving average process. How should the appropriate length of the moving average process be chosen? This depends upon the degree of smoothing of the data which is desired, and upon the nature of the fluctuations. The longer the period of the moving average process the greater the smoothing of the data, since the greater is the number of terms in the averaging process. In the case of unemployment data the fluctuations are probably fairly consistent from year to year since, for example, school leavers arrive on the unemployment register at the same time every year, causing a jump in the figures. A twelve-month moving average process would therefore be appropriate to smooth this data series.

Table 11.2 shows how the twelve-month moving average series is calculated. The calculation is the same in principle as the three-month moving average, but there is one slight complication, that of **centring** the data. Column 1 of the table repeats the raw data from Table 11.1. In column 2 is calculated the successive twelve-month totals. Thus the total of the first twelve observations is 27,503.3 and this is placed in the middle of 1991, between the months of June and July. The sum of observations 2–13 is 28,217.5 and falls between July and August, and so on. Notice that it is impossible to calculate any total before June/July by the moving average process. Values at the beginning and end of the period in question are always lost by this method of smoothing. The greater the length of the moving average process the greater the number of observations lost.

It is inconvenient to have this series falling between the months, so it is centred in column 3. This is done by averaging every two consecutive months' figures, so the June/July and July/August figures are averaged to give the July figure, as follows:

$$\frac{27,503.3 + 28,217.5}{2} = 27,860.4$$

This centring problem always arises when the length of the moving average process is an even number. One could instead use a 13-month moving average, which would give similar results, but it seems more natural to use a 12-month average for monthly data.

Column 4 of Table 11.2 is equal to column 3 divided by 12, and so gives the average of twelve consecutive observations, and this is the moving average series.

Comparison of the original data with the smoothed series shows the latter to be free of the short term fluctuations present in the former. The two series are graphed together in Fig. 11.3.

The chart shows the upward trend clearly and also reveals how this trend is levelling off. This is easier to see now that the vertical axis has been truncated a little. Note also that the trend appears to start levelling off around the end of 1992, while actual unemployment is *increasing* quite rapidly. Actual unemployment does not start

Table 11.2   Calculation of the 12-month moving average

	Unemployment	12-month total	Centred 12-month total	Moving average
Jan 91	1,959.7	–	–	–
Feb 91	2,045.4	–	–	–
Mar 91	2,142.1	–	–	–
Apr 91	2,198.5	–	–	–
May 91	2,213.8	–	–	–
Jun 91	2,241.0	–	–	–
		27,503.3		
Jul 91	2,367.5		27,860.4	2,321.7
		28,217.5		
Aug 91	2,435.1		28,550.1	2,379.2
		28,882.6		
Sep 91	2,450.7		29,165.3	2,430.4
		29,448.0		
Oct 91	2,426.0		29,717.0	2,476.4
		29,986.0		
Nov 91	2,471.8		30,233.1	2,519.4
		30,480.1		
Dec 91	2,551.7		30,698.7	2,558.2
		30,917.3		
Jan 92	2,673.9		31,120.6	2,593.4
		31,323.8		
Feb 92	2,710.5		31,529.0	2,627.4
		31,734.2		
Mar 92	2,707.5		31,932.6	2,661.0
		32,130.9		
Apr 92	2,736.5		32,325.1	2,693.8
		32,519.3		
May 92	2,707.9		32,715.5	2,726.3
		32,911.6		
Jun 92	2,678.2		33,127.4	2,760.6
		33,343.2		
Jul 92	2,774.0		33,537.3	2,794.8
		33,731.4		
Aug 92	2,845.5		33,897.5	2,824.8
		34,063.5		
Sep 92	2,847.4		34,208.1	2,850.7
		34,352.7		
Oct 92	2,814.4		34,484.7	2,873.7
		34,616.7		
Nov 92	2,864.1		34,721.1	2,893.4
		34,825.4		
Dec 92	2,983.3		34,918.8	2,909.9
		35,012.2		
Jan 93	3,062.1		35,089.9	2,924.2
		35,167.5		
Feb 93	3,042.6		35,224.8	2,935.4
		35,282.0		
Mar 93	2,996.7		35,314.4	2,942.9
		35,346.7		
Apr 93	3,000.5		35,336.3	2,944.7
		35,325.9		
May 93	2,916.6		35,278.6	2,939.9
		35,231.2		
Jun 93	2,865.0		35,130.9	2,927.6
		35,030.6		
Jul 93	2,929.3	–	–	–
Aug 93	2,960.0	–	–	–
Sep 93	2,912.1	–	–	–
Oct 93	2,793.6	–	–	–
Nov 93	2,769.4	–	–	–
Dec 93	2,782.7	–	–	–

to drop until February 1993. The moving average thus *anticipates* the movements in unemployment. This is not really so surprising since future values of unemployment are used in the calculation of the moving average figure for each month.

The trend has thus been disentangled from the raw data. Since the decomposition of the data into its four component parts is never perfect, there is probably some of the cyclical component also left in the moving average series, and possibly also small

Fig. 11.3
Unemployment and its
12-month moving average

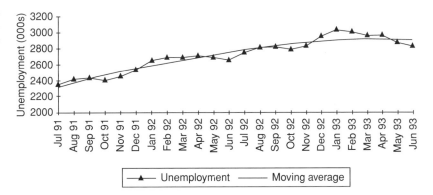

Isolating seasonal factors

elements of the seasonal and random components. The trend component is the predominant part, however, and thus the smoothed series will be referred to as the trend.

Having obtained the trend, the original data may be divided by the trend values (Table 11.2) to leave only the seasonal and random components. The cycle is assumed to be absent or included with the trend. This can best be seen by manipulating equation (11.2). Ignoring the cyclical component (which is difficult to analyse because of its possible varying length) we have

$$(11.3) \quad X = T \times S \times R$$

Dividing the original data series X by the trend values T therefore gives the seasonal and random components:

$$(11.4) \quad \frac{X}{T} = S \times R$$

Table 11.3 gives the results of this calculation. Column 3 of the table shows the ratio of the actual observations to the trend values (the trend values for January–June 1991 and July–December 1993 were calculated using data from outside the sample range, which are not shown). The value for January 1991, 1.006, shows the unemployment level in that month to be 0.6% above the trend. The March 1991 figure is 3.2% above trend, while the June figure (0.990) is 1% below trend. Other months' figures can be interpreted in the same way. Closer examination of the table shows that unemployment tends to be above its trend in January to April, below trend in June, October and November and otherwise on or about the trend line. This reflects in part the seasonal nature of the demand for labour (more jobs are available in the summer months).

The next task is to disentangle the seasonal and random components which make up the data in the final column of the table. The seasonal factor S can be obtained by averaging the three $S \times R$ components (for 1991, 1992 and 1993) for each month. For example, for January, the seasonal component is obtained as follows:

$$(11.5) \quad S = \frac{1.006 + 1.031 + 1.047}{3} = 1.028$$

The implicit assumption is that the random component has an expected value of

Table 11.3 Isolating the seasonal and random components

	Unemployment	Trend	Ratio
Jan 91	1,959.7	1,948.1	1.006
Feb 91	2,045.4	2,011.5	1.017
Mar 91	2,142.1	2,076.2	1.032
Apr 91	2,198.5	2,140.1	1.027
May 91	2,213.8	2,202.5	1.005
Jun 91	2,241.0	2,262.7	0.990
Jul 91	2,367.5	2,321.7	1.020
Aug 91	2,435.1	2,379.2	1.024
Sep 91	2,450.7	2,430.4	1.008
Oct 91	2,426.0	2,476.4	0.980
Nov 91	2,471.8	2,519.4	0.981
Dec 91	2,551.7	2,558.2	0.997
Jan 92	2,673.9	2,593.4	1.031
Feb 92	2,710.5	2,627.4	1.032
Mar 92	2,707.5	2,661.0	1.017
Apr 92	2,736.5	2,693.8	1.016
May 92	2,707.9	2,726.3	0.993
Jun 92	2,678.2	2,760.6	0.970
Jul 92	2,774.0	2,794.8	0.993
Aug 92	2,845.5	2,824.8	1.007
Sep 92	2,847.4	2,850.7	0.999
Oct 92	2,814.4	2,873.7	0.979
Nov 92	2,864.1	2,893.4	0.990
Dec 92	2,983.3	2,909.9	1.025
Jan 93	3,062.1	2,924.2	1.047
Feb 93	3,042.6	2,935.4	1.037
Mar 93	2,996.7	2,942.9	1.018
Apr 93	3,000.5	2,944.7	1.019
May 93	2,916.6	2,939.9	0.992
Jun 93	2,865.0	2,927.6	0.979
Jul 93	2,929.3	2,911.9	1.006
Aug 93	2,960.0	2,896.3	1.022
Sep 93	2,912.1	2,878.7	1.012
Oct 93	2,793.6	2,858.5	0.977
Nov 93	2,769.4	2,836.4	0.976
Dec 93	2,782.7	2,813.8	0.989

zero, so that by averaging we remove it, leaving only the seasonal component. The seasonal component for January each year is therefore 2.8% and there are negative, positive and positive random errors in 1991, 1992 and 1993 respectively.

Table 11.4 shows the seasonal factors for each month using the method shown above. For comparison, the seasonal factors for unemployment using data for the years 1982–84 are shown alongside (these were calculated in the first edition of this book). There is a fairly similar pattern, indicating that the seasonal pattern of unemployment has not changed significantly. There is some slight change in the summer months, which may reflect changes in entitlement to unemployment benefit by school leavers and others.

Seasonal adjustment   With the foregoing knowledge the original data can now be seasonally adjusted. This procedure eliminates the seasonal component from the original series leaving only

Table 11.4 Monthly seasonal factors for unemployment

	1991–93	1982–94
January	1.028	1.042
February	1.028	1.033
March	1.022	1.019
April	1.021	1.009
May	0.997	0.983
June	0.980	0.963
July	1.006	0.982
August	1.018	0.983
September	1.006	1.001
October	0.979	0.992
November	0.982	0.997
December	1.004	1.002

the trend, cyclical and random components. Seasonal adjustment is now simple – the original data are divided by the seasonal factors shown in Table 11.4 above. Equation (11.6) demonstrates the principle:

$$(11.6) \quad \frac{X}{S} = T \times C \times R$$

Table 11.5 shows the seasonally adjusted figures. The final column of the table adds the seasonally adjusted figures produced by the Central Statistical Office and published in the Employment Gazette. Although slightly more sophisticated methods are used, the results are similar to those we have calculated. Figure 11.4 graphs unemployment and the seasonally adjusted series.

Note that in October 1991 the jobless total fell, but the seasonally adjusted figures showed a rise over the previous month. The adjusted figures give the better picture, for unemployment continued to rise up until the beginning of 1993. The same phenomenon can be observed between September and October 1992 as well.

Fig. 11.4
Unemployment and seasonally adjusted unemployment

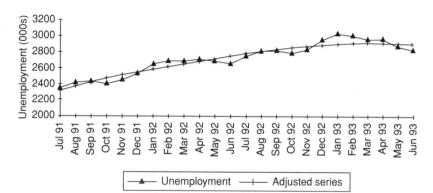

Table 11.5   Seasonally adjusted unemployment

	Unemployment	Seasonal adjustment factor	Adjusted series	Employment Gazette adjusted series
Jan 91	1,959.7	1.028	1,906.2	1,882.1
Feb 91	2,045.4	1.028	1,989.0	1,977.1
Mar 91	2,142.1	1.022	2,095.0	2,092.1
Apr 91	2,198.5	1.021	2,153.9	2,159.9
May 91	2,213.8	0.997	2,220.9	2,231.5
Jun 91	2,241.0	0.980	2,287.4	2,299.9
Jul 91	2,367.5	1.006	2,353.2	2,367.5
Aug 91	2,435.1	1.018	2,392.9	2,415.7
Sep 91	2,450.7	1.006	2,435.5	2,451.9
Oct 91	2,426.0	0.979	2,478.6	2,486.1
Nov 91	2,471.8	0.982	2,516.0	2,521.8
Dec 91	2,551.7	1.004	2,541.8	2,547.9
Jan 92	2,673.9	1.028	2,600.9	2,586.8
Feb 92	2,710.5	1.028	2,635.8	2,635.4
Mar 92	2,707.5	1.022	2,647.9	2,651.8
Apr 92	2,736.5	1.021	2,681.0	2,687.1
May 92	2,707.9	0.997	2,716.5	2,717.3
Jun 92	2,678.2	0.980	2,733.6	2,731.7
Jul 92	2,774.0	1.006	2,757.2	2,765.3
Aug 92	2,845.5	1.018	2,796.2	2,812.6
Sep 92	2,847.4	1.006	2,829.7	2,840.6
Oct 92	2,814.4	0.979	2,875.5	2,871.7
Nov 92	2,864.1	0.982	2,915.3	2,908.4
Dec 92	2,983.3	1.004	2,971.8	2,971.7
Jan 93	3,062.1	1.028	2,978.5	2,962.6
Feb 93	3,042.6	1.028	2,958.7	2,959.0
Mar 93	2,996.7	1.022	2,930.8	2,933.7
Apr 93	3,000.5	1.021	2,939.6	2,941.9
May 93	2,916.6	0.997	2,925.9	2,919.7
Jun 93	2,865.0	0.980	2,924.3	2,915.1
Jul 93	2,929.3	1.006	2,911.6	2,917.2
Aug 93	2,960.0	1.018	2,908.8	2,921.5
Sep 93	2,912.1	1.006	2,894.0	2,902.0
Oct 93	2,793.6	0.979	2,854.2	2,850.9
Nov 93	2,769.4	0.982	2,818.9	2,812.9
Dec 93	2,782.7	1.004	2,772.0	2,770.8

Note: The adjusted series is obtained by dividing the 'Unemployment' column by the 'Seasonal adjustment factor' column.

Fitting a moving average to a series using *Excel*

Many software programs can automatically produce a moving average of a data series. *Microsoft Excel* does this using a 12-period moving average which is not centred but located at the end of the averaged values. For example, the average of the January–December 1991 figures is placed against December 1991, not between June and July as was done above. This cuts off 11 observations at the beginning of the period but none at the end. Figure 11.5 compares the moving averages calculated by *Excel* and by the centred moving average method described earlier.

Fig. 11.5 *A comparison of moving average methods*

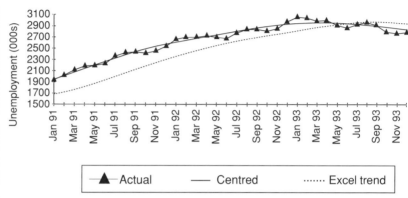

The *Excel* method appears less satisfactory: it is always lagging behind the actual series, in contrast to the centred method. However, it has the advantage that the trend value for the latest month can always be calculated.

An alternative method for finding the trend

Chapter 9 on regression showed how a straight line could be fitted to a set of data as a means of summarising it. This offers an alternative means of smoothing data and finding a trend line. The dependent variable in the regression is unemployment, which is regressed on a time trend variable. This is simply measured 1, 2, 3,. . ., 36 and is denoted by the letter t. January 1991 is therefore represented by 1, February 1991 by 2, etc. Since the trend appears to be non-linear, however, a fitted linear trend is unlikely to be accurate for forecasting. The regression equation can be made non-linear by including a t^2 term, for example. For January 1991 this would be 1, for February 1991 it would be 4, etc. The equation thus becomes

(11.7) $X_t = a + bt + ct^2 + e_t$

where e_t is the error term which, in this case, is composed of the cyclical, seasonal and random elements of the cycle. The trend component is given by $a + bt + ct^2$. The calculated regression equation is (calculation not shown)

(11.8) $X_t = 1,879.0 + 75.8t - 1.37t^2 + e_t$

The trend values for each month can easily be calculated from this equation, by inserting the values $t = 1$, 2, 3, etc. as appropriate. January 1991, for example, is found by substituting $t = 1$ and $t^2 = 1$ into equation (11.8), giving

(11.9) $X_t = 1,879.0 + 75.8 \times 1 - 1.37 \times 1 + 0 = 1,953.3$

which compares to1,948.1 using the moving average method. For July 1991 ($t = 7$) we obtain

(11.10) $X_t = 1,879.0 + 75.8 \times 7 - 1.37 \times 7^2 + 0 = 2,342.1$

compared to the moving average estimate of 2,321.7. The two methods give results which are slightly different, but not by much.

One final point to note is that the regression method has the advantage of not losing observations at the beginning and end of the sample period.

Forecasting

It is possible to forecast future levels of unemployment using the methods outlined above. Each component of the series is forecast separately and the results multiplied together. As an example the level of unemployment for August 1994 will be forecast.

The trend can only be forecast using the regression method, since the moving average method requires future values of unemployment, which is what is being forecast! August 1994 corresponds to time period $t = 44$, so the forecast of the trend by the regression method is

(11.11) $X_t = 1,879.0 + 75.8 \times 44 - 1.37 \times 44^2 + 0 = 2,557.65$

The seasonal factor for August is 1.018 so the trend figure is multiplied by this, giving

(11.12) $2,557.65 \times 1.018 = 2,602.71$

The cyclical component is ignored and the random component set to a value of 1 (in the multiplicative model, zero in the additive model). This leaves 2,602.71 as the forecast for August 1994. In the event the actual figure was 2,638.3, so the forecast is reasonably accurate. The error is only 1.4% of the predicted value.

Some observations on time-series analysis

The above analysis has taken a fairly mechanical approach to the analysis of time series, and has not sought the reasons *why* the data might vary seasonally. The seasonal adjustment factors are therefore a measure of ignorance as much as of knowledge, so further investigation might be worthwhile and help in the business of forecasting. Some examples will bring this out.

Unemployment varies seasonally because of (among other things) greater employment opportunities in summer (e.g. deck chair attendants) and school leavers entering the register in September. The availability of summer jobs might be predictable (based on forecasts of the number of tourists, weather, etc.), and the number of school leavers next year can presumably be predicted by the number of pupils at present in their final year. These sorts of considerations should provide better forecasts rather than blindly following the rules set out above.

Another example of seasonality is company behaviour, which can be influenced by accounting periods and tax rules. A large amount of investment might be observed in the last quarter of a tax year as companies bring forward investment plans to take advantage of tax reliefs. This is especially true when changes to the tax system are introduced. For example, the 1984 Budget changed the rules regarding capital allowances, so that companies could no longer write off 100% of capital investment in the first year. Because the allowances were phased out over a period of three years, it was expected that companies would bring forward their investment plans, leading to a rise in the figures for investment. Knowledge of this sort of behaviour can aid interpretation of the statistics and improve forecasting.

Many time series will exhibit monthly variation simply because the months are of different length. Overseas trade statistics, for example, are first adjusted for the number of working days in each month. Otherwise a lot of time might be spent wondering why exports and imports were regularly lower in February! The unemployment figures analysed above should not suffer from this defect, since they measure a stock of unemployed, rather than a flow.

Another important consideration is whether a series should be adjusted as a whole, or different parts of the series adjusted separately. For example, either one could seasonally adjust the balance of trade deficit, or one could adjust exports and imports separately. The seasonally adjusted trade balance would then be the difference between these two adjusted series. One advantage of the latter method is that different trends and seasonal factors might affect exports and imports, so that the balance of trade figure is a mixture of the two effects. In the official UK trade statistics this approach is adopted and extended. Exports are broken down under 27 different commodity categories, each of which is individually seasonally adjusted, before the (now seasonally adjusted) categories are summed to give seasonally adjusted exports. For imports there are 28 categories. Even this does not exhaust the possibilities, for it could be argued that seasonality is related not to commodity category but to the source or destination country. This would imply disaggregating the statistics by area, seasonally adjusting, and then aggregating again. The disaggregation by commodities method is preferred in the official statistics, but this shows that there is a variety of possible methods which need to be considered.

Using adjusted or unadjusted data

Seasonal adjustment can also introduce problems into data analysis as well as resolve them. Although seasonal adjustment can help in interpreting figures, if the adjusted data are then used in further statistical analysis they can mislead. It is well known, for example, that seasonal adjustment can introduce a cyclical component into a data series which originally had no cyclical element to it. This occurs because a large (random) deviation from the trend will enter the moving average process for twelve different months (or whatever is the length of the moving average process), and this tends to turn occasional, random disturbances into a cycle. Note also that the adjusted series will start to rise before the random shock in these circumstances.

The question then arises as to whether adjusted or unadjusted data are best used in, say, regression analysis. Use of unadjusted data means that the coefficient estimates may be contaminated by the seasonal effects; using adjusted data runs into the kind of problems outlined above. A suitable compromise is to follow the method outlined in Chapter 10: use unadjusted data with seasonal dummy variables. In this case the estimation of parameters and seasonal effects is dealt with simultaneously and generally gives the best results.

A further advantage of this regression method is that it allows the significance of the seasonal variations to be established. An F-test for the joint significance of the seasonal coefficients will tell you whether any of the seasonal effects are statistically significant. If not, seasonal dummies need not be included in the regression equation.

Finally, it should be remembered that decomposing a time series is not a clear cut procedure. It is often difficult to disentangle the separate effects, and different methods will give different results. The seasonally adjusted unemployment figures given in the Monthly Digest of Statistics are slightly different from the series calculated here, due to slightly different techniques being applied. The differences are not great and the directions of the seasonal effects are the same even if the sizes are slightly different.

EXERCISES

Exercise 1

The following table contains data for consumers' non-durables expenditure in the UK, in constant prices.

	Q1	Q2	Q3	Q4
1985			32,515	38,380
1986	32,868	33,711	34,093	40,148
1987	33,678	34,567	35,540	42,363
1988	35,426	35,909	36,581	43,667
1989	35,764	37,185	36,884	44,333
1990	36,128	37,495	37,248	44,081
1991	36,119	36,913	36,756	43,826
1992	35,349	36,905	36,794	44,428
1993	36,139	37,405		

(a) Graph the series and comment upon any apparent seasonal pattern. Why does it occur?

(b) Use the method of centred moving averages to find the trend values for 1986–92.

(c) Use the moving average figures to find the seasonal factors for each quarter (use the multiplicative model).

(d) By approximately how much does expenditure normally increase in the fourth quarter?

(e) Use the seasonal factors to obtain the seasonally adjusted series for non-durable expenditure.

(f) Were retailers happy or unhappy at Christmas in 1990? How about 1992?

Exercise 2

Repeat exercise 1 using the additive model. In 1(c) above, *subtract* the moving average figures from the original series. In (e), subtract the seasonal factors from the original data to get the adjusted series. Is there a big difference between this and the multiplicative model?

Exercise 3

The following data relate to car production in the UK (not seasonally adjusted).

	1989	1990	1991	1992	1993
January		105,222	113,472	95,245	109,127
February		95,452	109,160	114,192	111,091
March		126,014	123,531	133,881	144,303
April		102,544	111,138	108,902	113,301
May		107,563	111,996	105,324	130,415
June		116,952	125,077	129,203	134,732
July	94,855	90,393	102,007	118,514	
August	73,761	81,711	57,388	53,156	
September	101,817	102,153	90,613	103,716	
October	111,974	133,356	97,130	117,647	
November	124,286	142,417	116,376	116,799	
December	74,845	91,833	79,012	95,301	

(a) Graph the data for 1990–92 by overlapping the three years (as was done in Fig. 11.2) and comment upon any seasonal pattern.

(b) Use a 12-month moving average to find the trend values for 1990–92.

(c) Find the monthly seasonal factors (multiplicative method). Describe the seasonal pattern that emerges.

(d) By how much is the August production figure below the July figure in general?

(e) Obtain the seasonally adjusted series. Compare it with the original series and comment.

(f) Compare the seasonal pattern found with that for consumers' expenditure in exercise 1.

Exercise 4   Repeat exercise 3 using the additive model and compare results.

Exercise 5
(a) Using the data of exercise 1, fit a linear regression line through the data. Interpret the meaning of the slope of this line. (Use only the observations from 1986–92.)

(b) Calculate the seasonal factors (multiplicative model) based upon this trend. How do they compare to the values found in exercise 1?

(c) Predict the value of consumers' expenditure for 1993 Q4.

(d) Calculate the seasonal factors using the additive model.

Exercise 6
(a) Using the data from exercise 3 (1990–92 only), fit a linear regression line to obtain the trend values. By how much, on average, does car production increase per year?

(b) Calculate the seasonal factors (multiplicative model). How do they compare to the values in exercise 3?

(c) Predict car production for March 1994.

Exercise 7   A computer will be needed to solve this and the next exercise.

(a) Using the data in exercise 1, estimate a regression equation including a time trend and three seasonal dummy variables (for quarters 1, 2 and 3). How does the slope coefficient compare with that found in exercise 5 above? (Use data for 1986–92 only.)

(b) How does the t-ratio on the slope coefficient compare with the value found in exercise 5? Account for the difference.

(c) Compare the coefficients on the seasonal dummy variables with the seasonal factors found in exercise 5 (d).

Exercise 8
(a) How many seasonal dummy variables would be needed for the regression approach to the data in exercise 3?

(b) Do you think the approach would bring as reliable results as it did for consumers' expenditure?

Project: Obtain quarterly (unadjusted!) data for a suitable variable (some suggestions are given below) and examine its seasonal pattern. Write a brief report on your findings. You should:

(a) Say what you *expect* to find, and why.

(b) Compare different methods of adjustment.

(c) Use your results to try to forecast the value of the variable at some future date.

(d) Compare your results, if possible, with the 'official' seasonally adjusted series. Some suitable variables are the money stock, retail sales, rainfall, interest rates, house prices.

APPENDIX: TABLES

Table A1 Random number table

This table contains 1000 random numbers within the range 0–99. Each number within the range has an equal probability of occurrence. The range may be extended by combining successive entries in the table. Thus 7,399 becomes the first of 500 random numbers in the range 0–9,999. To obtain a sample of random numbers, choose an arbitrary starting point in the table and go down the columns collecting successive values until the required sample is obtained. If the population has been numbered, this method can be used to select a random sample from the population. Alternatively, the method can simulate sampling experiments such as the tossing of a coin (an even number representing a head and an odd number a tail).

73	23	41	53	38	87	71	79	3	55	24	7	7	17	19	70
99	13	91	13	90	72	84	15	64	90	56	68	38	40	73	78
97	16	58	2	67	3	92	83	50	53	59	60	33	75	44	95
73	10	29	14	9	92	35	47	21	47	82	25	71	68	87	53
99	79	29	68	44	90	65	33	55	85	7	57	77	84	83	5
71	97	98	60	62	18	49	80	4	51	8	74	81	64	29	45
41	26	41	30	82	38	52	81	89	64	17	10	49	28	72	99
60	87	77	81	91	57	6	1	30	47	93	82	81	67	4	3
95	84	74	92	15	10	37	52	8	10	96	38	69	9	65	41
59	19	2	61	40	67	80	25	31	18	1	36	54	31	100	27
35	3	54	83	62	28	21	23	91	46	73	85	11	63	63	49
66	18	31	17	72	15	8	46	10	3	64	22	100	62	85	16
3	4	42	8	4	6	40	73	97	0	37	34	91	56	48	98
28	20	23	98	86	41	41	13	53	61	16	92	95	31	79	36
74	49	86	5	74	82	12	58	80	14	94	4	88	95	9	32
80	80	2	47	91	100	76	84	0	57	17	69	87	29	52	39
65	67	0	39	11	10	54	80	74	56	55	91	94	52	32	18
67	44	89	50	7	73	70	52	18	28	89	43	54	60	20	10
48	33	61	66	2	71	74	91	31	45	63	2	97	62	30	90
3	18	54	19	17	87	3	91	41	64	78	10	99	24	1	20
69	35	12	53	97	30	96	69	59	55	65	64	30	3	100	17
15	0	33	86	93	73	52	57	77	77	83	10	64	54	85	18
87	79	51	68	5	23	50	15	68	67	14	59	42	61	83	2
69	52	34	86	34	34	78	51	48	65	57	91	8	74	72	36
11	1	11	43	51	85	6	47	72	43	34	54	20	56	31	81
59	14	78	32	94	24	19	44	16	49	65	16	30	86	0	65
18	86	62	47	96	46	73	67	79	40	45	82	96	61	34	60
99	63	2	81	58	93	81	37	53	20	64	87	3	27	19	55
34	55	14	29	10	59	7	69	13	8	54	97	56	7	57	16
88	90	6	98	32	55	37	17	35	93	31	66	67	84	15	14

Table A1 continued

78	30	30	78	41	59	79	77	21	89	76	59	30	9	64	9
67	10	37	14	62	3	85	2	16	74	40	85	30	83	29	5
93	50	83	76	42	86	92	41	27	73	31	70	25	40	11	88
35	68	98	18	67	22	95	34	19	27	21	90	66	20	32	48
32	52	29	78	68	96	94	44	38	95	27	85	53	76	63	78
92	100	75	77	26	39	61	33	88	66	77	76	25	67	90	1
40	73	28	5	50	73	92	32	82	23	78	30	26	52	28	94
57	41	64	50	78	35	12	60	25	4	5	82	82	57	68	43
82	41	67	79	30	43	15	72	98	48	6	22	46	92	43	41
100	11	21	44	43	51	76	89	4	90	48	31	19	89	97	45
94	8	20	67	32	42	39	6	38	25	97	10	18	85	9	60
21	59	27	39	13	81	2	47	83	12	17	54	84	68	56	29
63	62	36	6	57	96	6	36	24	13	70	32	90	92	81	86
91	42	57	99	55	31	58	21	21	65	70	4	37	28	59	9
91	27	61	86	36	57	11	35	92	15	79	30	19	85	39	49
97	39	12	28	35	37	90	93	88	20	99	76	81	61	95	70
64	89	32	80	9	66	73	71	84	69	70	12	10	56	59	56
45	34	1	32	80	99	39	52	25	87	76	91	22	26	46	67
21	65	14	1	78	35	35	63	21	66	34	3	47	51	24	37
85	64	69	93	47	82	55	87	22	56	53	85	43	66	23	66
21	37	62	29	44	39	4	4	99	3	6	82	67	53	14	0
23	8	62	9	19	31	81	92	63	10	65	78	79	96	65	33
84	14	92	85	9	16	51	70	26	60	7	7	55	66	5	51
70	37	11	7	93	63	48	12	35	95	32	5	64	5	63	28
80	27	32	92	81	27	55	98	71	22	66	64	78	79	34	73
66	13	16	48	74	51	78	83	42	31	97	72	25	75	34	40
1	51	47	84	82	27	77	40	99	13	66	52	56	27	2	19
84	26	0	38	55	30	45	80	50	20	17	78	87	4	88	86
95	28	57	33	51	39	18	12	37	100	89	63	22	50	10	22
45	76	48	43	18	24	19	1	65	93	16	48	8	60	32	76

Table A2 The standard Normal distribution

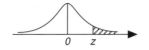

z	0.00	0.01	0.02	0.03	0.04	0.05	0.06	0.07	0.08	0.09
0.0	.5000	.4960	.4920	.4880	.4840	.4801	.4761	.4721	.4681	.4641
0.1	.4602	.4562	.4522	.4483	.4443	.4404	.4364	.4325	.4286	.4247
0.2	.4207	.4168	.4129	.4090	.4052	.4013	.3974	.3936	.3897	.3859
0.3	.3821	.3783	.3745	.3707	.3669	.3632	.3594	.3557	.3520	.3483
0.4	.3446	.3409	.3372	.3336	.3300	.3264	.3228	.3192	.3156	.3121
0.5	.3085	.3050	.3015	.2981	.2946	.2912	.2877	.2843	.2810	.2776
0.6	.2743	.2709	.2676	.2643	.2611	.2578	.2546	.2514	.2483	.2451
0.7	.2420	.2389	.2358	.2327	.2296	.2266	.2236	.2206	.2177	.2148
0.8	.2119	.2090	.2061	.2033	.2005	.1977	.1949	.1922	.1894	.1867
0.9	.1841	.1814	.1788	.1762	.1736	.1711	.1685	.1660	.1635	.1611
1.0	.1587	.1562	.1539	.1515	.1492	.1469	.1446	.1423	.1401	.1379
1.1	.1357	.1335	.1314	.1292	.1271	.1251	.1230	.1210	.1190	.1170
1.2	.1151	.1131	.1112	.1093	.1075	.1056	.1038	.1020	.1003	.0985
1.3	.0968	.0951	.0934	.0918	.0901	.0885	.0869	.0853	.0838	.0823
1.4	.0808	.0793	.0778	.0764	.0749	.0735	.0721	.0708	.0694	.0681
1.5	.0668	.0655	.0643	.0630	.0618	.0606	.0594	.0582	.0571	.0559
1.6	.0548	.0537	.0526	.0516	.0505	.0495	.0485	.0475	.0465	.0455
1.7	.0446	.0436	.0427	.0418	.0409	.0401	.0392	.0384	.0375	.0367
1.8	.0359	.0351	.0344	.0336	.0329	.0322	.0314	.0307	.0301	.0294
1.9	.0287	.0281	.0274	.0268	.0262	.0256	.0250	.0244	.0239	.0233
2.0	.0228	.0222	.0217	.0212	.0207	.0202	.0197	.0192	.0188	.0183
2.1	.0179	.0174	.0170	.0166	.0162	.0158	.0154	.0150	.0146	.0143
2.2	.0139	.0136	.0132	.0129	.0125	.0122	.0119	.0116	.0113	.0110
2.3	.0107	.0104	.0102	.0099	.0096	.0094	.0091	.0089	.0087	.0084
2.4	.0082	.0080	.0078	.0075	.0073	.0071	.0069	.0068	.0066	.0064
2.5	.0062	.0060	.0059	.0057	.0055	.0054	.0052	.0051	.0049	.0048
2.6	.0047	.0045	.0044	.0043	.0041	.0040	.0039	.0038	.0037	.0036
2.7	.0035	.0034	.0033	.0032	.0031	.0030	.0029	.0028	.0027	.0026
2.8	.0026	.0025	.0024	.0023	.0023	.0022	.0021	.0021	.0020	.0019
2.9	.0019	.0018	.0018	.0017	.0016	.0016	.0015	.0015	.0014	.0014
3.0	.0013	.0013	.0013	.0012	.0012	.0011	.0011	.0011	.0010	.0010

Source: Economic statistics and Econometrics, 1968

Table A3 **Percentage points of the *t* distribution**

The table gives critical values of the *t* distribution cutting off an area α in each tail, shown by the top row of the table.

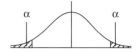

Area (α) in each tail

v	0.4	0.25	0.1	0.05	0.025	0.01	0.005	0.0025	0.001	0.0005
1	0.325	1.000	3.078	6.314	12.706	31.821	63.657	127.320	318.310	636.620
2	0.289	0.816	1.886	2.920	4.303	6.965	9.925	14.089	22.327	31.598
3	0.277	0.765	1.638	2.353	3.182	4.541	5.841	7.453	10.214	12.924
4	0.271	0.741	1.533	2.132	2.776	3.747	4.604	5.598	7.173	8.610
5	0.267	0.727	1.476	2.015	2.571	3.365	4.032	4.773	5.893	6.869
6	0.265	0.718	1.440	1.943	2.447	3.143	3.707	4.317	5.208	5.959
7	0.263	0.711	1.415	1.895	2.365	2.998	3.499	4.029	4.785	5.408
8	0.262	0.706	1.397	1.860	2.306	2.896	3.355	3.833	4.501	5.041
9	0.261	0.703	1.383	1.833	2.262	2.821	3.250	3.690	4.297	4.781
10	0.260	0.700	1.372	1.812	2.228	2.764	3.169	3.581	4.144	4.587
11	0.260	0.697	1.363	1.796	2.201	2.718	3.106	3.497	4.025	4.437
12	0.259	0.695	1.356	1.782	2.179	2.681	3.055	3.428	3.930	4.318
13	0.259	0.694	1.350	1.771	2.160	2.650	3.012	3.372	3.852	4.221
14	0.258	0.692	1.345	1.761	2.145	2.624	2.977	3.326	3.787	4.140
15	0.258	0.691	1.341	1.753	2.131	2.602	2.947	3.286	3.733	4.073
16	0.258	0.690	1.337	1.746	2.120	2.583	2.921	3.252	3.686	4.015
17	0.257	0.689	1.333	1.740	2.110	2.567	2.898	3.222	3.646	3.965
18	0.257	0.688	1.330	1.734	2.101	2.552	2.878	3.197	3.610	3.922
19	0.257	0.688	1.328	1.729	2.093	2.539	2.861	3.174	3.579	3.883
20	0.257	0.687	1.325	1.725	2.086	2.528	2.845	3.153	3.552	3.850
21	0.257	0.686	1.323	1.721	2.086	2.518	2.831	3.135	3.527	3.819
22	0.256	0.686	1.321	1.717	2.074	2.508	2.819	3.119	3.505	3.792
23	0.256	0.685	1.319	1.714	2.069	2.500	2.807	3.104	3.485	3.767
24	0.256	0.685	1.318	1.711	2.064	2.492	2.797	3.091	3.467	3.745
25	0.256	0.684	1.316	1.708	2.060	2.485	2.787	3.078	3.450	3.725
26	0.256	0.684	1.315	1.706	2.056	2.479	2.779	3.067	3.435	3.707
27	0.256	0.684	1.314	1.703	2.052	2.473	2.771	3.057	3.421	3.690
28	0.256	0.683	1.313	1.701	2.048	2.467	2.763	3.047	3.408	3.674
29	0.256	0.683	1.311	1.699	2.045	2.462	2.756	3.038	3.396	3.659
30	0.256	0.683	1.310	1.697	2.042	2.457	2.750	3.030	3.385	3.646
40	0.255	0.681	1.303	1.684	2.021	2.423	2.704	2.971	3.307	3.551
60	0.254	0.679	1.296	1.671	2.000	2.390	2.660	2.915	3.232	3.460
120	0.254	0.677	1.289	1.658	1.980	2.358	2.617	2.860	3.160	3.373
∞	0.253	0.674	1.282	1.645	1.960	2.326	2.576	2.807	3.090	3.291

Table A4   Critical values of the χ^2 distribution

The values in the table give the critical
values of χ^2 which cut off the area in the
right-hand tail given at the top of the column.

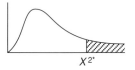

χ^{2^*}

Area in right-hand tail

v	0.995	0.990	0.975	0.950	0.900	0.750	0.500
1	392704.10^{-10}	157088.10^{-9}	982069.10^{-9}	393214.10^{-8}	0.0157908	0.1015308	0.454936
2	0.0100251	0.0201007	0.0506356	0.102587	0.210721	0.575364	1.38629
3	0.0717218	0.114832	0.215795	0.351846	0.584374	1.212534	2.36597
4	0.206989	0.297109	0.484419	0.710723	1.063623	1.92256	3.35669
5	0.411742	0.554298	0.831212	1.145476	1.61031	2.67460	4.35146
6	0.675727	0.872090	1.23734	1.63538	2.20413	3.45460	5.34812
7	0.989256	1.239043	1.68987	2.16735	2.83311	4.25485	6.34581
8	1.34441	1.64650	2.17973	2.73264	3.48954	5.07064	7.34412
9	1.73493	2.08790	2.70039	3.32511	4.16816	5.89883	8.34283
10	2.15586	2.55821	3.24697	3.94030	4.86518	6.73720	9.34182
11	2.60322	3.05348	3.81575	4.57481	5.57778	7.58414	10.3410
12	3.07382	3.57057	4.40379	5.22603	6.30380	8.43842	11.3403
13	3.56503	4.10692	5.00875	5.89186	7.04150	9.29907	12.3398
14	4.07467	4.66043	5.62873	6.57063	7.78953	10.1653	13.3393
15	4.60092	5.22935	6.26214	7.26094	8.54676	11.0365	14.3389
16	5.14221	5.81221	6.90766	7.96165	9.31224	11.9122	15.3385
17	5.69722	6.40776	7.56419	8.67176	10.0852	12.7919	16.3382
18	6.26480	7.01491	8.23075	9.39046	10.8649	13.6753	17.3379
19	6.84397	7.63273	8.90652	10.1170	11.6509	14.5620	18.3377
20	7.43384	8.26040	9.59078	10.8508	12.4426	15.4518	19.3374
21	8.03365	8.89720	10.28293	11.5913	13.2396	16.3444	20.3372
22	8.64272	9.54249	10.9823	12.3380	14.0415	17.2396	21.3370
23	9.26043	10.19567	11.6886	13.0905	14.8480	18.1373	22.3369
24	9.88623	10.8564	12.4012	13.8484	15.6587	19.0373	23.3367
25	10.5197	11.5240	13.1197	14.6114	16.4734	19.9393	24.3266
26	11.1602	12.1981	13.8439	15.3792	17.2919	20.8434	25.3365
27	11.8076	12.8785	14.5734	16.1514	18.1139	21.7494	26.3363
28	12.4613	13.5647	15.3079	16.9279	18.9392	22.6572	27.3362
29	13.1211	14.2565	16.0471	17.7084	19.7677	23.5666	28.3361
30	13.7867	14.9535	16.7908	18.4927	20.5992	24.4776	29.3360
40	20.7065	22.1643	24.4330	26.5093	29.0505	33.6603	39.3353
50	27.9907	29.7067	32.3574	34.7643	37.6886	42.9421	49.3349
60	35.5345	37.4849	40.4817	43.1880	46.4589	52.2938	59.3347
70	43.2752	45.4417	48.7576	51.7393	55.3289	61.6983	69.3345
80	51.1719	53.5401	57.1532	60.3915	64.2778	71.1445	79.3343
90	59.1963	61.7541	65.6466	69.1260	73.2911	80.6247	89.3342
100	67.3276	70.0649	74.2219	77.9295	82.3581	90.1332	99.3341

Table A4 continued

v	.250	0.100	0.050-	0.025	0.010	0.005	0.001
1	1.32330	2.70554	3.84146	5.02389	6.63490	7.87944	10.828
2	2.77259	4.60517	5.99146	7.37776	9.21034	10.5966	13.816
3	4.10834	6.25139	7.81473	9.34840	11.3449	12.8382	16.266
4	5.38527	7.77944	9.48773	11.1433	13.2767	14.8603	18.467
5	6.62568	9.23636	11.0705	12.8325	15.0863	16.7496	20.515
6	7.84080	10.6446	12.5916	14.4494	16.8119	18.5476	22.458
7	9.03715	12.0170	14.0671	16.0128	18.4753	20.2777	24.322
8	10.2189	13.3616	15.5073	17.5345	20.0902	21.9550	26.125
9	11.3888	14.6837	16.9190	19.0228	21.6660	23.5894	27.877
10	12.5489	15.9872	18.3070	20.4832	23.2093	25.1882	29.588
11	13.7007	17.2750	19.6751	21.9200	24.7250	26.7568	31.264
12	14.8454	18.5493	21.0261	23.3367	26.2170	28.2995	32.909
13	15.9839	19.8119	22.3620	24.7356	27.6882	29.8195	34.528
14	17.1169	21.0641	23.6848	26.1189	29.1412	31.3194	36.123
15	18.2451	22.3071	24.9958	27.4884	30.5779	32.8013	37.697
16	19.3689	23.5418	26.2962	28.8454	31.9999	34.2672	29.252
17	20.4887	24.7690	27.5871	30.1910	33.4087	35.7185	40.790
18	21.6049	25.9894	28.8693	31.5264	34.8053	37.1565	42.312
19	22.7178	27.2036	30.1435	32.8523	36.1909	38.5823	43.820
20	23.8277	28.4120	31.4104	34.1696	37.5662	39.9968	45.315
21	24.9348	29.6151	32.6706	35.4789	38.9322	41.4011	46.797
22	26.40393	30.8133	33.9244	36.7807	40.2894	42.7957	48.268
23	27.1413	32.0069	35.1725	38.0756	41.6384	44.1813	49.728
24	28.2412	33.1962	36.4150	39.3641	42.9798	45.5585	51.179
25	29.3389	34.3816	37.6525	40.6465	44.3141	46.9279	52.618
26	30.4346	35.5632	38.8851	41.9232	45.6417	48.2899	54.052
27	31.5284	36.7412	40.1133	43.1945	46.9629	49.6449	55.476
28	32.6205	37.9150	41.3371	44.4608	48.2782	50.9934	56.892
29	33.7109	39.0875	42.5570	45.7223	49.5879	52.3356	58.301
30	34.7997	40.2560	43.7730	46.9792	50.8922	53.6720	59.703
40	45.6160	51.8051	55.7585	59.3417	63.6907	66.7660	73.402
50	56.3336	63.1671	67.5048	71.4202	76.1539	79.4900	86.661
60	66.9815	74.3970	79.0819	83.2977	88.3794	91.9517	99.607
70	77.5767	85.5270	90.5312	95.0232	100.425	104.215	112.317
80	88.1303	96.5782	101.879	106.629	112.329	116.321	124.839
90	98.6499	107.565	113.145	118.136	124.116	128.299	137.208
100	109.141	118.498	124.342	129.561	135.807	140.169	149.449

Table A5(a) Critical values of the *F* distribution (upper 5% points)

The entries in the table give the critical values of *F* cutting off 5% in the right-hand tail of the distribution. v_1 gives the degrees of freedom in the numerator, v_2 those in the denominator

v_2 \ v_1	1	2	3	4	5	6	7	8	9
1	161.45	199.50	215.71	224.58	230.16	230.99	236.77	238.88	240.54
2	18.513	19.000	19.164	19.247	19.296	19.330	19.353	19.371	19.385
3	10.128	9.5521	9.2766	9.1172	9.0135	8.9406	8.8867	8.8452	8.8123
4	7.7086	6.9443	6.5914	6.3882	6.2561	6.1631	6.0942	6.0410	5.9988
5	6.6079	5.7861	5.4095	5.1922	5.0503	4.9503	4.8759	4.8183	4.7725
6	5.9874	5.1433	4.7571	4.5337	4.3874	4.2839	4.2067	4.1468	4.0990
7	5.5914	4.7374	4.3468	4.1203	3.9715	3.8660	3.7870	3.7257	3.6767
8	5.3177	4.4590	4.0662	3.8379	3.6875	3.5806	3.5005	3.4381	3.3881
9	5.1174	4.2565	3.8625	3.6331	3.4817	3.3738	3.2927	3.2296	3.1789
10	4.9646	4.1028	3.7083	3.4780	3.3258	3.2172	3.1355	3.0717	3.0204
11	4.8443	3.9823	3.5874	3.3567	3.2039	3.0946	3.0123	2.9480	2.8962
12	4.7472	3.8853	3.4903	3.2592	3.1059	2.9961	2.9134	2.8486	2.7964
13	4.6672	3.8056	3.4105	3.1791	3.0254	2.9153	2.8321	2.7669	2.7144
14	4.6001	3.7389	3.3439	3.1122	2.9582	2.8477	2.7642	2.6987	2.6458
15	4.5431	3.6823	3.2874	3.0556	2.9013	2.7905	2.7066	2.6408	2.5876
16	4.4940	3.6337	3.2389	3.0069	2.8524	2.7413	2.6572	2.5911	2.5377
17	4.4513	3.5915	3.1968	2.9647	2.8100	2.6987	2.6143	2.5480	2.4943
18	4.4139	3.5546	3.1599	2.9277	2.7729	2.6613	2.5767	2.5102	2.4563
19	4.3807	3.5219	3.1274	2.8951	2.7401	2.6283	2.5435	2.4768	2.4227
20	4.3512	3.4928	2.0984	2.8661	2.7109	2.5990	2.5140	2.4471	2.3928
21	4.3248	3.4668	3.0725	2.8401	2.6848	2.5727	2.4876	2.4205	2.3660
22	4.3009	3.4434	3.0491	2.8167	2.6613	2.5491	2.4638	2.3965	2.3419
23	4.2793	3.4221	3.0280	2.7955	2.6400	2.5277	2.4422	2.3748	2.3201
24	4.2597	3.4028	3.0088	2.7763	2.6307	2.5082	2.4226	2.3551	2.3002
25	4.2417	3.3852	2.9912	2.7587	2.6030	2.4904	2.4047	2.3371	2.2821
26	4.2252	3.3690	2.9752	2.7426	2.5868	2.4741	2.3883	2.3205	2.2655
27	4.2100	3.3541	2.9604	2.7278	2.5719	2.4591	2.3732	2.3053	2.2501
28	4.1960	3.3404	2.9467	2.7141	2.5581	2.4453	2.3593	2.2913	2.2360
29	4.1830	3.3277	2.9340	2.7014	2.5454	2.4324	2.3463	2.2783	2.2229
30	4.1709	3.3158	2.9223	2.6896	2.5336	2.4205	2.3343	2.2662	2.2107
40	4.0847	3.2317	2.8387	2.6060	2.4495	2.3359	2.2490	2.1802	2.1240
60	4.0012	3.1504	2.7581	2.5252	2.3683	2.2541	2.1665	2.0970	2.0401
120	3.9201	3.0718	2.6802	2.4472	2.2899	2.1750	2.0868	2.0164	1.9588
∞	3.8415	2.9957	2.6049	2.3719	2.2141	2.0986	2.0096	1.9384	1.8799

Table A5(a) continued

v_2 \\ v_1	10	12	15	20	24	30	40	60	120	∞
1	241.88	243.91	245.95	248.01	249.05	250.10	251.14	252.20	253.25	254.31
2	19.396	19.413	19.429	19.446	19.454	19.462	19.471	19.479	19.487	19.496
3	8.7855	8.7446	8.7029	8.6602	8.6385	8.6166	8.5944	8.5720	8.5494	8.5264
4	5.9644	5.9117	5.8578	5.8025	5.7744	5.7459	5.7170	5.6877	5.6581	5.6281
5	4.7351	4.6777	4.6188	4.5581	4.5272	4.4957	4.4638	4.4314	4.3985	4.3650
6	4.0600	3.9999	3.9381	3.8742	3.8415	3.8082	3.7743	3.7398	3.7047	3.6689
7	3.6365	3.5747	3.5107	3.4445	3.4105	3.3758	3.3404	3.3043	3.2674	3.2298
8	3.3472	3.2839	3.2184	3.1503	3.1152	3.0794	3.0428	3.0053	2.9669	2.9276
9	3.1373	3.0729	3.0061	2.9365	2.9005	2.8637	2.8259	2.7872	2.7475	2.7067
10	2.9782	2.9130	2.8450	2.7740	2.7372	2.6996	2.6609	2.6211	2.5801	2.5379
11	2.8536	2.7876	2.7186	2.6464	2.6090	2.5705	2.5309	2.4901	2.4480	2.4045
12	2.7534	2.6866	2.6169	2.5436	2.5055	2.4663	2.4259	2.3842	2.3410	2.2962
13	2.6710	2.6037	2.5331	2.4589	2.4202	2.3803	2.3392	2.2966	2.2524	2.2064
14	2.6022	2.5342	2.4630	2.3879	2.3487	2.3082	2.2664	2.2229	2.1778	2.1307
15	2.5437	2.4753	2.4034	2.3275	2.2878	2.2468	2.2043	2.1601	2.1141	2.0658
16	2.4935	2.4247	2.3522	2.2756	2.2354	2.1938	2.1507	2.1058	2.0589	2.0096
17	2.4499	2.3807	2.3077	2.2304	2.1898	2.1477	2.1040	2.0584	2.0107	1.9604
18	2.4117	2.3421	2.2686	2.1906	2.1497	2.1071	2.0629	2.0166	1.9681	1.9168
19	2.3779	2.3080	2.2341	2.1555	2.1141	2.0712	2.0264	1.9795	1.9302	1.8780
20	2.3479	2.2776	2.2033	2.1242	2.0825	2.0391	1.9938	1.9464	1.8963	1.8432
21	2.3210	2.2504	2.1757	2.0960	2.0540	2.0102	1.9645	1.9165	1.8657	1.8117
22	2.2967	2.2258	2.1508	2.0707	2.0283	1.9842	1.9380	1.8894	1.8380	1.7831
23	2.2747	2.2036	2.1282	2.0476	2.0050	1.9605	1.9139	1.8648	1.8128	1.7570
24	2.2547	2.1834	2.1077	2.0267	1.9838	1.9390	1.8920	1.8424	1.7896	1.7330
25	2.2365	2.1649	2.0889	2.0075	1.9643	1.9192	1.8718	1.8217	1.7684	1.7110
26	2.2197	2.1479	2.0716	1.9898	1.9464	1.9010	1.8533	1.8027	1.7488	1.6906
27	2.2043	2.1323	2.0558	1.9736	1.9299	1.8842	1.8361	1.7851	1.7306	1.6717
28	2.1900	2.1179	2.0411	1.9586	1.9147	1.8687	1.8203	1.7689	1.7138	1.6541
29	2.1768	2.1045	2.0275	1.9446	1.9005	1.8543	1.8055	1.7537	1.6981	1.6376
30	2.1646	2.0921	2.0148	1.9317	1.8874	1.8409	1.7918	1.7396	1.6835	1.6223
40	2.0772	2.0035	1.9245	1.8389	1.7929	1.7444	1.6928	1.6373	1.5766	1.5089
60	1.9926	1.9174	1.8364	1.7480	1.7001	1.6491	1.5943	1.5343	1.4673	1.3893
120	1.9105	1.8337	1.7505	1.6587	1.6084	1.5543	1.4952	1.4290	1.3519	1.2539
∞	1.8307	1.7522	1.6664	1.5705	1.5173	1.4591	1.3940	1.3180	1.2214	1.0000

Table A5(b)   Critical values of the *F* distribution (upper 2.5% points)

The entries in the table give the critical values
of *F* cutting off 2.5% in the right-hand tail of
the distribution. v_1 gives the degrees of freedom
in the numerator, v_2 in the denominator.

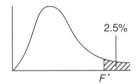

2.5%

F^*

v_1 / v_1	1	2	3	4	5	6	7	8	9
1	647.79	799.50	864.16	899.58	921.85	937.11	948.22	956.66	963.28
2	38.506	39.000	39.165	39.248	39.298	39.331	39.355	39.373	39.387
3	17.443	16.044	15.439	15.101	14.885	14.735	14.624	14.540	14.473
4	12.218	10.649	9.9792	9.6045	9.3645	9.1973	9.0741	8.9796	8.9047
5	10.007	8.4336	7.7636	7.3879	7.1464	6.9777	6.8531	6.7572	6.6811
6	8.8131	7.2599	6.5988	6.2272	5.9876	5.8198	5.6955	5.5996	5.5234
7	8.0727	6.5415	5.8898	5.5226	5.2852	5.1186	4.9949	4.8993	4.8232
8	7.5709	6.0595	5.4160	5.0526	4.8173	4.6517	4.5286	4.4333	4.3572
9	7.2093	5.7147	5.0781	4.7181	4.4844	4.3197	4.1970	4.1020	4.0260
10	6.9367	5.4564	4.8256	4.4683	4.2361	4.0721	3.9498	3.8549	3.7790
11	6.7241	5.2559	4.6300	4.2751	4.0440	3.8807	3.7586	3.6638	3.5879
12	6.5538	5.0959	4.4742	4.1212	3.8911	3.7283	3.6065	3.5118	3.4358
13	6.4143	4.9653	4.3472	3.9959	3.7667	3.6043	3.4827	3.3880	3.3120
14	6.2979	4.8567	4.2417	3.8919	3.6634	3.5014	3.3799	3.2853	3.2093
15	6.1995	4.7650	4.1528	3.8043	3.5764	3.4147	3.2934	3.1987	3.1227
16	6.1151	4.6867	4.0768	3.7294	3.5021	3.3406	3.2194	3.1248	3.0488
17	6.0420	4.6189	4.0112	3.6648	3.4379	3.2767	3.1556	3.0610	2.9849
18	5.9781	4.5597	3.9539	3.6083	3.3820	3.2209	3.0999	3.0053	2.9219
19	5.9216	4.5075	3.9034	3.5587	3.3327	3.1718	3.0509	2.9563	2.8801
20	5.8715	4.4613	3.8587	3.5147	3.2891	3.1283	3.0074	2.9128	2.8365
21	5.8266	4.4199	3.8188	3.4754	3.2501	3.0895	2.9686	2.8740	2.7977
22	5.7863	4.3828	3.7829	3.4401	3.2151	3.0546	2.9338	2.8392	2.7628
23	5.7498	4.3492	3.7505	3.4083	3.1835	3.0232	2.9023	2.8077	2.7313
24	5.7166	4.3187	3.7211	3.3794	3.1548	2.9946	2.8738	2.7791	2.7027
25	5.6864	4.2909	3.6943	3.3530	3.1287	2.9685	2.8478	2.7531	2.6766
26	5.6586	4.2655	3.6697	3.3289	3.1048	2.9447	2.8240	2.7293	2.6528
27	5.6331	4.2421	3.6472	3.3067	3.0828	2.9228	2.8021	2.7074	2.6309
28	5.6096	4.2205	3.6264	3.2863	3.0626	2.9027	2.7820	2.6872	2.6106
29	5.5878	4.2006	3.6072	3.2674	3.0438	2.8840	2.7633	2.6686	2.5919
30	5.5675	4.1821	3.5894	3.2499	3.0265	2.8667	2.7460	2.6513	2.5746
40	5.4239	4.0510	3.4633	3.1261	2.9037	2.7444	2.6238	2.5289	2.4519
60	5.2856	3.9253	3.3425	3.0077	2.7863	2.6274	2.5068	2.4117	2.3344
120	5.1523	3.8046	3.2269	2.8943	2.6740	2.5154	2.3948	2.2994	2.2217
∞	5.0239	3.6889	3.1161	2.7858	2.5665	2.4082	2.2875	2.1918	2.1136

Table A5(b) continued

v_1 v_2	10	12	15	20	24	30	40	60	120	∞
1	968.63	976.71	984.87	993.10	997.25	1001.4	1005.6	1009.8	1014.0	1018.3
2	39.398	39.415	39.431	39.448	39.456	39.465	39.473	39.481	39.400	39.498
3	14.419	14.337	14.253	14.167	14.124	14.081	14.037	13.992	13.947	13.902
4	8.8439	8.7512	8.6565	8.5599	8.5109	8.4613	8.4111	8.3604	8.3092	8.2573
5	6.6192	6.5245	6.4277	6.3286	6.2780	6.2269	6.1750	6.1225	6.069?	6.0153
6	5.4613	5.3662	5.2687	5.1684	5.1172	5.0652	5.0125	4.9589	4.9044	4.8491
7	4.7611	4.6658	4.5678	4.4667	4.4150	4.3624	4.3089	4.2544	4.1989	4.1423
8	4.2951	4.1997	4.1012	3.9995	3.9472	3.8940	3.8398	3.7844	3.7279	3.6702
9	3.9639	3.8682	3.7694	3.6669	3.6142	3.5604	3.5055	3.4493	3.3918	3.3329
10	3.7168	3.6209	3.5217	3.4185	3.3654	3.3110	3.2554	3.1984	3.1399	3.0798
11	3.5257	3.4296	3.3299	3.2261	3.1725	3.1176	3.0613	3.0035	2.9441	2.8828
12	3.3736	3.2773	3.1772	3.0728	3.0187	2.9633	2.9063	2.8478	2.7874	2.7249
13	3.2497	3.1532	3.0527	2.9477	2.8932	2.8372	2.7797	2.7204	2.6590	2.5955
14	3.1469	3.0502	2.9493	2.8437	2.7888	2.7324	2.6742	2.6142	2.5519	2.4872
15	3.0602	2.9633	2.8621	2.7559	2.7006	2.6437	2.5850	2.5242	2.4611	2.3953
16	2.9862	2.8890	2.7875	2.6808	2.6252	2.5678	2.5085	2.4471	2.3831	2.3163
17	2.9222	2.8249	2.7230	2.6158	2.5598	2.5020	2.4422	2.3801	2.3153	2.2474
18	2.8664	2.7689	2.6667	2.5590	2.5027	2.4445	2.3842	2.3214	2.2558	2.1869
19	2.8172	2.7196	2.6171	2.5089	2.4523	2.3937	2.3329	2.2696	2.2032	2.1333
20	2.7737	2.6758	2.5731	2.4645	2.4076	2.3486	2.2873	2.2234	2.1562	2.0853
21	2.7348	2.6368	2.5338	2.4247	2.3675	2.3082	2.2465	2.1819	2.1141	2.0422
22	2.6998	2.6017	2.4984	2.3890	2.3315	2.2718	2.2097	2.1446	2.0760	2.0032
23	2.6682	2.5699	2.4665	2.3567	2.2989	2.2389	2.1763	2.1107	2.0415	1.9677
24	2.6396	2.5411	2.4374	2.3273	2.2693	2.2090	2.1460	2.0799	2.0099	1.9353
25	2.6135	2.5149	2.4110	2.3005	2.2422	2.1816	2.1183	2.0516	1.9811	1.9055
26	2.5896	2.4908	2.3867	2.2759	2.2174	2.1565	2.0928	2.0257	1.9545	1.8781
27	2.5676	2.4688	2.3644	2.2533	2.1946	2.1334	2.0693	2.0018	1.9299	1.8527
28	2.5473	2.4484	2.3438	2.2324	2.1735	2.1121	2.0477	1.9797	1.9072	1.8291
29	2.5286	2.4295	2.3248	2.2131	2.1540	2.0923	2.0276	1.9591	1.8861	1.8072
30	2.5112	2.4120	2.3072	2.1952	2.1359	2.0739	2.0089	1.9400	1.8664	1.7867
40	2.3882	2.2882	2.1819	2.0677	2.0069	1.9429	1.8752	1.8028	1.7242	1.6371
60	2.2702	2.1692	2.0613	1.9445	1.8817	1.8152	1.7440	1.6668	1.5810	1.4821
120	2.1570	2.0548	1.9450	1.8249	1.7597	1.6899	1.6141	1.5299	1.4327	1.3104
∞	2.0483	1.9447	1.8326	1.7085	1.6402	1.5660	1.4835	1.3883	1.2684	1.0000

Table A5(c) Critical values of the F distribution (upper 1% points)

The entries in the table give the critical values of F cutting off 1% in the right-hand tail of the distribution. v_1 gives the degrees of freedom in the numerator, v_2 in the denominator.

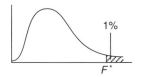

1%

F^*

v_1 \ v_1	1	2	3	4	5	6	7	8	9
1	4052.2	4999.5	5403.4	5624.6	5763.6	5859.0	5928.4	5981.1	6022.5
2	98.503	99.000	99.166	99.249	99.299	99.333	99.356	99.374	99.388
3	34.116	30.817	29.457	28.710	28.237	27.911	27.672	27.489	27.345
4	21.198	18.000	16.694	15.977	15.522	15.207	14.976	14.799	14.659
5	16.258	13.274	12.060	11.392	10.967	10.672	10.456	10.289	10.158
6	13.745	10.925	9.7795	9.1483	8.7459	8.4661	8.2600	8.1017	7.9761
7	12.246	9.5466	8.4513	7.8466	7.4604	7.1914	6.9928	6.8400	6.7188
8	11.259	8.6491	7.5910	7.0061	6.6318	6.3707	6.1776	6.0289	5.9106
9	10.561	8.0215	6.9919	6.4221	6.0569	5.8018	5.6129	5.4671	5.3511
10	10.044	7.5594	6.5523	5.9943	5.6363	5.3858	5.2001	5.0567	4.9424
11	9.6460	7.2057	6.2167	5.6683	5.3160	5.0692	4.8861	4.7445	4.6315
12	9.3302	6.9266	5.9525	5.4120	5.0643	4.8206	4.6395	4.4994	4.3875
13	9.0738	6.7010	5.7394	5.2053	4.8616	4.6204	4.4410	4.3021	4.1911
14	8.8618	6.5149	5.5639	5.0354	4.6950	4.4558	4.2779	4.1399	4.0297
15	8.6831	6.3589	5.4170	4.8932	4.5556	4.3183	4.1415	4.0045	3.8948
16	8.5310	6.2262	5.2922	4.7726	4.4374	4.2016	4.0259	3.8896	3.7804
17	8.3997	6.1121	5.1850	4.6690	4.3359	4.1015	3.9267	3.7910	3.6822
18	8.2854	6.0129	5.0919	4.5790	4.2479	4.0146	3.8406	3.7054	3.5971
19	8.1849	5.9259	5.0103	4.5003	4.1708	3.9386	3.7653	3.6305	3.5225
20	8.0960	5.8489	4.9382	4.4307	4.1027	3.8714	3.6987	3.5644	3.4567
21	8.0166	5.7804	4.8740	4.3688	4.0421	3.8117	3.6396	3.5056	3.3981
22	7.9454	5.7190	4.8166	4.3134	3.9880	3.7583	3.5867	3.4530	3.3458
23	7.8811	5.6637	4.7649	4.2636	3.9392	3.7102	3.5390	3.4057	3.2986
24	7.8229	5.6136	4.7181	4.2184	3.8951	3.6667	3.4959	3.3629	3.2560
25	7.7698	5.5680	4.6755	4.1774	3.8550	3.6272	3.4568	3.3439	3.2172
26	7.7213	5.5263	4.6366	4.1400	3.8183	3.5911	3.4210	3.2884	3.1818
27	7.6767	5.4881	4.6009	4.1056	3.7848	3.5580	3.3882	3.2558	3.1494
28	7.6356	5.4529	4.5681	4.0740	3.7539	3.5276	3.3581	3.2259	3.1195
29	7.5977	5.4204	4.5378	4.0449	3.7254	3.4995	3.3303	3.1982	3.0920
30	7.5625	5.3903	4.5097	4.0179	3.6990	3.4735	3.3045	3.1726	3.0665
40	7.3141	5.1785	4.3126	3.8283	3.5138	3.2910	3.1238	2.9930	2.8876
60	7.0771	4.9774	4.1259	3.6490	3.3389	3.1187	2.9530	2.8233	2.7185
120	6.8509	4.7865	3.9491	3.4795	3.1735	2.9559	2.7918	2.6629	2.5586
∞	6.6349	4.6052	3.7816	3.3192	3.0173	2.8020	2.6393	2.5113	2.4073

Table A5(c) continued

v_2 \ v_1	10	12	15	20	24	30	40	60	120	∞
1	6055.8	6106.3	6157.3	6208.7	6234.6	6260.6	6286.8	6313.0	6339.4	6365.9
2	99.399	99.416	99.433	99.449	99.458	99.466	99.474	99.482	99.491	99.499
3	27.229	27.052	26.872	26.690	26.598	26.505	26.411	26.316	26.221	26.125
4	14.546	14.374	14.198	14.020	13.929	13.838	13.745	13.652	13.558	13.463
5	10.051	9.8883	9.7222	9.5526	9.4665	9.3793	9.2912	9.2020	9.1118	9.0204
6	7.8741	7.7183	7.5590	7.3958	7.3127	7.2285	7.1432	7.0567	6.9690	6.8800
7	6.6201	6.4691	6.3143	6.1554	6.0743	5.9920	5.9084	5.8236	5.7373	5.6495
8	5.8143	5.6667	5.5151	5.3591	5.2793	5.1981	5.1156	5.0316	4.9461	4.8588
9	5.2565	5.1114	4.9621	4.8080	4.7290	4.6486	4.5666	4.4831	4.3978	4.3105
10	4.8491	4.7059	4.5581	4.4054	4.3269	4.2469	4.1653	4.0819	3.9965	3.9090
11	4.5393	4.3974	4.2509	4.0990	4.0209	3.9411	3.8596	3.7761	3.6904	3.6024
12	4.2961	4.1553	4.0096	3.8584	3.7805	3.7008	3.6192	3.5355	3.4494	3.3608
13	4.1003	3.9603	3.8154	3.6646	3.5868	3.5070	3.4253	3.3413	3.2548	3.1654
14	3.9394	3.8001	3.6557	3.5052	3.4274	3.3476	3.2656	3.1813	3.0942	3.0040
15	3.8049	3.6662	3.5222	3.3719	3.2940	3.2141	3.1319	3.0471	2.9595	2.8684
16	3.6909	3.5527	3.4089	3.2587	3.1808	3.1007	3.0182	2.9330	2.8447	2.7528
17	3.5931	3.4552	3.3117	3.1615	3.0835	2.0032	2.9205	2.8348	2.7459	2.6530
18	3.5082	3.3706	3.2273	3.0771	2.9990	2.9185	2.8354	2.7493	2.6597	2.5660
19	3.4338	3.2965	3.1533	3.0031	2.9249	2.8442	2.7608	2.6742	2.5839	2.4893
20	3.3682	3.2311	3.0880	2.9377	2.8594	2.7785	2.6947	2.6077	2.5168	2.4212
21	3.3098	3.1730	3.0300	2.8796	2.8010	2.7200	2.6359	2.5484	2.4568	2.3603
22	3.2576	3.1209	2.9779	2.8274	2.7488	2.6675	2.5831	2.4951	2.4029	2.3055
23	3.2106	3.0740	2.9311	2.7805	2.7017	2.6202	2.5355	2.4471	2.3542	2.2558
24	3.1681	3.0316	2.8887	2.7380	2.6591	2.5773	2.4923	2.4035	2.3100	2.2107
25	3.1294	2.9931	2.8502	2.6993	2.6203	2.5383	2.4530	2.3637	2.2696	2.1694
26	3.0941	2.9578	2.8150	2.6640	2.5848	2.5026	2.4170	2.3273	2.2325	2.1315
27	3.0618	2.9256	2.7827	2.6316	2.5522	2.4699	2.3840	2.2938	2.1985	2.0965
28	3.0320	2.8959	2.7530	2.6017	2.5223	2.4397	2.3535	2.2629	2.1670	2.0642
29	3.0045	2.8685	2.7256	2.5742	2.4946	2.4118	2.3253	2.2344	2.1379	2.0342
30	2.9791	2.8431	2.7002	2.5487	2.4689	2.3860	2.2992	2.2079	2.1108	2.0062
40	2.8005	2.6648	2.5216	2.3689	2.2880	2.2034	2.1142	2.0194	1.9172	1.8047
60	2.6318	2.4961	2.3523	2.1978	2.1154	2.0285	1.9360	1.8363	1.7263	1.6006
120	2.4721	2.3363	2.1915	2.0346	1.9500	1.8600	1.7628	1.6557	1.5330	1.3805
∞	2.3209	2.1847	2.0385	1.8783	1.7908	1.6964	1.5923	1.4730	1.3246	1.0000

Table A5(d)   Critical values of the F distribution (upper 0.5% points)

The entries in the table give the critical values of F cutting off 0.5% in the right–hand tail of the distribution. v_1 gives the degrees of freedom in the numerator, v_2 in the denominator.

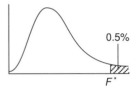

0.5%

F^*

v_1 / v_1	1	2	3	4	5	6	7	8	9
1	16211	20000	21615	22500	23056	23437	23715	23925	24091
2	198.50	199.00	199.17	199.25	199.30	199.33	199.36	199.37	199.39
3	55.552	49.799	47.467	46.195	45.392	44.838	44.434	44.126	43.882
4	31.333	26.284	24.259	23.155	22.456	21.975	21.622	21.352	21.139
5	22.785	18.314	16.530	15.556	14.940	14.513	14.200	13.961	13.772
6	18.635	14.544	12.917	12.028	11.464	11.073	10.786	10.566	10.391
7	16.236	12.404	10.882	10.050	9.5221	9.1553	8.8854	8.6781	8.5138
8	14.688	11.042	9.5965	8.8051	9.3018	7.9520	7.6941	7.4959	7.3386
9	13.614	10.107	8.7171	7.9559	7.4712	7.1339	6.8849	6.6933	6.5411
10	12.826	9.4270	8.0807	7.3428	6.8724	6.5446	6.3025	6.1159	5.9676
11	12.226	8.9122	7.6004	6.8809	6.4217	6.1016	5.8648	5.6821	5.5368
12	11.754	8.5096	7.2258	6.5211	6.0711	5.7570	5.5245	5.3451	5.2021
13	11.374	8.1865	6.9258	6.2335	5.7910	5.4819	5.2529	5.0761	4.9351
14	11.060	7.9216	6.6804	5.9984	5.5623	5.2574	5.0313	4.8566	4.7173
15	10.798	7.7008	6.4760	5.8029	5.3721	5.0708	4.8473	4.6744	3.5364
16	10.575	7.5138	6.3034	5.6378	5.2117	4.9134	4.6920	4.5207	4.3838
17	10.384	7.3536	6.1556	5.4967	5.0746	4.7789	4.5594	4.3894	4.2535
18	10.218	7.2148	6.0278	5.3746	3.9560	4.6627	4.4448	3.2759	4.1410
19	10.073	7.0935	5.9161	5.2681	4.8526	4.5614	4.3448	4.1770	4.0428
20	9.9439	6.9865	5.8177	5.1743	4.7616	4.4721	4.2569	4.0900	3.9564
21	9.8295	6.8914	5.7304	5.0911	4.6809	4.3931	4.1789	4.0128	3.8799
22	9.7271	6.8064	5.6524	5.0168	4.6088	4.3225	4.1094	3.9440	3.8116
23	9.6348	6.7300	5.5823	4.9500	3.5441	4.2591	4.0469	3.8822	3.7502
24	9.5513	6.6609	5.5190	4.8898	4.4857	4.2019	3.9905	3.8264	3.6949
25	9.4753	6.5982	5.4615	4.8351	4.4327	4.1500	3.9394	3.7758	3.6447
26	9.4059	6.5409	5.4091	4.7852	4.3844	4.1027	3.8928	3.7297	3.5989
27	9.3423	6.4885	5.3611	4.7396	4.3402	4.0594	3.8501	3.6875	3.5571
28	9.2838	6.4403	5.3170	4.6977	4.2996	4.0197	3.8110	3.6487	3.5186
29	9.2297	6.3958	5.2764	4.6591	4.2622	3.9831	3.7749	3.6131	3.4832
30	9.1797	6.3547	5.2388	4.6234	4.2276	3.9492	3.7416	3.5801	3.4504
40	8.8279	6.0664	4.9758	4.3738	3.9860	3.7129	3.5088	3.3498	3.2220
60	8.4946	5.7950	4.7290	4.1399	3.7599	3.4918	3.2911	3.1344	3.0083
120	8.1788	5.5393	4.4972	3.9207	3.5482	3.2849	3.0874	2.9330	2.8083
∞	7.894	5.2983	4.2794	3.7151	3.3499	3.0913	2.8968	2.7444	2.6210

Table A5(d) continued

v_2 \ v_1	10	12	15	20	24	30	40	60	120	∞
1	24224	24426	24630	24836	24940	25044	25148	25253	25359	25464
2	199.40	199.42	199.43	199.45	199.46	199.47	199.47	199.48	199.49	199.50
3	43.686	43.387	43.085	42.778	42.622	42.466	42.308	42.149	41.989	41.828
4	20.967	20.705	20.438	20.167	20.030	19.892	19.752	19.611	19.468	19.325
5	13.618	13.384	13.146	12.903	12.780	12.656	12.530	12.402	12.274	12.144
6	10.250	10.034	9.8140	9.5888	9.4742	9.3582	9.2408	9.1219	9.0015	8.8793
7	8.3803	8.1764	7.9678	7.7540	7.6450	7.5345	7.4224	7.3088	7.1933	7.0760
8	7.2106	7.0149	6.8143	6.6082	6.5029	6.3961	6.2875	6.1772	6.0649	5.9506
9	6.4172	6.2274	6.0325	5.8318	5.7292	5.6248	5.5186	5.4104	5.3001	5.1875
10	5.8467	5.6613	5.4707	5.2740	5.1732	5.0706	4.9659	4.8592	4.7501	4.6385
11	5.4183	5.2363	5.0489	4.8552	4.7557	4.6543	4.5508	4.4450	4.3367	4.2255
12	5.0855	4.9062	4.7213	4.5299	4.4314	4.3309	4.2282	5.1229	4.0149	3.9039
13	4.8199	4.6429	4.4600	4.2703	4.1726	4.0727	3.9704	3.8655	3.7577	3.6465
14	4.6034	4.4281	4.2468	4.0585	3.9614	3.8619	3.7600	3.6552	3.5473	3.4359
15	4.4235	4.2497	4.0698	3.8826	3.7859	3.6867	3.5850	3.4803	3.3722	3.2602
16	4.2719	4.0994	3.9205	3.7342	3.6378	3.5389	3.4372	3.3324	3.2240	3.1115
17	4.1424	3.9709	3.7929	3.6073	3.5112	3.4124	3.3108	3.2058	3.0971	2.9839
18	4.0305	3.8599	3.6827	3.4977	3.4017	3.3030	3.2014	3.0962	2.9871	2.8732
19	3.9329	3.7631	4.5866	3.4020	3.3062	3.2075	3.1058	3.0004	2.8908	2.7762
20	3.8470	3.6779	3.5020	3.3178	3.2220	3.1234	3.0215	2.9159	2.8058	2.6904
21	3.7709	3.6024	3.4270	3.2431	3.1474	3.0488	2.9467	2.7408	2.7302	2.6140
22	3.7030	3.5350	3.3600	3.1764	3.0807	2.9821	2.8799	2.7736	2.6625	2.5455
23	3.6420	3.4745	3.2999	3.1165	3.0208	2.9221	2.8197	2.7132	2.6015	2.4837
24	3.5870	3.4199	3.2456	3.0624	2.9667	2.8679	2.7654	2.6585	2.5463	2.4276
25	3.5370	3.3704	3.1963	3.0133	2.9176	2.8187	2.7160	2.6088	2.4961	2.3765
26	3.4916	3.3252	3.1515	2.9685	2.8728	2.7738	2.6709	2.5633	2.4501	2.3297
27	3.4499	3.2839	3.1104	2.9275	2.8318	2.7327	2.6296	2.5217	2.4079	2.2867
28	3.4117	3.2460	3.0727	2.8899	2.7941	2.6949	2.5916	2.4834	2.3690	2.2470
29	3.3765	3.2110	3.0379	2.8551	2.7594	2.6600	2.5565	2.4479	2.3331	2.2102
30	3.3440	3.1787	3.0057	2.8230	2.7272	2.6278	2.5241	2.4151	2.2998	2.1760
40	3.1167	2.9531	2.7811	2.5984	2.5020	2.4015	2.2958	2.1838	2.0636	1.9318
60	2.9042	2.7419	2.5705	2.3872	2.2898	2.1874	2.0789	1.9622	1.8341	1.6885
120	2.7052	2.5439	2.3727	2.1881	2.0890	1.9840	1.8709	1.7469	1.6055	1.4311
∞	2.5188	2.3583	2.1868	1.9998	1.8983	1.7891	1.6691	1.5325	1.3637	1.0000

Table A6   **Critical values of Spearman's rank correlation coefficient**

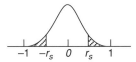

Entries in the table show critical values of Spearman's rank correlation coefficient. The value at the top of each column shows the significance level for a two-tail test. For a one-tail test, the significance level is half that shown.

N	10%	5%	2%	1%
5	0.900	—	—	—
6	0.829	0.886	0.943	—
7	0.714	0.786	0.893	—
8	0.643	0.738	0.833	0.881
9	0.600	0.683	0.783	0.833
10	0.564	0.648	0.745	0.818
11	0.523	0.623	0.763	0.794
12	0.497	0.591	0.703	0.780
13	0.475	0.566	0.673	0.746
14	0.457	0.545	0.646	0.716
15	0.441	0.525	0.623	0.689
16	0.425	0.507	0.601	0.666
17	0.412	0.490	0.582	0.645
18	0.399	0.476	0.564	0.625
19	0.388	0.462	0.549	0.608
20	0.377	0.450	0.534	0.591
21	0.368	0.438	0.521	0.576
22	0.359	0.428	0.508	0.562
23	0.351	0.418	0.496	0.549
24	0.343	0.409	0.485	0.537
25	0.336	0.400	0.475	0.526
26	0.329	0.392	0.465	0.515
27	0.323	0.385	0.456	0.505
28	0.317	0.377	0.448	0.496
29	0.311	0.370	0.440	0.487
30	0.305	0.364	0.432	0.478

Source: Annals of Statistics, 1936 and 1949

Table A7   **Critical values for the Durbin–Watson test at 5% significance level**

Sample size	Number of explanatory variables									
	1		2		3		4		5	
n	d_L	d_U	d_L	d_U	d_L	d_U	d_L	d_U	d_L	d_U
10	0.879	1.320	0.697	1.641	0.525	2.016	0.376	2.414	0.243	2.822
11	0.927	1.324	0.758	1.604	0.595	1.928	0.444	2.283	0.316	2.645
12	0.971	1.331	0.812	1.579	0.658	1.864	0.512	2.177	0.379	2.506
13	1.010	1.340	0.861	1.562	0.715	1.816	0.574	2.094	0.445	2.390
14	1.045	1.350	0.905	1.551	0.767	1.779	0.632	2.030	0.505	2.296
15	1.077	1.361	0.946	1.543	0.814	1.750	0.685	1.977	0.562	2.220
20	1.201	1.411	1.100	1.537	0.998	1.676	0.894	1.828	0.792	1.991
25	1.288	1.454	1.206	1.550	1.123	1.654	1.038	1.767	0.953	1.886
30	1.352	1.489	1.284	1.567	1.214	1.650	1.143	1.739	1.071	1.833
35	1.402	1.519	1.343	1.584	1.283	1.653	1.222	1.726	1.160	1.803
40	1.442	1.544	1.391	1.600	1.338	1.659	1.285	1.721	1.230	1.786
50	1.503	1.585	1.462	1.628	1.421	1.674	1.378	1.721	1.335	1.771
100	1.654	1.694	1.634	1.715	1.613	1.736	1.592	1.758	1.571	1.780
200	1.758	1.778	1.748	1.789	1.738	1.799	1.728	1.810	1.718	1.820

ANSWERS TO EXERCISES

Chapter 1

Exercise 1

(a)

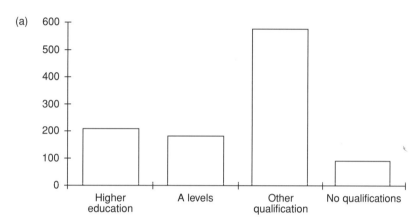

Comparison is complicated by different numbers, but there are relatively more women in the 'Other' education category, relatively less in the other three.

(b)

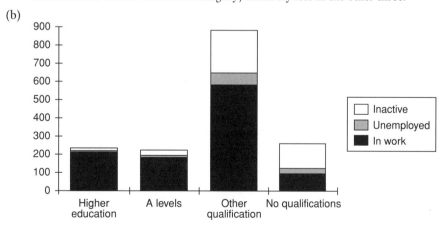

The biggest difference is the larger number of 'inactive' women, mostly engaged in child-rearing, one would suspect.

(c)   The 'inactive' women show up again.

(d)

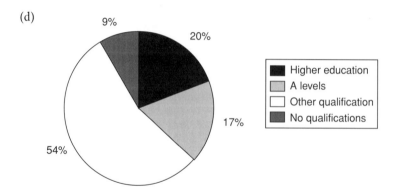

Relatively fewer women have no qualifications, A levels and higher education, but relatively more have other qualifications.

Exercise 3

(a) Higher education, 88%.

(b) Those in work, 20%.

Exercise 5

The difference between bar chart and histogram should be similar to those for the 1988 distribution. Overall shape similar (heavily skewed to right). Comparison difficult because of different wealth levels (due to inflation) and because grouping into classes can affect precise shape of graph.

Exercise 7

(a) Mean 16.399 ($£$000); median 8.92; mode 1–3 ($£$000) group has the greatest frequency density. They differ because of skewness in the distribution.

(b) Q1 = 3.295, Q3 = 18.339, IQR = 15.044; variance = 653.88; s.d. = 25.552; cv = 1.56.

(c) $95{,}469.32/25.55^3 = 5.72 > 0$ as expected.

(d) Comparison in text.

(e) This would increase the mean substantially (to 31.12), but the median and mode would be unaffected.

Exercise 9

57.62 pence/litre.

Exercise 11

(a) $z = 1.5$ and -1.5 respectively.

(b) Using Chebyshev's theorem with $k = 1.5$, we have that at least $(1 - 1/1.5^2) = 0.56$ (56%) lies within 1.5 standard deviations of the mean, so at most 0.44 (44 students) lies outside the range.

(c) Chebyshev's theorem applies to *both* tails, so we cannot answer this part. You cannot halve the figure of 0.44 because the distribution may be skewed.

Exercise 13

(a)

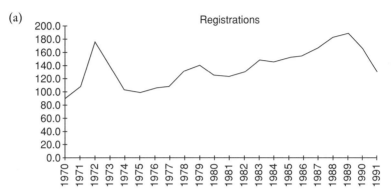

Strong upward trend from 1974–89, but substantial falls in 1972–74 and 1989–91. The market appears quite volatile, therefore. Note that this shows the *volume* of car registrations. *If* the 1972–76 pattern is repeated, one might expect car registrations to turn up again in 1992–93.

(b)

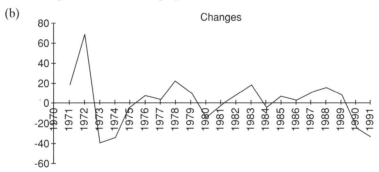

This figure shows the substantial volatility of the series, around an average not much above zero. 1989–91 looks less like 1971–73 on this graph. The log graphs are very similar to the levels graphs. There is not always an advantage to drawing these. Here, the time period is relatively short and the growth rate rather small.

Exercise 15

(a) 1.81% p.a. (but 4.88% p.a. between 1975 and 1989).

(b) 0.187 (around the arithmetic mean).

(c) Registrations appear more volatile, as measured by the cv (10.33 for car registrations, 0.663 for investment). Possible reasons: investment covers several categories and fluctuations in one may offset those in another; the registrations series is shorter, so a big random fluctuation has a larger effect; investment is nominal and the price influence may help to smooth out the series.

Exercise 17

(a) Non-linear, upward trend. Likely to be positively autocorrelated. Variation around the trend is likely to grow over time (heteroscedasticity).

(b) Similar to (a), except trend would be shallower after deflating. Probably less heteroscedasticity because price variability has been removed, which may also increase the autocorrelation of the series.

(c) Unlikely to show a trend in the *very* long run, but there might be one over, say, five years, if inflation is increasing. Likely to be homoscedastic, with some degree of correlation.

Exercise 19

(a) Using $S_t = S_0 (1 - r)^t$, hence $S_0 = S_t / (1 + r)^t$. Setting $S_t = 1,000$, $r = 0.07$ gives $S_0 = 712.99$. Price after two years: £816.30. If r rose to 10% the bond would fall to $1000/1.1^3 = 751.31$.

(b) The income stream should be discounted to the present using

$$\frac{200}{1+r} + \frac{200}{(1+r)^2} + \ldots + \frac{200}{(1+r)^5} = 820.04,$$ so the bond should sell for £820.04.

It is worth more than the previous bond because the return is obtained earlier.

Exercise 21

(a) 17.9% p.a. for BMW, 14% p.a. for Mercedes.

(b) Depreciated values are

BMW 525i	22,275	18,284	15,008	12,319	10,112	8,300
Merc 200E	21,900	18,833	16,196	13,928	11,977	10,300

which are close to actual values. Depreciation is initially slower than the average, then speeds up, for both cars.

Exercise 23

$$E\left(x + k\right) = \frac{\sum\left(x + k\right)}{n} = \frac{\sum x + nk}{n} = \frac{\sum x}{n} + k = E\left(x\right) + k$$

Exercise 25

The mistake is comparing non-comparable averages. A first-time buyer would have an above average mortgage and purchase a below average priced house, hence the amount of buyer's equity would be small.

Answers to exercises on Σ notation

Exercise A1

20, 90, 400, 5, 17, 11.

Exercise A3

88, 372, 16, 85.

Exercise A5

113, 14, 110.

Exercise A7

$$\frac{\sum f(x-k)}{\sum f} = \frac{\sum fx - k\sum f}{\sum f} = \frac{\sum fx}{\sum f} - k$$

$$\frac{\sum f(x-\mu)^2}{\sum f} = \frac{\sum f(x^2 - 2\mu x + \mu^2)}{\sum f} = \frac{\sum fx^2 - 2\mu\sum fx + \mu^2\sum f}{\sum f}$$

$$= \frac{\sum fx^2}{\sum f} - 2\mu^2 + \mu^2 = \frac{\sum fx^2}{\sum f} - \mu^2$$

Answers to exercises on logarithms

C1   −0.8239, 0.17609, 1.17609, 2.17609, 3.17609, 1.92284, 0.96142, impossible!
C3   −1.89712, 0.40547, 2.70705, 5.41610, impossible!
C5   0.15, 12.58925, 125.8925, 1258.925, 10^{12}.
C7   15, 40.77422, 2.71828, 22026.4658.
C9   3.16228, 1.38692, 1.41421, 0.0005787, 0.008.

Chapter 2

Exercise 1

(a)

	1987	1988	1989	1990	1991	1992
Exports	100	100.5	105.1	110.5	109.5	112.4
Imports	100	112.5	120.9	121.5	114.8	121.5

(b) No. Using the indexes, information about the *levels* of imports and exports is lost.

Exercise 3

(a)–(c)

Year	E	P_L	P_P	Q_L	Q_P
1984	100	100	100	100	100
1985	104.0	104.2	104.3	99.8	99.9
1986	85.9	85.9	86.7	99.0	100.0
1987	85.8	83.0	85.0	101.0	103.3

Exercise 5

(a)

Year	Coal	Petroleum	Electricity	Gas
1984	100	100	100	100
1985	102.8	101.4	103.9	107.9
1986	100.1	48.8	104.1	90.3
1987	95.8	52.2	100.1	83.4
1988	86.9	36.8	103.9	82.6
Shares	0.105	0.255	0.377	0.264

(b)   Answer as in exercise 3(a).

Exercise 7

The chain index is 100, 110, 115, 123.1, 127.7, 136.9, 139.2, using 1990 as the common year. Using one of the other years to chain yields a slightly different index. There is no definitive right answer.

Exercise 9

Expenditure on energy in 1991 was £6,059.08 m. The Laspeyres index increased from 105.7 to 109.3 between 1991 and 1992, an increase of 3.4%. Hence industry should be compensated 1.4% of 6,059.08 = 84.8. A similar calculation using the Paasche index yields compensation of 124.8. Note that we are not using proper Laspeyres or Paasche indexes between 1991 and 1992.

Exercise 11

The index number series are as follows:

	Cash expen-diture	Real expen-diture	Volume of expen-diture	Real expen-diture per capita	Volume of expen-diture per capita	Needs index	Spending deflated by need
	(a)	(b)	(c)	(d)	(d)	(e)	(e)
1987	100.0	100.0	100.0	100.0	100.0	100.0	100.0
1988	109.8	102.6	99.4	102.4	99.2	100.2	99.2
1989	120.5	105.7	101.9	105.1	101.3	100.5	101.4
1990	132.7	107.5	104.5	106.6	103.6	100.8	103.6
1991	150.4	113.6	108.8	111.9	107.1	101.6	107.1

(a) $109.8 = 23{,}601/21495 \times 100$; $120.5 = 25{,}906/21495 \times 100$; etc.

(b) This series is obtained by dividing col. 1 by col. 2 (and setting 1987 as the reference year). Clearly, much of the increase in col. 1 is due to inflation.

(c) This series is col. 1 divided by col. 3. Since the NHS price index rose faster than the GDP deflator, the volume of expenditure rises more slowly than the real figure.

(d) Per capita figures are obtained by dividing by the population, col. 4.

(f) Needs index could be improved by finding the true cost of treating people of different ages.

Exercise 13

(a) 1,702.20.

(b) Yes, 102.20.

Exercise 15

18.3%.

Exercise 17

(a)

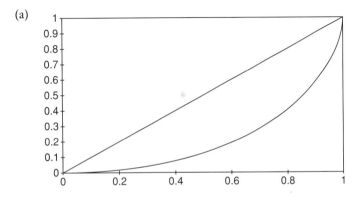

Gini = 0.56.

(b) The old have had a lifetime to accumulate wealth whereas the young haven't. This does not apply to income.

Exercise 19

(a) The Gini coefficients are 44.8%, 35.4%, 33.6% and 34.0% respectively.

(b) These differ from the values given in Table 2.24 (from *Economic Trends*), substantially so in the case of original and post-tax income. The figures based on quintiles are all lower than the figures in *Economic Trends*, as expected, although the bias is large in some cases. Drawing a smooth, freehand Lorenz curve based on the quintiles data for original income results in a Gini coefficient of around 46%, closer to the calculated figure than the *Economic Trends* figure. The results seem puzzling.

Exercise 21

79.3%.

Chapter 3

Exercise 1

(a) 4/52 or 1/13.

(b) 12/52 or 3/13.

(c) 1/2.

(d) $4/52 \times 3/52 \times 2/52 = 3/17576$ (0.017%).

(e) $(4/52)^3 = 0.000455$.

Exercise 3

(a) 0.25, 0.4, 5/9.

(b) 'Probabilities' are 0.33, 0.4, 0.5, which sum to 1.23. These cannot be real probabilities, therefore. The difference leads to an (expected) gain to the bookmaker.

(c) Suppose the true probabilities of winning are proportional to the odds, i.e. 0.33/1.23, 0.4/1.23, 0.5/1.23, or 0.268, 0.325, 0.407. If £1 were bet on each horse, then the bookie would expect to pay out $0.268 \times 3 + 0.325 \times 1.5 + 0.407 \times 0.8 = 1.6171$, plus one of the £1 stakes, £2.62 in total. He would thus gain 38 pence on every £3 bet, or about 12.7%.

Exercise 5

A number of factors might help: statistical ones such as the ratio of exports to debt interest, the ratio of GDP to external debt, the public sector deficit, etc., and political factors such as the policy stance of the government.

Exercise 7

(a) is the more probable, since it encompasses her being active *or* not active in the feminist movement. Many people get this wrong, which shows how one's preconceptions can mislead.

Exercise 9

The advertiser is a trickster and guesses at random. Every correct guess ($P = 0.5$) nets a fee, every wrong one costs nothing except reimbursing the fee. The trickster would thus keep half the money sent in. You should be wary of such advertisements!

Exercise 11

(a) $E(\text{winnings}) = 0.5^{20} \times £1\text{bn} + (1 - 0.5^{20}) \times -£100 = £853.67$.

(b) Despite the positive expected value, most would not play because of their aversion to risk. Would you?

Exercise 13

(a), (b), and (d) are independent, though legend says that rain on St Swithins day means rain for the next forty!

Exercise 15

(a) There are 15 ways in which a 4–2 score could be arrived at, of which this is one. Hence the probability is 1/15.

(b) Six of the routes through the tree diagram involve a 2–2 score at some stage, so the probability is 6/15.

Exercise 17

Pr(guessing all six) $= 6/50 \times 5/49 \times \ldots \times 1/45 = 1/15,890,700$. Pr(six from ten guesses) $= 10/50 \times 9/49 \times \ldots \times 5/45 = 151,200/11,441,304,000$. This is exactly 210 times the first answer, so there is no discount for bulk gambling!

Exercise 19

	Prior	Likelihood	Prior × likelihood	Posterior
Fair coin	0.5	0.25	0.125	0.2
Two heads	0.5	1.00	0.500	0.8
Total			0.625	

Exercise 21

(a) Using Bayes' theorem the probability is $p/(p + (1 - p)) = p$.

(b) Again using Bayes' theorem we obtain $p^2/(p^2 + (1-p)^2)$.

(c) If $p < 0.5$ then (b) < (a). The agreement of the second witness *reduces* the probability that the defendant is guilty. Intuitively this seems unlikely. The fallacy is that they can lie in many different ways, so Bayes' theorem is not applicable here.

Exercise 23

(a) EVs are 142, 148.75 and 146 respectively. Hence B is chosen.

(b) The minima are 100, 130, 110, so B has the greatest minimum. The maxima are 180, 170, 200 so C is chosen.

(c) The regret table is

	Low	Middle	High	Max.
A	30	5	20	30
B	0	0	30	30
C	20	15	0	20

so C has the minimax regret figure.

(d) The EV assuming perfect information is 157.75, against an EV of 148.75 for project B, so the value of information is 9.

Exercise 25

The probability of *no* common birthday is $365/365 \times 364/365 \times 363/365 \times \ldots \times 341/365 = 0.43$. Hence the probability of at least one birthday in common is 0.57, or greater than one-half. Most people underestimate this probability by a large amount. (This result could form the basis of a useful source of income at parties. . .)

Chapter 4

Exercise 1

The graph looks like a pyramid, centred on the value of 7, which is the mean of the distribution. The probabilities of scores of 2, 3, . . ., 12 are (out of 36): 1, 2, 3, 4, 5, 6, 5, 4, 3, 2, 1 respectively. The probability that the sum is nine or greater is therefore 10/36. The variance is 5.83.

Exercise 3

The distribution should be sharply peaked (at or just after the timetabled departure time) and should be skewed to the right.

Exercise 5

Similar to the train departure time, except that it is a discrete distribution. The mode would be 0 accidents, and the probability above 1 accident per day very low indeed.

Exercise 7

The probabilities are 0.33, 0.40, 0.20, 0.05, 0.008, 0.000, 0.000 of 0–6 sixes respectively.

Exercise 9

(a) $\Pr(0) = 0.9^{15} = 0.21$, $\Pr(1) = 15 \times 0.9^{14} \times 0.1 = 0.34$, hence $\Pr(0 \text{ or } 1) = 0.55$.

(b) By taking a larger sample or tightening the acceptance criteria, e.g. only accepting if the sample is defect free.

(c) 7% .

(d) The assumption of a large batch means that the probability of a defective component being selected does not alter significantly as the sample is drawn.

Exercise 11

The y-axis co-ordinates are:

0.05   0.13   0.24   0.35   0.40   0.35   0.24   0.13   0.05

This gives the outline of the central part of the Normal distribution.

Exercise 13

(a) 5%.

(b) 30.85%.

(c) 93.32%.

(d) 91.04%.

(e) Zero! (You must have an *area* for a probability.)

Exercise 15

(a) $z = 0.67$, area $= 25\%$.

(b) $z = -1$, area $= 15.87\%$.

(c) $z_L = -0.67$, $z_U = 1.67$, area $= 70.11\%$.

(d) Zero again!

Exercise 17

(a) $\overline{IQ} \sim N(100, 16^2/10)$.

(b) $z = 1.98$, $\Pr = 2.39\%$.

(c) 2.39% (same as (b)).

(d) 95.22%. This is much greater than the previous answer. This question refers to the distribution of sample means, which is less dispersed than the population.

(e) Since the marginal student has an IQ of 108 (see previous question) nearly all university students will have an IQ above 110 and so, to an even greater extent, the sample mean will be above 110. Note that the distribution of students' IQ is not Normal but skewed to the right, since it is taken from the upper tail of a Normal distribution. The small sample size means we cannot safely use the Central Limit theorem here.

(f) 105, *not* 100. The expected value of the last 9 is 100, so the average is 105.

Exercise 19

(a) $r \sim B(10, \frac{1}{2})$.

(b) $r \sim N(5, 2.5)$.

(c) Binomial: $\Pr = 82.8\%$; Normal: 73.57% (82.9% using the continuity correction).

Exercise 21

(a) By the Binomial, $\Pr(\text{no errors}) = 0.99^{100} = 36.6\%$. By the Poisson, $nP = 1$, so $\Pr(x = 0) = 1^0\,3 \times ^{-1}/0! = 36.8\%$.

(b) $\Pr(r = 1) = 100 \times 0.99^{99} \times 0.01 = 0.370$; $\Pr(r = 2) = 100C2 \times 0.99^{98} \times 0.01^2 = 0.185$. Hence $\Pr(r \leq 2) = 0.921$. Poisson method: $\Pr(x = 1) = 1^1 \times e^{-1}/1! = 0.368$; $\Pr(x = 2) = 1^2 \times e^{-1}/2! = 0.184$. Hence $\Pr(x \leq 2) = 0.920$. Hence the probability of more than two errors is about 8% using either method. Using the Normal method we would have $x \sim N(1, 0.99)$. So the probability of $x > 2.5$ (taking account of the continuity correction) is given by $z = (2.5 - 1)/\sqrt{0.99} = 1.51$, giving an answer of 6.55%, a significant underestimate of the true value.

Exercise 23

(a) Normal.

(b) Uniform distribution between 0 and 1 (look up the $=RAND()$ function in your software documentation).

(c) Mean = 0.5, variance = 5/12 = 0.42 for parent, mean = 0.5, variance = 0.42/5 for sample means (Normal distribution)

Chapter 5

Exercise 1

(a) It gives the reader some idea of the reliability of an estimate.

(b) The population variance (or its sample estimate) and the sample size.

Exercise 3

An estimator is the rule used to find the estimate or a parameter. A good estimator does not *guarantee* a good estimate, only that it is correct *on average* (if the estimator is unbiased) and close to the true value (if precise).

Exercise 5

$E(w_1 x_1 + w_2 x_2) = w_1 E(x_1) + w_2 E(x_2) = w_1 \mu + w_2 \mu = \mu$ if $w_1 + w_2 = 1$.

Exercise 7

$40 \pm 2.57 \times \sqrt{10^2 / 36} = [35.71, \ 44.28]$. If $n = 20$, the t distribution should be used, giving $40 \pm 2.861 \times \sqrt{10^2 / 20} = [33.60, \ 46.40]$.

Exercise 9

$40 \pm 2.57 \times \sqrt{0.4 \times 0.6 / 50} = [0.22, \ 0.58]$.

Exercise 11

$(25 - 22) \pm 1.96 \times \sqrt{12^2 / 80 + 18^2 / 100} = [-1.40, \ 7.40]$.

Exercise 13

$(0.67 - 0.62) \pm 2.57 \sqrt{\dfrac{0.67 \times 0.33}{150} + \dfrac{0.62 \times 0.38}{120}} = [-0.10, \ 0.20]$.

Exercise 15

$30 \pm 2.131 \times \sqrt{5^2 / 16} = [27.34, \ 32.66]$.

Exercise 17

$(45 - 52) \pm 2.048 \sqrt{40.32 / 12 + 40.32 / 18} = [-2.15, \ -11.85]$. 40.32 is the pooled variance.

Chapter 6

Exercise 1

(a) False, you can alter the sample size.

(b) True.

(c) False, you need to consider the Type II error probability also.

(d) True.

(e) False, it's the probability of a Type I error.

(f) False, the confidence level is $1 - \Pr(\text{Type I error})$ or the probability of accepting H_0 when true.

Exercise 3

H_0: fair coin, $(\Pr(H) = \frac{1}{2})$, H_1: two heads $(\Pr(H) = 1)$. $\Pr(\text{Type I error}) = (\frac{1}{2})^2 = \frac{1}{4}$; $\Pr(\text{Type II error}) = 0$.

Exercise 5

(a) Rejecting a good batch or accepting a bad batch.

(b) H_0: $\mu = 0.01$ and H_1: $\mu = 0.10$ are the hypotheses. Under H_0, $\Pr(0$ or 1 defective in sample$) = 0.911$, hence 8.9% chance of rejecting a good batch. Under H_1, $\Pr(0$ or $1) = 0.034$, hence 3.4% chance of accepting a bad batch. One could also use the Normal approximation to the Binomial, giving probabilities of 7.78% and 4.95%..

(c) $\Pr(\text{Type I error}) = 26\%$; $\Pr(\text{Type II error}) = 4.2\%$.

(d) (i) Try to avoid faulty batches, hence increase the risk of rejecting good batches, the significance level of the test.

   (ii) Since there are alternative suppliers it can increase the risk of rejecting good batches (which upsets its supplier).

   (iii) Avoid accepting bad batches.

Exercise 7

$z = 1.83$, hence prob-value is 3.36%.

Exercise 9

100%. You will always reject H_0 when false.

Exercise 11

$z = 1 < 1.96$, the critical value at the 95% confidence level.

Exercise 13

$z = 0.59$, not significant, do not reject.

Exercise 15

$z = (115 - 105)/\sqrt{21^2/49 + 23^2/63} = 2.4 > 1.64$, the critical value, hence reject with 95% confidence.

Exercise 17

$$z = \frac{0.57 - 0.47}{\sqrt{\dfrac{0.57 \times (1 - 0.57)}{180} + \dfrac{0.47 \times (1 - 0.47)}{225}}} = 2.12.$$

This is significant using either a one or a two tail test. Whether you used a one or a two tail test reveals something about your prejudices! The proportions passing are the actual outcomes for 1992 in the UK, based on 1.85 million tests altogether. You might have an interesting class discussion about what these statistics prove!

Exercise 19

(a) $t = -5/\sqrt{10^2/20} = -2.24 < -2.093$, the critical value, hence reject H_0.

(b) The parent distribution is Normal.

Exercise 21

$S^2 = 38.8$, and $t = 8.29$, so H_0 is rejected.

Exercise 23

(a) $t_{20} = 1.18$.

(b) $t_{10} = 1.63$. Neither is significant at the 5% level, though the latter is closer. Note that only one worker performs worse, but this one does substantially worse, perhaps due to other factors.

Exercise 25

(a) It would be important to check *all* the predictions of the astrologer. Too often, correct predictions are highlighted ex-post and incorrect ones ignored.

(b) Like astrology, a fair test is important, where it is possible to pass or fail, with known probabilities. Then performance can be judged.

(c) Samples of both taken-over companies and independent companies should be compared, with as little difference between samples as possible.

Chapter 7

Exercise 1

GNP versus GDP; gross or net national product; factor cost or market prices; coverage (UK, GB, England and Wales); current or constant prices are some of the issues.

Exercise 3

The following are index number series for UK and US GDP

	1985	1986	1987	1988	1989	1990	1991	1992	1993
UK	91.5	95.4	100	105.0	107.3	107.7	105.4	104.9	
US	94.3	97.0	100	103.9	106.6	107.9	107.1	109.8	113.1

Exercise 5

$n = 1.96^2 \times 400/2^2 = 385$.

Chapter 8

Exercise 1

The 95% c.i. for the variance is $\dfrac{39 \times 20^2}{59.34} \leq \sigma^2 \leq \dfrac{39 \times 20^2}{24.43}$ where 24.43 and 59.34 are the limits cutting off 2.5% in each tail of the χ^2 distribution, so the c.i. for σ is [16.21, 25.29].

Exercise 3

$\chi^2 = 15.46 > 3.84$, the 95% critical value.

Exercise 5

Using the data as presented, with expected values of 565, yields $\chi^2(3) = 1.33$, not significant. However, adding the dissatisfied customers (24, 42, 20, 54) and constructing a contingency table yields $\chi^2(3) = 22.94$, highly significant. The differences between the small numbers of dissatisfied customers adds most to the test statistic. The former result should be treated with suspicion since it is fairly obvious that there would be small numbers of dissatisfied customers.

Exercise 7

$\chi^2(4) = 8.12$ which is not significant at the 5% significance level. There appears to be no relationship between size and profitability.

Exercise 9

(a) The correct observed and expected values are

   47.0 (54.9)   72.0 (64.1)
   86.0 (76.6)   80.0 (89.4)
    4.0 (5.5)   8.0 (6.5)

and this yields a χ^2 value of 5.05 against a critical value of 5.99 (5% significance level, 2 degrees of freedom).

(b) Omitting the non-responses leads to a 2×2 contingency table with a test statistic of 4.22, against a critical value of 3.84, yielding a significant result.

Exercise 11

$F = 55/48^8 = 1.15 < 2.76$, the 1% critical value for 24 and 29 degrees of freedom. There is no significant difference, therefore.

Exercise 13

(a) Between sum of squares = 335.8; within sum of squares = 2088; total sum of squares = 2424. $F = (335.8/3)/(2,088/21) = 1.126 < 3.07$, the critical value for 3, 21 degrees of freedom.

(b) A significant result would indicate some difference between the classes, but this could be due to any number of factors which have not been controlled for, e.g. different teachers, different innate ability, different gender ratios, etc.

Chapter 9

Exercise 1

(b) We would expect similar slopes to those using Todaro's data, but the graphs for growth and the income ratio don't look promising.

(c) There seems to exist a psychological propensity to overestimate the degree of correlation. See (d) to see if you did.

(d) $r = -0.73, -0.25, -0.22$ for GNP, growth, the income ratio respectively. Note that $r < 0$ for the income ratio, in contrast to the result in the text.

(e) $t = -3.7, -0.89, -0.78$, so only the first is significant. The critical value is 1.78 (for a one tail test).

Exercise 3

(a) Very high and positive.

(b) A medium degree of negative correlation (bigger countries can provide more for themselves).

(c) Theoretically negative, but empirically the association tends to be weak, especially using the real interest rate. There might be lags in (a) and (c). (b) would best be estimated in cross-section.

Exercise 5

Rank correlations are:

	Birth rate
GNP	−0.727473
Growth	−0.314286
Inc. ratio	−0.323077

These are similar to the ordinary r values. Only the first is significant at 5%.

Exercise 7

(a)

	GNP	Growth	Income ratio
a	47.18	42.88	45.46
b	−0.006	−1.77	−1.40
R^2	0.53	0.061	0.047

These results are quite different from what was found before! GNP appears the best, not worst, explanatory variable.

(b)–(c)

	GNP	Growth	Income ratio
s_e	7.83	11.11	11.20
s_b	0.0017	1.99	1.82
t	−3.71	−0.89	−0.77
F	13.74	0.78	0.59

Only in the case of GNP is the t-ratio significant. The same is true for the F-statistic.

(d) You should be starting to have serious doubts! Two samples produce quite different results. We should think more carefully about how to model the birth rate and what data to apply it to.

(e) Using all 26 observations gives:

	GNP	Growth	IR
a	42.40	43.06	36.76
b	−0.01	−2.77	−0.20
R	0.31	0.28	0.002
F	11.02	9.52	0.04
S_b	0.00	0.90	1.01
t	−3.32	−3.08	−0.20

The results seem quite sensitive to the data employed. We should try to ensure that we get a *representative* sample for estimation.

Exercise 9

(i) 47.16 (34.71).

(b) 37.58 (32.61).

(c) 35.67 (33.76).

(Predictions in brackets obtained from Todaro's data). Again, different samples, different results, which doesn't inspire confidence.

Chapter 10

Exercise 1

(a) $B = 46.77 − 0.0064 \, \text{GNP} − 0.55 \, \text{growth} + 0.34 \, IR$

s.e.   (0.002)   (1.66)   (1.54)

$R^2 = 0.54$, $F = 3.91$

(i) Calculating elasticities: GNP: $−0.0064 \times 17{,}050/551 = −0.19$; growth: $−0.55 \times 27.9/551 = −0.03$; IR: $0.34 \times 61.1/551 = 0.04$. All seem quite small, although the first suggests a 10% rise in GNP should lower the birth rate by 2%.

(ii) Only GNP appears significant. Note that the R^2 value is only just greater than in the simple regression on GNP.

(iii) The F statistic is just significant at the 5% level (3.71 is the critical value).

(b) It looks like the growth and income ratio variables should be dropped.

(c) We need restricted and unrestricted ESS values for this test. $\text{ESS}_R = 736.17$ (from exercise 7 of Chapter 9: $\text{ESS} = s_e^2 (n − 2)$). $\text{ESS}_U = 726.96$ (from above regression). Hence $F = \dfrac{(736.17 − 726.96)/2}{726.96/3} = 0.019$, less than the critical value so the variables can be omitted.

(d) $B = 43.61 − 0.005 \, \text{GNP} − 2.026 \, \text{growth} + 0.69 \, \text{IR}$

            (0.0017)   (0.845)   (0.81)

$R^2 = 0.48$, $F = 6.64$, $n = 26$

The GNP and IR coefficients are of similar orders of magnitude and significance levels. The growth coefficient changes markedly and is now significant. The F

statistic for exclusion is 3.365, against a critical value of 3.44 at 5%, suggesting both could be excluded, in spite of the significant *t*-ratio on the growth variable.

(e) Not much progress has been made. More planning of the research is needed.

(f) Women's education, religion and health expenditures are possibilities.

Exercise 3

47.48 from 14 countries; 42.35 from all 26 countries.

Exercise 5

(a) A set of dummy variables, one for each class.

(b) Difficult, because crime is so heterogeneous. One could use the number of recorded offences, but this would equate murder with bicycle theft. It would be better to model the different types of crime separately.

(c) A proxy variable could be constructed, using such factors as the length of time for which the bank governor is appointed, whether appointed by the government, etc. This would be somewhat arbitrary, but possibly better than nothing.

Exercise 7

(a) Time-series data, since the main interest is in *movements* of the exchange rate in response to changes in the money supply. The relative money stock movements in the two countries might be needed.

(b) Cross-section (cross-country) data would be affected by enormous cultural and social differences, which would be hard to measure. Regional (within country) data might not yield many observations and might simply vary randomly. Time- series data might be better, but it would still be difficult to measure the gradual change in cultural and social influences. Best would be cross-section data on couples (both divorced and still married).

(c) Cross-section data would be of more interest. There would be many observations, with substantial variation across hospitals. This rich detail would not be so easily observable in time-series data.

Exercise 9

Suitable models would be:

(a) $C = b_0 + b_1 P + b_2 F + b_3 L + b_4 W$ where C: total costs, P: passenger miles flown; F: freight miles flown; L: % of long haul flights; W: wage rates faced by the firm. This would be estimated using cross-section data, each airline constituting an observation. P^2 and F^2 terms could be added, to allow the cost function to be non-linear. Alternatively, it could be estimated in logs to get elasticity estimates. One would expect $b_1, b_2, b_4 > 0, b_3 < 0$.

(b) $IM = b_0 + b_1 GNP + b_2 FEMED + b_3 HLTHEXP$ where IM: infant mortality (deaths per thousand births); FEMED: a measure of female education (e.g. the literacy rate); HLTHEXP: health expenditure (ideally on women, as % of GNP). One would expect $b_1, b_2, b_3 < 0$. This would be a cross-country study. There is likely to be a 'threshold' effect of GNP, so a non-linear (e.g. log) form should be estimated.

(c) $BP = b_0 + b_1 \Delta GNP + b_2 R$ where BP: profits; ΔGNP: growth; R: the interest rate. This would be estimated on time-series data. BP and growth should be measured in real terms, but the nominal interest rate might be appropriate. Bank profits depend upon the spread of interest rates, which tends to be greater when the rate is higher.

Exercise 11

(a) Higher U reduces the demand for imports; higher OECD income raises the demand for UK exports; higher materials prices (the UK imports materials) lowers demand, but the effect on expenditure (and hence the BoP) depends upon the elasticity. Here, higher P leads to a greater BoP deficit, implying inelastic demand; higher C (lower competitiveness) worsens the BoP.

(b) iii.

(c) U: linear; Y: non-linear.

(d) Since B is sometimes negative, a log transformation cannot be performed. This means elasticity estimates cannot be obtained directly. Since B is sometimes positive, sometimes negative, an elasticity estimate would be hard to interpret.

(e) 1.80, a surplus.

Chapter 11

Exercise 1

(a) The fourth quarter figure is much higher than the others, due to Xmas sales.

(b) The first few trend values (from 1986 Q1) are: 34,566, 34,984, 35,306, 35,515, 35,802,. . .The last few are (for 1992) . . . , 38,214, 38,294, 38,468, 38,629.

(c) Q1: 0.938; Q2: 0.961; Q3: 0.961; Q4: 1.143.

(d) 14% above average for the year, or about 18% above the other three quarters.

(e) 35,044, 35,080, 35,460, 35,131, . . ., 37,689, 38,404, 38,269, 38,876 (figures for 1986 and 1992).

(f) Unhappy in 1990 (S.A. figure fell from previous quarter and from previous Xmas), better in 1992 (S.A. figure rising again).

Exercise 3

(a) August and December have low production levels, October and November the highest.

(b) Trend values are 102,755, 102,900, 103,245, 104,150, . . . , 108,989, 109,607, 110,835, 112,112.

(c) Seasonal factors are as follows:

January	February	March	April	May	June
0.987	1.003	1.211	1.016	1.024	1.168
July	August	September	October	November	December
0.976	0.600	0.923	1.077	1.160	0.817

August is low because production and stocks build up to the new registration letter on 1 August. Sales are low after August.

(d) $0.6/0.976 = 61\%$, so the August figure is about 39% down on July.

(e) The SA series is 106,565, 95,130, 104,067, 100,914, . . . , 112,421, 109,215, 100,703, 116,701.

(f) The pattern is not so well defined because it is a monthly series and because an aggregated series such as consumers' expenditure has less of a random pattern.

Exercise 5

(a) The regression equation is $Y = 35,194.2 + 170.7X$, so expenditure rises by 170 each quarter on average.

(b) The seasonal factors are 0.937, 0.961, 0.961, 1.141, almost identical to the moving average method. This is because a linear trend fits the data well and the seasonal pattern is very well defined.

(c) The fitted value for $t = 32$ is $35,194.15 + 170.75 \times 32 = 40,658.02$. Multiplying this by 1.141, the seasonal factor for Q4 gives 46,394.8. The true value turned out to be 45,485 so we have an overestimate.

(d) The seasonals from the additive model are: $-2,366.4$, $-1,486.7$, $-1,484.5$, 5,337.6.

Exercise 7

(a) The equation is $Y = 41,254.1 + 125.6t - 7,839.5Q1 - 6,914.7Q2 - 6867.3Q3$. The slope is less than in the simple regression.

(b) The standard error and t-ratio are much better in the multiple regression; including the seasonal dummies this has firmed up the slope estimate.

(c) The comparison is as follows:

	Q1	Q2	Q3	Q4
Simple regression	$-2,366.4$	$-1,486.7$	$-1,484.5$	5,337.6
Dummy coefficients	$-7,839.5$	$-6,914.7$	$-6,867.3$	0

The patterns are quite similar: both show, for example, that expenditure in Q4 is about 6,850 higher than in Q3.

INDEX

THE LEARNING CENTRE
HAMMERSMITH AND WEST
LONDON COLLEGE

GLIDDON ROAD
LONDON W14 9BL

0181 741 1688